Good Kids from Bad Neighborhoods

This is a study of successful youth development in poor, disadvantaged neighborhoods in Denver and Chicago – a study of how children living in the worst neighborhoods develop or fail to develop the values, competencies, and commitments that lead to a productive, healthy, and responsible adult life. While there is a strong focus on neighborhood effects, the study employs a multicontextual model to take into account the effects of other social contexts embedded in the neighborhood that also influence development. The unique and combined influence of the neighborhood, family, school, peer group, and individual attributes on developmental success is estimated. The view that growing up in a poor, disadvantaged neighborhood condemns one to a life of repeated failure and personal pathology is revealed as a myth, as most youth in these neighborhoods are completing the developmental tasks of adolescence successfully.

Delbert S. Elliott is Distinguished Professor Emeritus of Sociology and Research Professor at the Institute of Behavioral Science at the University of Colorado.

Scott Menard received his B.A. from Cornell University and his Ph.D. from the University of Colorado, Boulder, both in Sociology.

Bruce Rankin is an Assistant Professor of Sociology at Koç University, Istanbul, Turkey, and a Research Fellow at the Malcolm Wiener Center for Social Policy, John F. Kennedy School of Government, Harvard University.

Amanda Elliott is a Research Analyst at the Institute of Behavioral Science at the University of Colorado.

William Julius Wilson is Lewis P. and Linda L. Geyser University Professor at Harvard University.

David Huizinga is a Senior Research Associate at the Institute of Behavioral Science at the University of Colorado.

Good Kids from Bad Neighborhoods

Successful Development in Social Context

DELBERT S. ELLIOTT
University of Colorado, Boulder

SCOTT MENARD
University of Colorado, Boulder

BRUCE RANKIN
Koç University

AMANDA ELLIOTT
University of Colorado, Boulder

WILLIAM JULIUS WILSON
Harvard University

DAVID HUIZINGA
University of Colorado, Boulder

CAMBRIDGE
UNIVERSITY PRESS

CAMBRIDGE UNIVERSITY PRESS
Cambridge, New York, Melbourne, Madrid, Cape Town, Singapore, São Paulo

Cambridge University Press
32 Avenue of the Americas, New York, NY 10013-2473, USA

www.cambridge.org
Information on this title: www.cambridge.org/9780521863575

First published 2006

Printed in the United States of America

A catalog record for this publication is available from the British Library.

Library of Congress Cataloging in Publication Data
Good kids from bad neighborhoods : Successful development in social context /
Delbert S. Elliott ... [et al.].
    p.   cm.
Includes bibliographical references and index.
ISBN-13: 978-0-521-86357-5 (hardback)
ISBN-10: 0-521-86357-0 (hardback)
ISBN-13: 978-0-521-68221-3 (pbk.)
ISBN-10: 0-521-68221-5 (pbk.)
1. Youth with social disabilities – United States.   2. Community organization –
United States.   3. Children – United States – Social conditions.   4. Neighborhood –
United States.   I. Elliott, Delbert S., 1933–   II. Title.
HV1431.G63   2007
362.74 – dc22   2006005653

ISBN-13   978-0-521-86357-5 hardback
ISBN-10   0-521-86357-0 hardback

ISBN-13   978-0-521-68221-3 paperback
ISBN-10   0-521-68221-5 paperback

Contents

v

List of Tables and Figures

FIGURES

Foreword

The last several decades have witnessed a pervasive transformation in the organization of knowledge and the process of social inquiry. In salutary contrast to their traditional – and parochial – preoccupation with disciplinary concerns, the social sciences have increasingly begun to take complex social problems as the starting point in their confrontation with the empirical world. Indeed, with regard to a particular discipline, that of sociology, Neil Smelser expressed doubt not long ago that this name would denote an identifiable field in the future, and he predicted that "scientific and scholarly activity will not be disciplinary in character but will, instead, chase problems" (1991, pp. 128–29). In the same vein, the prestigious Kellogg Commission noted pointedly that ". . . society has problems; universities have departments" (1997, p. 747). It is largely from the focus on complex problems of concern to society that whole new fields of knowledge have emerged in recent decades – among them behavioral science – and that *trans*disciplinary perspectives have, of logical necessity, come to inform and shape empirical inquiry. This volume by Elliott and colleagues exemplifies these recent developments and beautifully instantiates the *trans*disciplinary perspective of contemporary behavioral science.

Reflecting these trends, and self-consciously committed to furthering them, the MacArthur Foundation Research Network on Successful Adolescent Development in High-Risk Settings undertook a large-scale and extended program of collaborative, transdisciplinary research. The concerted aim of its various research projects was to further understanding about how young people growing up in circumstances of disadvantage, adversity, and even danger, nevertheless manage to do well, that is, to keep out of serious trouble, to stay on track, and to prepare themselves for the transition into young adult roles – in short, how they manage to "make it" (Jessor, 1993).

This volume is the third in a series reporting findings from those collaborative, converging, transdisciplinary endeavors, all in pursuit of that concerted aim – the illumination of successful adolescent development despite settings of disadvantage and diversity. The first volume, *Managing to Make It: Urban Families and Adolescent Success* (Furstenberg et al., 1999), while also considering multiple contexts of adolescent life in inner-city Philadelphia, had a primary focus on the family context and, especially, on the strategies parents employ to safeguard and ensure their adolescents' future in the face of limited resources and constrained opportunity. The second volume in the series, *Children of the Land: Adversity and Success in Rural America* (Elder and Conger, 2000), explored the responses of farm and small-town families in rural central Iowa to raising their adolescents during the drastic farm crisis of the 1980s that had decimated their financial resources and drove many from the land.

Elliott and his colleagues began their project with a key focus on the neighborhood context in both Denver and Chicago, but the logic of their theoretical and analytic framework required them to examine closely the other important contexts of daily adolescent life as well – the family, the school, and the peer group. By first articulating and then testing a comprehensive, transdisciplinary framework for explaining neighborhood effects, and also engaging the larger ecology of youth development, these authors have provided us with a landmark accomplishment in social inquiry. It is an achievement that will surely set the standard for future investigations of the role that the everyday settings of social life play in shaping the way young people grow up.

The contributions of this work are theoretical, analytical, and empirical, and some of these will be noted. But first, it is important to position it in relation to widely shared stereotypes about the urban poor. There has been an unfortunate tendency to emphasize dysfunction and failure as characteristic of those living in poverty and of the institutions – families, schools, communities – in which they are embedded. Compounding this stereotype has been a perspective that erases individual variation among the disadvantaged, seeing them as essentially homogeneous – a monolithic subgroup of the larger population. This volume makes clear that nothing could be further from reality, and in this regard its findings, fully consonant with those of the earlier volumes in the series, are a welcome and compelling corrective.

From the outset, and by deliberate contrast, the MacArthur Network projects sought to account for the observable success of so many young people despite circumstances of poverty and adversity in their everyday lives. As one scholar had earlier noted about adolescent black males growing up poor, "Given these cumulative disadvantages, it is remarkable that the proportion of black male adolescents who survive to become well-adjusted individuals and responsible husbands and fathers is so high, or that the percentage who drop out of school, become addicted to drugs, involved in crime, and end up in jail is not considerably greater" (Taylor,

1991, p. 156). The concurrence of the authors of this volume with that perspective is evident in the conclusion they draw from their comprehensive findings: "...a majority of youth from the worst neighborhoods appear to be on track for a successful transition into adulthood" (Chapter 1).

Rejecting the myths of homogeneity and of failure and dysfunction among the poor as being no more than caricatures, the present research instead established those factors at the contextual and individual levels, which underlie and explain the extensive variation in successful developmental outcomes that are, in fact, obtained among youth in high-risk settings. Their research strategy was to develop a multilevel, multicontext framework that conceptually could link attributes of neighborhoods (in this case, level of disadvantage) to adolescent developmental outcomes (in this case, level of success). This theory is elaborated cumulatively, chapter by chapter, from a model of the neighborhood, to a neighborhood plus family model, to models that then add the school and the peer contexts, culminating ultimately in the specification of the full conceptual framework for the explanation of neighborhood effects on youth development. *This transdisciplinary theory of neighborhood effects, assimilating constructs from sociology, social psychology, anthropology, geography, and epidemiology, must be seen as a major contribution in its own right.* It advances this field of research beyond its usual reliance on single dimensions, such as the concentration of poverty, to characterize neighborhoods in more complex ways; it permits the appraisal of indirect neighborhood effects, especially those that may be mediated through other contexts embedded in the neighborhood – the family, the school, or the peer group; and perhaps most important, it specifies the mechanisms or processes that constitute the chain of influence between neighborhood, on the one hand, and the course and content of adolescent development, on the other.

Despite a long history and a recent resurgence of social science interest in the neighborhood, its conceptualization and specification have remained problematic. Even the geographic delineation of urban neighborhoods, usually relying on census units, differs across studies; indeed, in this very volume, the Chicago site employed the larger unit of census tract, whereas the Denver site used the smaller unit of block group. What is ultimately at issue, and what runs throughout the authors' grapplings with the neighborhood notion, is how to ensure that the specification of neighborhood employed *is relevant to the experience and actions of its residents*, and it is in this regard that they make another important contribution. For the geographic delineation of a neighborhood, invoking the criterion of relevance to experience/action clearly favors employing the smaller unit wherever possible. That criterion also influenced the descriptive characterization of neighborhoods – a multidimensional characterization is likely to be more relevant to experience/action than any one of its components.

But most important are the implications of that criterion for the constitution of neighborhoods *theoretically*. Descriptive attributes of neighborhoods, such as dilapidated housing, have to be seen as remote or distal in the causal chain, their influence on experience/action requiring mediation by theoretical constructs, such as neighborhood social organization and neighborhood culture, which are causally closer, that is, more proximal to experience/action. This theoretical mediation is clearly illustrated in the full, multicontextual model at which the authors arrive. The descriptive characteristics of the neighborhood are represented as causally most distal from the adolescent developmental outcomes of interest, and their influence is represented as mediated by the theoretically defined properties of neighborhoods, that is, their organization and their culture. This is a contribution to thinking about neighborhoods that should help shift the balance more toward theoretically guided specification and away from the customary reliance on descriptive characteristics that happen to be readily available.

The authors' concern with the theoretical properties of neighborhoods advances understanding in yet another way. It makes clear the critical difference between the compositional effects of neighborhoods (the effects that derive from the individual-level characteristics of the people who happen to live there or might have moved there, their socioeconomic status, for example, or their ethnicity) and what might be called "true" neighborhood effects (those that reflect the organized interactions among its residents, their informal social networks, for example, or the degree of their consensus on values). These are *neighborhood-level* properties, what the authors of this volume refer to as "emergents," and it is these that capture what the construct of neighborhood should mean if it, indeed, means something more than the average of the characteristics of the people who live in it. Here is yet another contribution of this volume; it not only makes this distinction a guiding premise of the research, but the measures devised and the design of the analyses permit a clear separation between these two types of neighborhood effects.

This volume is rich with compelling findings that force our thinking in new directions about the influence of neighborhoods on successful adolescent development. The research reaffirms our expectation from the literature that neighborhoods do matter. But it also reveals that they matter quite differently, if we are seeking to explain neighborhood-level differences in rates of a developmental outcome (i.e., differences between neighborhoods) or seeking to explain differences in a developmental outcome at the individual level (i.e., differences between individuals). The neighborhood measures, taken together, are shown to provide a significant account of neighborhood-level differences in rates of success and, as expected, rates of successful development are indeed higher in better neighborhoods. But

what emerges most strikingly about neighborhoods as a source of influence on successful adolescent development is *how modest that influence is
at the individual level.* In short, what the research reveals is that most of
the individual-level variation in success occurs *within neighborhoods, not
between neighborhoods,* and the implications of that finding are enormous. It
requires rejecting the idea that there is an inexorable linkage between growing up in a poor neighborhood and being destined for poor developmental outcomes. Indeed, the magnitude of within-neighborhood variation in
successful outcomes – in both advantaged and disadvantaged neighborhoods – is such that the neighborhood per se, disadvantaged or otherwise,
cannot be considered to mortgage an adolescent's developmental future.
A more salutary finding would be difficult to envision.

    It is in their exploration and dissection of the within-neighborhood vari-
ation that the authors of this volume make perhaps their most significant
contribution to neighborhood research. By designing the project to permit examination not only of the neighborhood context itself, but also of
the social contexts that are embedded within it – families, schools, and
peer groups – the investigators were able to advance knowledge in several
important ways. First, they were able to show that most of whatever effects
neighborhoods have on adolescent developmental outcomes are indirect –
mediated by their effects on the other contexts they encompass. Second, in
examining those other contexts, they found that, within any given neighborhood, there can be considerable variation in quality vis-à-vis successful
developmental outcomes. That is to say, the quality of parenting in families, for example, or of the climate of schools, or of the modeling by peer
groups within a neighborhood remains highly variable; said otherwise,
the quality of its social contexts is not, or is only weakly, determined by
the quality of the neighborhood. Thus, to explain within-neighborhood
variation in successful developmental outcomes requires an account of
within-neighborhood variation in families, schools, and peer groups – and
this is precisely what these investigators have been able to do. Third, they
have been able to establish that there is variability among these contexts
in quality such that knowing, for example, that there are dysfunctional
families in a neighborhood tells little about the quality of its schools or of
its peer groups. In short, there seems to be only what, in the Network's
studies, came to be referred to as "loose coupling," not just between a
neighborhood and these other social contexts, but also among these other
contexts themselves Such findings underline the importance of attending
to within-neighborhood differentiation – conceptually and empirically –
in any study of neighborhood effects.

    A bountiful harvest of findings about neighborhood effects, beyond
those already noted, and with clear implications for social policy and for
community interventions, awaits the reader. These include findings about

the relative importance of the different social contexts of adolescent life; about the variables in those contexts that are most influential in shaping an adolescent's course of development along a trajectory of success; about how different predictors are engaged when the outcome being predicted is different, say, problem behavior instead of personal competence; about the difference developmental stage seems to make; and about much more. Along the way, the reader will find the volume inviting, accessible, and transparent, reflecting the care taken by its authors to provide a synopsis at the beginning of each chapter, to build the argument chapter by chapter, to summarize their major findings in the final chapter, and to reserve most technical material for the Appendixes.

As is the case with all research, especially research dealing with the complexities of the social environment, there are limitations to the conclusions that can be drawn from this study; these are sensitively acknowledged and clearly confronted by the authors. However, it needs to be emphasized here that the main findings of the study are unusually compelling. This stems, first, from the attention given to operationalizing the physical, compositional, and theoretical or emergent attributes of neighborhoods, and then to directly measuring them; it stems also from the authors having constituted innovative and comprehensive measures of adolescent developmental success. The study gains its most substantial increment in compellingness by having carried out the test of its explanatory model in two very different urban sites – Denver and Chicago – and in both advantaged and disadvantaged neighborhoods in both sites. The major findings remain consistent across those tests. Finally, the study's findings are consistent with those reported in the two earlier volumes, thereby supporting the reach of the authors' transdisciplinary explanatory model and further extending its generality.

In addressing an important social problem in the way that they have, D. S. Elliott and colleagues have not only strengthened our grasp on successful youth development in disadvantaged neighborhoods, but they have, at the same time, enriched behavioral science.

Richard Jessor
September 2005

References

Elder, G. H. Jr., and Conger, R. D. (2000). *Children of the Land: Adversity and Success in Rural America*. Chicago: University of Chicago Press.
Furstenberg, F. F. Jr., Cook, T. D., Eccles, J., Elder, G. H. Jr., and Sameroff, A. (1999). *Managing to Make It: Urban Families and Adolescent Success*. Chicago: University of Chicago Press.

Jessor, R. (1993). Successful adolescent development among youth in high-risk settings. *American Psychologist*, 48, 117–26.

Kellogg Commission. As cited in Abelson, P. H. (1997). Evolution of higher education. *Science*, 277, 747.

Smelser, N. J. (1991). Sociology: Retrospect and prospect. In R. Jessor (ed.), *Perspectives on Behavioral Science: The Colorado Lectures*. Boulder, CO: Westview Press.

Taylor, R. L. (1991). Poverty and adolescent Black males: The subculture of disengagement. In P. B. Edelman and J. Ladner (eds.), *Adolescence and Poverty: Challenge for the 1990s*. Washington, DC: Center for National Policy Press.

Acknowledgments

This study was one of several coordinated multicontextual studies undertaken by the John D. and Catherine T. MacArthur Foundation's Network on Successful Adolescent Development chaired by Richard Jessor. Dick's vision of a new integrated social science perspective was exciting and contagious, and his leadership in directing the Network was truly inspirational. Were it not for his encouragement and good-humored prodding, this book would not have been completed. We are grateful for his unflagging support.

We (Elliott and Wilson) are also indebted to the other members of this network – Albert Bandura, James Comer, Thomas Cook, Jacquelynne Eccles, Glen Elder, Frank Furstenberg, Norman Garmezy, Robert Haggerty, Betty Hamburg, Arnold Sameroff, and Marta Tienda – for the stimulating intellectual discussions and debates in a genuine interdisciplinary exchange of ideas that led to new insights in our thinking about contextual influences on youth development and behavior. Much of the conceptualization for this study came out of the work of this network, and together we developed and tested a number of key measures that were shared by the other studies coming out of the network. We give our thanks to all of these distinguished scholars for their contributions to the conceptualization and design of this study, and to the MacArthur Foundation for their funding of this specific study.

After completing the neighborhood surveys, we decided to conduct an in-depth ethnographic study of five selected Denver neighborhoods in an effort to integrate both survey and ethnographic data in our analysis of neighborhood effects on development. Our thanks go to Julie Henly who managed this part of the study and to Katherine Irwin, Kristi Jackson, and Deborah Wright who, together with Julie, did the observational work and in-depth individual and focus group interviews. This team did an outstanding job under difficult circumstances and delivered a rich, high-quality data set, which has been only partially mined in this book.

Special thanks go to Eda Homan who managed all the detailed checking of references and final editing and formatting of the manuscript. This dull work was done with care and good humor.

Finally, we thank all the youth and parents in Denver and Chicago who were willing to answer so many questions and share their experiences and opinions about their neighborhoods with us. We ought never take this goodwill on the part of our respondents for granted.

Del Elliott
Scott Menard
Bruce Rankin
Amanda Elliott
William Julius Wilson
David Huizinga

1

Growing Up in Disadvantaged Neighborhoods

We have this one little guy, 13 years old ... You can just see him, every day, trying to decide which is more glamorous, the Youth Council or the Foote Street Posse. The Foote Street Posse boys offer him five hundred dollars a week to be a lookout. All we offer is knowledge. They win, hands down, most every time.

Finnegan, *Cold New World*, 1998:26

INTRODUCTION

There is widespread concern that the social fabric of American community life has deteriorated, and this breakdown in neighborhood quality is directly responsible for the high rates of youth crime, substance abuse, unemployment, teenage pregnancy, welfare dependence, and mental health problems that characterize many of our inner-city neighborhoods. The neighborhood is generally assumed to play an essential role in raising children, and when the strong interpersonal ties, shared socialization values and processes, and effective appropriation and utilization of community resources fail to materialize or develop in the neighborhood, children are put at risk for poor developmental outcomes and dysfunctional lifestyles. The saying, "It takes a village to raise a child," captures this perspective on the importance of neighborhoods for a successful course of child and youth development.

This is the perspective typically taken by youth and parents in the study reported in this book. For both, the neighborhood is seen as an important context that shapes family and peer activities and individual developmental outcomes. The following exchange took place in a focus group meeting in one of our Chicago study neighborhoods. The focus group leader asked the teens in the group to describe their neighborhood. The initial responses indicated that it was a place with a lot of abandoned buildings, gangs, and drug dealers. Then the conversation turned as follows:

FG LEADER: What else? Drugs. Gangs. Abandoned buildings.

VOICE: It's not a very good place to raise children.

FG LEADER: Would the group agree with that? It's not a good place to raise children?

VOICE: Yeah.

FG LEADER: Why is that?

FEMALE: There's too many bad influence, too many drug dealers, too many...

MALE: Too much violence....

FEMALE: My little sister and brother already think the gangs are cute. They walk around trying to do gang handshakes... gang phrases.

FG LEADER: How old are they?

FEMALE: My little brother is 10, and my little sister just made 14.

FG LEADER: ... we've talked a little bit – actually a lot – about how hard it is being a teenager growing up here. Do you think it's hard for your parents, also?

VOICES: Yes.

FEMALE: It's hard because a lot of parents who do care about their kids, but know they've gone the wrong way, they have to worry about if their sons or daughters don't come in at night if she's gonna have to identify the body or what. She don't know if the kids will come in alive or...

FG LEADER: So, it's hard on them just because it's so hard on you, and they're all worried about you.

FEMALE: And they're scared. They want better for us. But my parents can't do any better. I mean, in terms of jobs, my parents can't afford to live somewhere else....

The youth who participated in the above focus group discussion tell us what it is like to live in Longmont,[1] a poor disadvantaged inner-city neighborhood. Their poignant descriptions of the problems in their neighborhood clearly suggest that the odds of failure and adoption of dysfunctional lifestyles are greater for youth in such environments. When asked what comes to mind when they think of their neighborhood, the teenagers blurted out such things as abandoned buildings, drug dealers, gangs, violence, school dropouts, teen pregnancies, and the absence of community organizations. They also discussed the lack of security and the problem of safety in neighborhood schools, as well as the absence of parks and playgrounds in the neighborhood. It was also clear that the teenagers in this focus group discussion had a conception of what constitutes a "good" neighborhood. They mentioned ethnic diversity, positive organizations like the YMCA, adequate housing, and jobs to employ people – things that their community lacked.

The focus group leader had to prompt the teenagers to think about things that were positive in their neighborhood. Several talked about the positive influence of some of the parents in the neighborhood. It appeared from their discussion that they believe their parents face a much greater challenge in raising children than do parents in more stable working- and middle-class neighborhoods, where attempts at normal child-rearing are not constantly undermined by social forces that interfere with a healthy course of child development. The teenagers in the focus group discussion all agreed that their community was *not* a good place for raising children. Their feelings are consistent with the views expressed by adult residents in other disadvantaged neighborhoods in this study. Our findings suggest that what many impoverished inner-city neighborhoods have in common is a general feeling among the adults that they have little control over their immediate environment, including the environment's negative influence on their children.

Nonetheless, despite the problems in neighborhoods like Longmont, many of the children living in high-poverty neighborhoods do in fact succeed in conventional terms and become productive and responsible adults. Our findings suggest that approximately half of youth living in high-poverty Denver neighborhoods were on a successful developmental trajectory. By understanding the factors that enable these youth to overcome the adversity they face, we can design more appropriate interventions and policies to maximize a successful course of child and youth development for all our children.

OVERCOMING ADVERSITY IN DISADVANTAGED NEIGHBORHOODS

At present, relatively little is known about how adolescents overcome adversity in high-risk neighborhoods.[2] Most neighborhood studies focus on the failures and pathologies of those living in poor neighborhoods. *The primary objective of this study is to understand how some youth living in disadvantaged neighborhoods succeed when others do not.* It is a study of success, not failure. But our focus is not solely on high-poverty neighborhoods such as Longmont. In order to fully comprehend the factors and processes that lead to successful adolescent outcomes in high-risk areas, one also needs to understand how and why adolescents in other neighborhoods succeed or fail.

The fact is that many middle-class suburban neighborhoods do not have a recreation center, library, bank, or grocery store in their immediate neighborhood. Can the presence or absence of these institutional facilities, called for by the teens and parents in Longmont, explain the difference in the likelihood of success for neighborhood children? Many middle-class youth have access to these places only by virtue of their (or their parents or friends) access to cars, whereas this form of access is much less likely for families living in neighborhoods like Longmont. This suggests that the significant social contexts in middle-class communities may not be the neighborhood but the school, the nearest recreation center, and the other places where families gather and interact. Without the comparison with more affluent neighborhoods, the general role of neighborhood influences on child and youth development can not be established; nor can the possibility of differential effects by type of neighborhood be explored.

Some high-poverty, disadvantaged neighborhoods have higher rates of successful adolescent development than others. Even poor neighborhoods differ substantially in the number and effectiveness of informal networks, access to conventional institutions, and the presence or absence of gangs and criminal organizations. These more proximate contextual differences make it easier (or harder) for families and peer groups to function in positive ways and for youth to grow up and become responsible adults. Moreover, neighborhood research has shown that these emergent neighborhood properties change over time and have different effects on different age groups.[3] In short, there is a good deal of variation across neighborhoods, both poor and affluent, in the organizational structures, informal processes, cultures, and lifestyles that emerge from the interactions of residents. The extent to which these features of neighborhood life are determined by the physical and social ecology of the neighborhood, and the role the neighborhood ecology and emergent organization and culture play in promoting a successful development, has yet to be established. We will review the available theory and research on neighborhood effects that supports this conclusion in subsequent chapters.

Our focus in this book is on the neighborhood as a sociogeographic place that provides the context for individual experiences, group interaction, and social development. The social context embodies the structural and cultural constraints and opportunities that influence developmental outcomes. These constraints and opportunities include those that enhance or impede participation in social institutions, that provide or deny access to institutional resources (such as schools, religious organizations, businesses, civic groups, recreational facilities, museums, the arts, and other enrichment programs). These constraints and opportunities also determine the extent to which adults in the neighborhood are integrated by a set of shared obligations, expectations, and social networks – factors that affect the degree of formal and informal social control in the neighborhood and the types of values and behavior that are promoted and rewarded.

As the teens in the Longmont focus group noted, the socialization patterns of parents are likely influenced by the constraints and opportunities encountered in their neighborhoods. We expect that average parents will have more success in raising their children when they reside in neighborhoods where strong institutions support and sustain their efforts. Styles of socialization may differ depending on the neighborhood and these differences may result in different social outcomes for children. Moreover, styles and strategies of socialization that are effective in middle-class suburban neighborhoods may be less effective in promoting the welfare of children in poor inner-city neighborhoods. In short, by focusing on the neighborhood as a sociogeographic setting, we shall see how it both directly and indirectly influences the developmental course of children living there.

Our focus goes beyond the search for neighborhood contextual effects. We propose to examine the combined contextual effects of the neighborhood and the other major social contexts that influence child and youth development – the family, school, and adolescent peer group. The explanatory model for this study is thus a multicontextual model in which critical features of each of these contexts are identified and both individual and combined contextual effects are considered. In this multicontextual model, the effects of neighborhoods may turn out to be direct, indirect, insignificant, or even spurious. If we find significant neighborhood effects, we expect that families, schools and peer groups will mediate or moderate a significant proportion of these ecological effects on development.

THE POTENTIAL CONTRIBUTION OF THIS STUDY

There are important differences of opinion about the significance of neighborhoods as socialization contexts and the advisability of mounting neighborhood-based initiatives to help at-risk children and families. The evidence for neighborhood-level differences in *rates* of crime, teen pregnancy, educational attainment, health problems, child abuse, and neglect is compelling. Clearly, there are differences between neighborhoods on rates of involvement in these behaviors.[4] The same can **not** be said for the evidence that neighborhoods matter much for individual-level outcomes, that is, that the level of poverty in the neighborhood accounts for whether individual residents do or do not become involved in these behaviors, once ascribed individual traits (race/ethnicity, socioeconomic class, and gender), family resources, socialization practices, and the influence of other more proximate social contexts have been taken into account.[5] Moreover, there are major differences in the conclusions from ethnographic accounts of neighborhood influences on individual development and lifestyles and survey studies examining these individual-level effects while controlling for other relevant factors; ethnographic studies suggest relatively strong neighborhood effects and survey research suggests very modest ones.

Some have argued that because of the development of mass transportation, nearly universal access to cars, TV, film, videos, the internet, and the emergence of huge retail outlets (Wal Mart, K-Mart, Lowe's, and Home Depot) as well as the service industry, the physical, geographical neighborhood is no longer the *functional* neighborhood. Modern contexts for family- and peer-group interaction are the workplace and special interest locations (schools and school-based activities, recreational centers, churches, concerts, shopping centers, and video arcades). From this perspective, physical neighborhoods are no longer meaningful socialization contexts.

In the light of these differences in findings about the importance of neighborhoods, there is reason to question whether it takes a village to raise a child and whether neighborhood revitalization efforts are likely to be effective.[6] There is a clear need for further research to determine (1) if neighborhoods are still meaningful socialization contexts, in both our modern suburban areas and our high-poverty inner cities; (2) if so, how it is that physical and ecological characteristics influence the social organization and culture of the neighborhood; and (3) how these emergent neighborhood characteristics operate to shape family, school, and peer group socialization processes and content, and directly or indirectly contribute to a successful or unsuccessful course of individual development. Answers to these questions should shed light on the current debates about when and how to intervene in neighborhoods to improve youth developmental outcomes.

PRIMARY STUDY OBJECTIVES

This study of neighborhoods differs from most earlier studies in several important ways. First, most studies of the ecology of the neighborhood have focused narrowly on the compositional effects of concentrated poverty. Without question, differences in socioeconomic composition are a critical feature of neighborhoods, one that has been linked to variation in many child development outcomes. However, the neighborhood ecology is more varied and complex than is captured by this one dimension. There are both theoretical and practical reasons for considering other compositional characteristics, if we are to gain a better understanding of the general ecology of the neighborhood, and how it drives the dynamics of growing up. The residential stability of the neighborhood, for example, turns out to be as important as poverty for some developmental outcomes in this study. Our conceptualization and measurement of neighborhood ecology is thus multidimensional and we demonstrate that the classification of neighborhoods as good or bad places for raising children based on these multiple ecological dimensions does a better job of accounting for neighborhood differences in development than does poverty alone.

We also include a measure of the physical environment when examining how the neighborhood ecology influences families and youth. While the early work of Park and Burgess (1924), Shaw and McKay (1942), and others in the Chicago School[7] considered the physical conditions in the neighborhood as an important dimension of its ecology, more recent neighborhood research on youth development often ignores this feature.[8] Again, we find that physical differences between neighborhoods turn out to be more important than concentrated poverty for explaining differences in some child-development outcomes. *One distinguishing feature of this study is thus the multidimensional conceptualization and measurement of the neighborhood ecology as a physical and social context where people live and interact.*

Second, relatively few neighborhood studies have actually identified and measured the specific structures and processes that link the social compositional and physical features of the neighborhood ecology to family socialization patterns, school quality, types of peer groups, and child development outcomes. We develop and test a complex model of neighborhood effects. This model specifies how features of the neighborhood ecology influence social interaction processes in the neighborhood to form the specific informal organization and culture that emerges. This model can also be used to show how this emergent organization and culture shape the socialization processes and development of youth living in the neighborhood, either directly or indirectly.

Third, while our primary focus is on the neighborhood context and its influence on youth development, our full model is a multicontextual model of development that includes measures of the family, school, and peer contexts, as well as the neighborhood context. *We thus consider how the neighborhood ecology, organization, and culture influence family socialization processes, the quality of schools and the types of peer groups emerging in the neighborhood, and how these multiple contexts combine to shape developmental outcomes for neighborhood youth.* Few studies of child development have considered the complex interplay of these multiple socialization settings. Most consider only the family, although a few include child-care settings and/or early school contexts.[9] We test this multicontextual model at both the neighborhood level and the individual level with good success.

Finally, the developmental outcomes for this study are different from many earlier studies that have focused primarily on how concentrated neighborhood poverty contributes to the social pathologies and arrested development of the poor – parental neglect, dysfunctional families, unemployment, mental and physical mental health problems, school dropout, delinquent gangs, crime, violence, drugs, and other indicators of developmental failure. In contrast, *this is a study of successful development.* Specifically, it is a study of how youth growing up in the worst neighborhoods, as judged by the neighborhood's social composition and physical ecology, develop the skills, values, commitments, and competencies necessary for a healthy, productive life and avoid the entanglements of health-compromising behavior and lifestyles that often derail a positive course of development for youth living in these neighborhoods. In this respect, this study follows the line of inquiry initiated by Reckless and his colleagues in their classic article, *The Good Boy in a High Delinquency Area*,[10] although their theoretical perspective was quite limited and has virtually no overlap with the explanatory model developed and tested here. One of the surprises in this study is that *a majority of youth from the worst neighborhoods appear to be on track for a successful transition into adulthood.* Our specific objective is to understand how this occurs. Better neighborhoods do have better developmental success rates, but living in an ecologically poor or disadvantaged neighborhood does not preclude high-quality parenting, good schools, supportive peer networks, and good individual development outcomes. Moreover, dysfunctional social contexts do not cluster to the extent often envisioned by social scientists.

ORGANIZATIONAL STRUCTURE OF THIS BOOK

We will justify the claims made here in subsequent chapters where the research on neighborhood, family, school, and peer group influences on child and youth development is reviewed. The next chapter will describe the study, its specific objectives, critical definitions, data sources, sampling strategy, and study measures. Special attention is given to the problem of conceptualizing and identifying neighborhoods as a unit of analysis. In Chapters 3–8, we provide reviews of existing research on each social context and build our explanatory model of multicontextual effects, starting with the most distal context (neighborhood ecology in Chapter 3), then adding the family context, the school context, and finally, the peer context in subsequent chapters. Chapter 9 presents the test of the full multicontextual model, with all contexts and individual attributes considered simultaneously. In each of the findings chapters, we consider contextual influences on developmental success at both the neighborhood level and the individual level. Chapter 10 highlights our major findings and discusses the implications for program development and policy formation. We conclude that chapter with some recommendations for future research on successful youth development.

With the exception of the final chapter, each of the chapters begins with a synopsis of the information found in that chapter. The reader can quickly determine what will be covered in that chapter and decide whether or not to read the detailed account. It is possible to skip right to the last two chapters, but this would result in missing some important findings that are masked when all of the contexts and individual attributes are included in a single model. To facilitate a smooth reading, references are largely confined to notes and technical information is found either in the notes or Appendixes. For those with technical skills, taking the time to read these notes and examine the tables in the Appendixes will provide a more detailed understanding of our findings and interpretations.

Notes

1. The names of study neighborhoods have been changed to comply with human subjects guarantees of confidentiality.
2. An important exception involves the work on resilience (for example, Werner and Smith, 1992; Rutter, 1979; and Garmezy, 1985). However, these early studies focused primarily on family and school protective factors rather than neighborhood contextual conditions. More recent work on resilience has considered community-level factors, for example, see Wolkow and Ferguson (2001).
3. Brooks-Gunn, Duncan, and Aber, 1997a.
4. For a review of this evidence, see Bursik and Grasmick, 1993 and Sampson, 2001.
5. Simcha-Fagan and Swartz (1986), Furstenberg et al. (1999), Brooks-Gunn et al., 1997a, b; Booth and Crouter, 2001.
6. Booth and Crouter have recently published a book raising this question: *Does it Take a Village?* (2001).
7. See Bursik and Grasmick (1993:6–8) for a brief description of this early work and those contributing to this school of thought.
8. There are important exceptions, primarily those recent studies that focus on neighborhood disorder and the "broken windows" perspective (Bratton, 1998). This work views residents' fear of crime as a reaction to neighborhood physical conditions and observed incivilities (for example, see Skogan, 1990 and Taylor, 2001). However, the focus of these studies is largely limited to the effects of neighborhood physical conditions on crime and fear of crime.
9. For example, the recent NICHD Study of Child Care and Child Development (2005) considered the family and child-care contexts, and some limited schools setting influences, but ignored neighborhood and peer contexts entirely.
10. Reckless et al., 1957.

Growing Up in Denver and Chicago

The MacArthur Neighborhood Study

SYNOPSIS

The Neighborhood Study is one of a series of integrated studies about youth development in multiple social contexts – neighborhoods, families, schools, and peer groups. This work was undertaken by the MacArthur Foundation Research Network on Successful Adolescent Development. This study developed and tested the most detailed and comprehensive model of neighborhood influences on families, schools, peer networks, and individual developmental outcomes. Denver and Chicago were selected as study sites and probability samples of neighborhoods in each city were selected as study neighborhoods. The rationale for selecting these two cities and the neighborhoods in each city is described.

A neighborhood is both a physical place and a social context; its boundaries have both geographical and social dimensions. Different ways of identifying geographical boundaries are explored and different census-based boundaries are compared with resident's perceived boundaries. Based on this analysis of the validity of different approaches to identifying neighborhoods, we decided to use census block groups and tracts to define and select neighborhoods for this study.

In Denver, 33 neighborhoods (census block groups) were selected with an average size of 27 square blocks. The samples of youth and families from each of these neighborhoods contained, on average, 19 families and 25 youth for a total sample of 662 families and 820 youth aged 10–18. Forty neighborhoods (census tracts) were selected in Chicago, with an average size of 14 square blocks. The sample of families and youth from each of these neighborhoods included, on average, 14 families and 21 youth aged 11–16, for a total sample of 545 households and 830 youth. Demographic descriptions of these neighborhoods are provided, with a focus on rates of affluence and poverty and racial/ethnic composition.

The information collected and available for this study involves four different sources: U. S. Census data for the years 1970, 1980, and 1990; personal interviews with parents of adolescents living in these neighborhoods; interviews with their teenage children; and in-depth interviews and focus groups (qualitative data) involving a separate sample of adults and adolescents living in six selected study neighborhoods. The study thus involves multiple sources of information and both survey and qualitative types of data. This ensures that our findings are rigorous and well grounded in the experiences of adolescents and adults living in these neighborhoods.

A common set of measures was developed and used in both Denver and Chicago. Additional measures were developed that were unique to Denver, taking advantage of additional data available for this site. These measures are described in the following chapters as they become relevant to the discussion. Finally, the general approach to this study and to the presentation of findings are described.

2

Growing Up in Denver and Chicago
The MacArthur Neighborhood Study

Male Adolescent – Broadmore: Uh, I'd say living here I have a whole lot better chance (for success) than living in another neighborhood.

Female Adolescent – Longmont: If I'm going to be successful and have kids, I don't want them to grow up here. I'm not trying to dis my neighborhood, but I can't have no kids and think I'm safe over here.

INTRODUCTION

This study of how kids living in bad neighborhoods manage to grow up successfully involves neighborhoods in two large, urban cities – Denver and Chicago. Initiated in 1991, it is one of a set of integrated studies of the MacArthur Foundation Research Network on Successful Adolescent Development. The main goal in all of these studies was to understand how youth growing up in poor, disadvantaged neighborhoods often manage to complete a successful course of adolescent development in spite of the social and economic adversity that characterizes their home environment. All of these studies used an ecological/developmental framework that viewed youth development as the result of many complex interactions, focusing on both individual attributes and dispositions as well as the set of conditions and social processes occurring in the multiple social contexts in which children and adolescents live. These physical and social contexts – the family, the school, and peer networks – were viewed as nested within and/or influenced by neighborhoods.[1] This ecological life-course paradigm is described more fully in Chapter 3.

Denver and Chicago were selected as study sites for several reasons. First, the authors were involved in ongoing neighborhood studies in both cities. Thus it was possible to do some preliminary work building on these existing studies and to use their sampling frames when drawing the new samples for this study.[2] Further, we had already established the necessary contacts and collaboration with the city officials and local neighborhood organizations that facilitated the implementation of these new studies. Second, both Denver and Chicago are large urban cities with a significant number of high-poverty, ethnically diverse neighborhoods. We also chose Denver and Chicago because the high-poverty neighborhoods in these two cities differed in some potentially important ways. Those in Chicago typically involved older, more established neighborhoods with many high-rise public housing projects; in Denver, these neighborhoods are relatively newer and are predominantly characterized by single-family dwellings and low-level apartment buildings.

There are some advantages in conducting the study in *two* urban cities. First, two sites offer a test of the generality of the model of neighborhood effects developed for this study, and the conditions and strategies employed by individuals and families who successfully overcome the negative predicted effects of living in a bad neighborhood. There are too many instances where neighborhood findings from a single city are generalized broadly. A study of two sites with similar measures and analyses provides a modest test at best, but two is clearly better than one. Second, the discovery of city differences in neighborhood structure, culture, and social processes can lead to refinements in our conceptual model of neighborhood effects. Should the general effect of poverty on youth development be different in Denver and Chicago, this would lead to a search for the source of this difference in local governmental policies and practices, historical development of high-poverty areas, different geographical characteristics (like resident density), demographic trends in housing markets, and other factors that were not controlled in the study and differed by city.

IDENTIFYING THE GEOGRAPHICAL BOUNDARIES
OF NEIGHBORHOODS

"Neighborhood" is both a physical place and a social context. Its boundaries have both geographical and social dimensions. Surprisingly, there is little agreement among researchers about how to identify the physical or geographical boundaries of an urban neighborhood or even about its typical size.[3] In the long tradition of neighborhood research, a number of definitions have been used, ranging from the "next-door" neighborhood consisting of those homes or apartments immediately adjacent to one's own residence; to a small cluster of residential blocks;[4] to the "walking-distance" neighborhood typically defined as the elementary school catchment area;[5] to a single census tract;[6] and finally to groups of census tracts or zip code areas.[7] Bursik and Grasmick (1993:5) tell the story of a reporter who was frustrated at the inability of a Carnegie Institute panel of experts to agree on a working definition of the neighborhood as a physical area with clear physical boundaries. The reporter suggested a practical definition offered him in private by a worker in the Puerto Rican Labor Office: "A neighborhood is where, when you go out of it, you get beat up."

There is, however, now some consensus about what a neighborhood is. Drawing upon Bursik and Grasmick's excellent review of the problem of identifying urban neighborhoods, we suggest three conceptual themes about which there is general agreement. First, a neighborhood is a relatively small physical area in which persons inhabit dwellings. They are small, residential environments nested within larger communities. Second, there is a social life that emerges within the neighborhood as the residents interact with one another. Thus, the physical size of the neighborhood is small enough to allow residents to interact on a *face-to-face* basis. The collective life of a neighborhood exists in the almost daily encounters with neighbors, the watching out for each other's children, working and partying together, borrowing food and tools, participating in neighborhood organizations and activities, and collaboration in interactions with the school, church, and other institutions in the larger community. Residents develop an informal social network with common interests in and shared expectations about their neighborhood and its relationship to the larger community. Ahlbrandt and Cunningham report that half of the residents in their Pittsburgh sample reported visiting regularly with neighbors and engaging in many of their "life activities" in and near their neighborhood.[8] Finally, the neighborhood has an identity and some historical continuity. In many communities, neighborhoods acquire names that are widely recognized and used in everyday conversation and by the media to locate persons and events within the city. These names sometimes have an official status, as is the case in Chicago and Denver, reflecting housing developments or city planning areas. They also have their own history of development and change over time, which generates a reputation for being desirable or undesirable, safe or dangerous, and affluent or poor places to live. These officially named neighborhoods are often quite large and are not consistent with the first theme identified above; in other cases they are small enough to be characterized by face-to-face interaction.

Establishing some geographical area, some physical boundaries to differentiate one neighborhood from another, is the minimum criterion for selecting neighborhoods to study and to determine whether an individual lives in one neighborhood or another. In practice, the "small physical size" characterization of neighborhoods is problematic. Most earlier quantitative studies of neighborhoods have used census tracts or groups of tracts as neighborhoods. The most ambitious neighborhood study to date, the Project on Human Development in Chicago Neighborhoods, combined 865 census tracts into 343 "Neighborhood Clusters," with an average of 2.5 tracts and 8,000 persons in each cluster.[9]

Recently, neighborhood researchers have started to question the appropriateness of using census tracts to identify neighborhoods.[10] Census tracts typically involve 4,000 or more residents,[11] a relatively large area with far too many people to be involved in face-to-face interactions and the resulting type of collective life described above. Although it is true that the original tracking by the Census Bureau more than 70 years ago attempted to capture homogeneous social areas where there was some sense of a collective life and neighborhood culture, many of these areas have changed dramatically over the years. Present tract boundaries may not capture coherent interacting or cultural neighborhoods. They are not internally homogeneous units; neither structural nor organizational features are likely to be evenly distributed within tracts or groups of tracts.[12] On the other hand, areas with widely acknowledged identities and historical traditions, such as *Woodlawn* or *Oak Park* in Chicago and *Cole* or *Five-Points* in Denver, typically involve more than a single tract and frequently include parts of tracts. Today, areas that have acquired a widely held reputation or identity are often quite large, both geographically and in numbers of residents living in these areas. There may well be more informal neighborhoods within these historical areas involving smaller geographical areas that are known only to those residents living in areas within or immediately adjacent to the neighborhood. Otherwise, the identity criterion for establishing neighborhoods appears to be inconsistent with the other two criteria in our modern cities.

A number of alternatives exist to using census units (tracts, block groups, or blocks) to identify neighborhoods. For example, residents living in an area might be asked in a household survey or ethnographic study to locate the boundaries of their neighborhood.[13] Whether there is enough consensus among residents to make this a feasible alternative for neighborhood research efforts has yet to be established, but there is at least some evidence that this may be a viable alternative.[14] It is also possible to ask city planners and local land-use experts to map the community into neighborhoods. Taylor[15] reports considerable agreement between residents and city planners about neighborhood geographical boundaries. Another approach is to rely upon formal neighborhood organizations to specify their neighborhood boundaries.[16] There are many such neighborhood organizations in Denver, for example, but there are also many areas identified as neighborhoods by the city planning office that have no formal neighborhood organization.

In practice, neighborhood research has relied almost exclusively on census tracts to identify neighborhoods without paying much attention to how well these geographical areas reflect the sociological conceptualization of neighborhoods. In part, census neighborhoods were used because these geographical areas are already identified and data on residents and dwellings are collected and aggregated to these geographic units every decade. There is indeed a rich, historical archive of census data going back to 1930. However, there has been little effort to validate the use of census tracts as geographic neighborhoods, to compare this approach to identifying neighborhoods with alternative approaches such as those described above, or even to systematically compare different census units like blocks, block groups, tracts, and groups of tracts that reflect major differences in area size.

VALIDATING NEIGHBORHOOD BOUNDARIES

Using data from a community sample in Denver,[17] we explored several ways of identifying neighborhoods and compared their validity in a "construct validation" study. We then replicated this construct validation study with data from the Chicago Neighborhood Study. The results of this work are summarized here; other sources offer a more detailed description of this study and findings.[18]

First, we asked respondents in both Denver and Chicago a series of questions about the size of their neighborhood and its physical and demographic characteristics. Each adult respondent was asked:

"When you think about your neighborhood, are you thinking about (1) the block or street you live on? (2) this block or street and several blocks or streets in each direction? (3) the area within a 15-minute walk from your house? or (4) an area larger than this?"

This set of questions was designed to yield responses that roughly matched (1) a census block, (2) a census block group, (3) a census tract, and (4) a group of census tracts, respectively.

The most frequent response in both Chicago and Denver was "this block or street and several blocks or streets in each direction," a geographical area roughly equivalent to a typical census block group (see Figure 2.1). A majority of respondents in both cities identified their neighborhood as a geographical area involving a single block or block group. Less than 15 percent identified their neighborhood as an area larger than the area they could walk in 15 minutes (a census tract).[19]

Most residents perceive their neighborhood as a relatively small geographical area. The vast majority (85 percent) identify an area that is as small as a single block and no larger than a census tract. Other studies of perceived neighborhood boundaries report similar findings. For example, Birch et al., interviewed residents in Houston, Dayton, and Rochester, asking them to identify the "... boundaries or borders of your neighborhood." Those living in single-family dwellings typically identified the houses immediately around their house or those on their block; apartment dwellers typically identified their apartments and persons on their floor, wing, or in their building.[20] Not surprisingly, people tend to make their own house the center of their neighborhood. This makes sense if social interactions are the central defining criteria for establishing neighborhood boundaries.[21]

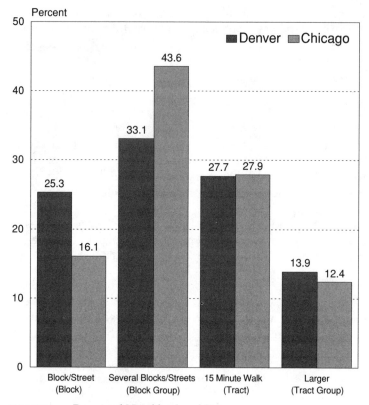

FIGURE 2.1. Perceived Neighborhood Size

How stable are these perceptions of neighborhood size? Over a one-year interval, Denver residents who had not moved were asked the same question about neighborhood size, with almost 60 percent providing a consistent response on both interviews.[22] Among those changing their response, there was a tendency to choose a smaller, rather than a larger neighborhood area at the second interview. In any event, considerable stability emerged in resident perceptions about neighborhood boundaries over time, but it is not perfect or absolute. This finding might reflect real changes in neighborhood physical characteristics and/or social dynamics over the one-year interval. It also might be the result of some unreliability or ambiguity in the question about neighborhood size.

    We also found some evidence that residents change their perception of neighborhood boundaries when they answer different kinds of questions about their neighborhood.[23] As we covered different topics in the interview that were related to the respondents' neighborhood, we asked them again at the end of each set of questions which of the above neighborhood areas they were thinking about when answering these questions. Later in the interview, when we asked about institutional programs or agencies located in their neighborhood, residents tended to identify a larger area than they identified at the beginning. About half of those originally identifying their neighborhood as a block or block group identified an area larger than a block group after this set of questions. By contrast, when asked about neighborhood youths' chances of realizing their educational and occupational goals, there was a slight tendency to select smaller areas. Questions about respondents' informal networks and activities in the neighborhood or the extent to which their neighbors shared their values and norms generated a high level of consistency with their original response (85–90 percent). These findings indicate that the geographical boundaries of the perceived neighborhood shift somewhat as residents describe different features of their neighborhood. They appear to be somewhat flexible, both over time and depending on the issues involved. Still, there is enough consensus and stability in perceived neighborhood boundaries to study neighborhoods as discrete physical and social contexts.

Individual perceptions of neighborhood boundaries also tend to vary by race and class.[24] Black residents are more likely to choose smaller neighborhoods (a block or block group) while whites (Anglos) select larger ones (typically tracts).[25] The trend for Hispanics is bimodal; they tend to select either a single block or a multitract area. Lower socioeconomic status (SES) residents are more likely to perceive their neighborhoods as blocks or block groups whereas higher SES residents view their neighborhoods as block groups or tracts. Perceived neighborhood size appears unrelated to the level of poverty in the neighborhood even though it is related to individual SES. Our analysis also revealed that blacks, lower SES respondents, and those living in high-poverty neighborhoods, are the most consistent in their perception of neighborhood size, both over time and across question content. Perhaps the physical neighborhood is a more salient social context for people relegated to these neighborhoods, or for these people, the physical and functional neighborhoods are the same. In any case, poor black respondents living in high-poverty neighborhoods are most likely to view their neighborhood as a single block or block group and to use this definition consistently throughout the interview when asked about different neighborhood characteristics and activities.

Using these data on perceived neighborhood boundaries, we constructed a perceived neighborhood typology and compared different census unit neighborhoods on several perceived criteria to evaluate their validity for a study of neighborhood effects. Respondents were assigned to a block group, tract, or multitract neighborhood, based on their response to the above question. We wanted to determine if assigning residents to these different census units had any effect on the correspondence between their aggregated descriptions of their "neighborhood" in our 1990 survey and official 1990 census descriptions for these census units. We reasoned that the greater the agreement between individual perceptions and the census reports of selected neighborhood characteristics for a particular census unit, the more valid that unit of neighborhood for our study.

Respondents were asked a series of questions that paralleled information available from the census. For example, we asked respondents how many families in their neighborhood were single-parent families, were poor, were on welfare, were black (Hispanic, Asian, or white), were renting, had five or more occupants per house, and had moved in or out of the neighborhood in the past year. We then tested to see if resident perceptions were more *accurate* (consistent with census data) when they had selected a block group, a tract, or a multitract as their neighborhood. The correspondence between individual perceptions and census-recorded characteristics was greatest for those identifying block groups as their neighborhoods. The differences between block group and tract neighborhoods were in some cases relatively small, and the correspondence was consistently and substantially higher for these two neighborhood units than for multitract neighborhoods.

We also looked for differences in the *homogeneity* of perceived neighborhood characteristics for these different neighborhood units. In this case, we were concerned with how similar individual perceptions are within neighborhoods and how different they are between neighborhoods. There should be less variation in these descriptions of the neighborhood when residents who live in the same objective neighborhood are describing it than if persons who live in different neighborhoods are describing their separate objective neighborhoods. In this analysis, we found the same pattern noted above – assignment to block groups produced more within-neighborhood similarity and between-neighborhood differences in perceptions of neighborhood characteristics than did assignment to tracts or multiple tract groups. Moreover, in this analysis, differences between block group and tract neighborhoods were more substantial, suggesting that block groups were more homogeneous neighborhood units than census tracts.

QUALITATIVE DATA ON NEIGHBORHOOD BOUNDARIES

We also explored neighborhood boundaries in a qualitative study of five selected neighborhoods in the larger Denver sample of neighborhoods. This study involved a series of adult and adolescent focus groups, in-depth semistructured interviews, and personal observations in each of these five neighborhoods. In order to compare residents' own sense of neighborhood boundaries with census boundaries, we asked participants in each of these (census block group) neighborhoods to draw a map of their neighborhood, showing the streets involved, businesses (if any), churches, schools, recreation centers, places where kids hang out, and any other important landmarks. During the adult focus group discussion about what it was like for adults to raise children in their neighborhood, or in youth focus groups about what it was like growing up in that neighborhood, participants also indicated where specific events were located on this map. For example, if there was a serious fight or drive-by shooting in the neighborhood, we attempted to locate it on this map; if there was a crack house in the neighborhood, a house fire that neighbors helped put out, or a person who let kids use his garage and tools to work on their bikes or cars, we attempted to locate these places on the map.

In some neighborhoods, it proved quite difficult to get agreement among participants about neighborhood boundaries. In others there was a general consensus about boundaries. Figures 2.2 and 2.3 illustrate the overlap in census-type boundaries and resident-perceived boundaries in Parkview,

FIGURE 2.2. Parkview Teen Map

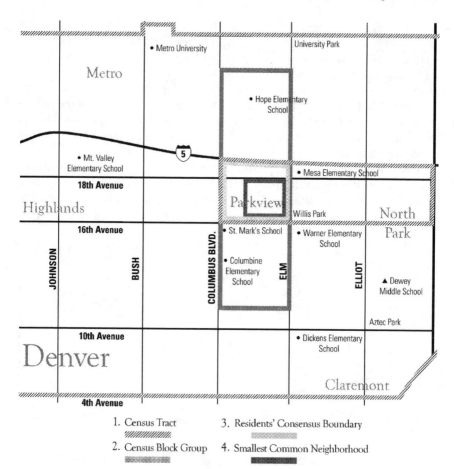

1. Census Tract   3. Residents' Consensus Boundary

2. Census Block Group   4. Smallest Common Neighborhood

FIGURE 2.3. Parkview Adult Map

one of these selected Denver neighborhoods, as perceived by adolescents and parents. On each map, four boundaries are identified: (1) the census tract, (2) the census block group, (3) the residents' general consensus about the boundary, and (4) the neighborhood area common to the individual perceived boundaries of **all** residents sampled. In general, there is a high consensus between parents and adolescents living in Parkview about these boundaries.

Consensus about boundaries was higher when there was an effective neighborhood organization, a neighborhood watch program, or some other type of organized activity in the neighborhood. Sometimes particular physical characteristics helped to establish clear neighborhood boundaries, like freeways, major streets, and particular housing characteristics.[26]

In one of the neighborhoods, residents participating in the focus-group discussion about neighborhood boundaries viewed what we had considered a single neighborhood in the survey as two separate neighborhoods. This opinion was shared by our qualitative research team after spending considerable time in this area. We had selected Northside for this in-depth study because our survey findings indicated it was a relatively high-poverty, racially-mixed neighborhood where youth appeared to have good developmental outcomes. This was an unexpected finding, and we wanted to probe into the nature of community life in this neighborhood. At the focus-group meeting, Alejandra (a pseudonym), a 38-year-old Latina mother of three living in the Northside block group, said almost nothing and was visibly uncomfortable during the meeting. When interviewed later, Alejandra said she was very angry with the Northside parents who talked about life in a neighborhood that was not at all like life in *her* neighborhood. She said they had failed to acknowledge the extreme differences between Allenspark (what she called her neighborhood) and Northside and did not respect her opinions about "neighborhood life." She vehemently maintained that her neighborhood was the small, densely populated area containing several rows of crisp white townhouses called Allenspark, which she considered separate from the block group area we called Northside.

Allenspark is a nine-acre, low-income housing project with children's playgrounds at the end of each row of townhouses, and an indoor gym and swimming pool. It is located entirely within the census block area we call Northside. In the mapping exercise, Northside residents' descriptions of boundaries and important neighborhood locations and events rarely included this housing project.[27] Likewise, residents of Allenspark mapped the few-block area around the project as their neighborhood and spoke with some contempt of the larger Northside neighborhood, describing these residents as outsiders. In general, both Northside and Allenspark residents agreed that these two areas functioned as separate neighborhoods. This distinction was clearly made by the director of the Allenspark gym:

I can't imagine how they'd see themselves as a part of the broader neighborhood. Most of them – a classic example was Halloween. A lotta kids went trick or treating right here. They didn't leave and go across the street... They don't know the people across the street... They just see the people across the street. They don't know – I've asked them, "You know the kids across the street? You ever play with 'em?" "No." There's 300 kids HERE to play with! And it's just easier... and if you look at it from the standpoint of a child, why should they go across the street? I think they see it as this is just the neighborhood we live in. They don't HAVE to interact with those people. AND those people don't have to interact with THEM.

Life was very different in these two parts of the census block group we originally called Northside. Both were racially and ethnically mixed, but the levels of poverty, unemployment, and single-parent families were much higher in Allenspark, and the developmental outcomes for youth living here were substantially lower than for the rest of Northside. The unexpected survey finding that led to the selection of this neighborhood for an in-depth study turned out to be an artifact of the way neighborhood boundaries had been established. The relatively good developmental outcomes involved primarily Northside youth and families; the high levels of neighborhood disadvantage were a reflection of the more extreme conditions and composition of Allenspark. Considered as two separate neighborhoods, the relationship between levels of disadvantage and youth developmental outcomes were now more in line with theoretical expectations.

Our qualitative studies in the other four neighborhoods selected indicated that these block-group neighborhoods corresponded reasonably well with resident perceptions of neighborhood boundaries. Levels of consensus in the mapping of neighborhoods was quite low in one of these neighborhoods, but there was no general agreement that more than one neighborhood existed within the census block group defined area.[28]

DISCUSSION

It is generally accepted that neighborhood units of greatest salience to residents are socially constructed, and these units may not be captured well in official census boundaries.[29] These analyses indicate that neighborhoods, as perceived by residents, are relatively small geographical areas. For the vast majority, these neighborhoods are the size of a single census tract or smaller. Coulton et al.,[30] report a similar finding using a resident mapping procedure. Multitract areas, which would include large housing developments and zip code areas, were seldom identified as neighborhoods and have consistently lower levels of construct validity than do block groups or single tracts. Unfortunately, officially designated neighborhoods in most cities (including Denver and Chicago) are multitract areas. These areas are probably better conceptualized as communities, each comprised of several neighborhoods.

Among census units, the block group appears to provide the best approximation of a neighborhood's boundaries and size as perceived by residents.[31] Block groups typically have one tenth of the population of census tracts. However, some evidence exists, primarily from our qualitative studies, that even this geographical area may be too large in Denver and provides a rather crude correspondence with perceived neighborhood boundaries. Still, the observed differences in construct validity between block groups and tracts are in most cases relatively small. If one is limited to using unmodified census units, block groups appear to be the most valid unit of neighborhood, followed by tracts.[32] Multitract units are the least valid census unit of neighborhood in this construct validation study.

Neighborhoods as perceived by residents appear to have somewhat flexible boundaries. Although we found some shifting of borders depending on the content of the question, the consistency was quite high for three of the four content areas investigated. Only when asking about agencies and community programs located in the neighborhood did we see a substantial redefinition (expansion) of boundaries. In the focus groups, the level of consensus among residents about exact boundaries was also sometimes low, but in all cases there was relatively high consensus about some minimum geographical area. There seems to be a clear "core" neighborhood area, but the outer boundaries appear more ambiguous.

The assumption that neighborhoods have some relatively constant or uniform size seems unwarranted.[33] There is, of course, considerable variation in the geographical size of block groups and tracts, but the amount of variation in the size of block groups and tracts in Denver is relatively small compared to the variation observed in perceived neighborhoods and between perceived and census-defined neighborhoods. Even with a sample of relatively small census units, we discovered at least one block group that contained two separate neighborhoods as perceived by residents. Any reasonable sample of perceived neighborhoods is likely to include some block-size, some block-group-size and some tract-size neighborhoods. But, without some prior ethnographic work, or at least some extended focus groups and observational studies in an area – or "windshield" surveys conducted by driving through and observing the physical characteristics and personal interactions in the area[34] – it would be impossible to map neighborhoods this way, using different combinations of census units.

It is no small task to obtain such data prior to drawing a representative (probability) sample of neighborhoods. For example, it would require ethnographic data (or focus-group data) for all residential areas in the cities of Denver and Chicago, all obtained within a relatively recent and short time interval to ensure that the mapping of neighborhood boundaries reflected the situation at the time the sample would be drawn. Even then, we would want to define neighborhoods in variable combinations of census units if possible, so as to make use of the available census data. These data are critical to obtaining independent measures of the physical and social context as well as historical changes in these characteristics.

SELECTING STUDY NEIGHBORHOODS

In the present study, we are using the best available census-unit definitions of neighborhoods, but we acknowledge that these neighborhood boundaries may not always correspond well to perceived neighborhood boundaries. Conceptually, perceived neighborhoods should have better construct validity, and we view our neighborhoods as relatively crude approximations of perceived neighborhoods. However, our qualitative data do not suggest that we have missed the mark in any serious way; the block group and perceived neighborhoods were generally similar, particularly given the ambiguities in perceived outer boundaries in some of our neighborhoods. Coulton et al.,[35] arrive at this same conclusion after comparing perceived and census-defined neighborhoods in Cleveland.

In addition, because our theoretical conceptualization of the neighborhood focuses on the *emergent* structure and culture that results from the interaction of residents, it seems appropriate to use a neighborhood unit that involves a relatively small geographical area where residents can have face-to-face interaction and joint participation in "life activities" in and around their neighborhood. We agree with Taylor (1997) that studies of the social processes, structure, and culture of neighborhoods should employ geographical areas where face-to-face interaction is at least a possibility.

In Denver, the sample of neighborhoods involves 33 block groups (BGs) representing, on average, a geographical area of 27 contiguous square blocks. The neighborhoods selected are representative of all block groups and areas in the city and county of Denver that meet minimum youth population requirements.[36] A representative (random) sample of families with children aged 10–18 was selected from each neighborhood. On average, the sample of families in each Denver neighborhood includes 19 families and 25 youth; the total across-neighborhood sample includes 662 families and 820 youth. For some analyses, particularly those that require a larger number of cases within each neighborhood, we combine those BGs that lie within the same census tract into a single unit, typically involving two BGs, creating a census tract sample.

In Chicago, the neighborhood sample includes 40 census tracts (CTs) with an average size of 14 square blocks. The sample was restricted to predominantly African American neighborhoods below the poverty line and disproportionately African American neighborhoods above the poverty line.[37] A random sample of neighborhoods (CTs) was selected from each of these two types of neighborhoods. From each sample neighborhood, a random sample of African American families with children aged 11–16 was selected. The high-poverty sample included 382 households and 569 youth; the low-poverty sample included 163 households and 261 youth. The total sample thus includes 545 households and 830 youth, an average of 14 families and 21 youth per neighborhood.

Although neighborhoods in Denver are block groups and in Chicago are census tracts, the average geographical size of the neighborhood is larger in Denver than Chicago (27 vs. 14 square blocks). This is primarily the result of differences in housing density in these two samples. Although different defined census areas are used, both studies employ the "best definition" of neighborhood as described earlier – small geographical areas the size of census tracts or smaller. The average number of households and youth per neighborhood are also similar across sites, suggesting that neighborhood site comparisons made in later chapters are reasonable. The neighborhoods in Denver are representative of the total set of neighborhoods with above minimum rates of youth residents in the city and county of Denver; the full range of neighborhoods as defined by income and race or ethnicity is represented in the sample. The sample of Chicago neighborhoods is representative of high poverty, predominantly African American neighborhoods and low poverty neighborhoods with a relatively high proportion of African American families. This sample is not representative of all neighborhoods or even all predominantly African American neighborhoods in Chicago, it is representative of neighborhoods with relatively large proportions of African American families that differ by median income levels.

DATA SOURCES AND MEASURES

The information used in this study involves four different sources: U.S. Census data for the years 1970, 1980, and 1990; personal interviews (survey data) with the sample of parents living in these neighborhoods; interviews with their children (aged 10–18 in Denver and 11–16 in Chicago); and in-depth interviews (qualitative data) from adults and adolescents (aged 10–18) living in selected study neighborhoods.[38] The survey data involve structured interviews with the representative sample of both parents and adolescents living in sample neighborhoods in Denver and Chicago. The qualitative data involve semistructured, in-depth interviews with purposive or "snowball" samples of both parents and adolescents living in selected study neighborhoods, data from recorded focus group meetings involving groups of adults and groups of adolescents from these neighborhoods, and personal observations of the physical characteristics and social interaction patterns in these neighborhoods. The analysis thus involves multiple sources of information and attempts to integrate quantitative and qualitative methods and data so that our findings are both rigorous and well grounded in the experiences of adolescents and adults living in these neighborhoods. These data will become increasingly important in subsequent chapters as we explore youth perceptions of how their neighborhood organization and culture influences their families, peers, and schools, and how their involvement in each of these social contexts affects their lives and future life chances.

A core set of common measures was developed for each site using the census and survey data. In addition to the set of core measures common to both Denver and Chicago, several site-specific measures were obtained, taking advantage of some unique features of each site and allowing for each site to pursue research topics unique to that site. For example, race and ethnic differences in neighborhood composition can be explored only on the Denver site. We will describe each of these measures as they become relevant to our discussion.

GENERAL ORGANIZATION OF STUDY FINDINGS

Our ultimate aim is to understand how it is that some youth overcome the negative influences and limitations inherent in living in high-poverty, disadvantaged neighborhoods. However, we begin with a more general analysis, describing how the neighborhood environment influences the course of youth development. Some neighborhood characteristics are linked to poor developmental outcomes, others to good outcomes, and some have no effect on developmental outcomes. After we identify and understand how certain features of the neighborhood adversely affect development, we can assess how some youth avoid or are buffered from these expected effects.

In addition to individual resiliency, we anticipate that well-functioning families, good schools, and participation in conventional peer groups all function to offset or limit the negative effects of living in a bad neighborhood. However, neighborhood influences can also affect parenting practices, school quality, and peer group characteristics, rendering them more or less effective in providing a healthy conventional course of development for children and youth. Some neighborhood effects thus operate directly on adolescents and others operate indirectly by reinforcing or undermining their family's functioning, the social climate of the schools they attend, and the types of peer groups that emerge in their neighborhood. A complex model of multiple contextual effects is required to understand both direct and indirect effects, and particularly how the neighborhood influences the structure and functioning of families, schools, and peer groups, and how these contexts, in turn, influence the course of youth development.

We will build this multicontextual model incrementally in Chapters 3–8. We begin by considering the direct effects of neighborhood poverty, disadvantage, and physical deterioration on successful developmental outcomes (Chapters 3 and 4). In subsequent chapters, we will add the effects of neighborhood organization and culture (Chapters 5 and 6), the structure and functioning of families (Chapter 7), and finally, the effects of school climate and peer groups (Chapter 8). In Chapter 9, we will consider the full multicontextual model of youth development, assessing both direct and indirect neighborhood effects as well as the unique and combined effects of all of these social contexts on youth development outcomes. This model also estimates the influence of individual attributes and dispositions of youth, above and beyond the effects of the social contexts in which they live. Here we will address directly our central question: How many youth living in high-risk, disadvantaged neighborhoods successfully pass through adolescence, and how are more successful youth different from less successful youth? The final chapter (Chapter 10) will summarize our findings and discuss neighborhood-level intervention strategies and policies that should facilitate higher rates of successful youth development for children and youth living in disadvantaged neighborhoods.

Notes

1. Although the Philadelphia Family Management Study, the Prince Georges County School Study, the Prince Georges County Parent Study, and the Iowa Farm Family Study all considered each of these contexts and shared some common contextual measures, each study had a unique focus, giving more emphasis to a specific context and developing a fuller conceptualization and measurement of the conditions and processes that influence youth development in that setting. The Denver and Chicago Neighborhood Study is the Network study that focused primarily on the neighborhood context. This study developed and tested the most detailed and comprehensive model of neighborhood influences on families, schools, peer networks, and individual developmental outcomes

2. The MacArthur Research Program on Successful Adolescent Development funded a preliminary neighborhood study that involved an add-on data collection component to Wave 3 of the Denver Youth Survey (Office of Juvenile Justice and Delinquency Prevention, David Huizinga, PI). The Denver Neighborhood Study is a later study funded by the John D. and Catherine T. MacArthur Foundation with supplemental funding from the Office of Juvenile Justice and Delinquency Prevention. This study involved a separate sample of neighborhoods that was representative of the full range of neighborhoods in the City and County of Denver (see note 36). Both MacArthur studies in Denver were directed by Del Elliott. The Chicago Youth Achievement Study, referred to hereafter as the Chicago Neighborhood Study, was also funded by the MacArthur Foundation. This study built upon the earlier Urban Poverty and Family Life Study in Chicago. Both Chicago studies were directed by William Julius Wilson.

3. Hallman, 1984; Bursik and Grasmick, 1993; Lee, 2001. Lee in particular notes the "slipperiness" of the neighborhood concept (p. 32).

4. Keller, 1968; Rivlin, 1987.

5. Morris and Hess, 1975.

6. Skogan, 1990; Bursik and Grasmick, 1993; Jencks and Peterson, 1991.

7. Hogan and Kitagawa, 1985; Schuerman and Kobrin, 1983; Corcoran et al., 1987; Sampson, 2001.

8. Ahlbrandt and Cunningham, 1980.

9. Sampson, Raudenbush, and Earls, 1997.

10. For example, see Bursik and Webb, 1982; Bursik and Grasmick, 1993; Elliott and Huizinga, 1990; Suttles, 1968; and Tienda, 1991; Lee, 2001.

11. Schmid, 1960; Furstenberg et al., 1999.

12. Denton and Massey, 1991; Allen and Turner, 1995; Cook, Shagle, and Değirmencioğlu, 1997; Lee and Campbell, 1998; Lee, 2001.

13. This approach has been used by Coulton et al., 1997; Lee et al., 1991; Downs and Stea, 1973; Burton et al., 1997.

14. See Coulton et al., 1997; Taylor, 1981.
15. Taylor, 1997; Taylor and Browser, 1981.
16. Taylor, 1997.
17. The construct validation study reported here was based on these data from Wave 3 of the Denver Youth Survey and on later data from the Chicago Neighborhood Study.
18. For a more detailed description of this study, see Campbell, Henley, Elliott, and Irwin, 2003.
19. Respondents in the Project on Human Development in Chicago Neighborhoods reported that the mean number of blocks in their neighborhoods was 25, a number much larger than reported by residents in this study. However, the definition of neighborhood given to the respondents was quite different; it included "... the general area around your house where you might perform routine tasks, such as shopping, going to the park, or visiting with neighbors" (Sampson, 2001).
20. Birch et al., 1979. Residents also identified a variety of secondary boundaries: (1) the point where apparent differences in market value of homes changed, (2) an area bearing a name recognized in the larger community, (3) school district boundaries, (4) civic association areas, (5) major traffic arteries, and (6) a section of the city.
21. Hallman, 1984.
22. These data were from the Denver Youth Survey, Waves 2 and 3. This analysis involves using categories that approximate the three census units being compared: block group, census tract, and multitracts. The first two response categories were thus combined into a block group category.
23. Lee (2001) reports a similar finding.
24. See Lee et al., 1991, for similar findings to those reported here. Lee and Campbell (1998) report differences by sex and age, but not by race for Nashville.
25. Consistent with this finding, Lee (2001) reports that black networks in Nashville neighborhoods were typically smaller and more intimate than those of whites.
26. For a discussion of neighborhood boundaries in this study see Irwin, 2004.
27. Birch et al. (1979) report that in this survey of residents in Houston, Dayton, and Rochester, everyone excluded any area where they wouldn't want to live, no matter how close, when asked to identify neighborhood boundaries.
28. Coulton et al. (1997) report on a resident mapping study in Cleveland where the perceived boundaries of the neighborhood appeared to approximate the size of a census tract and was approximately four times the area of a block group. Most often, the perceived neighborhood incorporated parts of more than one tract and multiple block groups. However, if the perceived neighborhood was restricted to the common area defined by residents (with at least 70 percent agreement), the overlap with the block group was greater than with the tract.
29. See Rapoport, 1997 and Lee, 2001.
30. See Coulton et al., 1997.
31. Coulton et al. (1997) come to a different conclusion in their study of Cleveland.

32. This is the unit recommended by Brooks-Gunn et al. (1997a). In principle, the smallest census unit available to a study is probably the best.

33. For example, see Lee (2001). In the Lee and Campbell (1998) study of neighborhoods in Nashville, the perceived size of the neighborhood ranged from one block to more than 900 blocks. The range in the Denver neighborhood study mapping exercise was much smaller, typically one to forty blocks.

34. Burton et al., 1997.

35. Coulton et al., 1997.

36. The Denver sample of neighborhoods is a stratified probability sample of households. Based on a social ecology analysis, block groups were assigned to one of nine strata, defined by high, medium, and low levels of disorganization and high, medium and low rates of officially recorded crime. Due to cost considerations, social areas and BGs with very low rates of youth per household (less than 0.08) were excluded from the sample. Modified census tracts, those portions of a tract lying within a single stratum and containing qualified BGs, were identified. Within each stratum, two modified census tracts were selected with probability proportional to size and from each of these census tracts, two BGs were selected with probability proportional to size. A random sample of households was selected from each selected BG with sampling rates chosen to provide approximately 25 youth aged 10, 12, 14, 16, or 18 per BG living in selected households. With appropriate weighting, selected persons and neighborhoods (BGs) are representative of persons and neighborhoods in the areas of Denver with eight or more youth per 100 households. Selected neighborhoods include the full range of neighborhoods from the very affluent to the very poor, from predominantly white to predominantly black or Latino. One BG was dropped from the study because of a very small number of resident families and in three cases, adjacent BGs were combined to produce a single neighborhood so as to achieve an adequate number of families and eligible youth. The resulting number of BGs/neighborhoods was thus 33. The mother (or primary caregiver) and all eligible youth living in the household were included in the eligible sample of families and youth.

37. The Chicago sample of neighborhoods involved two strata. The first stratum was a high-poverty, African American stratum and included all neighborhoods (Census Tracts) with 50 percent or more African American families and 20 percent or more families below the poverty line. The second was a low-poverty, African American stratum that included tracts with 30 percent or more African American families and median incomes of $30,000 or more. The sample of households selected within these strata was restricted to African American households with one or more eligible youth aged 11–16. Mothers and up to two eligible youth from each eligible household were included in the family and youth samples. The size of neighborhoods ranged from one to 67 square blocks.

38. In Denver, there was little overlap in respondents who participated in the surveys and the ethnographic studies. The survey interviews were completed in 1991. The ethnographic data were collected in 1995 in selected Denver study neighborhoods. Using the survey data, these neighborhoods were selected to include high disadvantaged neighborhoods in which there were (1) good and

(2) poor youth developmental outcomes; and low disadvantaged neighborhoods in which there were (3) good and (4) poor youth developmental outcomes. A fifth neighborhood was selected to provide a comparison of mixed ethnic/racial neighborhoods with good outcomes. There was already a mixed neighborhood with poor developmental outcomes in the earlier selected neighborhoods.

The ethnographic data for the Chicago site comes from two studies, the Urban Poverty and Family Life Study and the Community Redevelopment and Revitalization Study, which included subjects living in the Woodlawn and North Kenwood/Oakland neighborhoods. These subjects were selected as a purposive sample of residents representing all racial groups and three employment status groups (steadily employed, steadily unemployed, and intermittently employed) in these communities. There is some potential overlap in neighborhoods as the 1993 study involved neighborhoods with 20 percent or more poverty, but the exact overlap is not known.

Good and Bad Neighborhoods for Raising Children

SYNOPSIS

Some neighborhoods are good places to raise children. Living in these areas increases the chances that children will grow up to be healthy, responsible, and productive adults. Other neighborhoods are bad places to raise children – places where they are exposed to violence, dysfunctional lifestyles, negative role models, unfriendly neighbors, and poor quality schools. Children living in these neighborhoods may have little opportunity to acquire the personal skills and experiences necessary for effective participation in mainstream community life. In this chapter, we identify features that distinguish between good and bad neighborhoods as environments for raising children and adolescents.

Three features of the neighborhood influence the course of development for children: (1) its demographic composition, (2) the condition of its physical environment, and (3) its social organization and culture. We focus on the first two features in this chapter and on the third in Chapter 5. The set of compositional conditions associated with bad neighborhoods we refer to as neighborhood disadvantage. The physical condition is called neighborhood deterioration. Concentrated poverty is one indicator of disadvantage, but there are also other compositional or demographic characteristics of a neighborhood that have negative influences on youth development. We identify these characteristics and describe the mechanisms linking each of these demographic compositional features to developmental processes and outcomes. The extent to which these conditions cluster in a neighborhood defines its level of disadvantage.

The other defining characteristic of a bad neighborhood is its physical condition. Neighborhood deterioration refers to buildings being in disrepair or abandoned, uncollected trash on the streets, and open spaces that are littered and vandalized. These are signs that the physical neighborhood is not being maintained and that the quality of community services delivered to the neighborhood is low. Again, we describe the mechanisms by which these physical conditions influence youth development. Neighborhoods that are disadvantaged also tend to be deteriorated and it is this combination of conditions that typically marks a neighborhood as a bad place for raising children.

Disadvantage and deterioration constitute the initial set of neighborhood effects that we examine in our study of successful youth development in disadvantaged neighborhoods. This model of neighborhood effects is tested in Chapter 4.

3

Good and Bad Neighborhoods for Raising Children

Adult female – Westside: I always think of it (neighborhood) as being safe and nice. That's the main thing.

Adult male – Martin Park: This isn't really a neighborhood, you know. Mr. Rogers has a neighborhood. We don't have neighborhoods as far as I know. This is a house where I live and where we do the best we can from day to day.

INTRODUCTION

Neighborhoods are a central feature of urban and suburban life. Their development is a natural phenomenon, arising out of our living in close proximity to others and our need to establish relationships with others to sustain our individual and collective lives. Some neighborhoods are better than others in supporting the lives and maximizing the potential of those who live there; these neighborhoods have been created, nurtured, and sustained over long periods of time. Others have been neglected, abused, and essentially abandoned; and still others have developed structures and cultures that actually encourage dysfunctional lifestyles.

Below are short descriptions of two of the neighborhoods included in this study. They are both ethnically diverse, lower income/working-class neighborhoods that are immediately adjacent to each other, but life is very different in these two neighborhoods.

NORTHSIDE

This neighborhood is a stable neighborhood made up primarily of Hispanic and white families. Most residents are employed in blue-collar jobs and many families supplement their income with informal activities like selling arts and crafts, transcribing work, and piece-work done at home. Pockets of poverty exist in the neighborhood, with poor families living in the few large apartment complexes in a neighborhood where single-family dwellings are most common. Most residents know their neighbors and are active in neighborhood and community organizations like the PTA, church, school fund-raisers, scouts, and school sports. There is high consensus among parents about what they want for their children: having good schools and a safe neighborhood. Parents know their children's teachers and in most cases the principals at their schools. They are aware of some drug and crime problems in the neighborhood but do not think of their neighborhood as a particularly dangerous place, and they reject the assertion by some outsiders that it is a drug- and crime-ridden neighborhood.

ADULT WOMAN: We moved here in 1964...when we moved into the neighborhood, it was predominantly Italians and Jews. We were very comfortable. Northside was the school. And over the years I've seen it that we're Italians, we're Jewish, we're Mexicans...we're, uh, blacks...we're very diverse.

ADULT WOMAN: When you have, especially elementary school-age kids, seems like you get to know people more...actually our boys...started meeting everyone around before we did...Oh, you're so and so's parents, you know. After a while there was a teenage gal in high school across from the back end of our lot...she'd watch them (her boys) a good part of the time, you know. And she took them around and everybody knew them, you know.

ADOLESCENT MALE: It's a good neighborhood. It's safe and there's no crime out here, not many strangers walking down the street. Neighborhood watch program is around and so my uh, mom made that, set up this block here.

Like their parents, adolescents in Northside are very active, juggling demands of family, school, sports, and jobs. Their friends typically include youth from the neighborhood. They often drink and party on weekends, but they are also committed to doing well in school, sports, and other conventional activities. Most look forward to attending college and starting careers and families, reflecting the types of expectations their parents have for them.

The subculture of their school differs from that of their neighborhood. Northside High contains many nonconventional cultures and opportunities for drug use, drug sales, gangs, guns, and violent encounters with other adolescents. Some Northside youth are attracted to such activities, but most are not. There is some reported victimization at school, but most youth seem insulated from the drugs, violence, and gangs found there.

ADULT WOMAN: My husband coached soccer for five years. That used to be a part, a real large part of our activity and time that we put in with that. My youngest son, he's in soccer right now at Northside High and, he goes after school every day, so ... so we're – go to the games and stuff like that every – you know, week, either two or three – usually two games a week. He does go to Young Life at Northside ... (My older son), he is in the internship program, which is through CEC (High School Program) ... He's at the hospital – he's at Northside Hospital. He – instead of going to school ... he goes with an anesthesiologist, he goes there to see if he wants to be a – you know, a doctor.

ADULT WOMAN: Our daughter's been pretty much involved with stuff that we're involved with and stuff that she's not hanging around just to hang around, you know. She's here, she's at school. Yeah, either for school for sports or she's up like at St. Jude's Hospital because she's involved in an Explorer Post.

ADOLESCENT MALE: Well, there is a lot of, you know, drug selling ... And there is kids that work and so have jobs and they do get honest money. But again, there are those kids who do that kind of stuff ... You know, if they want – if the will is there and they want to get a job, the opportunity is there and like we were talking about earlier, some of the things I'm grateful that Northside High offers, well that is one of the things where they have a program also where the teacher will get you a job. She'll go out and she'll talk to the manager. She'll get you an application, you know. She'll do everything, you know ... Most of my close friends that I confide in or whatever, you know, are people like, you know, kids my age from my church and stuff ... they (drug dealers), you know, ... they don't live in this area.

ALLENSPARK

As noted in Chapter 2, this neighborhood was initially considered a part of Northside but is quite distinct in the minds of residents. It is a densely populated, ethnically diverse, poor, city-planned neighborhood project. There are some physical differences between Northside and Allenspark. The buildings in Allenspark are two-story, multiple-family-type buildings compared to the predominantly single-family, single-story structures in Northside. Like Northside, the buildings are in good repair and the lawns are watered and mowed. Although it is immediately adjacent to Northside, it is not integrated into the larger Northside community. While adolescents living in this neighborhood attend the same schools, parents typically are not involved in neighborhood or community organizations or even aware of the organizations in which Northside parents participate. While there are some organized activities and recreational facilities in this neighborhood (a gym in the projects, a social service agency, and a swimming pool), few adolescents use these facilities. They are, however, used by younger children. Teen gangs (Asian and Latino), random violence, drug use and sales, car theft, tagging, vandalism, school dropout, and teen pregnancy are common components of adolescent life in Allenspark. Many adults (and youth) are intimidated by the gangs and adolescents in the neighborhood and abide by a "code of silence" out of fear of retaliation. Informal relations among neighbors are characterized by distrust, conflict, and racial tension. Most residents want to move out of the neighborhood.

ADULT WOMAN: Living in Allenspark is okay... during the day it's all right. But during the night, there's a lot of break-ins, especially in cars... just got my car stolen.

INTERVIEWER: When you got your car stolen, or other cars have been broken into – does anyone call the police?

ADULT WOMAN: Right away. But we feel like they don't do nothin, because they'll just say "Oh, they've just ripped off another poor Mexican," you know! – "tough luck."

INTERVIEWER: Do they come?

ADULT WOMAN: Yeah, about two hours after you call them. Some of the parents go right along with their kids, too, to rip off houses. Some of the parents around here are dealing. I mean, they're not any better than their kids on it. That's what bugs the hell outta me. I mean, what cracks me up is the cops – the cops from Allenspark [the project police] know exactly who they are, and they're still here!

ADOLESCENT FOCUS GROUP: I don't like police officers... they think they're all bad 'cause they're police officers. They think they can pull you over whenever they feel like it and stuff... Sometimes you don't even have to be doin' anything. 'Cause we like to jump like this, they think we're in a gang or something... Mexicans and Asians used to fight... If one of them would mess with another one, everybody'd get in it and there's just a big fight. A big, big fight. It's worse now. It's just not – it's not racial. Like we'll call them chinkers and they'll call us beaners and we'll call them micks or japs or dog eaters and stuff like that... You kinda don't feel – I don't feel safe, you know, because they start talking in that language. You know they talking about you, you know they using all the language, you know, but you don't know – you really don't understand what they're saying.

Life is very different in these two neighborhoods, both for adults and for adolescents. There are real physical dangers, fear, and racial tensions in Allenspark that are not present in Northside although both are racially/ethnically diverse. Adolescents (and adults) seem to be engaged in different activities and parents appear to employ different strategies to promote a successful course of development for their children. In sum, the chances of growing up to be a responsible, productive, healthy adult appear to be quite different for youth in these two neighborhoods.

How did these adjacent neighborhoods come to be so different? Are these differences purely a function of the types of persons who move in and out of the neighborhood and the levels of physical deterioration and disrepair? Is the difference largely one of the wealth or poverty of residents? Are the chances of a successful adolescent development really different in neighborhoods like these?

We will begin to answer such questions in this chapter, describing what makes a good or bad neighborhood for raising children. Our focus in this chapter is on the ecology of the neighborhood. This refers to the demographic composition and physical condition of the neighborhood, that is, on the types of people and families that live in the neighborhood and whether it is well-kept or run-down. We will describe how these features of the neighborhood influence a successful course of youth development. In Chapter 5, we will consider another feature of neighborhoods that influences the course of youth development – the informal organization and culture of the neighborhood – but we begin with neighborhood composition and physical condition and argue that these two ecological features of neighborhoods largely determine whether an effective informal organization and supportive culture will emerge in the neighborhood. In later chapters, we will consider the effects of all three neighborhood characteristics on parenting and family socialization practices, the culture of the school and peer group organization within the neighborhood, and how the multiple layers of social contexts (neighborhood, family, school, and peer) together affect youth development outcomes. This conceptualization of a neighborhood thus directs our inquiry into how youth living in high-risk, disadvantaged neighborhoods can beat the odds, overcome these risks, and complete a successful course of adolescent development.

THE NEIGHBORHOOD AS A DEVELOPMENTAL CONTEXT

We view neighborhoods from an ecological-developmental perspective.[1] The neighborhood is seen as a transactional setting that influences individual behavior and development both directly and indirectly through its influence on several other social contexts that often are nested within neighborhoods, for example, families, schools, and peer groups. Further, although our focus here is on how the demographic composition and physical environment influence individual developmental outcomes, individual actions and events also influence the composition and physical environment of the neighborhood. The neighborhood–individual relationship is thus dynamic and interdependent.[2]

To separate contextual and individual effects on adolescent development, we outline our conceptualization of neighborhood effects, beginning with compositional and physical environmental effects in this chapter and continuing in Chapter 5, where we consider organizational and cultural effects. This view of how neighborhoods influence youth development draws upon several theoretical traditions, including social disorganization,[3] social disorder,[4] and urban poverty and inequality.[5]

TYPES OF NEIGHBORHOOD EFFECTS

We identify three types of neighborhood effects on youth development, three sets of conditions that determine whether a neighborhood is a good or bad place to raise children. These conditions involve the demographic composition of the neighborhood, the physical characteristics of the neighborhood, and the social organization and culture of the neighborhood. Together, these features of neighborhoods create a social context that can be either supportive of conventional socialization processes and a successful course of youth development, or one that can impede and undermine these processes and outcomes.

Society's concern about the consequences of growing up in bad neighborhoods is primarily a concern with specific physical and compositional characteristics of neighborhoods. It is a concern over neighborhoods with high rates of poverty, high unemployment, single-parent families, rundown and abandoned buildings, graffiti, gangs, and high rates of crime.[6] These are ecological indicators of neighborhood *disadvantage* (composition) and *deterioration* (physical conditions) in a neighborhood, which undermine or threaten a successful course of development for youth. We begin our discussion of neighborhood effects by looking at the possible influences of these two features of neighborhoods on successful youth development.

ADVANTAGED AND DISADVANTAGED NEIGHBORHOODS

The demographic composition of a neighborhood refers to the collective characteristics of persons and families living in the neighborhood, for example, to the proportion of residents who are children, retired, unemployed, poor, married, on welfare, or parents of young children. The decision to live in a given neighborhood is not random, nor are individuals and families equally free to live in any neighborhood they might choose. The choice of neighborhood is restricted in certain ways and these restrictions lead to segregated neighborhoods with markedly different compositional characteristics. We will characterize neighborhoods as advantaged or disadvantaged based upon these compositional characteristics and their assumed influence on child and youth development. This difference is widely acknowledged by realtors and home buyers who know intuitively that the neighborhood they live in will influence the development and security of their children.

What accounts for differences in neighborhood composition? Early sociological theories, like those of Park and Burgess (1924), identified economic competition as the fundamental social process underlying the formation of neighborhoods, and levels of poverty or wealth as the primary distinguishing characteristic of neighborhoods. From this perspective, the critical demographic characteristics of the neighborhood are established by the laws of supply and demand for scarce, desirable space. Persons with limited economic resources are relegated to neighborhoods with the cheapest housing and the least physically attractive space; those with better economic resources are able to live in more attractive areas and afford more expensive housing.[7] This economic sorting of individuals and families results in neighborhoods that tend to be internally homogeneous with respect to income, class, and other indicators of economic status; and there are big differences across neighborhoods on these indicators, ranging from neighborhoods where most residents are very poor to neighborhoods where most are very wealthy. Historically, most theory and research on neighborhood composition effects focused on this economic sorting process (hereafter referred to as *selection*) and on poverty and affluence as the most salient compositional feature of neighborhoods that influenced childhood socialization and development.

While the differences between good and bad neighborhoods clearly involve economics, more recent theory and research indicates that other factors are also involved.[8] Although a heavy concentration of poor families in a given neighborhood should have an effect on socialization practices, role models, and resources available to youth, this is not the only compositional feature of neighborhoods that has the potential of limiting or undermining a successful course of youth development.

Today, the neighborhood selection and sorting process is more complex than the "free and open competitive housing market" described by sociologists and demographers prior to World War II. Recent research on social disorganization and urban inequality suggests a number of additional selection factors that affect neighborhood composition: the structure of the job market, for example, the elimination or relocation of skilled manufacturing jobs;[9] patterns of family composition and disruption, e.g., single parents; multiple-family households; number of children per family/household;[10] racial and ethnic segregation;[11] and the impact of political processes such as urban renewal, rent controls, zoning restrictions, and other housing policies.[12] Together, these economic, social, and political conditions and processes operate to sort individuals and families into particular neighborhoods and this selection process accounts for the distinctive compositional characteristics of neighborhoods that influence youth development.

Neighborhood disadvantage is thus a multidimensional trait involving a complex *set* of compositional characteristics. It is not simply a matter of poverty or the concentration of poverty, although this is a key indicator of neighborhood disadvantage.[13] We propose to include a broader set of economic, political, and cultural variables in our definition of disadvantage and to specify the mechanisms or processes that link these particular features of neighborhood composition to poor developmental outcomes for youth.

DEFINING DISADVANTAGE

In their classic analysis of neighborhood effects on socialization processes and outcomes, Shaw and McKay[14] identified three critical neighborhood-level indicators of disadvantage: high poverty levels, high rates of residential instability, and racial and ethnic heterogeneity. To these three we have added a measure of family composition – the proportion of single-parent families.[15] Each of these four compositional characteristics is a risk factor for poor developmental outcomes. We will consider each of these indicators of neighborhood disadvantage in turn.

Neighborhood Poverty

The primary mechanism linking neighborhood poverty to poor youth development outcomes is its restriction on economic and social resources within the neighborhood. More affluent neighborhoods have more tangible physical amenities, like cleaner and better maintained parks, supervised play areas, and safer streets. More importantly, they are served by better (resource-rich) schools, provide more contacts with conventional work networks, have better police protection, and have greater access to public transportation.[16]

In addition to scarce economic resources, poor neighborhoods have limited social resources that derive from or are associated with their limited economic resources. Living in an affluent as compared to a poor neighborhood provides some measure of social status to individuals and may increase their job prospects.[17] Exposure to neighbors who have limited education and are frequently unemployed provides poor role models and results in low educational and work expectations.[18] The high levels of economic and social stress and the limited resources for dealing with these stresses result in low expectations for and quality of health care.[19]

The influence of neighborhood poverty on youth development involves both a *contagion effect* and an institutional *deprivation effect*.[20] These mechanisms work through the social organization and culture that emerge in the neighborhood. In the first case (contagion), the interaction patterns in poor neighborhoods result in a set of norms that reflect low educational, health, and work expectations. These norms undermine high educational aspirations and achievement, appropriate health care, and the acquisition of work-related competencies for children living in these neighborhoods. In the second case (deprivation), the limited institutional investment in poor neighborhoods restricts educational and occupational opportunities for children living in these neighborhoods. Together, these normative constraints and limited opportunities are mutually reinforcing and seriously undermine the development of youth living in poor neighborhoods.

Racial and Ethnic Heterogeneity

The second indicator of neighborhood disadvantage is a high mix of different racial and ethnic groups in the neighborhood.[21] The specific mechanism involved here is a *culture conflict effect*. The presence of multiple cultures, each with a somewhat unique set of values and norms and frequently involving different languages, increases the likelihood that there will be limited communication among neighbors and low levels of consensus about appropriate neighborhood goals and standards of behavior. This limited interaction also impedes the formation of informal social networks in the neighborhood that could provide social support for individuals and families and social controls on appropriate behavior.

In addition to limiting network size, ethnic/racial diversity also tends to limit the breadth of social networks in neighborhoods.[22] Merry[23] provides a clear example of this effect in a mixed-race/ethnic public housing project with Chinese, African American, Hispanic, and white[24] residents. Although most of these families had lived in the project more than 10 years and were involved in daily contact when using the project facilities, friendship networks rarely crossed racial/ethnic boundaries and the levels of distrust between the different racial/ethnic groups were quite high. There were small informal friendship groups, but the breadth of the interpersonal network was quite restricted and Merry reports that youth committed serious crimes without fear of apprehension because of the anonymity within the project. A similar effect is noted by Kingston (2005). Lee and Campbell (1998) also report that despite circumstances favorable to integration in Nashville neighborhoods, friendship networks remained distinct for black and white residents. Even when living side by side in the same neighborhood, more than 80 percent of black and 95 percent of white ties were to same-race neighbors. They noted that mixed neighborhoods contain "multiple social worlds."

Racial and ethnic diversity thus tends to undermine the emergence of a common culture in the neighborhood and the formation of informal social networks that cross racial/ethnic lines. Children living in mixed racial and ethnic neighborhoods may be exposed to contradictory values and different standards of behavior. This situation undermines the family's socialization efforts as there are few and inconsistent reinforcements for their specific values and norms in the neighborhood.

We view racial and ethnic diversity as an indicator of neighborhood disadvantage that is independent of poverty, that is, it has an effect on neighborhood organization and culture that is above and beyond that of poverty. In Jargowsky's[25] recent analysis of high-poverty urban neighborhoods in the United States, he notes that a majority of residents in these neighborhoods are members of minority groups. However very few high-poverty neighborhoods (approximately 4 percent) are composed *exclusively* of one racial/ethnic group. In fact, nearly 30 percent of high-poverty neighborhoods have no dominant racial group. Among those high-poverty neighborhoods that had a dominant racial group (two thirds or more of the population), 65 percent were predominantly African American, 16 percent were predominantly Hispanic, and 19 percent were predominantly white. Thus, within high-poverty neighborhoods, there is considerable variation in the level of racial/ethnic diversity.

Residential Instability

Residential stability has a direct effect on the frequency and pattern of social interaction in the neighborhood. It takes time to develop meaningful relationships with others and to develop common goals and values. In neighborhoods where families and individuals stay only a short time and then move, social relationships and shared understandings may never emerge or have to be constantly renewed as neighbors come and go. The social networks that do emerge are likely to be more transient and superficial, with a limited level of personal commitment and social support. Residents have little motivation to develop friendships when they do not expect to stay in the neighborhood for long and will leave at the first opportunity. When the informal networks are weak, adults in the neighborhood do not know the children and youth living there and are less likely to intervene on their behalf or take responsibility for their behavior because they do not know the children's parents.[26] In sum, residential instability limits the creation and stability of interpersonal friendship (social support) networks in the neighborhood and the emergence of informal norms that guide and regulate behavior and promote positive developmental outcomes.[27]

Residential instability also undermines the development of parochial networks in a neighborhood.[28] These are the broader, less intimate relationships among residents and persons in the institutions serving the neighborhood, such as the schools, churches, and businesses. These persons, for example, local teachers, store clerks, parishioners, and local business employees, often do not live in the neighborhood. Without some continuity in these broader relationships, the linkage between the neighborhood and the social institutions serving the residents cannot be maintained. Residential instability thus undermines the potential influence of social institutions serving the neighborhood, isolating residents of the neighborhood from effective participation in these institutions.

Single-Parent Families

The high prevalence of single-parent families is often a distinguishing feature of high-poverty neighborhoods. Over half of all families with children living in high-poverty neighborhoods are female-headed families, compared to 15 percent in low-poverty neighborhoods.[29] But the mechanism linking a high prevalence of single-parent families to a weak neighborhood organizational structure and ineffective neighborhood norms involves more than the limited economic resources in the neighborhood and the contagion effect on educational and occupational expectations noted earlier for neighborhood poverty.

First, there is a social control effect: The larger the proportion of single-parent families in the neighborhood, the fewer adult caretakers are available in the neighborhood to monitor and supervise the activities of children and to protect them from victimization by others.[30] Single parents are also less able to participate in informal friendship networks in the neighborhood, and these networks are less likely to exist in neighborhoods where there is a high proportion of single-parent families. These informal networks provide social controls on behavior and a safety net for neighborhood youth; if they are not present in a neighborhood, the levels of social control are limited.

Second, there is a limited-opportunity effect that results from the inability of many single parents to participate in voluntary organizations and other parochial networks in the neighborhood because of time constraints and energy levels. These networks play a critical role in providing access to and social support for school and work opportunities and for sports and other activities in the community. Neighborhoods with a high proportion of single-parent families are less likely to develop and sustain these kinds of networks.[31]

In sum, we have taken a multidimensional approach to defining neighborhood disadvantage, identifying four compositional characteristics of neighborhoods that influence the way people interact with their neighbors. This approach to studying the effects of neighborhood composition on youth development is theoretically grounded. It specifies the mechanisms or processes linking these conditions to youth development and provides a more comprehensive perspective on variation in neighborhood disadvantage and its influence on the emerging neighborhood organization and culture than the use of a poverty measure alone.

A multidimensional focus on ecological disadvantage is also important because it allows for the possibility that not all high-poverty neighborhoods are characterized by residential instability, high levels of ethnic and racial diversity, and a high proportion of single-parent families. Not all poor neighborhoods are disadvantaged and not all disadvantaged neighborhoods are poor. While there is a tendency for these compositional conditions to cluster in specific neighborhoods,[32] there is also sufficient variation to assess the independent effects of these conditions, as we will do in the next chapter. These additional indicators of disadvantage may well have a greater influence on neighborhood organization or interact with poverty to produce particularly deleterious effects on neighborhood organization and adolescent development. Bronfenbrenner notes that one type of contextual risk may well compound the effects of other contextual risks, producing multiplicative effects on youth development.[33]

Finally, composition effects are the result of selection processes reflecting the general societal-level economic, social, and political processes that determine who lives in what neighborhood. Compositional effects are nevertheless genuine contextual effects that logically can be distinguished from individual-level effects. If children in poor families have different developmental outcomes when they live in a disadvantaged as compared to an affluent neighborhood (and other individual-level variables are constant), this difference is a true contextual effect. For example, Blankston and Caldas (1998) in a study of 18,000 10th graders in Louisiana, report that being surrounded by schoolmates from female-headed families had a negative effect on academic achievement that was independent and stronger than the effect of individual family structure.

PHYSICAL CONDITION: WELL-KEPT AND DETERIORATED
NEIGHBORHOODS

Neighborhoods are not only characterized by the types of people who live there, they are also physical places with distinguishing physical features. If you were to tell a person who knows the Chicago area that you live in Hyde Park or Woodlawn, that person would immediately envision a physical setting at each location – the types of houses, landscaping, areas where kids play and teenagers hang out, schools, stores, vacant lots, streets, and sidewalks. The person would also make some assumptions about your social status and the economic well-being of your family, based on the reputations of these areas. Neighborhoods thus have a spatial identity and most Chicago residents would be aware of major differences in the physical characteristics of these two specific neighborhoods.

We propose that the condition and spatial arrangements of the physical features of the neighborhood have an influence on both the decision (sometimes highly constrained) of residents to live there (neighborhood composition) and on the interpersonal contact and interaction patterns that emerge among neighbors. The physical environment of the neighborhood, together with the compositional characteristics of the neighborhood, shape the collective life of the residents and indirectly influence the socialization processes and developmental outcomes of the children living there.

Early studies of the neighborhood identified some physical features that were typically associated with compositional indicators of disadvantage and poor developmental outcomes for children and youth. Shaw and McKay[34] identified dilapidated and deteriorated housing and mixed-use areas (residential and commercial buildings or industrial plants sharing the same geographical space) as two features of the physical environment that led to high rates of population turnover (instability) and more directly influenced the social interaction and socialization processes in the neighborhood. Subsequent work has focused on the type of structure, age, and density of housing; the size, height, accessibility, and open spaces between buildings; the condition of the buildings, streets, and landscaping as detected by deteriorated, dilapidated, and abandoned buildings; litter and garbage on the streets; abandoned cars; broken streetlights and windows; graffiti and signs of vandalism; and land use.[35]

While the type of housing (e.g., single-family dwellings, multiple-family dwellings, high-rise housing projects) and the condition or quality of housing has been the primary focus of much of this research, residents use many neighborhood spaces in addition to their houses. How this space is used also has an influence on the quality of neighborhood life. The street is probably the most commonly used of these areas. Residents use the streets to enter and leave the neighborhood, for recreation, parties, the purchase of goods and services, and as a place for adolescents to "hang out."[36] There is evidence that lower-income residents are more likely to use the area in front of their houses, the porches, sidewalks, and streets; more affluent residents are more likely to use their private yards.[37] Neighborhood differences clearly exist in block layout, land use and circulation patterns, types of open spaces, and housing characteristics.

There are three processes by which the physical neighborhood influences youth development: social isolation, social control, and an amplification of disadvantage. The first two processes have a direct effect on the frequency and type of interaction that will emerge among residents. The last has the effect of escalating the levels of compositional disadvantage in the neighborhood.

SOCIAL ISOLATION

The physical environment in a neighborhood can operate to facilitate or limit the interaction among residents. It often determines which neighbors are most likely to meet (or not meet) and under what circumstances. This patterning of activities and interactions exists even before residents move into the neighborhood and actually meet. There are also immediate visual cues in the neighborhood that reflect the care and attention given to the

buildings and open spaces. Bad neighborhoods are immediately identified by the neglect, deterioration, and abuse of the physical environment.
Skogan refers to these particular visual cues as "physical incivilities."[38]
They include such things as buildings in disrepair or abandoned; broken
streetlights and windows; trash, litter and graffiti in public areas; run-down
yards; and evidence of vandalism to buildings and cars. These physical features of the neighborhood, which we will refer to as physical deterioration,
signal the newcomer that the streets and open spaces are not safe and that
no one cares about or has the means to control the destructive activities
going on in the neighborhood. Research indicates that under these conditions, the sense of one's "territory" shrinks to include only that space
residents can directly control, typically their own house or apartment.
Residents thus tend to withdraw from involvement in the neighborhood
out of fear and insecurity and restrict their children's activities to their own
homes and areas they can watch.[39]

   This withdrawal and sense of isolation was clearly expressed by an adult
woman living in Denver's Allenspark neighborhood, a housing project
where a number of these physical incivilities were present:

I'm an inside person, you know? I don't associate with really nobody around
here . . . I don't trust nobody . . . cause I don't know them. You know. I say "hi"
to them when I walk by their houses, but that's about it. Oh, God – they (the cops)
should have their own station here . . . the thing of it is, everybody runs around the
house, they close their doors, they turn off the lights, they don't answer the door.
So it like – they can't do anything. At all . . . there's fights, there's cars being tore up,
there's places being broken into, I mean – it's a joke around here.

   Research also confirms that residents living in physically deteriorated
areas are less likely to help their neighbors. This finding holds even for
highly disadvantaged neighborhoods; the greater the physical deterioration of these neighborhoods, the less helping among neighbors.[40] Physical
deterioration limits social interaction.

SOCIAL CONTROL

Newman reports that the greater the size of an apartment building or
multiple-unit housing project, the less residents make use of the common
areas, the less social interaction among neighbors, and the less sense of
control over both the interior and exterior public areas.[41] The critical issue
here is that the physical environment can either facilitate or restrict resident
surveillance. Open areas that cannot be watched or observed by residents
from their apartments, long dark hallways, poorly lighted stairwells, and
areas where no one is specifically responsible for monitoring activities all
reduce the levels of surveillance and the capacity for effective social control.

Large, high-rise subsidized housing projects typically provide very poor surveillance over internal and external public areas. This accounts, at least in part, for the diminished sense of control, limited use of open areas, and restricted interaction with neighbors in these projects.[42]

Physical incivilities and social incivilities go hand in hand in a person–environment reciprocal relationship. Social incivilities include the presence of gangs, prostitution, drug selling, homeless persons blocking doorways, panhandling, loitering, gambling, public drunkenness, and vandalism. These activities are a clear indication that the neighborhood lacks the organizational capacity and normative consensus required to control these activities.[43]

THE AMPLIFICATION OF DISADVANTAGE

Physical deterioration, social isolation, low levels of surveillance, high rates of victimization, and little risk of censure for uncivil behavior will, over time, produce changes in the social composition of the neighborhood. First, high levels of physical deterioration and social disorder in the neighborhood lead to declining property values. Second, some neighborhoods characterized by physical deterioration acquire a reputation for tolerating disorder and incivilities. Together, these conditions set in motion an out-migration of those families and individuals with the means to move to better, safer locations and an in-migration of troublemakers and persons with deviant lifestyles who are attracted to this kind of neighborhood. This change in composition results in an even lower commitment of residents to improving the physical environment, less surveillance and fewer guardians in the neighborhood, and a diminished capacity for social control.[44] The net effect is an amplification of the neighborhood's deterioration and disorder problems.

Thus, physical deterioration undermines the basic social interaction process by which residents in a neighborhood create a stable order and supportive culture. There is no guarantee that a physically attractive, well-designed and cared-for neighborhood will produce a safe and nurturing context for child development, but it is more likely to happen in this type of neighborhood because there are fewer immediate dangers to address and the physical environment facilitates more positive exchanges among residents, which typically leads to the emergence of a strong neighborhood organization and a supportive, prosocial culture.

DISCUSSION

Figure 3.1 summarizes our initial model of neighborhood effects on youth development. We have identified two types of neighborhood effects: (1) a

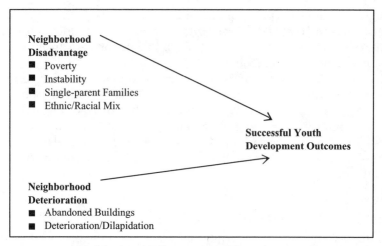

FIGURE 3.1. Neighborhood Effects on Youth Development: Initial Model

compositional effect that we have labeled neighborhood disadvantage, and (2) an effect of the physical environment that we refer to as neighborhood deterioration. We argue that the effect of neighborhood disadvantage and physical deterioration are effects that combine over time to disrupt a successful course of youth development.

In this model, concentrated poverty, by itself, does not produce a bad neighborhood for raising children. It is only one of several compositional and physical characteristics that combine to undermine the effectiveness of socialization processes, the presence of social controls, and the availability of conventional resources and opportunities. Poverty is linked most directly to a weak institutional presence and limited resources and opportunities in mainstream institutions. Poverty and physical disorder are also linked to the emergence of gangs and illegal activities in the neighborhood. But it is not the only feature of the neighborhood that accounts for the quality of the neighborhood as a developmental context that can generate strong and effective social networks and a conventional culture or lifestyle.

The instability (mobility), racial/ethnic mix, and the concentration of single-parent families with children are other conditions that directly undermine developmental processes. These are critical features of the neighborhood that influence family life and the creation of supportive social networks and culture. We thus expect that these features of the neighborhood ecology will also contribute to the quality of the neighborhood as a context for youth development.

We expect these indicators of disadvantage to cluster together in specific neighborhoods, that is, neighborhoods that are unstable are also likely to be poor, racially mixed, with a high proportion of single-parent families.

These compositional features of the neighborhood are all related to one another to some degree. We also believe, however, that each feature has a unique effect on the quality of neighborhood life and on young people's chances for completing the developmental tasks of childhood and adolescence successfully.

The most controversial proposition in this model of neighborhood effects is that racial or ethnic diversity is an indicator of neighborhood Disadvantage. This view is clearly at odds with current ideology and political strategies for reducing the racial and ethnic inequalities and segregation that exist in our neighborhoods and larger society. Since World War II, housing policies have been designed to facilitate and encourage racial and ethnic diversity within neighborhoods in the belief that increased interaction and exposure to persons of different cultural backgrounds would break down racial stereotypes; reduce intergroup hostility, prejudice, and discrimination; facilitate positive interpersonal interaction; and eliminate the residential segregation and social isolation from mainstream institutions traditionally experienced by minorities, especially persons of color. The critical question is, when other neighborhood conditions are equal, (for example, income levels or social class), does the cultural diversity of residents have some independent influence on youth developmental processes and outcomes? Does it contribute to a successful or unsuccessful course of youth development? Are there specific conditions under which this strategy is effective or not effective?

Much of the available research on this question confounds racial and ethnic diversity with poverty. There is general consensus that neighborhood poverty, particularly when highly concentrated in a neighborhood, has a negative influence on neighborhood resources and opportunities and this has a direct negative influence on youth development. For example, there is evidence that socioeconomic diversity (e.g., some exposure to successful, upwardly mobile adults) in the neighborhood may have beneficial effects on youth development, particularly on developmental outcomes for poor youth.[45] The unique, independent effect of racial and ethnic diversity is not well established in contemporary studies. What is known generally supports the proposition in our conceptual model of neighborhood effects – that diversity limits the formation and integration of informal networks and the development of normative and value consensus.[46] The proposition that racial diversity is linked to higher rates of delinquency in the neighborhood is also supported by this body of research. Much less is known about the effects of neighborhood diversity on other developmental outcomes. The evidence on school performance, for example, is quite mixed.[47]

We will consider this question carefully in the next chapter when we construct our measure of neighborhood disadvantage and we will include racial/ethnic diversity as an indicator of disadvantage only if the evidence supports its negative influence on youth development outcomes. Further, our conceptual model clearly specifies the hypothesized mechanism linking racial diversity with negative developmental outcomes. Even if the evidence supports the general proposition, there may be conditions under which these postulated effects do and do not occur. For example, when economic levels are roughly comparable, ethnic diversity may not have the hypothesized negative effects on development outcomes; or only when groups have a high level of commitment to maintaining their unique cultures does racial diversity lead to low levels of consensus and limited informal networks. Such findings would provide important insights into how we might design effective neighborhood-level interventions to promote higher rates of successful youth development.

Finally, these compositional and physical environment effects are both genuine *contextual* effects. They involve characteristics of neighborhoods rather than individuals. This distinction is important. Jargowsky warns "...it is very unwise to assume that all social problems observed in the ghetto are caused by the ghetto or by some ghetto culture. Some of the social pathologies of the ghetto are common to poor people or members of minority groups wherever they live."[48]

We have conceptualized disadvantage as an ecological contextual condition; more specifically as a concentration effect, reflecting the compounding of individual-level effects produced by economic and racial/ethnic selection and segregation processes. For example, poor families have limited resources and this is expected to have an effect on the developmental course of their children, no matter where they live. This is an individual- or family-level effect. If there is a clustering of poor families in particular neighborhoods, there would be an added effect of this concentration of poor families. Not only is a given child's family poor but most other families in her neighborhood are also poor, and that condition is expected to exacerbate the effects of poverty on development above and beyond the individual-level effect. Likewise, if children from poor families typically have better developmental outcomes when they live in more advantaged than disadvantaged neighborhoods, this difference reflects a true neighborhood-level effect; it cannot be explained by the families' poverty. Whenever we estimate the effect of poverty, it will require that we measure it as an effect above and beyond the individual-level effect. Race/ethnicity and family structure are also indicators of disadvantage that are expected to have both individual-level and neighborhood-level effects on youth development. The contextual effect of disadvantage will always be assessed as an effect above and beyond these individual-level effects.

The physical environment in the neighborhood is also conceptualized as an ecological contextual effect. Some aspects of the physical environment are fixed features that are largely independent of the composition of the neighborhood. At the same time, the care and maintenance of the buildings and the cleanliness of the streets and open areas are, at least in part, a reflection of the informal organizations and culture of the neighborhood; and the physical attractiveness of the neighborhood does influence the composition of the neighborhood. We thus expect some overlap between compositional and physical environmental effects. To the extent that living in a physically deteriorated neighborhood as compared to a well-kept, physically attractive neighborhood has an effect above and beyond the individual-level and concentrated disadvantage effects, we can isolate unique physical environment effects. We turn now to test our ideas about the influence of neighborhood disadvantage and deterioration on youth development outcomes.

Notes

1. Bronfenbrenner, 1986.
2. Bursik and Grasmick, 1993; Burton et al., 1997; Sampson, 2001.
3. Shaw and McKay, 1942; Bursik and Grasmick, 1993; Sampson and Groves, 1989.
4. Skogan, 1990; Wilson and Kelling, 1982.
5. Wilson, 1987, 1997; Jencks and Peterson, 1991; Massey and Denton, 1989; Jargowsky, 1997; Brooks-Gunn, Duncan, and Aber, 1997a; Sampson, 2001.
6. Jencks and Peterson, 1991; Brooks-Gunn, Duncan, and Aber, 1997a; Bursik and Grasmick, 1993; Skogan, 1990; Wilson, 1987, 1997.
7. For example, see Park and Burgess's (1924) theory of human ecology and Shaw and McKay's (1942) theory of social disorganization.
8. For a review of the structural characteristics of neighborhoods that contribute to disadvantage see Sampson and Morenoff, 1997.
9. Wilson, 1987, 1997.
10. Bursik and Grasmick, 1993; Land et al., 1990; Reiss and Tonry, 1986; Sampson and Lauritsen, 1994; Wilson, 1987; Sampson, 1987b, 2001; Kipke, 1999.
11. Massey and Denton, 1989, 1993; Massey, 1993; Massey, Gross, and Eggers, 1991; Sampson, 2001.
12. Bursik, 1989; Foley, 1973; Logan and Moloch, 1987; Sampson and Wilson, 1995; Skogan, 1986; Sampson, 2001.
13. Mainstream neighborhood research has focused narrowly on poverty, neglecting other dimensions of structural disadvantage that have a significant influence on youth development (Brooks-Gunn et al., 1997; Sampson, 2001).
14. Shaw and McKay, 1942. Many subsequent researchers have also used these three indicators to identify disadvantaged neighborhoods, for example, see Miethe and McDowell (1993).
15. A number of other neighborhood researchers have suggested that this compositional feature of neighborhoods is a key indicator of disadvantage. For example, see Bursik and Grasmick (1993) and Sampson (1985, 1987b, 2001).
16. Jencks and Mayer, 1990; Wilson, 1987, 1997; c.f. Jargowsky, 1996.
17. The evidence for this claim is limited and inconsistent. See Jencks and Mayer (1990).
18. Jargowsky, 1996; Halpern-Felsher et al., 1997.

19. Manski, 1995; Turner and Killian, 1987; Tedeschi and Felson, 1994.
20. Mayer and Jencks, 1989; Duncan, 1995.
21. Shaw and McKay, 1969; Bursik and Grasmick, 1993; Sampson and Groves, 1989; Bellair, 1997; Merry, 1981a; Smith and Jarjoura, 1988; Korbin, 2001; Kingston, 2005; Taylor, 2001.
22. Gans, 1962; Suttles, 1968; Merry, 1981a; Greenberg et al., 1982; Bellair, 1997; Lee and Campbell, 1998; Lee, 2001.
23. Merry, 1981a.
24. The term "white" as used in this book refers to the census category "non-Hispanic whites," i.e., persons who classify themselves as being white and not of Hispanic origin.
25. Jargowsky, 1996.
26. Sampson, 1986, 1987; Smith and Jarjoura, 1988; Bursik, 1984. Sampson (2001) recently called for a renewed look at residential stability as a key indicator of neighborhood disadvantage.
27. Shaw and McKay, 1942; Bursik and Grasmick, 1993; Simcha-Fagan and Schwartz, 1986.
28. Greenberg et al., 1982; Sampson, 2001.
29. Jargowsky, 1996.
30. Felson and Cohen, 1980; Sampson, 1985, 2001; Smith and Jarjoura, 1988.
31. Sampson and Groves, 1989; Bursik and Grasmick, 1993; Wilson, 1987; Sampson and Morenoff, 1997.
32. Gephart, 1997.
33. Bronfenbrenner, 1979; Massey, 2001.
34. Shaw and McKay, 1942.
35. For a review of this body of research, see Hallman (1984) and Taylor and Harrell (1996).
36. Gans, 1962; Suttles, 1968; Whyte, 1955.
37. Hester, 1975.
38. Skogan, 1990.
39. Skogan, 1990; Wilson and Kelling, 1982; Newman, 1972; Jacobs, 1961; Hallman, 1984.
40. Skogan, 1990.
41. Newman, 1979.
42. Rainwater, 1970; Taylor and Harrell, 1996; Yancey and Ericksen, 1979; Hallman, 1984.
43. See Skogan, 1990.
44. Stark, 1987; Felson and Cohen, 1980; Taylor and Harrell, 1996.
45. Brooks-Gunn, Duncan, and Aber, 1997a. See Klebanov et al. (1994) for some exceptions.
46. See Gans, 1962; Suttles, 1968; Maccoby et al., 1958; Merry, 1981a; Greenberg et al., 1982; Sampson and Groves, 1989; Taylor and Covington, 1988; Bellair, 1997; Brooks-Gunn et al., 1993, 1997; Klebanov et al., 1994; Duncan, 1994; Jarret, 1997; Lee and Campbell, 1998; Lee, 2001; Kingston, 2005.
47. See Bryk and Driscoll, 1988; Furstenberg et al., 1987; Hogan and Kitagawa, 1985; Mayer, 1997; Crane, 1991.
48. See Jargowsky, 1996:28.

The Effects of Growing Up in a Bad Neighborhood

Initial Findings

SYNOPSIS

How much difference does it make if one grows up in a disadvantaged neighborhood as compared to an affluent neighborhood? Does living in a physically deteriorated neighborhood as compared to a well-cared-for neighborhood undermine a successful course of development? These are the questions answered in this chapter, testing the model of neighborhood effects outlined in the last chapter.

We used two measures of successful development that were common to both Denver and Chicago: Prosocial Competence and Problem Behavior. The first is a composite measure combining five subscales measuring school grades, prosocial activities, self-efficacy, importance of school and work, and expected educational attainment. The second is a negative indicator and includes self-reports of delinquent behavior, drug use, and arrests. Three additional success measures are used for Denver. Personal Competence and Prosocial Behavior are expanded versions of Prosocial Competence, separating attitudinal indicators of competence from behavioral indicators and including several additional subscales. The final measure, On Track, measures the probability that a youth is "on track" developmentally for making a successful transition into adult roles.

Three classifications of neighborhoods are developed based on levels of income (Advantaged, Moderate, and Poor), disadvantage (Advantaged, Modest, and Disadvantaged) and deterioration (Deteriorated and Well-Kept). The appropriateness of using racial mix as an indicator of neighborhood disadvantage is examined and confirmed. Disadvantage is more strongly related to youth development than Poverty alone when compared on the Denver site.

The influence of living in different types of neighborhoods on developmental outcomes is estimated at two levels: the neighborhood level involving *rates* of successful development or the *average* level of success achieved; and the individual level, where the influence of the neighborhood on individual outcomes is estimated. The findings at the neighborhood level confirm the central hypothesis – on average, youth living in advantaged and well-kept neighborhoods have better developmental outcomes than those living in disadvantaged and deteriorated neighborhoods. Other important findings include:

- The strength of neighborhood effects was greater in Denver than Chicago.
- One exception – neither neighborhood measure predicted Problem Behavior in Denver.
- Neighborhood effects are stronger on attitudinal than behavioral indicators of success.

While most of the differences in developmental outcomes between good and bad neighborhoods are substantial, and in some cases quite large, they are clearly not monolithic or absolute.

At the individual level, the unique contextual effects of Disadvantage and Deterioration are small. Combined individual and contextual effects were more substantial, accounting for 9–27 percent of the variance in individual outcomes. Other important findings include:

- These effects are substantially larger for older than younger youth.
- There are significant gender and class interactions.
- Disadvantage and individual race/ethnicity effects are generally independent and additive.

The observed interaction between social class and neighborhood Disadvantage was consistent with a relative deprivation argument but it was primarily working-class youth living in Modest Neighborhoods who were at elevated risk for poor developmental outcomes, not poor youth in Disadvantaged Neighborhoods. The negative effects of Disadvantage were typically greater for females than males, except when Problem Behavior was the outcome.

4

The Effects of Growing Up in a Bad Neighborhood

Initial Findings

Adult Male – Martin Park: Yeah, that was bad (neighborhood). You couldn't even trust your kids. Across the street...you'd find, uh, young – young gang members or whatever you wanna call 'em shootin up in the alleys, ya know? Hadda chase 'em off, you know, you hadda stay in the apartment building because that was like the neighborhood, you know? Cause you couldn't – you didn't know what was gonna happen. There was always shooting and stuff like that.

INTRODUCTION

How much difference does it really make if one grows up in an advantaged as compared to a disadvantaged neighborhood? Are the chances of successful development substantially lower if one lives in a deteriorated compared to a well-kept neighborhood? Are these differences due to the type of neighborhood or simply a reflection of the fact that parents and children who, from the outset are more likely to succeed, choose to live in better neighborhoods?

In this chapter, we will present our initial findings on how identified neighborhood features influence youth development outcomes. Here we will focus on the ecological composition of the neighborhood, that is, on the clustering of persons with particular backgrounds, resources, and personal attributes in selected neighborhoods, and the effects of high levels of physical deterioration. Our reasons for believing that children growing up in advantaged and well-kept neighborhoods are more likely to acquire the skills, beliefs, capacity for moral reasoning, and experiences and opportunities required for effective participation in conventional adult life were outlined in the last chapter. Here we test the validity of these ideas, identifying disadvantaged and advantaged neighborhoods and comparing the rates of successful development for youth living in these neighborhoods.

We also compare the rates of successful development for youth living in deteriorated and well-kept neighborhoods. When people talk about good and bad neighborhoods for raising kids, they are typically describing these two features of the neighborhood.

When presenting findings, we will refer to neighborhood *effects* or *influences* on youth development success outcomes. We believe these terms are appropriate because we have developed a theoretical model of neighborhood effects, hypothesizing specific causal mechanisms that link neighborhood characteristics and processes to youth development outcomes, and examined these relationships. The evidence we present will either be consistent or inconsistent with these hypothesized effects. Although the evidence may *support* a causal claim, limitations in the study preclude making this interpretation of our findings.[1] On the other hand, the evidence may be sufficient to *reject* the causal claim of some of our hypotheses.

To differentiate between a theoretical concept and a specific measure of that concept, measures of success and contextual variables will always be capitalized. Specific types of contexts, such as Disadvantaged Neighborhoods, will also be capitalized. Measures of individual-level demographic variables such as age, gender, and ethnicity, will not be capitalized.

We start by examining the strength of disadvantage and deterioration effects on developmental outcomes, first on neighborhood-level rates of successful youth development, and then on individual-level success outcomes. In the latter analysis, we will separate individual-level effects from contextual-level effects so that these different kinds of influences on children and youth are not confused.

MEASURES OF SUCCESS, DISADVANTAGE, AND DETERIORATION

Measuring Successful Youth Development

In the first chapter we described developmental "success" as the completion of those individual and social developmental tasks that prepare one to become a productive, healthy, responsible, well-functioning adult. As discussed, this includes achieving a minimal level of personal competence, personal efficacy, social skills, a sense of personal well-being, the capacity for intimacy and social bonding, a commitment to conventional beliefs and the faculty for moral reasoning and action, a healthy lifestyle, and the avoidance of problem behavior. We noted earlier that these criteria for a successful development are widely endorsed in American society.[2]

Although this definition of success involves a number of dimensions, we decided to use a relatively modest level of attainment for each in defining success, attempting to identify the *minimum* level of competence and functioning necessary for effective participation in conventional adult society. We believe the standards we used to define success are thus very reasonable, ones that most youth should be capable of meeting.

The creation of our success measures involved several steps. First, we constructed specific scales as indicators of each of our success criteria. Some of these scales were common to both sites and some were unique to a particular site. These scales were then combined into larger composite measures.[3]

Two identical composite measures were developed for each site: (1) Prosocial Competence, which included five subscales assessing grades in school, involvement in prosocial activities (school, community, and religious), perceived self-efficacy, the importance attached to education and work, and one's expected level of educational attainment; and (2) Problem Behavior, which measures the youth's self-reported involvement in delinquency and drug use and any arrests for criminal behavior.[4]

Three additional measures of success are available only on the Denver site. Conceptually, the first two scales have the same content as the Prosocial Competence scale described above but include more items and separate the perception or belief indicators from the behavioral indicators, placing them in different scales. Personal Competence contains indicators of perceptions, expectations, and beliefs that will promote a successful transition into adult roles. It includes seven scales: self-esteem, self-efficacy, perceived popularity with friends, attachment to school, future educational expectations, perceived future opportunities given the neighborhood the youth lives in, and general perceived opportunities for the future. The second composite, Prosocial Behavior, reflects involvement in conventional behavior and contains four indicator scales: average grades in school; involvement in sports and other conventional activities within the school and community; involvement in religious activities; and involvement in family activities. In using the latter two composite scales in the analysis, we found it important to distinguish between beliefs and behavior; these two scales reflect different dimensions of successful development and contextual effects on beliefs and expectations are sometimes quite different from those on behavior. For this reason, we routinely present these two scales rather than the general Prosocial Competence scale when presenting findings for the Denver site. For Chicago, the general scale is the only measure of personal competence available. When it is instructive to directly compare the Denver and Chicago sites, we will present the findings for the general Prosocial Competence composite on both sites.

On Track is a third Denver-only composite that measures the probability that a youth is "on track" to make a successful transition into adult roles. This measure requires a little explanation. It is based on a predictive model derived from a national longitudinal study of American adolescents in which measures obtained during the adolescent years were used to predict later adult success.[5] Adult success in this longitudinal analysis involved four adult outcomes: (1) stable employment or financial stability, (2) commitment to conventional beliefs and aspirations, (3) involvement in a support network of friends or family, and (4) abstinence from problem

TABLE 4.1. *Measures of Individual Development Success*

	No. Items		Reliability	
Common Measures:	Chicago	Denver	Chicago	Denver
Prosocial Competence				
1. Personal Efficacy	3	3	.41	.63
2. Educational Expectations	1	1	n/a	n/a
3. Grades	1	1	n/a	n/a
4. Commitment to Conventionality	3	3	.63	.22
5. Involvement in Conventional Activity	4	4	n/a	n/a
Problem Behavior				
1. Delinquency	15	15	n/a	n/a
2. Drug Use	7	7	n/a	n/a
3. Arrests	1	1	n/a	n/a
Denver Only Measures:				
On Track (Probability of being "on track" for adult success)				
16–18 Year-Olds	–	4	–	.62
13–15 Year-Olds	–	3	–	.67
10–12 Year Olds	–	2	–	.73
Personal Competence				
1. Self-Esteem	–	6	–	.74
2. Self-Efficacy	–	3	–	.63
3. Perceived Popularity with Peers	–	9	–	.80
4. Attachment to School	–	7	–	.77
5. Future Educational Expectations	–	1	–	n/a
6. Future Opportunities Given Neighborhood	–	5	–	.71
7. Future Opportunities in General	–	8	–	.65
Prosocial Behavior				
1. Average Grades	–	1	–	n/a
2. Involvement in Sports/Activities	–	8	–	n/a
3. Involvement in Religious Activities	–	2	–	n/a
4. Involvement in Family Activities	–	2	–	n/a

substance use or involvement in serious illegal behavior.[6] As expected from a life course developmental perspective, adolescent measures that predicted adult success varied by age or stage of development. Based on these predictive equations, an age-specific On Track score was calculated for each adolescent in the Denver study. This score reflects the probability (0–100 percent) that this respondent is on track for making a successful transition into adulthood.

Table 4.1 outlines these measures and identifies the set of scales used as indicators for each composite measure.[7] Table A4.1 showing the relationships (correlations) between these scales is found in Appendix A.

The Measure of Neighborhood Disadvantage

In the last chapter, we argued that disadvantage was a multidimensional construct involving high poverty, family disruption, high rates of population turnover, and racial/ethnic heterogeneity. Our measure of Disadvantage is a composite of these four indicators as reported in the 1990 Census for each neighborhood on each site. The specific census indicators included: the percentage of families below the poverty line; the percentage of single-parent families with children under age 18; the rate of population turnover over the past five years; and the racial/ethnic mix in each neighborhood.[8] This neighborhood Disadvantage measure is the sum of the standardized values of these four census characteristics for each study neighborhood. A high score on this measure indicates a high level of disadvantage.

The Disadvantage measure worked well for Denver. Each indicator appeared to be validated as an independent measure of disadvantage and the necessary assumptions for combining these indicators into a single composite measure were satisfied. Further, each indicator was related to our measure of success in the expected way. These indicators were each negatively related to Personal Competence, Prosocial Behavior, and On Track, and positively related to Problem Behavior.[9] In Chicago, however, these hypothesized indicators of disadvantage were not all positively related to one another and our analysis suggested they reflected two different things. Poverty and single-parent families were positively related to each other, as in Denver, but they were either unrelated (nonsignificant) or negatively related to population turnover (mobility) and racial/ethnic mix. This set of relationships was also found for the whole city of Chicago, that is, it was not just a characteristic of the particular neighborhoods in the Chicago sample. Further, neither mobility nor racial/ethnic mix was significantly related to our measures of success in the Chicago sample. Simply put, these latter two ecological conditions do not appear to be indicative of disadvantage in Chicago neighborhoods, and it would be inappropriate to combine them with poverty and single-parent families in a composite scale measuring disadvantage.[10]

The relationships among poverty, mobility, and racial mix are more complicated in Chicago. While neighborhood poverty is not related to mobility, it is related to population decline.[11] This suggests that those without economic means are trapped in neighborhoods that have experienced high rates of out-migration, a "fleeing the ghetto" phenomenon (Wilson, 1987). These neighborhoods often appear to be stable when measured by the percent of families living there five years ago (our measure of mobility). However, this measure masks the declining population and changes in population composition and the quality of the neighborhood caused by the out-migration of the neighborhood's better-off residents. It is also the case that for blacks, racially mixed neighborhoods in Chicago are often better-off neighborhoods that are the destinations of stable working-class families looking to escape the problems of the inner city. Predominantly African American neighborhoods tend to be the high-poverty neighborhoods.

The situation appears to be different for whites, where predominantly white neighborhoods are more advantaged and racially mixed neighborhoods are relatively poorer. This suggests that living in a mixed racial neighborhood may have different implications and consequences for black as compared to white youth, a hypothesis we will consider later.

How unique is the set of relationships found in Chicago? Is Chicago the exception or is Denver? We checked the relationships between these four census indicators of disadvantage in 20 of the largest U.S. cities with significant minority populations.[12] At most, three of these 20 cities had a pattern of relationships similar to that found in Chicago. Although the Chicago pattern appears to be atypical, it is not unique. Still, high rates of poverty, single-parent families, mobility, and racial/ethnic mix typically cluster together in census tracts. There are only a few cities where they do not, but Chicago is one of these cities.[13]

To facilitate cross-site comparisons, we explored several options for a common measure and decided to use a single indicator – the percentage of families below poverty (Poverty).[14] Since we have both measures available in Denver, we could compare the predictive power of these two measures of neighborhood composition. Theoretically, we argued that the effect of Disadvantage, which includes family disruption, mobility, and racial/ethnic heterogeneity in addition to poverty, would predict youth development outcomes better than Poverty alone. This is important because, if incorrect, our theoretical reasoning about the processes and mechanisms linking ecological composition to neighborhood organization and culture, and eventually to individual development, would be suspect.

We tested this hypothesis directly by estimating the effect single-parent families, mobility, and racial/ethnic heterogeneity had on our successful youth developmental outcomes, above and beyond the effect of Poverty alone. The results of this analysis are shown in Figure 4.1.

This analysis demonstrates that in Denver, neighborhood Disadvantage is a better predictor of developmental outcomes than is Poverty alone. For two of the four success composites, Disadvantage is a significantly better predictor than Poverty, increasing the explained variance of Personal Competence from 43 to 56 percent and that of Prosocial Behavior from 22 to 41 percent. Neither Poverty nor Disadvantage is a very good predictor of Problem Behavior, and although the percentage of explained variance increased from 2 to 9 percent when including other indicators of disadvantage, this increase is not statistically significant. Finally, Poverty may be as good a predictor of On Track as is Disadvantage; that is, adding the other indicators of disadvantage does not improve significantly on the prediction

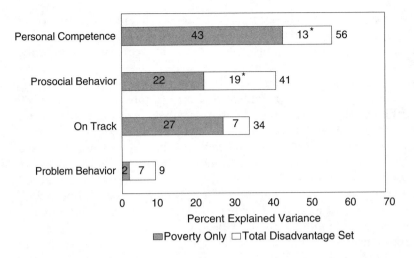

*Increase in explained variance is statistically significant, $p <= .05$.

FIGURE 4.1. The Predictive Power of Poverty and Disadvantage on Development Outcomes: Denver

made by Poverty alone. However, the other indicators, without Poverty, do as well in predicting On Track. Although not all of the increases in explained variance are statistically significant, the pattern is consistent. Overall, Disadvantage is more strongly related to a negative outcome on these success measures than is Poverty.

This analysis provides support for our view that high rates of mobility and racial/ethnic mix are ecological risk factors that reduce the likelihood of positive youth development outcomes in Denver. High mobility and racial/ethnic heterogeneity both had significant negative effects on specific developmental outcome rates that were above and beyond the effects of Poverty.[15]

As discussed in Chapter 3, the most controversial of these potential risk factors is the racial/ethnic mix in a neighborhood. Prior studies, including very recent ones, reveal considerable evidence that racial/ethnic heterogeneity within the neighborhood is related to negative developmental outcomes for youth, particularly for problem behavior.[16] To test this proposition more directly, we classified our study neighborhoods in Denver into four types: (1) predominantly white, (2) predominantly black, (3) predominantly Hispanic, and (4) mixed white/Hispanic.[17] The only truly mixed ethnic neighborhoods in Denver, that is, neighborhoods where no racial/ethnic group was predominant (60 percent or more), included mixed white and Hispanic families and individuals. We then calculated the average developmental outcome scores for individual youth living in these neighborhoods, based upon their individual race or ethnicity. To ensure that any observed differences were not the result of differences in individual socioeconomic status (SES), SES was also controlled statistically in the analysis (see Table A4.2 in Appendix A).

In Denver, both individual race/ethnicity and the predominant race/ethnic composition of the neighborhood significantly influenced developmental outcomes. The only exception involved Problem Behavior; for this outcome, the predominant racial makeup of the neighborhood had a significant influence but individual race or ethnicity did not. In mixed racial/ethnic neighborhoods, we found, on average, higher levels of involvement in Problem Behavior irrespective of individuals' racial/ethnic or socioeconomic background. The only other set of conditions with high average levels of involvement in Problem Behavior involved Hispanic youth living in predominantly black neighborhoods.

Congruence between individual race/ethnicity and the predominant race/ethnicity of the neighborhood was not always associated with better developmental outcomes. Non-Hispanic white (hereafter referred to as white) youth had good developmental outcomes in both predominantly white and predominantly Hispanic neighborhoods; but they did not do well in predominantly black or mixed neighborhoods. African American youth did best in predominantly white neighborhoods and quite well in predominantly black neighborhoods. However, their outcomes when living in predominantly Hispanic or mixed neighborhoods were most often negative. The developmental outcomes for Hispanic youth were most favorable when they lived in predominantly white or Hispanic neighborhoods; but they consistently experienced very negative outcomes when living in predominantly black neighborhoods and frequently when living in mixed neighborhoods. Overall, developmental outcomes for all youth, regardless of racial or ethnic background, were less favorable when they lived in mixed neighborhoods. Our decision to include racial mix as an indicator of Disadvantage was thus validated for the Denver site.

While racial/ethnic heterogeneity is a risk factor for poor development outcomes in the Denver sample, we do not know if this is true for the Chicago sample as well. Because the sample was limited to African American families in predominantly African American neighborhoods, we did not attempt to analyze the effects of racial/ethnic mix in Chicago. We will return to this issue later in this chapter when we consider the effects of neighborhood Disadvantage on individual-level outcomes and in even more depth in Chapters 5 and 6 when we consider the specific mechanisms by which racial mix might influence youth development.

In this chapter, we use both the Poverty and Disadvantage measures of neighborhood composition. Using the Poverty measure, neighborhoods were classified as Poor, Moderate, or Advantaged Neighborhoods on each

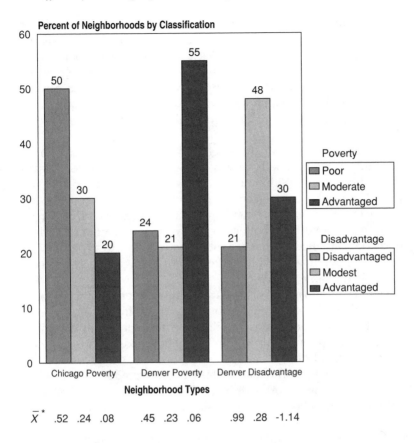

$^{*}\bar{X}$ = Average neighborhood proportion of families living below poverty or average neighborhood disadvantage score.

FIGURE 4.2. Types of Neighborhoods: Chicago and Denver

site. With this measure, we can make direct comparisons of types of neighborhoods across sites. For Denver, neighborhoods were also classified using the Disadvantage Composite into Advantaged, Modest, and Disadvantaged Neighborhoods.[18] The distribution of neighborhood types and their average Poverty or Disadvantage scores are presented in Figure 4.2.

The number and percent of Poor (high-poverty) Neighborhoods in our study samples is substantially higher in Chicago than Denver – half of Chicago neighborhoods compared to one-fourth of Denver's neighborhoods. This finding was expected, given the differences in sampling designs. Because the sample of neighborhoods in Denver is a representative sample of all neighborhoods, this proportion approximates the proportion of all Denver neighborhoods that are poor neighborhoods. This is not the case for Chicago. Because the vast majority of sample neighborhoods were predominantly black neighborhoods, poor African American neighborhoods were over-represented in our sample. When we present descriptive information by city, it is important to remember that the samples of neighborhoods from these two cities are different, with a larger proportion of Chicago neighborhoods classified as Poor Neighborhoods.

At the outset, we thought the levels of concentrated poverty in the Chicago study neighborhoods would be substantially greater than in Denver neighborhoods. Within neighborhoods classified as Poor Neighborhoods, that is, where 30 percent or more of families are below the federal poverty line, there is only a small difference in the actual mean percent of families below poverty; in both cities, the average poverty rate in those neighborhoods classified as Poor Neighborhoods is close to 50 percent. The mean levels of poverty within Moderate and Advantaged Neighborhoods are essentially the same in each city.

Denver and Chicago neighborhoods are quite different in other respects. For example, there are fewer public housing projects in Denver, and even in the Poor Neighborhoods, most families live in single-family dwellings. The density of the populations in these neighborhoods is thus quite different. By design, all of the Chicago neighborhoods are predominantly African American neighborhoods, whereas there are predominantly white, black, and Hispanic neighborhoods in the Denver sample as well as mixed racial/ethnic neighborhoods where no single group is predominant.

The classification based on the neighborhood Disadvantage scale in Denver results in a substantially different distribution of neighborhoods from that based on Poverty. While a similar number of neighborhoods are classified as Poor or Disadvantaged, these are not the same neighborhoods in all cases. Table 4.2 shows how neighborhoods are classified on each of these two variables. Overall, nearly half (45 percent) of Denver neighborhoods are in a different type of neighborhood on the disadvantage classification as compared to the poverty classification.[19] Most of these differences involve a switch to an adjacent category, but there is a substantial difference in how individual neighborhoods are classified by these two indices of ecological composition.

It is important to note that poverty is only moderately associated with high rates of population turnover ($r = .37$) and racial/ethnic mix ($r = .33$). It is more strongly associated with single parent families ($r = .70$). A significant proportion of high poverty neighborhoods in Denver are relatively stable areas with a predominant racial/ethnic composition. Youth in these high-poverty neighborhoods have better developmental outcomes than do youth living in neighborhoods where poverty is combined with residential instability and racial/ethnic heterogeneity.

TABLE 4.2. *Neighborhoods Classified by Poverty Level and Disadvantage*

		Disadvantage			
		Advantaged	Modest	Disadvantaged	Total
Poverty	Advantaged	10	6	2	18
	Moderate	0	5	2	7
	Poor	0	5	3	8
	TOTAL	10	16	7	33

Correlation $(r) = .515$ $(p = .002)$[20]

The Measure of Physical Deterioration

The measure of neighborhood physical Deterioration is derived from information obtained in the parent survey. Respondents were asked about a number of problems that sometimes occur in neighborhoods – for example, if there was high unemployment, little respect for laws and authority, abandoned houses, prostitution, run-down and poorly kept buildings, or delinquent gangs. For each characteristic, parents indicated if it was (1) a big problem, (2) somewhat of a problem or (3) not a problem in their neighborhood. Their responses to two of these questions, about abandoned houses and run-down and poorly kept buildings, were combined to create the measure of Deterioration. The measure reflects the average rating given these two items by adults living in each neighborhood. It reflects whether adults in the neighborhood think that abandoned houses and run-down, poorly kept buildings are a problem in their neighborhood.

We then classified all neighborhoods in Denver and Chicago as having a high or low perceived level of deterioration. Those neighborhoods with scores above the respective city mean were classified as Deteriorated Neighborhoods, and those with scores below the mean were classified as Well-Kept Neighborhoods. In Denver, this resulted in 15 Deteriorated and 18 Well-Kept Neighborhoods; in Chicago there were 22 Deteriorated and 18 Well-Kept Neighborhoods.

NEIGHBORHOOD POVERTY, DISADVANTAGE, AND DETERIORATION

How do these features of neighborhood composition and physical condition relate to one another? The overlap in neighborhood classifications is illustrated in Table 4.3. As might be expected, these classifications are related, although the relationship is not extremely high. With the poverty classification, none of the Advantaged Neighborhoods in Chicago has a high level of Deterioration. In comparison, half of the Moderate Neighborhoods and 80 percent of the Poor Neighborhoods in Chicago have high levels of Deterioration. In Denver, two of the eighteen Advantaged Neighborhoods had above-average (high) levels of Deterioration, while all of

TABLE 4.3. *Neighborhood Types by Deterioration, Poverty, and Disadvantage*

	Poverty						Disadvantage		
	Advantaged		Moderate		Poor		Advantaged	Modest	Disadvantaged
	Chi*	Den*	Chi	Den	Chi	Den		Denver Only	
Deterioration Low	8	16	6	0	4	2	10	7	1
High	0	2	6	7	16	6	0	9	6
Correlation (r):	Chi .605	(p = .000)	Den .629	(p = .000)	Chi	(p = .000)		.623 (p = .000)	

* Chi = Chicago; Den = Denver.

the Moderate and six of the eight Poor Neighborhoods have high levels of Deterioration.

The pattern of neighborhood-type combinations looks a little more like one would expect when the disadvantage classification is used for Denver, although the overall strength of the relationship is essentially the same. None of the Advantaged Neighborhoods has an above-average (high) level of physical Deterioration, whereas slightly over half of the Modest and 86 percent of the Disadvantaged Neighborhoods have high levels of Deterioration.[21]

In sum, the relationship between physical Deterioration and either Poverty or Disadvantage is moderately strong. Most neighborhoods that are classified as Poor or Disadvantaged are also classified as having above-average levels of Deterioration; and most neighborhoods classified as Advantaged have below-average levels of Deterioration. However, it is important to note that the overlap is not complete. Physical Deterioration and Disadvantage or Poverty are not simply measures of the same thing. Some Poor and Disadvantaged Neighborhoods have below-average levels of physical Deterioration and some Advantaged Neighborhoods have above-average levels of Deterioration. We can thus establish unique or independent effects of these two features of neighborhood social composition and physical condition.

NEIGHBORHOOD DISADVANTAGE, DETERIORATION, AND SUCCESSFUL YOUTH DEVELOPMENT: NEIGHBORHOOD LEVEL FINDINGS

Is one's chance of success related to the level of disadvantage and deterioration in the neighborhood in which one lives? Does it make a difference if one lives in Park Hill or Five Points in Denver? In Woodlawn or Oak Park in Chicago? How much of the variation in success can be attributed to the type of neighborhood in which one lives? If there is little or no difference in developmental outcomes by level of neighborhood disadvantage or deterioration, the idea that the concentration of poor, single-parent, highly mobile families in particular neighborhoods makes them bad neighborhoods for raising children has little merit.

Neighborhood-Level Effects: Poverty and Disadvantage

At the neighborhood level, we are asking about the aggregated rates of successful development across neighborhoods or whether youth in advantaged neighborhoods, on average, are more likely to be successful in completing the developmental tasks of adolescence than youth living in disadvantaged neighborhoods. For this analysis, our individual-level measures of success are aggregated to the neighborhood level so that each neighborhood has an average success score. These neighborhood-level success scores are then aggregated by type of neighborhood, and an average success score for each type of neighborhood – Advantaged, Modest, and Disadvantaged – is calculated. The resulting type-of-neighborhood success score is thus a description of the average level of success achieved by youth living in neighborhoods we have classified as Poor or Disadvantaged.

We will also report the highest and lowest neighborhood score (the range) for neighborhoods of a given type. This provides some idea of how much the average neighborhood-level success scores varied from one neighborhood to another *within* the set of Poor or Advantaged Neighborhoods. It also reveals how much overlap there is in average neighborhood success scores across types of neighborhoods. In focusing on average levels of success in Poor or Advantaged Neighborhoods, we are ignoring differences between individuals who live *within* a given type of neighborhood. We will consider these individual-level differences at a later point.

Figure 4.3 graphically presents the average success scores for Advantaged, Moderate, and Poor Neighborhoods (the vertical line) and the range of neighborhood success scores within each type of neighborhood (the horizontal bar). For all composite scales except On Track, these scores are standardized and have a mean of zero and a standard deviation of one. A score of zero is the average score for all neighborhoods in the Denver or Chicago sample. Standardized scores tell us how a given neighborhood or type of neighborhood compares to the average neighborhood in that city. Because the average neighborhood in Denver may have a different raw score from the average neighborhood in Chicago, these standardized scores are not directly comparable across sites. This option was chosen to facilitate within-site comparisons.

Success: Personal Competence Outcomes
Living in an Advantaged as compared to a Poor Neighborhood has a substantial positive effect on most of the developmental outcomes graphed in Figure 4.3. The typical Poor Neighborhood has a lower level of Prosocial Competence (both cities, Denver not shown) and lower levels of Personal Competence and Prosocial Behavior (Denver) than does an Advantaged Neighborhood.

In Chicago, the highest average level of Prosocial Competence is found in Advantaged Neighborhoods, but, unexpectedly, the lowest is found in Moderate rather than Poor Neighborhoods.[22] The average competence level for Poor Neighborhoods is close to zero, the overall average for Chicago. Further, the range of individual neighborhood-level scores is very broad in Poor Neighborhoods, completely overlapping the range of scores for Advantaged Neighborhoods and, for the most part, those of Moderate Neighborhoods. This means that there are some Poor Neighborhoods where the competence score is as high as or higher than that for the best

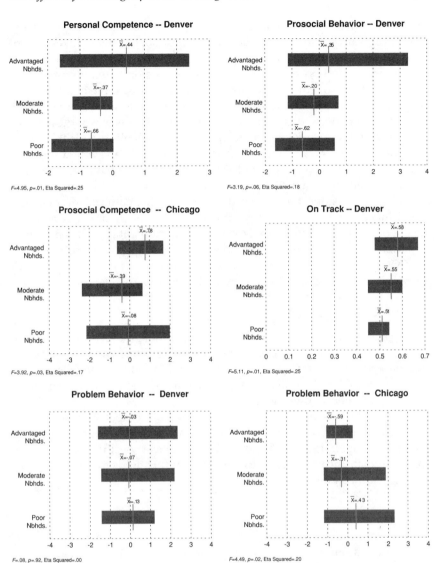

FIGURE 4.3. Neighborhood Adolescent Outcomes by Level of Poverty

Advantaged Neighborhood; it also means that there are other Poor Neighborhoods where the level of competence is much lower than that of the worst Advantaged Neighborhood. There is simply much more variation in average competence scores within Poor African American Neighborhoods than within Moderate or Advantaged black Neighborhoods in Chicago.

In Denver, the analysis involving Personal Competence and Prosocial Behavior, as well as Prosocial Competence (not shown), reveals the more expected pattern of differences – the typical Advantaged Neighborhood has the highest and the typical Poor Neighborhood, the lowest level of competence. We found great variation in average competency scores among Advantaged Neighborhoods and little variance among Moderate and Poor Neighborhoods. In some Advantaged Neighborhoods, the average competence scores are nearly as low as those in the worst (low end) Moderate and Poor Neighborhoods, and there are neighborhoods where the average score is very high. However, there are no Poor Neighborhoods where the score on any competence measure is as high as the overall average score for Advantaged Neighborhoods. Still, living in an Advantaged Denver Neighborhood is no guarantee of a high average level of Personal Competence.

We will consider the city differences in the patterns of averages and ranges for different types of neighborhoods in our summary of neighborhood-level effects of Poverty and Disadvantage. On both sites, significant neighborhood effects exist on the average level of competence. Knowing the type of neighborhood accounts for 17–25 percent of the variation in competence scores across neighborhoods.

Problem Behavior

In Chicago, there are lower average rates of Problem Behavior in Advantaged as compared to Poor Neighborhoods. Knowing the type of neighborhood accounts for 20 percent of the neighborhood variance in rates of Problem Behavior. Again, the range in neighborhood averages is greatest for Poor Neighborhoods and is quite restricted for Advantaged Neighborhoods, a pattern we observed earlier for Prosocial Competence. In contrast, there are no significant differences in average rates of Problem Behavior by type of neighborhood in Denver. We will look at specific components of this composite measure below to see if this finding holds for these separate indicators of Problem Behavior.

Being On Track

Differences in the probability of being On Track across Denver neighborhoods may seem a little surprising, but remember the minimal criteria for success used in this measure. In the poorest neighborhoods, the average probability for a minimally successful adolescent-to-adult transition is 51 percent. In Moderate Neighborhoods, the average probability is 55 percent and in Advantaged Neighborhoods it is 58 percent. The probability of success is clearly higher in more Advantaged Neighborhoods, but even very Poor Neighborhoods have only slightly lower probabilities of success. On average, living in an Advantaged as compared to a Poor Neighborhood increases the likelihood of being On Track by 7 percent. Type of neighborhood accounts for about 25 percent of the variance in the estimated average probability of being On Track for a successful adolescent development.

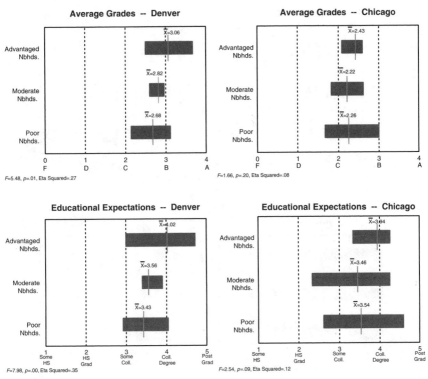

FIGURE 4.4. Selected Adolescent Outcomes by Level of Poverty-Subscales

We turn now to a consider a few specific components of these composite measures, selected because they are easily interpreted, directly comparable across sites, and demonstrate important differences in specific developmental outcomes by type of neighborhood. The analyses involving these scales are graphed in Figure 4.4.

Grades

In Poor Denver Neighborhoods, the typical average grade is a C+ (2.68 GPA). Most adolescents expect to complete some college, usually at a junior college or community college. In comparison, in Advantaged Neighborhoods the average grade at school is a B, and most adolescents expect to graduate from a four-year college.

Surprisingly, there are no significant differences in average grades by type of neighborhood in Chicago; the average grades in Poor, Moderate, and Advantaged Neighborhoods are all Cs. This suggests that schools in the Chicago sample neighborhoods may be using local norms, that is, different standards for grading. Not only are there greater differences in earned grades by type of neighborhood in Denver but the average grades

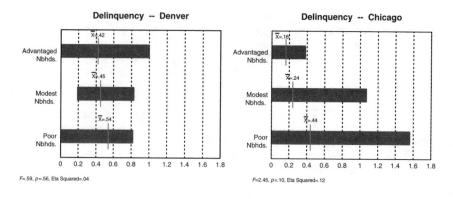

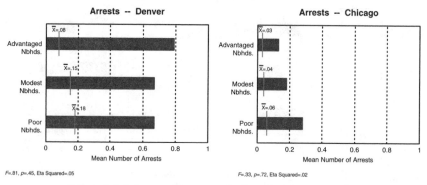

FIGURE 4.4. Selected Adolescent Outcomes by Level of Poverty-Subscales (*continued*)

are uniformly higher in Denver. In spite of this difference, the educational expectations in Poor and Advantaged Neighborhoods in Chicago are very similar to those in Denver – some college and college graduation, respectively. The connection between grades and educational attainment thus appears different in Chicago than in Denver. Type of neighborhood accounts for approximately 30 percent of the variation in average grades and educational expectations in Denver compared to about 10 percent in Chicago.

Delinquency and Arrest

In neither Denver nor Chicago are the differences in typical neighborhood rates of delinquency or arrest statistically significant. The Delinquency measure here is a variety measure, reflecting the number of different types of offenses reported by each youth, or at the neighborhood level, the average number of different types of offenses reported by neighborhood youth. Variety scores are highly correlated with frequency scores and provide a good measure of the overall level of involvement in delinquent activity.[23] The average number of different types of offenses reported in

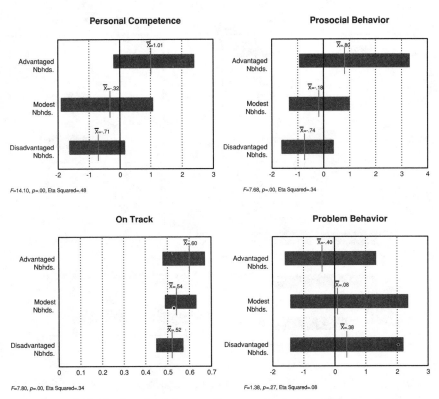

FIGURE 4.5. Neighborhood Adolescent Outcomes by Level of Disadvantage

different neighborhoods is substantially higher in Denver than Chicago neighborhoods, particularly for Advantaged and Moderate Neighborhoods. The average number of arrests in Denver neighborhoods is three times that in Chicago neighborhoods. We will discuss this unexpected difference between study sites in our summary of neighborhood-level findings.

Figure 4.5 shows the same neighborhood-level analysis using the neighborhood Disadvantage classification in Denver. While the pattern of findings is the same for our composite measures – significant neighborhood effects on all measures of successful development except Problem Behavior – neighborhood effects based on the Disadvantage classification are much stronger than for the poverty classification. Type of disadvantaged neighborhood accounts for nearly twice as much variance in these successful development composite measures as did the poverty classification, explaining between a third and one-half of the variance in these outcomes.

The greatest neighborhood differences are between Advantaged and other neighborhoods. While youth from Advantaged Neighborhoods

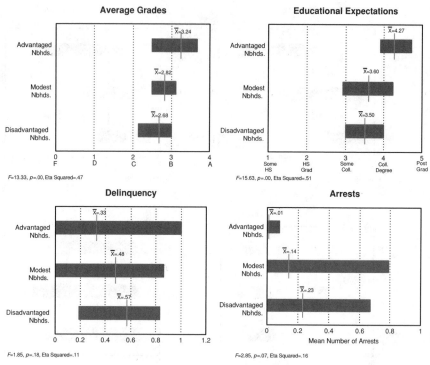

FIGURE 4.6. Selected Neighborhood Adolescent Outcomes by Level of Disadvantage-Subscales

consistently have the most favorable outcomes, the difference between typical outcomes for Modest or Disadvantaged Neighborhoods are usually much smaller. Finally, the range of average neighborhood outcomes is, with the exception of Problem Behavior, greatest in Advantaged Neighborhoods and most restricted in Disadvantaged Neighborhoods.

Neighborhood differences are also larger for the selected subscales (see Figure 4.6). On average, residents of Advantaged Neighborhoods are getting Bs and As in school and expect to graduate from college and get some postgraduate education. In comparison, those from Modest and Disadvantaged Neighborhoods are getting Cs and Bs (mostly Cs for those from Disadvantaged Neighborhoods) and expect to complete only some college work. Although residents of Advantaged Neighborhoods do not have an overwhelming advantage on these particular indicators of success, it is still substantial given the current job market. Type of neighborhood accounts for about half of the variance in average grades and educational expectations.

Although the difference in average levels of Problem Behavior between types of neighborhoods was not statistically significant, the difference in the arrest subscale is now significant. The rates of arrest are one per 100 in Advantaged Neighborhoods compared to 14 per 100 in Modest Neighborhoods and 23 per 100 in Disadvantaged Neighborhoods. These are very large differences. The range in average arrest rates in Advantaged Neighborhoods is very small; these neighborhoods *all* have very low arrest rates. The range in Modest and Disadvantaged Neighborhoods is very large, extending from zero to more than 60 per 100.

The above analysis suggests that in Denver, the measure of Disadvantage is a much more powerful predictor of neighborhood rates of successful development than is Poverty. In subsequent analyses of neighborhood-level effects in Denver, we will present findings based on this measure of neighborhood composition, as it is the better measure both conceptually and empirically. Only when there are important differences in neighborhood-level effects between Denver and Chicago will we compare the two cities using the Poverty measure, to provide some insight into the reasons for the difference.

NEIGHBORHOOD-LEVEL EFFECTS: PHYSICAL DETERIORATION

The effects of physical Deterioration on neighborhood rates of successful development are summarized in Figures 4.7 and 4.8. In Chicago, there are no significant differences in Prosocial Competence outcomes for Well-Kept as compared to Deteriorated Neighborhoods. This finding was not replicated in Denver – there were significant differences in Prosocial Competence by level of neighborhood Deterioration (not shown). Further, in Denver, the relationship between living in a Well-Kept or Deteriorated Neighborhood and average levels of Prosocial Competence holds for both the belief and behavioral components of this measure as reflected in the Personal Competence and Prosocial Behavior measures. There are no Deteriorated Neighborhoods in Denver where the average level of Personal Competence is above the overall city average. Moreover, there is relatively little overlap in the Well-Kept and Deteriorated Neighborhood means on this measure. The differences are not as great for Prosocial Behavior, but they are still significant. In Denver, living in a Well-Kept as compared to a Deteriorated Neighborhood is associated, on average, with the development of individual competencies, both attitudinal and behavioral; it accounts for about a third of the variance in Personal Competence and about a fourth of the variation in Prosocial Behavior.

Neighborhood Deterioration is also related to the probability of a successful transition into adulthood, but the difference is not great; the average On Track probability is 0.58 in Well-Kept Neighborhoods as compared to 0.53 in Deteriorated Neighborhoods. Still, living in a Well-Kept Neighborhood is associated with a higher probability of being

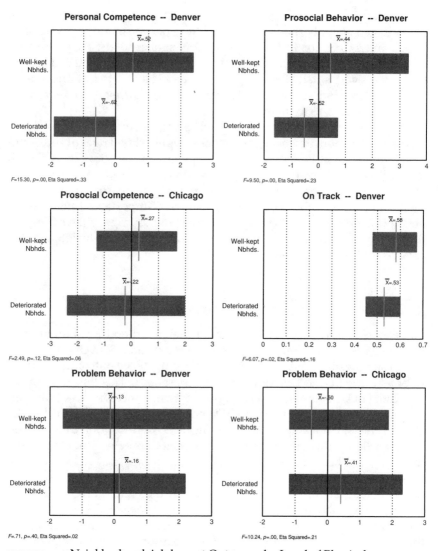

FIGURE 4.7. Neighborhood Adolescent Outcomes by Level of Physical Deterioration

On Track. Neighborhood Deterioration accounts for about 16 percent of the variation in being On Track.

Deterioration is not related to neighborhood rates of Problem Behavior in Denver; it is in Chicago. While the difference in Well-Kept and Deteriorated Chicago Neighborhoods is significant, the range of neighborhood averages is very similar and the relationship is not particularly strong. Deterioration accounts for about 20 percent of the variance in neighborhood rates of Problem Behavior in Chicago.

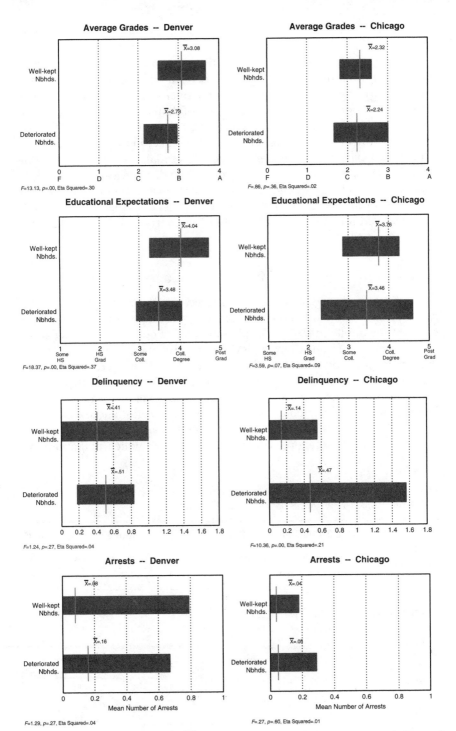

FIGURE 4.8. Selected Neighborhood Adolescent Outcomes by Level of Physical Deterioration – Subscales

Looking at the same set of specific components discussed earlier (Figure 4.8), we found that living in a Deteriorated Neighborhood is associated, on average, with lower grades (Denver only), lower educational expectations (both cities), and higher rates of delinquency (Chicago only). There were no differences in average arrest rates by neighborhood Deterioration in either city. The neighborhood differences in average grades and educational expectations in Denver are substantial, accounting for about a third of the variation in these outcomes. The differences in educational expectations and delinquency in Chicago are smaller, accounting for 9 to 21 percent of the variance. This pattern of differences is nearly identical to that observed for the relationship between Poverty or Disadvantage and these outcomes.

COMBINED DISADVANTAGE AND DETERIORATION EFFECTS

Our estimates of neighborhood-level effects in these analyses were all based on our neighborhood classifications. Within any type of neighborhood, for example, the set of Disadvantaged or Poor Neighborhoods, we ignored actual differences in the level of disadvantage or poverty among these neighborhoods. Neighborhoods of a given type were treated as if they were a homogeneous group of neighborhoods. Table 4.4 displays the strength of the relationship between the actual level of Disadvantage or Poverty in a neighborhood and the average or typical success outcome for youth living in this neighborhood without any grouping of neighborhoods by type or category. This is an analysis in which neighborhood

TABLE 4.4. *Correlations (r and R²) between Poverty, Disadvantage, Deterioration, and Neighborhood-Level Rates of Successful Development*

Youth Development Outcome	Deterioration		Poverty		Disadvantage	Combined[a]	
	Den	Chi	Den	Chi	Den	Den	Chi
	r^b	r	r	r	r	R^2	R^2
Prosocial Competence	−.584	−.489	−.633	−.173	−.760	.59	.24
Personal Competence	−.575	−	−.648	−	−.752	.58	−
Prosocial Behavior	−.545	−	−.483	−	−.644	.45	−
Problem Behavior	$.107^b$	.451	$.135^b$	.291	$.241^b$	$.06^b$	.22
On Track	−.464	−	−.550	−	−.550	.32	−

[a] Poverty and Deterioration in Chicago, Deterioration and Disadvantage in Denver.
[b] All are statistically significant, $p = .01$, except for Problem Behavior in Denver.

Disadvantage or Poverty is treated as a continuous variable rather than a categorical variable.

The pattern of results in the bivariate (r) and multiple correlations (R^2) in Table 4.4 is the same as that reported in the earlier analysis by type of neighborhood, but the significant relationships are uniformly stronger. There are no significant neighborhood effects in average levels of involvement in Problem Behavior – delinquency, drug use, and arrests – for Denver. But for Chicago, the relationships are significant and stronger than reported earlier, particularly for the Deterioration–Problem Behavior relationship. Surprisingly, the influence of Deterioration looks stronger than that for Poverty on both successful development outcome measures available for Chicago.

With one exception, Disadvantage is again a stronger predictor of successful development outcomes than is Poverty on the Denver site. The exception involves On Track where Poverty is as good a predictor as Disadvantage. The effects of Deterioration are sometimes as great as the effect of Poverty, but they are not as strong as those for Disadvantage (Denver).

The final column in Table 4.4 shows the combined effects of neighborhood composition and physical environment on average rates of successful development outcomes.[24] For rates of Prosocial and Personal Competence, 24 to 59 percent of the variance is explained by neighborhood Disadvantage/Poverty and Deterioration. For On Track, about a third of the variance is explained. Neither the individual nor combined effects of these two neighborhood features explains a significant percent of the variance in Problem Behavior in Denver. In Chicago, the composition and physical environment combined effects on Prosocial Competence and Problem Behavior are quite similar.

NEIGHBORHOOD-LEVEL EFFECTS: SUMMARY AND DISCUSSION

Living in an Advantaged as compared to a Poor or Disadvantaged Neighborhood is clearly associated with better youth development outcomes. Living in a well-taken-care-of neighborhood as compared to a run-down neighborhood is also associated with more favorable outcomes. Taken together, neighborhood composition and physical condition are good predictors of neighborhood rates of Personal Competence and involvement in constructive forms of behavior. The strength of this relationship was substantially greater in Denver than Chicago but holds for both cities. These two neighborhood features also predicted being On Track, a measure available only in Denver. In general, then, neighborhood composition and physical environment do appear to be reasonably good predictors, distinguishing between good and bad neighborhoods for raising children, at least for the developmental outcomes we have considered here.

We want to emphasize one important exception to this generalization. Neighborhood Disadvantage, Poverty, and Deterioration were not strong predictors of involvement in Problem Behavior in Denver. The direction of differences in neighborhood-level rates always indicated lower rates in Advantaged and Well-Kept Neighborhoods, but in only one analysis (arrest rates by level of Disadvantage) was the relationship statistically significant. In Chicago, rates of Problem Behavior were predicted by both Poverty and Deterioration, with the latter relationship being stronger. High rates of Problem Behavior (delinquency and drug use) were more likely to be found in neighborhoods with high levels of Deterioration than high rates of Poverty, although both types of neighborhoods were at risk for high levels of Problem Behavior.

It may surprise some that there is little between-neighborhood variation in delinquency, drug use, or arrest rates in Denver and relatively small differences between high- and low-poverty neighborhoods in Chicago. In fact, this is the typical finding in neighborhood studies of adolescent self-reported delinquency and drug use.[25] The evidence most supportive of a relationship between neighborhood composition or physical environment and problem behavior involves official record data (arrests) and adult populations.[26] The one subscale for which we found significant neighborhood-level differences in Denver was the arrest rate measure.

The fact that there were no significant differences in self-reported Delinquency but significant differences in the arrest rate, with Disadvantaged Neighborhoods having the highest rates, suggests that it is the probability of arrest that is related to neighborhood composition, not the rate of delinquent behavior.[27] Youth living in Disadvantaged Neighborhoods may be more vulnerable to official action for their delinquency than are youth living in more Advantaged Neighborhoods. However, this set of findings was not replicated in Chicago, nor was it replicated with the poverty classification in Denver. In Chicago, arrest rates did not differ by the level of Poverty or Deterioration in the neighborhood, whereas rates of delinquency did. Neither Poverty nor Deterioration was predictive of either Delinquency or arrest in Denver.

The weak findings relative to Problem Behavior may reflect, in part, a more general tendency for weaker neighborhood effects on behavioral markers of successful development than on beliefs, aspirations, and expectancies. In Denver, where the general composite measure of individual competencies was separated into behavioral and nonbehavioral indicators, neighborhood differences were uniformly smaller on the behavioral composite. Other studies have reported similar findings.[28] We will consider this possibility again in Chapter 6 where organizational and cultural effects are estimated.

The findings showed several differences in these neighborhood effects by city. First, the strength of the relationships were typically stronger in Denver than Chicago. Poverty and physical Deterioration together account for 22 to 24 percent of the variance in successful developmental outcomes in Chicago; Disadvantage and Deterioration account for 32 to 59 percent of the variance in outcomes (excluding Problem Behavior) in Denver. This may be a result of the differences in sampling designs in Denver and Chicago. The sample of neighborhoods in Denver is more heterogeneous than that in Chicago because the full range of neighborhoods is represented in the sample whereas the Chicago sample was drawn from relatively high- and low-poverty, predominantly black neighborhoods. As a result, the middle-income strata of predominantly African American neighborhoods is somewhat under-represented. The Denver sample is also more heterogeneous with respect to race and ethnicity. As a result, there may be more variation to explain across neighborhoods in Denver, which could account for stronger neighborhood effects. It is also possible that there is a race-by-neighborhood interaction in which the strength of neighborhood-level effects of Disadvantage and Deterioration are greater on whites and/or Hispanics than on African Americans. Recall that there were no differences in average grades for youth from Disadvantaged and Advantaged Neighborhoods in Chicago, whereas there were relatively large differences in Denver. We will explore this possibility in the next section when we estimate the effects of neighborhood Poverty, Disadvantage, and Deterioration on individual success outcomes.

Second, the rates of self-reported Delinquency and arrests are substantially higher in Denver than Chicago. This was a surprise. Prior studies using self-reported measures of delinquency typically find no race differences in general delinquency measures.[29] Further, official record studies uniformly find higher arrest rates for blacks than for whites or Hispanics.[30] Given these established findings in delinquency research, we expected to find similar rates of delinquency and higher rates of arrest in Chicago. Apart from the race differences in the Denver and Chicago samples, we might have expected higher rates of crime in Denver than Chicago. Victimization studies do find higher rates of criminal victimization, especially for property crimes, in the West than in the Midwest.[31] There are race differences in self-reported drug use, with blacks reporting lower rates of use than whites, a difference consistent with earlier findings.[32]

Third, the success scores for Poor Neighborhoods in Chicago were not always the least favorable; they were consistently the least favorable in the Poor and Disadvantaged Neighborhoods in Denver. However, given the extensive range of average success scores across Chicago neighborhoods classified as Poor, this one unexpected finding may not hold much significance. It is still the case that there were individual neighborhoods classified as Poor that had worse average outcome scores than any Moderate or Advantaged Neighborhood.

In sum, neighborhood composition and physical conditions do indeed predict successful developmental outcome rates, with Advantaged Neighborhoods typically having more favorable outcomes than Poor or Disadvantaged Neighborhoods. An Advantaged Neighborhood is, on average, a better place to raise children. These neighborhood differences are important and, in some instances, relatively large, but they are not monolithic or absolute. Living in an Advantaged as compared to a Disadvantaged Denver Neighborhood increased the average probability of being on course for a successful adulthood from 52 to 60 percent; living in a Well-Kept as compared to a Deteriorated Neighborhood increased this probability from 53 to 58 percent. Differences in average grades involved the difference between a B and a C (Denver only) and differences in future expectations for a college degree versus some college-level education. Neighborhood composition and physical conditions explain a good part of neighborhood-level differences in successful youth development, but there is much that is still unexplained and must involve other factors.

NEIGHBORHOOD EFFECTS ON INDIVIDUAL DEVELOPMENT

The previous analysis indicates that on average, more Advantaged, Well-Kept Neighborhoods have substantially better developmental outcomes. However, this analysis ignores the variation in individual outcomes *within* any given neighborhood and is essentially a comparison of average outcomes in different types of neighborhoods. To illustrate this difference, imagine two neighborhoods where the average or typical youth has a 2.0 (C) grade-point average. In the first, every youth living in this neighborhood is, in fact, earning all Cs. No youth are earning As, Bs, Ds, or Fs. By comparison in the second, half of them are earning As and Bs and half are earning Ds and Fs. In the first, there is no variation in individual academic performance within the neighborhood; every youth is getting the same identical grade, in this case a C. In the second, there are big differences in grades between neighborhood youth and, in fact, no one is actually getting Cs even though this is the average grade for all youth. If neighborhood composition effects on individual performance were very strong, most neighborhoods would have youth performance outcomes more like the first neighborhood than the second; that is, all youth would have similar grades, although not necessarily Cs. If neighborhood effects were relatively weak, there would be youth performance outcomes more like the second; there would be big differences in grades among youth living in the same neighborhood and youth with similar grades would just as likely be found outside as inside the neighborhood.

When estimating neighborhood compositional and physical environment effects on individual-level developmental outcomes, it is also essential that we take into account individual differences on the attributes we are aggregating in our neighborhood composition measure. For the individual youth or child, this means we must separate that part of any between-individual difference in success outcomes that is the direct result of being poor or from a single-parent family from that part that is the direct result of living in a neighborhood where most of the neighbors are also poor or single parent families. These are two separate effects: (1) the individual-level effect of being poor, African American, or from a single-parent family; and (2) the aggregated effect of living in a neighborhood context where persons with these characteristics are more or less concentrated, creating a social context that has its own additional (independent) effect on developmental outcomes. It is important that we separate these two effects and not confuse them. To do so would result in serious overestimates of the influence of neighborhood composition and physical environment on youth development. Many earlier studies of neighborhood effects on individual-level developmental outcomes found surprisingly small neighborhood influences, once these individual differences were taken into account.[33]

To separate the two types of effects, we employed two types of analyses, an Intraclass Correlation (ICC) analysis and a Hierarchical Linear Modeling (HLM) analysis.[34] ICCs estimate the extent to which individuals within a neighborhood are more similar to one another than to persons outside the neighborhood; it is a measure of within-neighborhood homogeneity (Cochran, 1977). An ICC of 1.0 would reflect a condition in which all (100%) people within a given neighborhood or type of neighborhood had the same score on an outcome measure, and this score was different from that for all people living outside that neighborhood – a condition in which all (100%) of the variance lies *between* neighborhoods. A value of zero would reflect a condition in which any two people in the same neighborhood are no more likely to have the same outcome score than any two individuals from different neighborhoods – all of the variance lies *within* neighborhoods. In practice, both sources of variation are present and the ICC indicates how much of this total variation lies between neighborhoods, that is, is a neighborhood effect. We will consider this approach to estimating individual and neighborhood effects on individual youth development outcomes first and then turn to the HLM analysis, which takes into account individual differences that might influence these estimates.

INITIAL ESTIMATES OF NEIGHBORHOOD INFLUENCES
ON INDIVIDUAL SUCCESS OUTCOMES

Intraclass Correlations for each individual success outcome are found in Table A4.3 in Appendix A. In both Denver and Chicago, the influence of neighborhood Disadvantage/Poverty on individual involvement in Problem Behavior is very weak with zero to 3 percent of the variance lying between neighborhoods. Thus the vast majority of the variance in Problem

Behavior in both cities lies within neighborhoods, not between them. Individual involvement in delinquency and drug use has little to do with differences in the level of Disadvantage or Poverty in the neighborhood.[35]

Some modest neighborhood composition effects are found in the development of individual competencies. Between 10 and 14 percent of the variance in Prosocial Competence (both cities), Personal Competence and Prosocial Behavior lies between neighborhoods. The effect of Disadvantage on the probability of being On Track is smaller, with slightly more than 5 percent of the variance in this developmental outcome attributable to the type of neighborhood in which a youth lives.

In general, the influence of neighborhood composition on individual developmental outcomes is small. There are some modest differences in the effects of Disadvantage on developmental outcomes by the youth's race or ethnicity. Disadvantage accounts for 8 to 13 percent of outcomes among white youth and zero to 3 percent for Hispanic youth. The effects of Deterioration look similar for blacks and whites, from 2 to 20 or 23 percent. The effects for Hispanics are again close to zero.

We found some interesting age and gender differences in compositional effects on specific developmental outcomes. In Denver, the effects of neighborhood Disadvantage are substantially greater on females than on males for all outcomes except Problem Behavior, accounting for 10 to 20 percent of the variation in On Track, Personal Competence, and Prosocial Behavior for females. In contrast, composition effects on males are all close to zero (1–6 percent). The gender effect in Chicago is the reverse with neighborhood Poverty having a stronger effect (20 percent) on male than on female levels of Prosocial Competence. The size of this gender effect is about the same in the two cities, but in opposite directions.

There also appears to be an age trend in the influence of composition on individual developmental outcomes in Denver, with the neighborhood influence becoming larger with increasing age. This trend is clearest for On Track, where the effect is close to zero for 10-year-olds and increases regularly to 18 percent for 18-year-olds. For all outcomes, except Problem Behavior, the strongest neighborhood influence is for 18-year-olds. Nearly a third of the variance in individual competence measures for 18-year-olds is between neighborhoods. In Chicago, ICCs are strongest for the oldest group (16-year-olds), except for Prosocial Competence, which is strongest at age 12. Neighborhood influence on our measures of individual competence is thus relatively strong for older youth.

HLM ANALYSES: ADJUSTED ESTIMATES OF NEIGHBORHOOD
AND INDIVIDUAL EFFECTS ON SUCCESS

Hierarchical Linear Modeling (HLM) is a type of analysis that allows us to get separate estimates of individual and neighborhood-level effects on individual success outcomes, providing assurance that our estimates of neighborhood-level influences on youth development outcomes are not simply a result of individual characteristics, like socioeconomic status, that influence these outcomes and also happen to vary across neighborhoods.[36] The individual attributes used in this analysis include the youth's age, gender, race/ethnicity, socioeconomic status, family structure, and length of residence in the neighborhood. Table 4.5 provides a summary of the HLM analyses, with estimates of the influence of neighborhood Disadvantage/Poverty and Deterioration on successful developmental outcomes, as well as the separate influence of the above individual-level characteristics, interactions between these individual characteristics and neighborhood compositional characteristics, and the variance that these different sources of influence share. The sum of these separate sources of explained variance is the total explained variance.

Taken together, neighborhood and individual-level influences account for 9–27 percent of the variance in individual success outcomes in Denver and 12–19 percent in Chicago. However, the unique effects of the physical environment (Deterioration) and demographic composition (Disadvantage/Poverty) are both very small, ranging from zero to 2 percent of the variance. In addition to these unique effects, neighborhood influences are also reflected in the interaction effects and some portion of the shared variance is also attributable to neighborhood influence. However, even if we added all of these potential neighborhood influences to obtain a maximum possible influence – a procedure that certainly overstates the true neighborhood effect – the influence of neighborhood Disadvantage/Poverty and Deterioration on these individual developmental outcomes is still a quite modest 5–10 percent (excluding Problem Behavior).

As expected from the neighborhood-level findings presented earlier, neighborhood Disadvantage/Poverty and Deterioration had no effect on Problem Behavior in Denver and close to no effect in Chicago (1 percent). All of the variance that is explained in Denver is attributable to individual-level attributes, that is, to the age, gender, race/ethnicity, family composition, socioeconomic status, and residential stability of individual youth. In contrast, neither individual-level attributes nor neighborhood features uniquely account for much of the explained variance in Chicago. The shared effect of these sources of influence accounts for most of the variance explained, that is, an effect of this set of influences that is not uniquely attributed to any single one of them.[37]

Individual-level attributes also have the strongest influence on Prosocial Behavior (Denver) and Prosocial Competence in both cities (Denver not shown); all other unique effects are relatively small. It would appear that the effects of individual characteristics are stronger on behavioral indicators of competence than attitudinal or belief indicators, consistent with our earlier observation of neighborhood-level findings that indicated

TABLE 4.5. *Individual, Compositional, and Physical Neighborhood Effects on Youth Development: Unique, Shared, and Total Variance Explained*

Disaggregated Neighborhood Effect	Personal Competence	Prosocial Behavior	Prosocial Competence		On Track		Problem Behavior	
	Den	Den	Den	Chi	Den	Chi	Den	Chi
Unique Physical Effect[a]	.00	.02	.00	.02	.00	.00	.00	.01
Unique Compositional Effect[b]	.00	.00	.00	.01	.00	.00	.00	.00
Unique Individual Effect[c]	.03	.18	.09	.12	.04	.14	.14	.02
Unique Interactional Effect[d]	.02	.02	.04	.00	.02	.00	.00	.01
Shared Effect	.08	.05	.05	.04	.03	.00	.00	.08
Total Explained Variance[e]	.14	.27	.18	.19	.09	.13	.13	.12

Columns grouped under: Individual Youth Developmental Outcomes

[a] The unique proportion of variance explained by neighborhood physical condition.
[b] The unique proportion of variance explained by neighborhood Disadvantage/Poverty (continuous measure).
[c] The unique effect of a set of individual compositional/selection variables which included: age, gender, race/ethnicity, socioeconomic status, family structure and length of residence in the neighborhood.
[d] The unique effect of the following individual by neighborhood Disadvantage/Poverty interactions: age by Disadvantage/Poverty, gender by Disadvantage, race/ethnicity by Disadvantage, socioeconomic status by Disadvantage, and family structure by Poverty.
[e] Figures for the unique and shared effects may not sum to equal the total explained variance due to rounding error.

neighborhood effects were stronger on attitudinal and perceptual indicators of youth competence. The fact that shared effects are stronger for attitudinal rather than behavioral indicators of competence is also consistent with this observation.

There are significant interaction effects for Prosocial Competence (not shown), On Track, and Prosocial Behavior that account for 2–4 percent of the variance in Denver. There are essentially no interaction effects in Chicago. The interaction effects in Denver indicate that the negative effects of living in a Disadvantaged Neighborhood are (1) worse for females than males, and (2) become worse with increasing age for both males and females. We saw these same effects in the ICC analyses presented earlier.[38] Further, as neighborhoods become more advantaged, the effects of one's own socioeconomic status (SES) on developmental outcomes become greater. Thus, the negative effect of low individual SES on individual competence is more pronounced in Advantaged than in Disadvantaged Neighborhoods. We found the same gender interactions for the Prosocial Behavior outcome but no age or SES interaction. The negative effects of Disadvantage on the probability for a successful transition into adulthood (On Track) were also stronger for females and grew more pronounced as youth approached their adult years.

EXPLORING THE INTERACTIONS

In an effort to explore the individual SES by neighborhood interactions in more depth, we examined the average individual success outcome for different SES groups in each type of neighborhood. In this analysis[39] we controlled for individual race/ethnicity to ensure that socioeconomic status and race/ethnicity effects were not confounded. This analysis revealed a strong influence of youths' SES on the development of competence when they lived in Advantaged Neighborhoods, as suggested earlier. However, the exact nature of the interaction was more complex. Those with moderate levels of SES did relatively poorly in Advantaged Neighborhoods.[40] The weakest relationship between the individual's SES and personal competence score was found in Modest rather than more Disadvantaged Neighborhoods. Individually advantaged youth (moderate and high SES) were least able to take advantage of their family's greater resources when living in Modest Neighborhoods. Typically, the worst outcomes were observed for those with moderate levels of SES living in Modest Neighborhoods. This pattern was nearly uniform for all developmental outcomes although the interactions were statistically significant only for the measure of Personal Competence. It is also this type of neighborhood and individual SES combination that results in the highest rate of Problem Behavior for those in the Denver sample.

Finally, there was one significant interaction between race/ethnicity and type of neighborhood (not shown in Table 4.5). Being African American and living in a Disadvantaged Neighborhood resulted in higher-than-expected levels of involvement in Problem Behavior. Apart from this one race-by-type-of-neighborhood effect, the HLM analysis revealed that the detrimental effects of individual minority status and neighborhood disadvantage are independent and additive. This means that for black and Hispanic youth living in a Disadvantaged Neighborhood, both their racial/ethnic status and the type of neighborhood have a negative influence on their developmental outcomes. Nevertheless, the effect of being African American on individual-level competence, positive behaviors, and being On Track outcomes, for example, is the same no matter which type of neighborhood is involved, whether Advantaged or Disadvantaged; and except for involvement in Problem Behavior, the effect of living in a Disadvantaged Neighborhood was the same for both white and African American youth. For most developmental outcomes then, being black and living in a Disadvantaged Neighborhood does not accentuate the effect of race above that operating in any other type of neighborhood. The one exception is significant, however, putting African American youth living in Disadvantaged Neighborhoods at particularly elevated risk of involvement in and apprehension for delinquency and drug use.

DISCUSSION: THE EFFECTS OF DISADVANTAGE/POVERTY AND
DETERIORATION ON INDIVIDUAL-LEVEL SUCCESS OUTCOMES

Neighborhood effects on *individual* developmental outcomes are modest, uniquely accounting for less than 3 percent of individual variation, and when including interaction and shared effects, no more than 5–10 percent, depending on which outcome is considered. This excludes Problem Behavior (Denver), which does not appear to be influenced by the type of neighborhood in which one lives. Still, the practical effect of growing up in a Disadvantaged or Poor Neighborhood compared to an Advantaged one involves *both* individual and neighborhood-level effects, and these combined effects are more substantial, ranging from 9 to 27 percent of the variance in the total sample. But these individual-level effects are predominantly selection effects, personal or family characteristics related to the sorting process involved in finding a neighborhood in which to live; they are not properly viewed as emergent neighborhood effects.

Neighborhood effects on individual development are substantially larger for specific subgroups of youth. In general, the closer youth are to the adolescent–adult transition, the stronger the overall neighborhood effect and the greater the unique effect of neighborhood Disadvantage/Poverty on the development of Personal Competence and the probability of being on course for a successful transition to adult roles.[41] Combined effects for older youth range from 17 to 28 percent of explained variance.[42]

There are several possible explanations for this age effect. First, it may reflect the cumulative effects of exposure to neighborhood disadvantage over time on individual attitudes, perceptions of life chances, perceived self-efficacy, and the development of those academic skills and competencies that prepare one for a successful transition into adult roles. It is interesting that this age gradient in neighborhood effects is *not* observed for involvement in Prosocial Behavior or Problem Behavior. Indeed, neighborhood effects on these developmental outcomes are quite small at every age. The observed effect of neighborhood Disadvantage on perceptions of self-efficacy, life chances, and school performance does not appear to be sudden or dramatic from age to age. It may involve a different life-course trajectory that puts youth from more Advantaged Neighborhoods in a better position to make a successful transition into adulthood. These different trajectories might well involve small initial differences that become larger over time and, by age 18, involve substantially different individual competencies, perceived opportunities, probabilities for stable work in the legitimate economy and participation in other conventional adult roles and community life. This interpretation views the age effect as a true neighborhood effect that emerges over time in disadvantaged areas.

A second explanation is that the salience of the neighborhood changes with stages of development. Conditions and events in the neighborhood have a greater direct impact on development during adolescence than they did during childhood.[43] The effect is not cumulative but changes as children approach the adult years. With the move to independence during this period of the life course, direct exposure to neighborhood norms and values increases. The increased exposure is the result of a complex interaction of biological, psychological, and social developmental changes occurring in adolescence, which result in a dramatic change in the potential influence of the "street," i.e., the neighborhood culture and opportunity structures that define appropriate life goals and lifestyles.

With the onset of puberty, ethnic and gender identity formation, the initiation of dating, and increasing independence from parents, there is evidence of an increase in the levels of ethnic and SES differentiation among teens, marked primarily by their peer group affiliations.[44] During adolescence, the neighborhood streets and school grounds become the primary contexts where adolescents gather, where they encounter the neighborhood norms and values directly without parental filtering and interpretation. As a result, the emergent influences of the neighborhood become greater during this period of the life course. Why these changes in direct exposure to neighborhood conditions do not influence both expectations and behavior is not clear. We will examine this interpretation of the age effect further when we consider the combined effects of neighborhood, family, and peer groups on successful adolescent developmental outcomes in later chapters.

It is also possible that this age effect reflects a selective in- and out-migration pattern within Disadvantaged/Poor Neighborhoods. If the more successful youth and families are more likely to leave these neighborhoods as the youth grow older, the residual group of remaining older youth would become increasingly homogeneous, producing the observed age gradient in neighborhood effects. Although we cannot dismiss this possibility without a careful longitudinal analysis of movement in and out of neighborhoods, the fact that the age effect in the HLM analysis appeared to involve neighborhood rather than individual-level effects argues against it.

We also found significant gender and SES effects. In general, the SES interaction findings are consistent with a relative deprivation argument; the negative effect of individual Poverty or Disadvantage on developmental outcomes is greater if one lives in an Advantaged than a Poor Neighborhood. However, the interaction was a complex one in which the combination of a moderate individual SES and living in a Modest Disadvantaged Neighborhood often revealed the lowest chance for successful development. Although poor (low SES) youth did not do as well as high SES youth when living in Advantaged Neighborhoods, this was the best neighborhood context for them, developmentally. This finding is similar to that of Duncan and Brooks-Gunn (1994), who report that having advantaged neighbors provides an added advantage for developmental outcomes. And it has important practical implications because more than half of metropolitan dwellers who are poor live in low-poverty neighborhoods.[45]

It is interesting to note that when we controlled for SES we found only one significant race-by-neighborhood interaction, although we looked systematically for them. Black youth living in Disadvantaged Neighborhoods were at elevated risk of involvement in Problem Behavior. However it was surprising that we found no other significant race/ethnicity interaction effects. The Philadelphia study (Furstenberg et al., 1999), which used many of the same neighborhood- and individual-level measures as used in this study, reported no race-by-neighborhood interactions. There was a consistent race/ethnicity main effect on development: minority youth have lower chances of successful development in all types of neighborhoods. But except for the one case involving black youth, neighborhood Disadvantage and Problem Behavior, minority youth do not appear to be at an elevated risk in Disadvantaged as compared to Advantaged Neighborhoods because of their minority status. Nor did we find any evidence for the claim that African American youth benefit less from having advantaged neighbors than do white youth.[46] Our analysis also did not support the claim that the co-occurrence of minority status and low SES family background makes youth particularly vulnerable to neighborhood effects.[47] In general, minority status and neighborhood Disadvantage effects are independent and additive, but they do not interact. There also were no significant interactions for family structure. Single-parent families had essentially the same effect on youth development when the family lived in an Advantaged as compared to a Disadvantaged Neighborhood. Neither were there any interactions involving length of residence in the neighborhood.

CONCLUSION

For many readers, the most surprising finding is that bad neighborhoods, as identified by Poverty, Disadvantage, and physical Deterioration, have such a small effect on individual-level success outcomes. Given the conventional wisdom and media portrayal about what it is like growing up in bad neighborhoods, how can this be? In one respect, our findings support this view: at the neighborhood level – the rates of successful development are substantially higher in good as compared to bad neighborhoods; residents of good neighborhoods have, on average, higher levels of personal competencies, mostly As and Bs at school, expectations of graduating from college, and expectations of getting advanced degrees. They are more likely to have conventional friends and are much less likely to be involved in problem behavior. Taken together, this involves a substantial advantage over the developmental outcomes associated with living in a bad neighborhood. The negative influence of bad neighborhoods on *rates* of successful development was relatively strong, accounting for 32–59 percent of the variance in Denver. It was substantially less in Chicago, accounting for about a quarter of the variance in developmental outcomes.

However, at the individual level, a different picture emerges. Bad neighborhoods account for only a small part of the variation in *individual* outcomes. Again, how can this be? First, this finding reflects the fact that much of what we saw at the neighborhood level was the result of individual-level attributes. Most families living in good neighborhoods have good economic and social resources, are well educated, and are committed to conventional values and lifestyles. Their children are likely to do well in any neighborhood. Once we separated the individual-level influences and the contextual effects of concentrated advantage, the pure contextual influence is quite modest.

Second, the use of neighborhood average scores or rates of successful development obscures the actual variation in individual outcomes within the neighborhood. In both Advantaged and Disadvantaged Neighborhoods, some youth are doing very well, some are just doing OK, and others are doing poorly. In fact, our measure of being on course for a successful transition into adulthood suggests that at least half of those youth living in Disadvantaged and Deteriorated Neighborhoods are doing OK. Our individual-level findings indicate that the variation in successful developmental outcomes within good or bad neighborhoods is typically greater than the variation between neighborhoods. Clearly, neighborhood Disadvantage and Deterioration as contextual influences do not have an all-powerful influence on development and behavior in this study.

It may be that the influence of neighborhoods has changed since the early studies by Shaw and McKay (1942) and others.[48] Much of this work was done prior to World War II and there have been many changes in community structure and composition since then. With the introduction of television, the widespread ownership of cars and telephones, and the development of mass transportation systems and other conveyors of mass culture, the sociogeographic neighborhood today may be less important as a developmental context than it was prior to the 1950s. However, the claims for strong neighborhood effects are still being made today, particularly in recent ethnographic studies.[49] Whether neighborhood effects on youth development have diminished in recent years or not, recent research findings from survey-based studies are quite consistent in reporting small effects on individual-level outcomes.[50] In fact, our estimates of neighborhood effects, particularly for older youth, are higher than those reported by most other survey studies. However all survey and demographic studies agree: there is great diversity in successful developmental outcomes within neighborhoods, even in high-poverty or high-disadvantaged neighborhoods.[51]

The large within-neighborhood differences in individual success may well be the result of differences in other social contexts that are "nested" within neighborhoods and moderate their effect on development – in family socialization and management practices, variation in social support and opportunities at school and the type of school climate, and involvement with different types of peer groups. To some extent, as we have already demonstrated in the HLM analysis, they are the result of differences in individual attributes, abilities, and motivation. We will consider these additional contextual and individual effects in later chapters.

While neighborhood composition and physical effects do not appear to be dramatic, they are still substantial; living in a Disadvantaged Neighborhood significantly reduces one's chances for a successful course of development. But how might we intervene at the neighborhood level so as to improve the chances of success for children and youth living there? How might we change the composition, structure, or culture of the neighborhood so as to mitigate the negative effects of ecological disadvantage on developmental outcomes? The answer to this question requires that we understand *how* neighborhood disadvantage influences development; that we identify the specific mechanisms or processes by which neighborhood poverty, mobility, racial/ethnic mix, and family composition are linked to individual development. We turn now to consider this question in the next chapter and test our full model of neighborhood influences on individual development in Chapter 6.

Notes

1. Because this is a cross-sectional study, the temporal order of variables is not established and we have not manipulated the independent variables as required

for a causal interpretation of study findings. The evidence presented can be judged consistent or inconsistent with the theoretical hypotheses and thus supportive or not supportive of the proposed explanatory model of neighborhood, family, school, and peer group effects on youth development outcomes. It is in this sense that we use the terms "effect" and "influence" throughout the remainder of this book. We are not making causal claims by using these terms.

2. For example, see Wilson, 1997; Harris, 1998; Furstenberg et al., 1999. The body of evidence for this claim was discussed in Chapter 1.

3. Most of these measures were taken directly from scales previously developed and validated in the National Youth Survey (Elliott et al., 1989) or the Denver Youth Survey (Huizinga et al., 1995). Several involve adaptations of NYS or DYS scales. The construction of our composite scales was based upon a principal components analysis and a confirmatory factor analysis that considered the indicator scales relationships to each other and the resulting relationships between composite measures. See Dunteman (1989) and Carmines and Zeller (1979).

4. The development of these two composite scales was based upon an initial factor analysis of a set of 12 individual scales common to both sites. The final selection involved a confirmatory factor analysis.

5. Elliott, Huizinga, and Menard, 1989.

6. These are relatively minimal criteria for "success," and could be considered criteria for doing OK or at least not experiencing major failures.

7. The reliability of some of the scales in Table 4.1 can not be calculated as indicated by "n/a" in the Table. The measure of reliability used is Cronbach's Alpha, an internal consistency test (Carmines and Zeller, 1979). It is not possible to calculate Alpha for single-item scales. It is also inappropriate to calculate an internal consistency reliability for scales involving simple numerical counts. In both cases, the only appropriate reliability measure would be a test–retest measure, which is not available for this cross-sectional study.

8. Sampson et al. (1997) use a similar measure of disadvantage (Concentrated Disadvantage) that included one additional variable – percent receiving public assistance. Garner and Raudenbush (1991) use a larger number of indicators in their measure or "Index" of disadvantage. Their index was comprised of twelve economic and demographic indicators from the U.S. Census. For our Disadvantage composite, a neighborhood's score on the diversity scale was calculated by counting the number of racial/ethnic groups (e.g., African American, white, Hispanic, and Asian) that account for 10 percent or more of the neighborhood population. It has a range 1–4. The range was quite constricted for the Chicago sample, due to the sample selection procedures used for this site.

9. The set of indicators hung together as a single underlying construct in a factor analysis and a confirmatory factor analysis (Theta = .734). This analysis was at the neighborhood level. Each was related to our success measures as expected. Except for the correlations with Problem Behavior, they ranged between .33 and .66 and were all statistically significant. The correlations with Problem Behavior were all positive, but only that with Single Parent Families was statistically significant.

10. This outcome was not expected. The conceptual work behind the multidimensional view of disadvantage was based upon work done in Chicago in the 1930s and 1940s (Park, 1926; Burgess, 1925; Park and Burgess, 1924; Shaw and McKay, 1942; Bursik and Grasmick, 1993) and confirmed in many subsequent studies in other locations. It does raise the critical issue of whether the racial/ethnic heterogeneity and mobility of a neighborhood are *always* risk factors for negative developmental outcomes. They do not appear to be ecological risk factors in Chicago in the 1990s.

11. The correlation (*r*) is .50.

12. This analysis involved 1990 tract-level data from the following cities: Atlanta, Boston, Dallas, Chicago, Denver, Detroit, Houston, Kansas City, Los Angeles, Miami, Minneapolis, New Orleans, New York, Philadelphia, Pittsburgh, St. Louis, San Diego, San Francisco, Seattle, and Washington, D.C.

13. Poverty and racial mix are typically not correlated in large cities where African Americans are the dominant minority (Jargowsky, 1996).

14. We also considered a two-factor index of disadvantage that combined poverty and single-parent families, as these two indicators loaded on a single factor on both sites and had uniform predictive relationships with our success measures. However, the two-factor index did no better predicting successful outcomes than the poverty indicator alone; and the neighborhood typology based upon the single poverty indicator produced a better distribution of neighborhood types than did the two-factor index. We also considered a disadvantage index using population decline instead of mobility in Chicago. This produced a single factor in Chicago which was then dichotomized into high- and low- disadvantage. Again, poverty as a single indicator of disadvantage was a stronger and more consistent predictor of neighborhood success outcomes than was this disadvantage index. Finally, we considered an employment-ratio measure, which reflected the proportion of adults in the neighborhood who were working. Again, this measure produced results that were very similar to those obtained with the Poverty measure in Chicago; it did not work as well as either Poverty or Disadvantage in Denver.

15. Racial Mix contributed a significant additional effect to both Prosocial Competence (*b* = −0.26) and Prosocial Behavior (*b* = −0.26); *Mobility* also added significant explained variance to Prosocial Competence (*b* = −0.22).

16. See Shaw and McKay, 1942; Gans, 1962; Suttles, 1968; Merry, 1981a; Sampson and Groves, 1989; Skogan, 1990; Bursik and Grasmick, 1993; Sampson, 2001.

17. A neighborhood classified as predominantly white, African American, or Hispanic had populations made up of 60 percent or more of that particular racial/ethnic group as established by the 1990 U.S. Census.

18. For the four-factor index, each of the indicators of disadvantage was dichotomized at the median and then summed to create a scale with a range of 4 to 8 for each neighborhood. Neighborhoods with scores of 4 and 5 were classified as Advantaged; 6 to 7 as Modest; and 8 as Disadvantaged Neighborhoods. On the single factor measure, neighborhoods with 30 percent or more families below poverty were classified as Poor Neighborhoods; those with 18 to 29 percent were classified as Moderate; and those with less than 18 percent below poverty were classified as Advantaged Neighborhoods.

19. In most cases, this difference involved a move to an adjacent type, e.g., if classified as a Poor Neighborhood, it was classified as a Modest Neighborhood and vice versa. An exception involved two Advantaged Neighborhoods in the poverty classification that are classified as Disadvantaged Neighborhoods in the disadvantage classification, as a result of their percent of single-parent families, high mobility and high racial mix. The correlation between the two classifications is .494 for ordinal variables (Kendall's tau-b).

20. This is the correlation for the three-way classification shown in Table 4.2. When the two classifications are treated as continuous variables, the correlation (r) is .823, $p = .000$.

21. The correlation (r) between the continuous measures of Disadvantage and Deterioration (.640, $p = .000$) is higher than that for Poverty and Deterioration (.514 $p = .002$).

22. While the overall relationship between type of neighborhood and average competence score is statistically significant, the specific difference between Moderate and Poor Neighborhoods may not be statistically significant.

23. For a review of various measures of delinquency and the relationship between measures see Elliott (1993), Elliott and Huizinga (1989), Hindelang, Hirschi, and Weis (1981), and Huizinga and Elliott (1986). Moffitt et al. (2001) list the following advantages of variety scores: (1) they capture involvement in multiple forms of crime so that trivial forms of behavior do not overweight the measure; (2) variety scores have better distributional properties for analyses than frequency scores (less skewness); (3) they are predictive of future delinquency; and (4) they are the preferred measure according to the classic study on delinquency measurement (Hindelang et al., 1981).

24. We consider only the total explained variance (R^2) here since unique individual effects will change as we add variables to the model. However, in the Denver analysis, Deterioration has no significant effect when Disadvantage is controlled, but the effect of Disadvantage remains when Deterioration is controlled. This suggests that it is Disadvantage, not Deterioration that predicts successful development outcome rates. In Chicago, the pattern of correlations suggests that Deterioration has a stronger influence on successful development outcomes than Poverty. These conclusions are tentative, however, and subject to change as we introduce additional variables into the analysis in subsequent chapters.

25. For example, see Simcha-Fagan and Schwartz, 1986; Loeber and Wikstrom, 1993; Sampson and Groves, 1989; Bursik and Grasmick, 1993; Murray and Short, 1995. There is more compelling evidence for the relationship between neighborhood composition and crime when official record data involving adults are used in the analysis.

26. Skogan, 1990; Schuerman and Kobrin, 1986; Sampson, Raudenbush, and Earls, 1997.

27. Farrington (1993) found that the type of neighborhood was related to the probability of arrest even after controlling for type of crime, race of offender, offender demeanor, and victim preference for arrest. Elliott (2000) has reported that the probability of arrest for each robbery and aggravated assault offense is approximately twice as high for African Americans as for whites, which is

consistent with a neighborhood composition effect on the probability of arrest. See also O'Brien, 1996.

28. Murray and Short, 1995; Furstenberg et al., 1999.

29. For a review of these studies, see Hindelang, Hirschi, and Weis, 1981; Huizinga and Elliott, 1987; Short, 1996; U.S. Surgeon General, 2001. African American males do typically report higher rates of very serious offenses (aggravated assault, robbery, rape) (Elliott, 1994). But general delinquency measures such as that used in this study are dominated by minor types of offenses and frequently do not even include these serious offenses because they are relatively rare events. Even if included, they have little influence on general delinquency measures (see Elliott and Ageton, 1980, for a discussion of this issue). Hindelang, Hirschi, and Weis (1981) report that African American males have significantly higher rates of under reporting than white males. This race differential in the validity of self-reported delinquency, if real, could account for some of the observed difference between Denver and Chicago, but not all of it, and we have argued elsewhere that the evidence for this differential validity claim is not very convincing (Elliott, 1982; Huizinga and Elliott, 1986; and Elliott, 1995).

30. Sickmund, Snyder, and Poe, 1997; Snyder and Sickmund, 1999; Blumstein et al., 1986.

31. Ennis, 1967; Kaufman et al., 2000.

32. Elliott, Huizinga, and Menard, 1989; Elliott, 1994; Johnston et al., 2000a,b.

33. Jencks and Mayer, 1990; Simcha-Fagan and Schwartz, 1986; Datcher, 1982; Gottfredson et al., 1991; Aber et al., 1992; Stouthamer-Loeber et al., 1993; Farrington, 1993; Duncan and Brooks-Gunn, 1994; Murray and Short, 1995; Laub and Lauritsen, 1998.

34. Bryk and Raudenbush, 1992. All of the models presented here are fixed slope and random intercept models.

35. Murray and Short (1995) report a similar finding in their analysis of alcohol use by community context. However, we did not find a consistent pattern of lower ICCs for behavioral outcomes in Denver, as compared to attitudinal or belief outcomes as reported by Murray and Short. This pattern was more evident in Chicago.

36. Five separate HLM models were estimated for each of our successful youth development outcomes: (1) the full model, which included all of the variables and all of the interactions; (2) the full model minus Deterioration; (3) the full model minus Disadvantage (or Poverty); (4) the full model minus the individual-level attributes; and (5) the full model minus the interactions. By comparing these different models, the amount of unique variance in individual success outcomes attributable to neighborhood Disadvantage, Deterioration, individual attributes, individual/neighborhood interactions and shared by all four sources was estimated.

37. We could partition the shared variance among the predictors (no shared variance), but we are not doing so here. We will present such analyses in Chapter 9.

38. However, the ICCs do not indicate the directionality of differences, that is, which groups are doing better or worse in this type of neighborhood.

39. We used an analysis of variance procedure, covarying race/ethnicity to compare outcome means for each SES group in each type of neighborhood. There

was a significant SES by neighborhood interaction for Personal Competence and this interaction was nearly significant for Prosocial Competence. This analysis is found in Appendix A, Table A4.4.

40. Poor youth living in Advantaged Neighborhoods did quite well compared to poor youth in other types of neighborhoods. However, there were too few cases in this combination of individual and contextual conditions to obtain a reliable estimate of its influence.

41. Halpern-Felsher et al. (1997) report a similar finding.

42. See Table A4.5 in Appendix A.

43. For a discussion of earlier observed age or developmental stage effects, see Brooks-Gunn et al. (1993) and Brooks-Gunn, Duncan, Levanthal, and Aber (1997).

44. For similar findings, see Eccles et al., 1997; Kao and Tienda 1998; Furstenberg et al., 1999.

45. Jargowsky, 1996.

46. Clark, 1992.

47. Brooks-Gunn et al., 1993, p. 148.

48. Park et al., 1925; Liebow, 1967; Wirth, 1928, 1938; Whyte, 1955.

49. Anderson, 1991, 1994; MacLeod, 1987; Williams and Kornblum, 1985; Kozol, 1995; and Kotlowitz, 1991.

50. Simcha-Fagan and Schwartz, 1986; Jencks and Mayer, 1990; Gottfredson et al., 1991; Farrington, 1993.

51. Jargowsky, 1996; McNeely, 1999.

Critical Dimensions of Neighborhood Organization and Culture

SYNOPSIS

Our central concern in this study of neighborhoods, is how youth living in bad neighborhoods can avoid or overcome the negative influences of this set of compositional and physical conditions and grow up to be healthy, well-functioning, productive adults. At the neighborhood level, the type of social organization and culture that emerges from the social interaction in the neighborhood provides a set of conditions that can either neutralize these ecological influences or aggravate them; can support and encourage a positive course of development or compound the negative influences of disadvantage and deterioration on youth development. These organizational structures include both formal and informal organizations. In good neighborhoods, the formal institutions that serve the neighborhood, such as schools, city recreational programs, local employers, businesses, and police, have a strong, visible presence and provide effective services to the neighborhood. Neighbors create a set of interconnected informal networks of adults and children that directly promote positive developmental outcomes, provide controls on dysfunctional behavior, and provide a "safety net" for families experiencing difficulties in raising their children. As neighbors interact, they also develop shared understandings about appropriate goals, attitudes and behavior for their children, creating a normative climate or culture, which sets boundaries on acceptable behaviors and expectations for achievement and particular lifestyles. Finally, in a good neighborhood, the organizational structures and common culture enable the neighborhood to effectively resist the intrusion of any organized criminal activity or other threats to the stability and order in the neighborhood. This potential for collective action ensures that the neighborhood remains a safe and supportive environment for raising children.

In many neighborhoods, the effects of disadvantage and physical deterioration combine to disrupt or prevent the formation and effective operation of neighborhood organizational structures, the creation of a common, conventional culture, and the ability to resist the intrusion of illicit and dysfunctional activities. In others, the residents are able to develop these organizational structures and this type of culture which facilitates a successful course of youth development. The effects of neighborhood disadvantage and deterioration are thus mediated by the emerging organization and culture of the neighborhood.

The specific mechanisms that link neighborhood organization and culture to individual development outcomes are identified. Together with neighborhood disadvantage and deterioration, they constitute the full set of neighborhood effects that will be examined in our study of successful youth development.

5

Critical Dimensions of Neighborhood Organization and Culture

Interviewer: Is there a lot of social interaction between neighbors?

Broadmore resident: There is around here, especially things... like nothing real formal, but a lot of people just out on the street in the summertime especially. Like if I see my neighbor across the street, we will make time to just say hi and talk a few minutes. And we actually did just have a neighborhood party last Saturday night (adult female).

Allenspark resident: I'm an inside person, you know? I don't... I don't associate with really anybody around here (adult female).

Allenspark resident: I don't pay attention to none of the adults here. I don't pay attention to nobody. I'm never outside walking around or anything really (teen female).

Martin Park resident: And one of the big problems here is some people find it easier to change by dropping their adherence to the values than to fight the fights. You know, they'd rather stay in at nights than go out and take the streets back. I don't play that game. I don't bother anybody, and I don't want anybody bothering me either (adult male).

INTRODUCTION

The potential influences of a good or bad neighborhood go beyond the effects of disadvantage and deterioration, although these are the features most people consider when classifying neighborhoods. Neighborhoods also involve social networks, shared understandings among neighbors and common activities. Over time, these interactions become patterned or "routine" and give rise to neighborhood norms and values; to friendship networks and a common culture. These features are less apparent to outside observers than the physical environment or general demographic composition of residents, but we believe they are more critical for a successful course of youth development.

When one moves into an established neighborhood, this organization and culture is often already in place. The new individual or family encounters it as a set of informal and formal relationships, norms and traditions that may appear relatively fixed. In fact, they are dynamic and constantly changing with the movement of individuals and families into and out of the neighborhood. They also reflect changes in the age, status, and lifestyles of the more permanent residents. Even in very stable neighborhoods the social organization and culture changes as residents age and go through the various stages of the life cycle. Although our focus here is on the effect of neighborhood organization and culture on individuals and families, we acknowledge that this relationship is dynamic and reciprocal.

The effects of neighborhood disadvantage are the results of the concentration of particular types of individuals in a given neighborhood. Deterioration reflects the influences of the physical environment. In contrast, neighborhood organization and culture reflect the social dimension of the neighborhood. They are *emergent* effects that result from the collective efforts of neighbors that can create a healthy, supportive setting for their children and themselves; effects which are above and beyond the effects of neighborhood composition and physical conditions (Jencks and Mayer, 1990). They are the result of social processes occurring within the neighborhood. For example, neighborhood residential stability (a demographic feature) facilitates the formation of informal networks and shared expectations for children's success (a social process), which then affects youth development outcomes (individual behavior) in that neighborhood. As noted earlier, emergent effects can have either positive or negative effects on successful development.

A GENERAL MODEL OF NEIGHBORHOOD EFFECTS

We believe organization and culture are the critical features of the neighborhood that determine a successful or unsuccessful course of youth development. They are the most immediate or proximate neighborhood influences on child development. The influence of disadvantage and deterioration is mediated by this social dimension of neighborhoods. They will have negative influences on individual development only to the extent they undermine collective action in the neighborhood. However, the success or failure of residents to achieve an effective organization and supportive culture is only partially determined by the compositional characteristics of residents and the physical features of the neighborhood. In most disadvantaged neighborhoods we expect to find weak social networks and unconventional cultures or lifestyles. We also expect to find some disadvantaged and deteriorated neighborhoods where residents have managed to develop

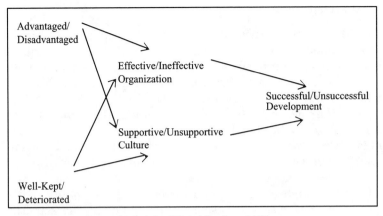

FIGURE 5.1. A General Model of Neighborhood Effects

relatively effective organizations and supportive cultures. Here children are growing up successfully, prepared to enter productive, responsible, and healthy adult roles in our communities.[1] Disadvantage and deterioration increase the likelihood that a neighborhood will fail to develop an effective social organization and supportive culture, but this effect is neither automatic nor absolute. A simplified model of these effects is presented in Figure 5.1. To the extent neighborhood organization and culture do mediate the effects of disadvantage and deterioration as described in Figure 5.1, we can expect that they will have no direct effects on developmental outcomes once the influence of organization and culture is taken into account. Likewise, the effects of organization and culture will be as great or greater than those of disadvantage and deterioration.

The results reported in the preceding chapter may well underestimate the overall effect of the neighborhood context as presented in Figure 5.1.

COMPONENTS OF ORGANIZATION AND CULTURE

We have identified four organizational and cultural characteristics of neighborhoods that are linked directly to youth developmental outcomes: (1) effective formal institutions, (2) informal promotion and control structures, (3) normative and value consensus, and (4) illegal modeling and performance structures. These are the critical features of neighborhood organization and culture that determine whether a neighborhood is a good or bad place to raise children.[2] The first three provide the first line of defense from the negative effects of disadvantage and deterioration; the fourth, illegal role models and illegitimate enterprises, promote dysfunctional lifestyles and behavior that interfere with a successful course of youth development.

Institutional Effectiveness

Neighborhood disadvantage has a direct effect on the capacity and quality of formal institutions which are charged with delivering basic services to the neighborhood – on neighborhood schools, recreational facilities, churches, local businesses, health-care services, transportation, police protection, and sanitation services. One defining characteristic of a good neighborhood for raising children is a high-quality institutional presence of these formal organizations in the neighborhood.

The limited economic resources, lack of political influence, and residential instability of families in disadvantaged neighborhoods make it difficult for public agencies to maintain a high quality of service or even sustain a physical presence in the neighborhood. Given the low spending power of residents, many local businesses leave for more profitable markets. The neighborhood economic base is insufficient to keep child care, preschool, public school, church, and recreational facilities adequately staffed and in good repair. The high rates of student (and parent) turnover continually disrupts the continuity and progression of learning in the classroom and parent involvement in their children's schooling. And the local organizations that once supplied job information and work opportunities for neighborhood residents are unable to sustain themselves either politically or economically.

Wilson reports on changes in the institutional presence in Longmont, a study neighborhood located on the south side of Chicago, that has become increasingly disadvantaged in recent years. In 1950, there were more than 800 commercial and industrial establishments in this neighborhood; today, only about a hundred are left and these are represented by small struggling businesses that employ only one or two persons.[3] Loic Wacquant, a member of Wilson's research team recalls:

> ... not so long ago ... crowds were so dense at rush hour that one had to elbow one's way to the train station ... now ... the commercial strip has been reduced to a long tunnel of charred stores, vacant lots littered with broken glass and garbage, and dilapidated buildings left to rot in the shadow of the elevated train line ... the handful of remaining establishments that struggle to survive are huddled behind wrought-iron bars ... The only enterprises that seem to be thriving are liquor stores and currency exchanges, these "banks of the poor" where one can cash checks, pay bills and buy money orders for a fee.[4]

The inability of residents to secure public goods and services that typically are provided by the business community or allocated by community, state and federal agencies located outside the neighborhood, seriously undermines the neighborhood's capacity for supporting a successful course of youth development. There are three specific mechanisms linking a weak, ineffective institutional presence to poor youth development outcomes: (1) limited public resources to support basic education, recreation, and health needs of youth and their families, (2) ineffective formal controls for maintaining order and safety in public places and deterring individual or group involvement in dysfunctional behavior, and (3) limited opportunities for advanced education or training and for better paying jobs in the mainstream society.

School funding in most states is based on local tax revenues. Because both the residential housing and the commercial tax base is low in disadvantaged neighborhoods, schools located in or serving these neighborhoods typically operate on a lower per-pupil budget,[5] lack up-to-date textbooks and teaching materials, and employ less qualified and competent teachers than more affluent neighborhood schools.[6] Given these limited educational resources, it is not surprising that students in these schools receive a lower quality of instruction, achieve lower grades and lower general achievement test scores, and have lower rates of graduation and higher rates of dropout.[7]

Schools located in or serving disadvantaged neighborhoods also have fewer after-school programs and supervised activities for students. Other institutions that provide recreational and supportive educational services to youth – YMCAs, Big Brothers Big Sisters, Little Leagues and other recreational programs, Boy Scouts and Girls Scouts, Boys and Girls Clubs – are less likely to be found in disadvantaged neighborhoods and those that are located in these neighborhoods typically have fewer resources than those in more affluent neighborhoods.[8] It is difficult to find safe meeting places in disadvantaged neighborhoods. Most youth serving organizations receive no sustained state or federal funding, and rely on local fundraising efforts and participant dues, both of which are problematic for residents in disadvantaged neighborhoods.[9]

There is also evidence that the quality of health-care services is relatively poor in disadvantaged neighborhoods.[10] In part, this is a reflection of the fact that many low-wage jobs do not provide health insurance. Wilson notes that many residents of disadvantaged neighborhoods choose welfare over low paying jobs specifically to obtain the health coverage.[11] This also reflects the fact that clinics and hospitals are often physically distant and difficult to access from these neighborhoods and that the quality of care provided through Medicare is not as high as that from private or corporate insurance programs.

In sum, children and teenagers living in disadvantaged neighborhoods typically do not have high quality child care, preschool programs or health-care, safe parks and recreation centers, supervised after school activities, organized athletic leagues, libraries with the latest books, videos and records, or part-time jobs with local merchants or businesses. All of these resources and services typically are available in more affluent neighborhoods, confirming a strong and effective institutional presence.

A weak institutional presence also means weak formal constraints on disruptive and disorderly behavior in public places. When schools, recreation centers, and public meeting places are not adequately staffed and resourced, the levels of monitoring and supervision become inadequate to maintain order. Chaiken[12] reports this is a major problem for youth-serving agencies trying to set up programs in disadvantaged neighborhoods. It is difficult to find safe meeting places. Levels of security are inadequate, vandalism and other property crime rates are high, and these social control problems drain already limited resources and make staff recruitment difficult.

It is also a problem in many inner-city schools serving disadvantaged neighborhoods. There is often little discipline or order in these schools as they are under staffed and lack the necessary resources to maintain a safe, controlled environment. The levels of social control are further undermined by high staff turnover rates. The stability and continuity of staff required for establishing and maintaining a conventional normative structure in the schools is simply not there. This is, in part, a result of the special needs and problems that children from disadvantaged neighborhoods bring with them to school; the demand for special resources and security is probably greater for schools serving disadvantaged neighborhoods than it is for more advantaged neighborhoods. However, the actual allocation of resources is typically less than that provided schools serving more affluent neighborhoods. Further, disadvantaged neighborhoods lack the political power to influence these funding decisions.

As noted earlier, teachers in disadvantaged neighborhood schools perceive the institutional investment and resulting education offered students to be of low quality.[13] And there is a clear relationship between the quality of education provided by a school and the safety of teachers and students. National surveys reveal that less than half of teachers and students in schools that are perceived as providing a low quality education, feel "very safe" at school.[14] Nearly a third of teachers in these schools report having been the victim of a violent act.

This lack of control creates a school climate in which teachers are unable to teach and students are unable to learn.[15] Two-thirds of teachers in these schools report that their colleagues are less likely to challenge or discipline students because of their fear of retaliation. Students report a reduced motivation to participate in class, difficulty maintaining attention in class, and finding excuses for staying home from school.[16] Disorder and victimization at school thus undermine the learning process.[17]

A weak institutional presence in the neighborhood is also associated with a high level of disorder in the public spaces within the neighborhood.[18] With few legitimate businesses, community organizations, and public facilities located in the neighborhood, the levels of surveillance over public areas on the part of persons with some responsibility for maintaining order is minimal. Those businesses that are surviving in disorganized neighborhoods – bars, liquor stores, pawn shops – are not particularly effective in playing this institutional monitoring role. In some instances, they actually contribute directly or indirectly to the crime, drugs, violence and other signs of disorder in the neighborhood, that is, they become the "hot spots" where unsupervised youth hang out and much of the crime and disorder takes place.

Finally, a weak institutional presence greatly restricts the opportunities for legitimate work, advanced education and training, better housing, and active participation in political activities.[19] All of these opportunities are provided primarily through our social institutions. To get into college, one must have a high school diploma or GED, meet specific course content entrance requirements, take ACT or SAT tests and achieve satisfactory scores, fill out application forms, and have good recommendations from high school teachers and counselors. Getting a job, particularly a higher-paying or higher-status job, has similar institutional requirements and certifications. Most will require a high school diploma or higher level of formal educational attainment, specific competencies that are acquired through one's formal educational, social skills to manage personal relationships while on the job, and access to the job market through institutional or personal networks.

When there is a strong education and work presence in the neighborhood, information about these opportunities and how to access them is readily available; where this presence is weak, educational and work opportunities can be quite limited. If youth have no contacts with adults in or outside the neighborhood who can serve as role models for educational achievement and work roles, or meaningful contacts with adults working in these institutions, they are unlikely to know about the opportunities for further education and jobs or how to go about securing them. The educational expectations for students in disadvantaged neighborhood schools often is such that neither the student nor his parents are even informed about college entrance requirements or available grants, scholarships, or other types of student aid. Further, the fact that few adults in the neighborhood are employed, means that neighborhood youth are frequently uninformed about jobs that are available, and the perception that there is no opportunity for further education and there are few jobs available, may lead youth to exert less effort at school.[20]

It should be clear that our focus here is not simply on the presence of institutions or businesses in the neighborhood, but on the presence of *effective* neighborhood resources, those that support or promote positive child development. In a study of Cleveland, Korbin (2001) notes that the presence of neighborhood businesses and facilities was often a mixed bag. Convenience stores, liquor stores, check cashing/bill paying (for a fee) facilities, and pawn shops may have some positive effects for residents, but, as noted above in the study of Woodlawn, they also can have significant negative influences on development for neighborhood children. Counting churches in the neighborhood can be very misleading, as they may have little involvement with neighborhood residents. The same can be said for some YMCAs and other recreational facilities. Even neighborhood parks can be perceived by residents as dangerous places they instruct their children to avoid.

Informal Promotion and Control Structures

The primary organizational structure that facilitates and regulates social development in the neighborhood is the dynamic set of social relationships that emerge (or fail to emerge) from interpersonal interactions between residents. In addition to the presence or absence of these informal social networks in the neighborhood and their size and breadth, the level of attachment and commitment to them and to the physical neighborhood as a viable community, operates to promote certain developmental outcomes and constrain others. We refer to these two informal organizational features of the neighborhood as *informal networks* and *neighborhood bonding*. Together, they function to promote and control developmental processes and outcomes in the neighborhood.

Informal Networks and Social Control

The processes of social control operating in the neighborhood have been clearly delineated by scholars and researchers working in the social disorganization tradition.[21] From this perspective, effective social control is rooted in the overlapping and interconnected system of friendship and family networks. These are reciprocal networks; they not only give support to individuals and families, but require that these individuals and families give support to others in the network. Through these networks, individuals maintain ties to others in the neighborhood and to persons in the larger community.[22] These informal family and friendship networks provide the most direct surveillance of neighborhood activities, supervision of children and youth, intervention into questionable activities that might be occurring in the neighborhood, and an awareness of who belongs in the neighborhood and who are strangers.

Hunter[23] has identified three levels of neighborhood social networks and the specific control mechanisms used by each. The first level involves informal, intimate, face-to-face, interpersonal networks where control is achieved through criticism, shaming, ridicule, avoidance, and possible rejection from the group (private networks). The second level consists of interlocking friendship networks with the broader, less intimate networks of persons in local institutions such as teachers, members of one's church, casual friends and acquaintances at work; here control is achieved through the allocation or threatened withdrawal of services and supports and mutual esteem or status (parochial networks). The neighborhood's linkages to city and county government agencies in the larger community make up the third level. Through these broader institutional relationships, residents can secure public resources and services from agencies located outside the neighborhood (public networks).

When these networks are interconnected and overlapping, they provide strong social controls on behavior within the neighborhood.[24] Parents know their children's friends and their friends' parents; children know their parents' friends and associates at work. In this type of integrated child–adult network, the norms are reinforced by many different adults and youth. Adults are willing to intervene in events and activities that threaten the well-being of neighborhood children. They know they have the permission of their neighbors to correct and admonish their children. It creates the situation where kids sometimes complain that "if I screw up in this neighborhood, my folks will know about it before I can get home."

When these informal structures are weak or fail to develop, there is no mechanism for exercising effective controls on behavior in the neighborhood. Further, there are no informal social organizations to support collective action in the neighborhood; no communication networks, established interaction patterns, stable relationships, or other means to determine what might be common problems or goals, and no means to mobilize the neighborhood residents to take action to defend the neighborhood or promote the successful development of their children. There is clear evidence that these informal networks tend to be less extensive and effective in disadvantaged neighborhoods.[25]

Informal Networks and Promoting Successful Development

Shaw and McKay (1942), Bursik and Grasmick (1993), Sampson (1985), Sampson et al. (1997), and others working in the disorganization tradition have focused almost exclusively on social controls, i.e., mechanisms that constrain behavior, specifically delinquent behavior. They give little attention to how these neighborhood networks might *promote* positive youth development and prosocial patterns of behavior. In fact, informal networks in a neighborhood operate to both constrain some behaviors and to promote others. Successful youth development, as we conceptualize it, involves both; certain behaviors, skills, beliefs, and experiences are considered positive indicators of a successful developmental course and are rewarded in supportive prosocial networks; others are viewed as negative indicators, things to be avoided if one is to be successful as an adult.

When describing the control mechanisms inherent in informal social networks, Hunter identified only the potential group sanctions associated with noncompliance of proscriptive norms, e.g., expressions of disapproval and criticism, threatened withdrawal of sentiment and social support, rejection, and abandonment. These are potential group punishments, but the group also has mechanisms for rewarding approved behaviors, beliefs, skills, and aspirations. These include expressions of approval, praise, extending increased social supports, and increased status and privilege.

Although the control function of informal networks may be the more important one for explaining delinquency, the promotion and support function is the more critical function for facilitating a positive, healthy course of youth development. An effective informal network usually does both but these two functions are somewhat independent and some networks put more emphasis on one than the other or are more effective in accomplishing one than the other. We will return to this issue in the Discussion Section.

Neighborhood Bonding and Cohesion

As social beings, neighbors do things together, and there is both a structural and an affective dimension to their interaction. Park and Burgess[26] saw the social interaction between neighbors leading both to the formation of social networks and to bonds of personal attachment to the neighborhood. Personal ties, or what we will refer to as neighborhood bonding, are to both the informal personal networks that develop in the neighborhood and the physical place. Although the formation of social networks and neighborhood bonding both emerge from the interaction of neighbors, they are separate emergent properties. Living in the same neighborhood sets the stage for social bonding but genuine friendship does not always result from neighborhood interaction. The presence of informal networks clearly facilitates the development of personal attachments but it does not guarantee high levels of neighborhood bonding. Further, it is possible to develop strong bonds to the physical neighborhood when the informal networks are weak and ineffective, because of other advantages associated with the physical location – its proximity to work, the quality of local schools, its physical attractiveness, and its general status within the larger community. Neighborhood bonding will thus vary across neighborhoods which have functioning informal social networks.

Bonding refers to affective sentiments such as liking, belonging, satisfaction, trust, and commitment. These personal feelings about the neighborhood result primarily from participation in the informal social networks, that is, from the personal investments of time and resources to the collective social life in the neighborhood and the maintenance of the physical environment. It takes time and effort to develop friendships with neighbors.[27] As neighbors do things together and invest more time and energy in the informal networks within the neighborhood, levels of satisfaction with and commitment to the neighborhood should increase.

Neighborhood bonding thus enhances the effectiveness of the informal networks in promoting and controlling specific behaviors and attitudes in the neighborhood. It provides a psychological investment in the network that produces a sense of neighborhood cohesion, trust, and solidarity in promoting and controlling socialization practices and developmental outcomes within the neighborhood. The development of these neighborhood organizations together with a strong attachment to them among neighbors, provides the basis for collective action and a sense of collective efficacy.[28] The levels of trust between neighbors provides the implicit authority to correct and admonish each others' children; and to encourage and praise them when they do well. Those persons with strong bonds to the neighborhood *like* living there and are unlikely to leave, even if they have the means to relocate to more expensive or physically attractive areas. Leaving the neighborhood means leaving their friends and support groups.

The Culture of the Neighborhood: Normative/Value Consensus

In most neighborhoods, there is a prevailing normative climate which sets boundaries on acceptable behavior and expectations for achievement and the attainment of specific goals.[29] Indeed, the effective regulation of developmental processes and behavior requires the development of shared expectations and standards for judging what is acceptable and unacceptable behavior as well as a mechanism for rewarding or punishing these behaviors. The informal networks in a neighborhood provide the mechanism for generating, enforcing and promoting these shared understandings, but they do not specify what is valued, what is expected, and what is threatening or prohibited. This is defined by the *culture* that emerges within the neighborhood.

By culture we refer to the *content* of socialization, to the values, norms, beliefs, moral evaluations, perceptions of opportunity, symbolic meanings, rituals of daily life and normative orientations shared by or professed by members of a social system. The system, in this case, includes the private and parochial networks in the neighborhood.[30] It is the culture of the neighborhood that embodies the social values of the neighborhood and promotes specific social practices and behaviors. It is the culture that accounts for the transmission of lifestyles from one generation to another.[31] The culture of the neighborhood defines the "character" of the neighborhood by providing authoritative models of human relationships and developmental outcomes.

Our focus here is specifically on cultural values and the norms that embody them. These informal rules for living in everyday situations specify which behaviors, skills, beliefs and experiences are to be encouraged and rewarded, and which are to be avoided, discouraged, and punished. They define the *content* of neighborhood socialization. At the neighborhood level, there are two separate issues involved: (1) the *types* of values and norms that come to be endorsed, and (2) the *level of consensus* within the neighborhood around these specific values and norms.

First, there are important differences in the types of behavior and values promoted across different neighborhoods. There is a "conventional" bias in the purely structural argument that the presence of strong, cohesive informal networks in a neighborhood provide a form of regulation that always promotes a healthy, conventional course of development and deters negative or dysfunctional developmental outcomes. This *assumes* that all private, parochial, and public networks have a value and normative orientation that supports a conventional developmental trajectory.[32] This is clearly *not* the case.

Shaw and McKay found stable neighborhoods with extensive private networks that had high rates of delinquency and crime. Many others have reported the same combination of characteristics.[33] There are two explanations offered for this finding: (1) that the private networks in these neighborhoods were not integrated into public networks and thus had no power or influence over the investments of public resources, and it was the limited institutional resources and opportunities that led to high rates of neighborhood crime; or (2) that there are differences in the culture of well-organized neighborhoods that lead to the promotion of different patterns of behavior and socialization outcomes.[34]

The first explanation is a purely structural one that ignores differences in culture across neighborhoods. Even if these neighborhood networks are not integrated, this condition does not account for the particular adaptation made to the limited resources and opportunities in disadvantaged neighborhoods. For example, Shaw and McKay also found some disadvantaged neighborhoods with strong private networks and limited public resources that *did not* have particularly high rates of delinquency and crime. Further, some high-crime neighborhoods had private, parochial, and public networks that were both cohesive and integrated; in fact, the most successful organized crime operations were in these types of neighborhoods where the criminal activities were embedded in the private networks and sanctioned and protected by (corrupt) public officials.[35] Thus a purely structural explanation cannot account for the observed variation in crime, delinquency, teen pregnancy, high school graduation rates, or other developmental outcomes across neighborhoods.

Youth gangs provide more direct evidence that well-organized primary networks can have unconventional value and normative orientations.

Gangs can be very well organized, effective social networks; they can serve many practical needs of members, generate strong allegiances and loyalty (social bonds), and can be very effective in regulating the behavior of members (social control). Typically, they do not have a conventional normative orientation. In fact, membership and status in the gang often requires participation in delinquent acts and other forms of problem behavior.[36]

Although many disadvantaged neighborhoods and most advantaged neighborhoods do not have formal gangs (i.e., groups with formal membership rituals, colors and other identifying signs or symbols, and a formal leadership structure), the peer networks in these neighborhoods may nevertheless tolerate or encourage unconventional values and behavior that are dysfunctional or disruptive for a successful course of youth development.[37] The culture and normative orientation of adolescent peer groups clearly vary across neighborhoods.

There is also more direct evidence that the private networks of adults in some neighborhoods promote or tolerate unconventional lifestyles. Shaw and McKay report finding well-organized neighborhoods that were characterized by "a coherent system of values supporting delinquent acts."[38] Ethnographic studies have also documented the existence of an oppositional culture marked by a rejection of mainstream values as reflected in cohabiting and childbearing outside of marriage, welfare dependency, unemployment, drug use, and crime.[39] There are clear instances where the adults in a neighborhood support the violence of juveniles toward outsiders as a way of protecting the character or identity of the neighborhood. For example, in the Chicago housing riots of the late 1940s and early 1950s, the young people arrested were fully supported by the adults in the neighborhood. With respect to attitudes and values, those arrested were representatives of the neighborhood not its deviants.[40] There is also evidence that the adults in some neighborhoods give tacit approval to the drug distribution and stolen goods networks functioning in the neighborhood, as this is a primary source of economic support.[41]

Even the public network in disorganized neighborhoods may provide little support for conventional developmental outcomes, as is often the case when organized crime is entrenched in the neighborhood, has corrupted the political offices, and has a strong influence on the police, unions, and businesses that operate in the neighborhood. Apart from what adults in these networks "say" about appropriate and inappropriate behavior, real-life practices that model promiscuous sexual activity, getting drunk, idleness, and quick and easy money from drugs and violence, may become part of the informal normative expectations.

A second dimension of neighborhood culture involves the level of *consensus* achieved about norms and values. When there is inconsistency within or across the set of informal networks in a neighborhood, the ability of this interconnected system to effectively promote a successful adolescent development is undermined. Both Shaw and McKay (1942) and Kobrin (1951) report that children living in disadvantaged neighborhoods are often exposed to contradictory values and standards for behavior. This is probably a more typical condition than that where the neighborhood has a high level of consensus around a uniformly deviant or oppositional culture.[42]

Further, consensus is critical to the development of friendships and the formation of primary networks. When the levels of consensus in the neighborhood are low, residents typically withdraw from interaction and participation in neighborhood private networks and activities, out of a fear of rejection, victimization, and distrust of fellow neighbors. Low consensus thus undermines neighborhood bonding and the development of effective friendships and mutual trust that are essential for the formation and effective functioning of the private and parochial networks in a neighborhood.

To the extent that different racial and ethnic groups in a neighborhood promote different cultural norms and values, there will be lower levels of normative consensus in the neighborhood. This is neither an automatic nor an inevitable result of racial or ethnic diversity. Some ethnically diverse neighborhoods have high levels of normative and value consensus,[43] but there is substantial evidence that ethnic diversity sometimes leads to a clash in values and norms.[44] Racial and ethnic diversity is thus linked to cultural diversity.

Illegal Activities and Opportunities

We noted earlier that crime and other dysfunctional lifestyle activity is most likely to emerge in disadvantaged neighborhoods. More specifically, dysfunctional lifestyles are most likely to emerge when the neighborhood is structurally and culturally disorganized, and lacks the collective power to resist or control these activities. Indeed, a neighborhood's inability to organize any effective resistance often draws small-time theft rings, gambling, prostitution, drug distribution networks and other illegal enterprises into these neighborhoods.[45]

Criminologists have identified two distinct types of high-crime neighborhoods that differ primarily in the degree to which there has been some integration of criminal and conventional value systems. The first type is the disadvantaged, disorganized neighborhood as described above. They have no effective informal networks, low levels of normative and value consensus, and a very limited institutional presence. There is virtually no possibility of any collective action by adults in this type of neighborhood to control undesirable behavior. There are too few established stable relationships, no common values or goals, very limited resources, and few connections through which to mobilize the larger community. Anything goes in this type of neighborhood. It is this type of neighborhood that Nathan Glazer describes in his account of riding the subway through disorganized neighborhoods:

"... (a neighborhood) environment one must endure for an hour or more each day is un-controlled and uncontrollable, and that anyone can invade it to do whatever damage and mischief the mind suggests."[46]

While this type of neighborhood attracts petty criminals, drug dealers, and those involved in deviant lifestyles, these persons and activities remain highly individualized; they do not involve organized networks of adults or organized adult activities. Families with conventional values and normative orientations live side-by-side with families and persons with unconventional or criminal values and deviant lifestyles. Neither group of residents has the power to establish a clear, unambiguous set of norms for the neighborhood, and children grow up exposed to both conventional and unconventional values and alternative lifestyles that reflect these different value systems.

This is the type of neighborhood in which youth gangs typically emerge and flourish.[47] Because they often represent the only stable social organization in the neighborhood, gangs come to exercise a substantial level of control over neighborhood activities. They alone have the means for mobilizing collective action in the neighborhood, but their normative orientation is not one that encourages conventional behavior or promotes a conventional lifestyle. The adults in organized-gang neighborhoods have little control over the gangs, are often victimized by these youth and live in fear of them. The following exchange between an interviewer and adult female in Allenspark captures much of this:

INTERVIEWER: Has there ever been any kind of neighborhood organization?

WOMAN: No. Well, see – I guess we're afraid to do that. . . . I'd personally be afraid.

INTERVIEWER: You'd be afraid that they would get back at you?

WOMAN: Yes!

INTERVIEWER: Has somebody – . . .

WOMAN: Oh yes! There's a lady that lives a few houses from here, and she calls the police, you know, for anything that goes on around here. So people found out who's the snitch, you know, around Allenspark.

INTERVIEWER: So what has happened to her?

WOMAN: They throw, you know, like rocks at her, they break her windows, they throw – I guess, I've seen, like notes, "like F-you, this, and F-you that," walk – they walk by and start calling her names. You know? So, so I don't want to start something like that.

INTERVIEWER: So does that keep you from doing certain things – that
you would have normally done? Or ...

WOMAN: Yeah. Because in the summertime, you know, she wasn't –
she was inside her, her house, her doors were already closed.
Some kids just walked by and broke her windows, and I was right
there! ...

INTERVIEWER: So what'd you think?

WOMAN: I said "Oh my goodness!" you know? And the kids saw me.
They weren't kids, they were teenagers. The saw me.

INTERVIEWER: Did they say anything to you?

WOMAN: They just looked at me. You know, they just looked at me, and
she called the police, and she – and she pointed at this, at me that I
was outside, while I was right there. And they came to me and the
kids were right there –

INTERVIEWER: Oh, and what did you say?

WOMAN: And they asked me "Did you see everything?" and I said,
"nope, I didn't see nothing!" And I walked back into my house. And
they were lookin at me. And forget it, if I talk, if I start saying about
it...

INTERVIEWER: You're next?!

WOMAN: My car'll be – and then my windows'll be broken, and so I said
"forget it!"

In contrast, the second type of high-crime neighborhood has developed
effective informal networks that are organized around illegitimate economic activities, for example, organized theft rings, gambling operations,
prostitution, and drug distribution networks. In some cases, this involves
the presence of a crime syndicate or an elaborate regional or national drug
distribution network. These are *organized* neighborhoods with a criminal
culture. The organization typically involves a loosely integrated set of private, parochial, and public networks involving family members, friendship cliques, local fences, illicit business operations, lax police enforcement
or protection, national suppliers, and corrupt politicians. These criminal
networks perform the same support and socialization functions as more
conventional networks; but they have a different normative and value orientation – a different culture.

The fact that these disadvantaged neighborhoods are relatively well-
organized provides some degree of order and control in the neighborhood.
For example, violent fighting gangs are not tolerated in organized crime
neighborhoods as they bring unwanted public attention and scrutiny to
the neighborhood.[48] These organized crime neighborhoods also provide a
new set of economic and social opportunities for adults and youth, a set of
relationships where illegal activities are modeled and successful criminal

activities are rewarded. They also promote a distinctive, unconventional lifestyle and culture that involves particular forms of approved behavior and definitions of "success," which involve immediate forms of gratification, that is, having lots of money to spend, flashy clothes, jewelry, fancy cars and extravagant spending.

However, this type of organization and culture requires some integration of conventional and criminal values among residents in the neighborhood. This value integration typically takes the form of a survival or expediency rationale. Residents often express indifference or even opposition to the stealing, violence, prostitution, gambling, and drug sales found in these neighborhoods, but these same individuals are either directly involved in these activities or rely on this economy for their economic support and tacitly accept it as a necessary evil.[49]

This type of neighborhood also requires a structural integration of conventional and criminal organizations at some level. Typically, this integration occurs at the public network level, with corrupt public officials that provide some protection for the criminal enterprises going on in the neighborhood, but this is not always the case. There are numerous examples of neighborhoods where there is a stable organized crime or drug distribution network that is encouraged, or at least tolerated, by most adults in the neighborhood, and where this illicit economy provides a significant part of the economic support for many individuals and families in the neighborhood.[50]

These two types of high-crime neighborhoods are both disadvantaged neighborhoods, but differ in their level of organization and cultural consensus. The first is the more frequent type of disadvantaged neighborhood. Neighborhoods with highly organized criminal networks are relatively rare. In both types of neighborhoods, youth are exposed to criminal values, criminal role models, and opportunities to participate in criminal activities – what Cloward and Ohlin refer to as criminal learning and opportunity structures.[51] However, in organized crime neighborhoods, there is more informal network support for these activities and greater opportunities to learn the skills and establish the relationships that facilitate a life of crime. Typically, opportunities for involvement in organized crime are quite limited in disorganized neighborhoods, there is less direct support for these activities among residents, and the risks of apprehension and incarceration are substantially greater.

Because opportunities for legitimate work are limited in disadvantaged neighborhoods, participation in the illicit economy is often more lucrative and immediate, requiring less effort and fewer institutional hurdles. The amounts of money to be made in dealing drugs, gambling, and prostitution are far greater than adolescents could expect from any conventional job for which they were qualified. A 25-year-old unmarried father from the West side of Chicago describes this situation:

> For years I been out here trying to find a steady job. Going back and forth all these temporary jobs and this 'n' that. Then you know you got to give money at home . . . you talkin' about food in the house too, you know, things like that . . . Well, lately like I said I have been trying to make extra money and everything. I have been selling drugs lately on the side after I get off work and, ah, it has been going all right . . . like I was saying you can make more money dealing drugs than your job, anybody. Not just me but anybody.[52]

In many disorganized neighborhoods then, youth are exposed to ambivalent or alternative value systems, both conventional and deviant lifestyles and limited opportunities in the conventional and the illicit opportunity systems. There are specific families and individuals in the neighborhood who will provide support for doing well at school, developing prosocial competencies and getting a conventional job; and there are others who will promote or model dropping out of school, dealing drugs and petty theft, and a lifestyle of immediate gratification. It is possible in such a neighborhood, depending on family resources and values, to achieve some success at school, and by a careful selection of friends, to craft an individual set of relationships that supports and enables a successful, conventional course of development. However, the chances of fashioning or encountering a uniformly conventional private network and obtaining access to conventional opportunities in such an environment is low.[53]

DISCUSSION

Focusing on both positive and negative dimensions of normative regulation within informal groups and networks has several implications for our understanding of how neighborhood organization and culture impact youth development. First, behaviors that are disapproved acquire this status, not only because they annoy the people on whom they are foisted, but also because they are viewed by the group as threats to a successful course of development. Sexual intercourse at an early age, substance use and abuse, bad attitudes, dropping out of school, thievery, violent behavior, and involvement in delinquent gangs are all generally disapproved, at least in part, because they have the potential for blocking or delaying the acquisition of conventional forms of personal competence, experience in conventional social roles necessary for future jobs, and the completion of specific developmental transitions that are important for adult functioning, like high school graduation.

Whether involvement in these problematic behaviors actually impedes or undermines a positive conventional developmental outcome is an important question. There is reason to believe that experimentation with these behaviors may *not* always interfere with a successful course of development.[54] Some fighting, use of alcohol and sexual experimentation are normative during adolescence. However, any sustained involvement in these behaviors, particularly the more serious forms, carries a high probability of disrupting a conventional course of development. Becoming a teenage mother or dropping out of school involves a disruption in the normal developmental process and a higher chance that the developmental tasks of adolescence will not be completed successfully. However, even these premature, side-tracking life course transitions may not be irreversible.[55] From this perspective, the central focus is on how the informal networks in a neighborhood *promote positive development*; the extent to which they also constrain negative behaviors is important, but primarily insofar as these restrictions affect the completion of a successful developmental course over time.

There is a very strong tendency for youth to mature out of these negative, problem behaviors as they approach their adult years. For those youth who make a successful transition into adult roles, involvement in these forms of behavior typically ends.[56] However, when youth fail to develop the personal competencies, social skills, moral reasoning, and commitment to conventional values that are essential for a successful transition into adulthood, or lack the opportunity for full-time jobs, independent living, self support, and stable intimate relationships, these types of negative behavior are much more likely to become permanent lifestyle behaviors.[57] The official justice system response to those continuing their substance abuse and criminal behavior into their adult years is much more serious and is likely to result in a prison sentence. Positive youth development that prepares one for the transition to conventional adult roles is thus linked directly to the continuity or discontinuity in problem behaviors initiated in adolescence. If involvement in problem behavior has not disrupted the completion of the normal developmental tasks of adolescence, these behaviors will likely terminate with a normal maturation process and the transition into adulthood; if these developmental tasks have not been completed, youth are not prepared for the transition into adulthood and problem behaviors will continue into the adult years and will become elements in a more permanent lifestyle.[58]

There is also the possibility of a serious imbalance in the types of normative regulation operating in informal networks, either within a single network or across the overlapping private, parochial and public networks. For example, it is possible that the informal group norms discourage delinquency and substance use but do not promote high school graduation or the development of those personal skills necessary for getting and holding a conventional job.[59] It's one thing to have group consensus about the negative effects of drugs and crime on children's future well-being, and another to have consensus on what skills, attitudes, experiences, opportunities, and social roles should be promoted, and to have highly visible neighborhood role models for these outcomes. It is also possible to promote positive developmental outcomes as abstract goals, but provide little or no guidance or support for the practical steps that must be taken to achieve them. This can occur when members of the informal networks have little knowledge or understanding about what is required to achieve certain goals and there are no role models available in the neighborhood. For example, it helps to understand that entry into college after high school requires that one take and pass particular courses and achieve a minimum GPA. Formal and informal networks that both discourage dysfunctional behavior and promote a positive course of development are most conducive to a successful adult life.

The emerging culture in a neighborhood is, at least in part, an adaptation to the neighborhood structure and organization. For example, when resources and opportunities in mainstream society are severely limited and informal networks are too weak to resist, an illicit economy is likely to emerge within the neighborhood. Under these conditions, adults in the private and parochial networks in the neighborhoods often come to accept or at least tolerate these activities as they are forced to depend upon them for economic support.[60]

As another example, Wilson, Massey, and Denton and others have argued that racial and ethnic segregation in neighborhoods leads to limited contacts with whites and mainstream society, and eventually to distinctive speech patterns and an alternative status system in the ghetto which is in opposition to the basic ideals and values of mainstream American society.[61] It is a culture that explains and legitimizes the social and economic conditions of ghetto blacks, viewing these behavior patterns and attitudes as the result of residential segregation rather than personal choices or failings. This culture of segregation attaches value and meaning to a way of life that the broader society views as deviant and dysfunctional.

Emergent neighborhood organization and culture effects are more amenable to change than concentration effects, and perhaps even physical environment effects. They do not depend primarily upon individual characteristics that residents bring with them to the neighborhood or the physical attractiveness of the neighborhood. Rather, they are the result of the evolving interaction patterns among residents that create informal social networks, neighborhood norms and other emerging forms of neighborhood organizational and cultural adaptations to community life. If the proportion of poor families was the same in two neighborhoods with similar levels of physical deterioration, but one had a very strong informal network that endorsed conventional norms, provided positive role models and support mechanisms that promoted a successful course of development, and the other lacked this type of informal network system, poor children and families should have better developmental outcomes in the former neighborhood than in the latter. This added effect could not be explained by the family's poverty level (an individual-level effect), the proportion of poor families in the neighborhood (a compositional effect) or its physical condition.

We do expect these three types of effects to overlap, that is, they will be related to each other or cluster in particular neighborhoods. But we believe each has a unique, independent effect on youth development within the neighborhood. In our test of this model, we will attempt to estimate these unique, separate effects as well as their combined effects.

SUMMARY

Our complete model of neighborhood effects is summarized in Figure 5.2. Each of the three types of neighborhood effects is identified together with the specific indicators or elements of each type that are causally linked to youth development processes and outcomes. In this model, the direct effects of neighborhood disadvantage and physical deterioration are primarily on the emerging organization and culture of the neighborhood, limiting the effectiveness of mainstream institutions, and undermining the formation of cohesive, effective social networks and the development of shared conventional values and expectations among residents. In this model, it is the neighborhood organization and culture that have the greatest and most direct influence on child and youth development.

The influences of the neighborhood in this model are far from being absolute or deterministic although we tend to describe them that way. Growing up in a bad neighborhood reduces the chances of a successful developmental outcome for reasons discussed above, but this effect is not expected to be uniform or deterministic. Outcomes are not the same for everyone in any type of neighborhood; but the odds of success, or the percentages of adolescents who experience a successful development, are expected to be higher for neighborhoods that are effectively organized and have high levels of normative and value consensus.

In addition, coming from a strong family, one that is effective in managing the resources and risks in the neighborhood and promoting a positive development should help one overcome neighborhood adversity. Getting into prosocial peer groups at school or in the neighborhood should buffer one from many of these negative neighborhood influences. But we also expect that family and peer influences are shaped by the larger neighborhood context in which families and peer groups live, so that these effects are, in part, indirect neighborhood effects. We will consider these multicontextual influences on development in later chapters.

First, we will test this general model about neighborhood effects on adolescent development. In the next chapter we will establish the relative significance and influence of each feature of the neighborhood context

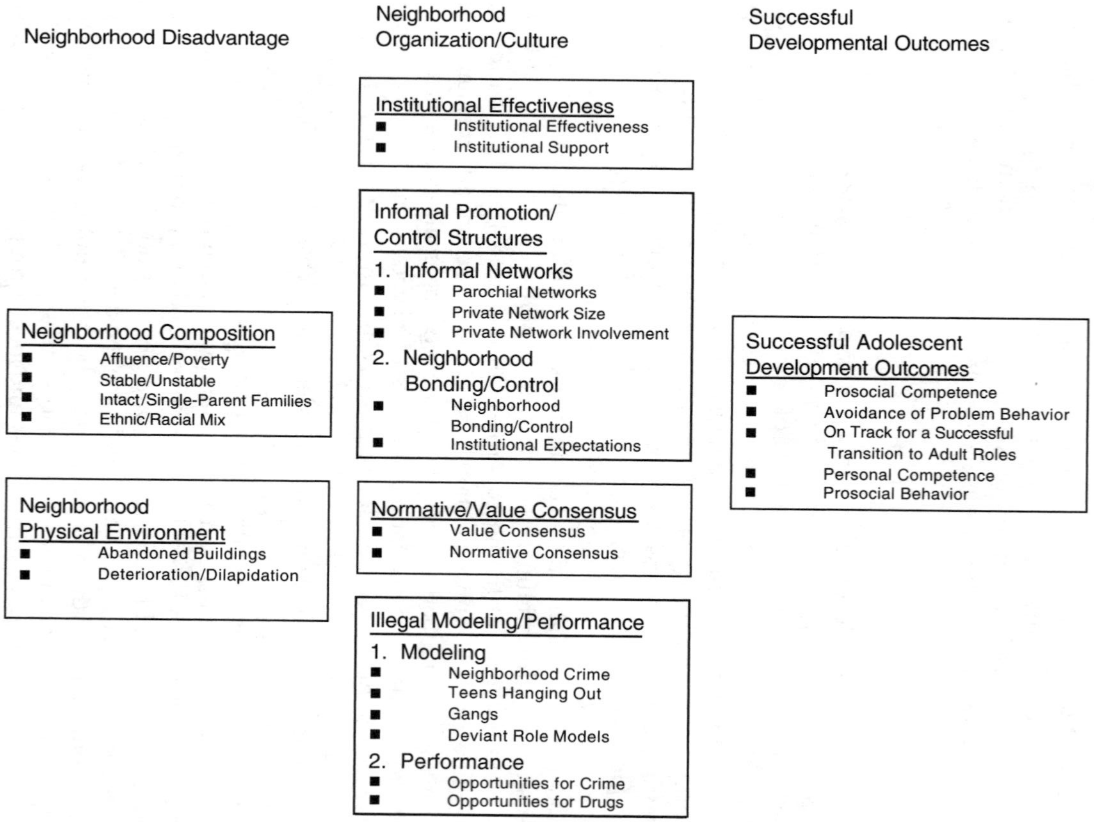

Neighborhood Disadvantage

Neighborhood
Organization/Culture

Successful
Developmental Outcomes

Institutional Effectiveness
- Institutional Effectiveness
- Institutional Support

**Informal Promotion/
Control Structures**
1. **Informal Networks**
   - Parochial Networks
   - Private Network Size
   - Private Network Involvement
2. **Neighborhood
   Bonding/Control**
   - Neighborhood
     Bonding/Control
   - Institutional Expectations

Normative/Value Consensus
- Value Consensus
- Normative Consensus

Illegal Modeling/Performance
1. **Modeling**
   - Neighborhood Crime
   - Teens Hanging Out
   - Gangs
   - Deviant Role Models
2. **Performance**
   - Opportunities for Crime
   - Opportunities for Drugs

Neighborhood Composition
- Affluence/Poverty
- Stable/Unstable
- Intact/Single-Parent Families
- Ethnic/Racial Mix

**Neighborhood
Physical Environment**
- Abandoned Buildings
- Deterioration/Dilapidation

**Successful Adolescent
Development Outcomes**
- Prosocial Competence
- Avoidance of Problem Behavior
- On Track for a Successful
  Transition to Adult Roles
- Personal Competence
- Prosocial Behavior

FIGURE 5.2. The Full Neighborhood Model

identified in the model. Some features of the neighborhood may be more critical to a successful adolescent development than others. Knowing this would help us develop neighborhood context interventions that will increase the rates of successful youth development. If our model is correct, interventions aimed at facilitating the development of effective organizations and supportive cultures in disadvantaged and deteriorated neighborhoods should improve the developmental outcomes for children. A concerted effort to establish effective informal networks and a conventional culture can turn potentially bad neighborhoods into relatively good ones for raising children. This may be a more viable neighborhood intervention strategy than attempting to change the neighborhood selection process or eradicate poverty and deterioration, as it is likely to be less politically charged and should have more dramatic and robust effects on developmental outcomes for youth.

Notes

1. Sampson, Raudenbush, and Earls (1997) report finding neighborhoods in Chicago that were largely African American and poor, that had relatively effective informal networks that were characterized by mutual trust and a willingness to intervene collectively to maintain order and supervise children in the neighborhood.
2. These contextual features are similar to those proposed by Sackney (1988) for educational contexts.
3. Wilson, 1997.
4. Wilson, 1997:5.
5. Connell and Halpern-Felsher, 1997.
6. The recruitment of highly qualified teachers is based both on the salary levels provided and the attractiveness of the school setting. Because most school districts have seniority systems, the most experienced teachers are typically drawn to the more attractive schools, which are in more affluent neighborhoods. See Connell and Halpern-Felsher, 1997; and Harris, 1998.
7. For a review of these studies, see Gephart, 1997; Brooks-Gunn et al., 1993; Clark, 1992; Crane, 1991; Ensminger et al., 1996; Garner and Raudenbush, 1991; and Duncan, 1994.
8. Chaiken, M. R., 1998. See also Carnegie Corporation, 1992, 1995; and Connell and Halpern-Felsher, 1997.
9. Chaiken, 1998.
10. Disadvantaged neighborhoods have higher rates of chronic conditions, self-reported health problems, and mental health problems. See Robert, 1998:18 and LeClere, Rogers, and Peters, 1997, 1998. Coulton and Pandey (1992) also report higher rates of low birth weight and infant death rates in high poverty neighborhoods (census tracts).
11. Wilson, 1997: 168.
12. Chaiken, 1998.
13. See Metropoliton Life Insurance Company, 1993; Kaufman et al., 2000.

14. Metropoliton Life Insurance Company, 1993:11.
15. Stephens, 1998; and Elliott et al., 1998ab.
16. Metropoliton Life Insurance Company, 1993:79; and Lorion, 1998.
17. For a review of this body of evidence, see Lorion, 1998.
18. Bursik and Grasmick, 1993; Skogan, 1990.
19. Wilson, 1987, 1997; Gephart, 1997; Brewster, Billy, and Grady, 1993.
20. Wilson, 1987, 1997.
21. Shaw and McKay, 1942; Bursik and Grasmick, 1993; and Sampson et al., 1997.
22. Kasarda and Janowitz, 1974; Hunter, 1997.
23. Hunter, 1985.
24. Coleman, 1990; Sampson, 1992; Hagan, 1993, 1998; Thornberry et al., 2003.
25. Sampson, 1986, 1987a; Sampson and Groves, 1989.
26. Park and Burgess, 1924.
27. Lewis and Salem, 1986; Sampson, 1986; Tittle, 1989; Kasarda and Janowitz, 1974.
28. Kasarda and Janowitz, 1974; Sampson and Morenoff, 1997; Sampson, Raudenbush, and Earls, 1997.
29. Jencks and Mayer, 1990; Brewster, Billy, and Grady, 1993.
30. Kroeber and Parsons, 1958; Gilmore, 1992:409; Swindler, 1986.
31. Shaw and McKay, 1942; Zorbaugh, 1976; Sampson and Morenoff, 1997.
32. Many criminologists take this purely structural position. See Bursik and Grasmick, 1993 and Sampson et al., 1997.
33. Shaw and McKay, 1942; Sutherland, 1939; Kobrin, 1951; Cloward and Ohlin, 1960; Whyte, 1955; Thrasher 1927; Anderson, 1991; MacLeod, 1995; Bursik and Grasmick, 1993; Burton, 1997; Korbin and Coulton 1996; Korbin, 2001.
34. This first position is taken by Bursik and Grasmick, 1993 and Whyte, 1955; the second is taken by Shaw and McKay, 1942 and Kobrin, 1951.
35. Sutherland, 1939; Shaw and McKay, 1969; Kobrin, 1951; Cloward and Ohlin, 1960.
36. Short, 1996; Klein, 1996; Anderson, 1994; Thornberry et al., 2003; Thornberry, 1998.
37. Elliott and Menard, 1996; Thornberry, 1998.
38. Shaw and McKay, 1969:173.
39. Anderson, 1976, 1991, 1994: MacLeod, 1995; Ogbu, 1985, 1994; Sullivan, 1989; Williams and Kornblum, 1985; Wilson, 1997; c.f., Snow and Anderson, 1993.
40. Suttles, 1968, 1972; Hirsch, 1993; Bursik and Grasmick, 1993.
41. Sullivan, 1989.
42. Shaw and McKay, 1969; Kobrin, 1951.
43. Wilson, 1987, 1997.
44. For example, see Hallman, 1984; Bellair, 1997; Gans, 1962; Suttles, 1968; Merry, 1981a; Maccoby et al., 1958; Bursik and Grasmick, 1993.
45. Stark (1987) refers to this as the deviance amplification process. Skogan (1990) further elaborates on this theme in his discussion of physical and social disorder in the neighborhood attracting those with deviant lifestyles.
46. Nathan Glazer as cited in Wilson and Kelling, (1982:29–38).
47. Klein, 1995; Cloward and Ohlin, 1960.

48. See Cloward and Ohlin (1960) for a discussion of the specific neighborhood conditions that give rise to different types of gangs.
49. Sutherland, 1939; Kobrin, 1951; Cloward, and Ohlin, 1960; Wacquant, 2002. Wacquant criticizes Anderson (1991) for his overly simple division of families into "decent" and "street" types, suggesting that boundaries between cultural systems and their behavioral manifestations are more fluid and situational. He notes that both of Anderson's types exist within the same families and the same individuals at different times and under different circumstances.
50. Sullivan, 1989; Johnston et al., 1998; Kozol, 1995; Williams and Kornblum, 1985; Whyte, 1955; Thrasher, 1927; Lukas, 1985; Suttles, 1968; Clay, 1998.
51. Cloward and Ohlin, 1960.
52. Wilson, 1997:58–59.
53. Spencer, 2001; Wacquant, 2002.
54. Newcomb and Bentler, 1988; Mihalic and Elliott, 1997; Thornberry et al., 2003.
55. Furstenberg, Brooks-Gunn, and Morgan, 1987; Elliott and Voss, 1974; Mihalic and Elliott, 1997.
56. Elliott, 1994; Sampson and Laub, 1993.
57. Sampson and Laub, 1991, 1997; Elliott, 1994.
58. Elliott, 1994.
59. Furstenberg, 1990.
60. Sutherland, 1939; Whyte, 1955; Thrasher, 1927; Cloward and Ohlin, 1960; Kobrin, 1951; Cohen, 1980; Elliott and Menard, 1996.
61. Wilson, 1987; Massey and Denton, 1993:176.

The Effects of Neighborhood Organization and Culture

SYNOPSIS

In the last chapter, we argued that socioeconomic disadvantage and physical deterioration influence youth development primarily through the patterns of social interaction among residents in the neighborhood. Over time, this interaction gives rise to a particular type of social organization and culture. A neighborhood with a strong institutional presence, informal networks of residents that promote a positive development and discourage dysfunctional behavior, consensus on neighborhood norms and values, and the ability to resist the introduction of drugs, crime and other negative influences in the neighborhood, is organized to promote a positive course of youth development. This type of organization/culture can protect youth from the potential negative effects of disadvantage and deterioration. Typically, however, disadvantaged neighborhoods have a weak and ineffective organization and unsupportive culture, as these demographic conditions tend to undermine and restrict social interaction between residents. The evidence for this set of relationships is presented in this chapter.

Measures of the organizational and cultural features of a neighborhood that provide a positive, supportive environment for youth development are described and include: Institutional Effectiveness, Informal Networks, Neighborhood Bonding and Control, Normative and Value Consensus, (limited) Illegal Modeling, and (limited) Illegal Performance Opportunities. A composite measure, General Organization, comprised of all six individual scales is also described. A neighborhood organizational typology is also developed using the six organization/culture measures, classifying neighborhoods as Organized, Regular, Weak, and Disorganized.

As expected, neighborhoods that are Disadvantaged and Deteriorated tend to be poorly organized and have unsupportive, sometimes nonconventional or deviant cultures. In Denver, both Disadvantage and Deterioration were associated with an ineffective neighborhood organization/culture, but in Chicago, it is Deterioration, not Poverty, that predicts a weak General Organization. In both cities, however, there were some Disadvantaged or Poor. Neighborhoods that had average or good levels of General Organization. Disadvantaged, Poor Neighborhoods *can* develop relatively good, supportive organizations and cultures, although this proved to be the exception rather than the rule.

Living in an Organized compared to a Disorganized Neighborhood does improve the rate of successful youth development. The size of this effect is greater in Denver than Chicago. Knowing both the type of organization/culture in a neighborhood and the levels of Disadvantage and Deterioration in the neighborhood, substantially improves our ability to predict neighborhood success rates using Disadvantage and Deterioration alone (by 10–27 percent). Unfortunately, using all of these neighborhood measures does not improve our prediction of *individual* successful development outcomes much (2 percent at most). The evidence does suggest that it is neighborhood organization/culture, not Disadvantage or Deterioration that account primarily for neighborhood influences on success outcomes for individuals. In sum, the full neighborhood model works well for explaining differences in rates of successful youth development across different neighborhoods, but it does not do too well in explaining which individual youth will be successful.

6

The Effects of Neighborhood Organization and Culture

Adult female – Allenspark: I try to stay outta here (neighborhood). Oh man, there's. . . . shootings, there's fights, there's cars being tore up, there's places being broken into, I mean – it's a joke around here. Some of the parents – some of the parents go right along with their kids, too, to rip off houses. Some of the parents around here are dealing. I mean, they're not any better than their kids on it.

Adult female – Westside: This neighborhood to me is like a place where I can come home every day from work and know that I'm safe and that my kids are OK. There are lots of friends around, just a real feeling of community. I always think of it (neighborhood) as being safe and nice. That's the main thing.

INTRODUCTION

Do good and bad neighborhoods typically have different kinds of social organization and culture? Are there differences in organization and culture *within* disadvantaged and deteriorated neighborhoods? If it can be shown that there are substantial differences in organization and culture by type of neighborhood, we can then determine if these differences account for (mediate) the effects of neighborhood disadvantage on successful youth developmental outcomes as hypothesized in the last chapter. Further, differences in neighborhood organization and culture *within* good and bad neighborhoods may account for some of the variability in developmental outcomes we found within these types of neighborhoods (Chapter 4). Identifying organizational features that protect youth from the effects of demographic disadvantage and physical deterioration would provide very useful information for community-level interventions to improve youth development outcomes in these high-risk neighborhoods. Finally, adding organizational and cultural effects to our general model of neighborhood effects may reveal stronger neighborhood influences than were observed for Disadvantage and Deterioration alone.

In general, we expect that an effective neighborhood organization and supportive culture will be associated with low levels of disadvantage and physical deterioration, for two reasons. First, individuals with greater economic resources are more likely to be attracted to neighborhoods with a desirable neighborhood organization and culture: low crime, high informal interaction, effective organizations and institutions, a sense of common values, and strong attachments to the community. Given a choice – and affluence and status does provide choice – people are more likely to choose well-organized neighborhoods than poorly organized neighborhoods.

Although it is true that neighborhood organization and culture are not directly observable, they can be inferred from the attractiveness of the physical environment and by talking to residents about what goes on in the neighborhood and how neighbors get along. In many cases, persons deciding to move into a neighborhood already have relatives or friends living there, and base their decision to move upon information obtained from them.

Second, even when economic resources are limited, residents in a neighborhood with good organizational features may be more effective in the way they use them. They may have better social resources and be better at motivating and mobilizing their neighbors to maintain the physical condition of the neighborhood, and may encourage them to stay rather than to move to another neighborhood. In terms of cause and effect, the pattern is probably circular, with organization both affecting and affected by the level of disadvantage and physical deterioration.

However, we believe that the principal direction of this effect is from deterioration and disadvantage to organization and culture, with physical deterioration and socioeconomic disadvantage placing real and perceived limits on the ability of neighborhood residents to develop a high quality neighborhood. Deterioration and disadvantage should not, however, fully determine neighborhood organization. There may be advantaged neighborhoods where the economic and social resources are present, but there is little interaction between neighbors and, as a result, a very weak neighborhood organization. Likewise, it should be possible for individuals in physically deteriorated and socioeconomically disadvantaged neighborhoods to work together to promote consensus, bonding, vigilance against illegal activity, and effective neighborhood organizations and institutions. In general, however, it will be more difficult to accomplish this when resources are limited, residential stability is low, and racial/ethnic diversity is high. When neighborhoods are successful in their efforts to promote neighborhood organization and a positive neighborhood culture, there should be long-term (not immediate) improvements in physical condition and, quite possibly, in the levels of concentrated socioeconomic disadvantage.[1]

MEASURES OF NEIGHBORHOOD ORGANIZATION

Our measures of neighborhood organization and culture represent those features of neighborhoods that were identified in our model of neighborhood effects presented in the last chapter: Institutional Effectiveness, Informal Promotion and Control Structures, Normative and Value Consensus, and Illegal Activities and Opportunities (see Figure 5.1).[2]

Institutional Effectiveness is a measure of the extent to which residents believe that if their children need help or are having problems – like getting pregnant, thinking about dropping out of school, looking for a job or wanting help to get into college – they can get this support from institutions serving their neighborhood. It also includes a measure of the perceived effectiveness of institutional representatives like teachers and police, and services such as healthcare and adequate transportation to and from their neighborhood.

As outlined in the last chapter, there are two measures of Informal Promotion and Control Structures. The first is called Informal Networks and the second Neighborhood Bonding and Control. Informal Networks reflects the presence of small, intimate social networks made up of friends and relatives (private networks), and less intimate networks of acquaintances that include, for example, children's teachers, employees of local businesses, staff at recreation centers, members of the local PTA, and clergy and members of churches or synagogues, where residents worship (parochial networks). It also reflects the levels of interaction and support provided by these private networks, for example, how often network members have been in each others' homes, have coffee or eat together, go out together for an evening, borrow tools, take care of each others' children, share intimate stories and problems, or borrow money. Finally, it includes information about other organizations and activities in the neighborhood.

Neighborhood Bonding and Control, includes resident expectations that neighborhood children will graduate from high school, will complete college or get a good paying job as an adult. It also includes a measure of residents' personal attachment to the neighborhood as indicated by their answers to questions such as "How satisfied are you with this neighborhood?" and "Would you move out of this neighborhood if you could?" Finally, it includes resident expectations that if someone were breaking into their house, selling drugs on the street, or fighting in front of their house, neighbors would intervene directly or call the police, and further, that neighbors would tell them if their children were getting into trouble. This measure captures both the normative promotion of successful development and the potential for social control in the neighborhood.

Normative and Value Consensus is comprised of two scales. The first assesses the level of consensus within the neighborhood about youth norms. Specific norms involved include those about sexual behavior, drinking, smoking and drug use, and getting pregnant. The second reflects the consensus among neighbors about values, such as the importance of getting a good education, having a good paying job, working hard, getting good grades, planning ahead, exercising good self control, and developing a good reputation in the community.

Our factor analysis of the interview questions about Illegal Activities and Opportunities revealed that there were two distinct types of influences involved. We called the composite measures of these two sets of indicators Illegal Modeling and Illegal Performance Opportunities. The distinction between Illegal Modeling and Illegal Performance Opportunities is similar to that described by Cloward and Ohlin (1960) in their discussion of illegitimate opportunity structures. They argued that illegitimate opportunity structures should be divided into two components, learning structures, in which people learn how to commit crimes and get away with it (probably unnecessary for some simpler types of crime), and performance structures, in which motivated offenders find opportunities to use their knowledge and exercise their choice to actually commit crime. Our two measures of the general Illegal Activities and Opportunities construct appear to reflect this important distinction. Illegal Modeling is a measure of exposure to criminal activity, gangs, and negative role models in the neighborhood, and Illegal Performance Opportunities reflects the opportunities to commit delinquent acts and use illicit drugs with little risk of apprehension. With this modification, there are six separate measures of neighborhood organization and culture.

We also developed a General Organization measure that is a composite of all of the six measures of neighborhood organization and culture identified above.[3] We frequently employ the General Organization measure in the analyses that follow because it provides a good overview of our findings, without having to review each of the separate measures of organization and culture. Whenever this is done, we have examined the relationships with each of the separate measures that contribute to this summary measure and have determined that the General Organization measure fairly represents these more specific findings.

Table 6.1 summarizes our composite measures of each of these constructs, showing the indicators used for each measure.[4] Each resulting composite measure was standardized with a mean of zero and a standard deviation of one.[5] They all have a common metric and interpretation *within* each city (Chicago and Denver, taken separately). A positive (+) score always refers to a higher than average level for that construct within each city, and a negative (−) score always indicates a lower than average score within each city. The larger the absolute value of the score, the greater

TABLE 6.1. *Neighborhood Organization/Culture Measures*

	Number of Items		Reliability (Cronbach's Alpha)	
	Chicago	Denver	Chicago	Denver
Institutional Effectiveness	2	2	.42	.38
1. Institutional Support	4	4	.80	.65
2. Institutional Effectiveness	3	3	.66	.66
Informal Promotion and Control				
A. Informal Networks	4	4	.68	.65
1. Institutional Presence	14	14	n/a	n/a
2. Private Network Size	4	4	n/a	n/a
3. Private Network Involvement	7	7	n/a	n/a
4. Parochial Networks	18	20	n/a	n/a
B. Neighborhood Bonding and Control	3	3	.77	.61
1. Institutional Expectations	3	3	.91	.88
2. Bonding to Neighborhood	4	4	.73	.69
3. Neighborhood Social Control	4	4	.92	.82
Normative and Value Consensus	2	2	.81	.72
1. Consensus on Youth Norms	1	1	n/a	n/a
2. Consensus on Conventional Values	1	1	n/a	n/a
Illegal Activities and Opportunities				
A. Illegal Modeling	3	4	.84	.83
1. Neighborhood Crime	5	5	.89	.83
2. Teens Hanging Out	1	1	n/a	n/a
3. Gangs in the Neighborhood	1	1	n/a	n/a
4. Negative Role Models*		5		n/a
B. Illegal Performance	2	2	.33	.47
1. Illegal Opportunities: Crime				
2. Illegal Opportunities: Drugs				
General Organization	6	6	.69	.83
1. Institutional Effectiveness				
2. Informal Networks				
3. Bonding/Control				
4. Normative/Value Consensus				
5. Illegal Modeling				
6. Illegal Performance				

* Denver only.

the departure from the city average. For example, a high positive value on Institutional Effectiveness would reflect a much higher than average perceived effectiveness of institutions serving the neighborhood; a score close to zero would reflect an average level of effectiveness; and a large negative score would reflect a very low level of effectiveness.

TABLE 6.2. *Types of Neighborhoods by Organization and Culture*

Organization and Culture	Types of Neighborhoods			
	Organized	Regular	Weak	Disorganized
Institutional Effectiveness	High	Average	Low	Low
Informal Networks	High	Average	Low	Low
Neighborhood Bonding/Control	High	Low	Average	Low
Normative/Value Consensus	High	Average	Low	Low
Illegal Modeling	Low	Average	Low	High
Illegal Performance Opportunities	Low	High	Low	Average
Number:				
Denver	8	13	6	6
Chicago	9	0	0	31

CLASSIFYING NEIGHBORHOODS BY SOCIAL ORGANIZATION
AND CULTURE

Just as we divided neighborhoods into three groups based on their levels of Poverty and Disadvantage, we also classified groups of neighborhoods based on levels of neighborhood organization and type of culture.[6] Table 6.2 describes the organizational/cultural types of neighborhoods and the numbers of each type found in Denver and Chicago.[7] We will refer to these groups of neighborhoods for both Chicago and Denver as neighborhood organizational types. All four neighborhood organizational types were found in Denver, but only two were found in Chicago. This may be an artifact of the sampling design for Chicago, as discussed earlier, in which neighborhoods were deliberately sampled from two contrasting types of census tracts, "poor" or "low income" tracts and "middle class" or "moderate income" tracts.

Organized and Disorganized Neighborhoods are essentially reverse mirror images of one another. Both are found in Denver and Chicago. Organized Neighborhoods have consistently high scores on Institutional Effectiveness, Informal Networks, Neighborhood Bonding/Control and Normative/Value Consensus and low scores on Illegal Modeling and Illegal Performance Opportunity measures; Disorganized Neighborhoods have the exact opposite pattern of scores. Regular Neighborhoods have scores on these measures that are close to the mean for Denver, except that they have scores slightly below average on Neighborhood Bonding and Control and high scores on Illegal Performance Opportunities. It is interesting that perceived opportunities for involvement in illegal behavior are greater in Regular than in Weak or Disorganized Neighborhoods (Denver). The thing that differentiates Weak and Disorganized Neighborhoods is their scores on the illegal learning and opportunities measures. Weak Neighborhoods do not look like neighborhoods that have the capacity to promote good development outcomes, but they do not appear to encourage involvement in delinquency or drug use. Disorganized Neighborhoods, in contrast, not only provide little support for a successful course of development, but also encourage involvement in illegal, dysfunctional behavior. The fact that neighborhoods can be differentiated on these organizational dimensions was anticipated in our model of neighborhood effects.[8] We argued earlier that promoting success did not always require a high level of control for problem behavior. Some problem behavior is normative. As long as it does not become so serious or chronic that it interferes with a timely completion of developmental tasks, it may not undermine a positive course of development. If our ideas about these two features are correct, Weak and Disorganized Neighborhoods may have different rates of Problem Behavior, but there should be little difference in their rates of successful development; and although Regular and Disorganized Neighborhoods may have similar rates of Problem Behavior, the rates of success should be substantially higher in Regular Neighborhoods. This is indeed the case as shown below.

NEIGHBORHOOD ORGANIZATION, PHYSICAL DETERIORATION,
AND DISADVANTAGE

The first question we address is whether concentrated Disadvantage and physical Deterioration are linked to weak neighborhood organization and nonsupportive cultures as suggested by our model of neighborhood effects. The evidence suggests that they are. We approached this question three different ways. The results of these analyses are summarized below.

First, we looked at the relationships between our three classifications of neighborhoods based on physical environment (Deterioration), demographic composition (Disadvantage) and social Organization. If our model of neighborhood effects is correct, most of the neighborhoods classified as Advantaged and Well-Kept should also be classified as Organized; and most neighborhoods classified as Disadvantaged/Poor and Deteriorated should be classified as Disorganized. This three-way classification of neighborhoods is presented in Table 6.3. As predicted, there is a clear clustering of neighborhoods on these three sets of characteristics. The most common type of neighborhood in Denver is one that is Well-Kept, Advantaged, and Organized. In Chicago the most common pattern is a Deteriorated, Poor, and Disorganized Neighborhood and the next most common is a Well-Kept, Advantaged, Organized Neighborhood. The vast majority (82 percent) of Denver neighborhoods are either: (1) Well-Kept, Modest or Advantaged socioeconomically, and Regular or Organized, or (2) Deteriorated, Disadvantaged or Modest socioeconomically, and Weak or Disorganized. Likewise, the

TABLE 6.3. *Three-Way Classification of Neighborhood Types**

Physical Environment

DENVER	Well-Kept			Deteriorated		
	Socioeconomic Composition			Socioeconomic Composition		
Organization	Advan.	Modest	Disadv.	Advan.	Modest	Disadv.
Disorganized	0	0	0	0	2	4
Weak	0	1	0	0	4	1
Regular	3	5	1	0	3	1
Organized	7	1	0	0	0	0

CHICAGO	Well-Kept			Deteriorated		
	Socioeconomic Composition			Socioeconomic Composition		
Organization	Advan.	Moderate	Poor.	Advan.	Moderate	Poor.
Disorganized	1	5	3	0	6	16
Organized	7	1	1	0	0	0

* Cell entries: Number of neighborhoods in each classification.

majority (75 percent) of neighborhoods in Chicago are either: (1) Well-kept, Advantaged or Moderate, and Organized or (2) Deteriorated, Moderate or Poor, and Disorganized. In neither city are there any Deteriorated Neighborhoods that are Organized. Moreover, in Denver, there are no Well-Kept Neighborhoods that are Disorganized.

The tendency for these three features to co-occur in neighborhoods is not absolute. There are some important exceptions. Chicago has one neighborhood that is Well-Kept and Advantaged but Disorganized. There is also a Well-Kept, Poor Neighborhood that is Organized. A similar set of neighborhoods can be found in Denver: a Well-Kept, Disadvantaged with Regular Organization neighborhood and a Deteriorated, Disadvantaged with Regular Organization Neighborhood. *It is thus possible for a deteriorated or disadvantaged neighborhood to develop a good level of social organization, but it is relatively rare.* This analysis of the overlap in neighborhood classifications indicates that most Disadvantaged and Deteriorated neighborhoods are also Disorganized.

The second analysis treats neighborhood organization as a continuous variable, using the neighborhood organization measures rather than the organizational classification. This allows for greater variation in organizational outcomes across neighborhoods classified by physical environment or demographic composition. Figure 6.1 shows the average, minimum, and maximum General Organization score for neighborhoods classified on the basis of physical Deterioration and Disadvantage. This analysis suggests two general conclusions. First, as expected, neighborhood organization and culture are typically better in neighborhoods that are physically attractive and well-kept. In Denver, the average General Organization score for Well-Kept Neighborhoods is higher than the maximum for Deteriorated Neighborhoods, and the average for Deteriorated Neighborhoods is lower than the minimum for Well-Kept Neighborhoods. This indicates a relatively strong relationship between Disadvantage and Deterioration and the quality of neighborhood organization and culture. There are similar effects in Chicago, although the relationships are not quite as strong and there is a little more overlap in the range of General Organization scores.[9]

In Denver, nearly all of the Disadvantaged Neighborhoods have low levels of General Organization. Likewise, nearly all of the Advantaged Neighborhoods have good General Organization and Modest Neighborhoods have close to average levels of General Organization. The highest levels of General Organization are found only in Advantaged Neighborhoods and the lowest levels are found only in Disadvantaged Neighborhoods. For Chicago, the results are similar, but again the effects are not as strong. This appears to be the result of the greater overlap in ranges across neighborhood types in Chicago.[10]

Overall, this second analysis revealed the relationships we expected to find.[11] The differences between good and bad physical neighborhoods,

140   *Good Kids from Bad Neighborhoods*

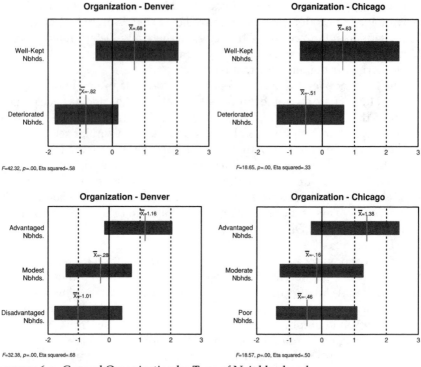

FIGURE 6.1. General Organization by Type of Neighborhood

and between socioeconomically Advantaged and Disadvantaged Neighborhoods, are especially pronounced for Institutional Effectiveness, Neighborhood Bonding and Control, and Illegal Modeling.[12] Differences are less pronounced for Informal Networks, Normative Consensus, and Illegal Performance. Physical conditions account for 58 percent of the variation in General Organization in Denver and 33 percent in Chicago. Disadvantage accounts for 68 percent of the organizational variance in Denver and 50 percent in Chicago.

The third analysis involves multiple regression.[13] This is a type of analysis where we use the full range of scores for Disadvantage/Poverty, Deterioration and indicators of organization for *each* neighborhood rather than lumping neighborhoods together in categories like Deteriorated or Advantaged and then comparing the average score for all neighborhoods in one category with the average for another category. This analysis tells us how well we can predict a neighborhood's organizational effectiveness based upon knowing the neighborhood's physical condition and demographic composition. Figure 6.1 above indicates that both physical Deterioration and socioeconomic Disadvantage are related to neighborhood organization

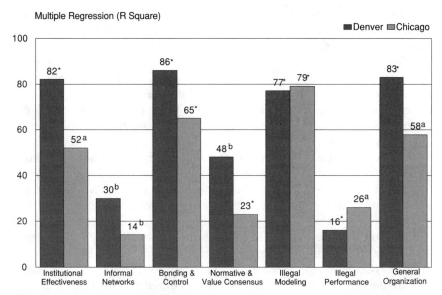

FIGURE 6.2. Neighborhood Disadvantage/Poverty and Deterioration Predicting Neighborhood Organization and Culture

when considered separately, but when we consider the two together, are both important as predictors of neighborhood organization? The results of this analysis are presented in Figure 6.2 (see Table A6.3 in Appendix A).

Our ability to predict measures of neighborhood organization from Disadvantage and Deterioration varies with the neighborhood organization components we are trying to predict. For both Denver and Chicago, the level of predictability is high for Institutional Effectiveness, Neighborhood Bonding and Control, Illegal Modeling, and General Organization. It is lower but still substantial for the other indicators. In Denver, Disadvantage makes a significant contribution to all of the indicators of neighborhood organization and culture. Deterioration contributes to all but Informal Networks and Normative/Value Consensus. Living in a run down or Well-Kept Denver Neighborhood is not related to how effective Informal Networks are or the level of consensus on norms and values in the neighborhood.

In Chicago, Deterioration is the more consistent predictor, making a significant contribution to all indicators except Informal Networks. Surprisingly, Poverty does not make a significant contribution to Institutional Effectiveness or Illegal Performance indicators, or to the measure of General Organization. It is also interesting to note that the effectiveness of Informal Networks at both sites is predicted by level of socioeconomic Disadvantage or Poverty, but not level of Deterioration. But the level of predictability for this indicator is low, particularly for Chicago.

We had expected Disadvantage or Poverty to be the stronger and more consistent predictor of organization at both sites. The finding that Deterioration was not a significant predictor of Informal Networks at either site when Disadvantage was taken into account was thus not unexpected. It indicates that the demographic composition of a neighborhood is a more important determinant of social interaction in the neighborhood than is the physical environment. However, the finding that Poverty is not a consistent predictor of different dimensions of neighborhood organization and culture in Chicago when Deterioration is taken into account was surprising. Deterioration, not Poverty, is the more consistent predictor in Chicago. There was one other unexpected finding. Physical Deterioration had a weak negative influence on Illegal Performance in Denver. This suggests that there may be more opportunities for committing crimes in Denver neighborhoods that are in *better* physical condition. This finding, although not altogether unreasonable, is not entirely consistent with our theoretical model.

The General Organization measure summarizes these findings pretty well: Disadvantage and Deterioration both contribute to the prediction of neighborhood organization in Denver and together account for 83 percent of the variation in General Organization; in Chicago, the only statistically significant predictor of General Organization is Deterioration, which accounts for 58 percent of the variation. In general, Disadvantage is the stronger predictor in Denver, whereas Deterioration is stronger in Chicago. These two features of the neighborhood do a better job of predicting neighborhood organization in Denver than in Chicago.

SUMMARY AND DISCUSSION

In general, neighborhoods that are Disadvantaged and Deteriorated are also poorly organized and have ineffective and sometimes nonconventional cultures. This finding is supported by both the survey data reported here and our analysis of the qualitative data from six specific neighborhoods. With the exception of the negative relationship between Deterioration and Illegal Performance (Denver) and between Informal Network Size and Poverty (Chicago), all of the observed relationships are consistent with the model of neighborhood effects presented in Chapter 5. The latter finding suggest, that poor neighborhoods may be more likely to have strong social networks when one racial group predominates, as is the case for the Chicago sample.

We were surprised that it was Deterioration, not Poverty, that accounted for differences in organization and culture in Chicago. Once Neighborhood

Deterioration was taken into account, Poor Neighborhoods were no more likely to have weak organizations and cultures than more Advantaged Neighborhoods. This may be the result of the sampling design in Chicago, because African Americans were the dominant racial group in nearly all of these neighborhoods. Cultural diversity was thus restricted in some respects for Chicago neighborhoods. In Denver, Disadvantage was the stronger predictor but both Disadvantage and Deterioration contributed to variation in measures of organization and culture. Together they accounted for most (83 percent) of this variation. In Chicago, this prediction was substantially weaker (58 percent).

Our analysis of the focus-group and in-depth personal interviews revealed three important insights to these survey findings. First, it appears that women play the central role in building informal networks and establishing normative and value consensus in the neighborhood. This may be the result of a greater physical presence or of a greater sociability (Bursik and Grasmick, 1993). It might also be the case that there are fewer working moms in more Advantaged than Disadvantaged Neighborhoods. If so, this could account, at least in part, for the observed differences in the strength of the informal networks in Disadvantaged and Advantaged Neighborhoods.

Adult respondents in the survey were predominantly women. This suggests that the survey results may overstate the general levels of network participation and cohesion in these neighborhoods. This would not negate the finding that there are substantial *differences* in the strength of these networks in Advantaged and Disadvantaged Neighborhoods, but the actual level of neighborhood interaction and cohesion for the average resident may be lower. It also is possible that these differences could be explained by a gender-by-type of neighborhood interaction, where males play a more important role in Disadvantaged and women in Advantaged Neighborhoods, but this seems very unlikely. The qualitative data suggest that women in *all* types of neighborhoods play a larger role in informal network activity.

Although the survey findings indicated that Disadvantage was typically associated with limited institutional resources in the neighborhood, the situation in Allenspark, one of our Disadvantaged Neighborhoods, did not fit this expectation. Each cluster of buildings in this housing project had their own playground, there was a gym with a hired recreational director, a swimming pool with a lifeguard, and a Center with a library, meeting rooms, and other facilities. Although classified as a Disadvantaged Neighborhood, Allenspark had more community resources than most neighborhoods. It clearly was not disadvantaged in this respect. However, when we consider youth development outcomes later in this chapter, it will become clear that these resources were not used or "effective" resources for teens living in Allenspark.

The third qualitative finding concerns the influence of racial diversity on neighborhood organizational and culture. We noted earlier that the inclusion of this feature of neighborhood composition as an indicator of Disadvantage was controversial, and that we would examine its relationship to other measures of context quality to validate its inclusion as an indicator of Disadvantage. Our neighborhood effects model predicts that racial/ethnic mix undermines informal neighborhood interaction, contributing to an ineffective neighborhood organization. Our analysis of survey data confirmed this expectation.[14]

Evidence from the focus groups and in-depth interviews found that ethnicity strongly influenced life in one of our two Disadvantaged Neighborhoods (Allenspark) where residents were primarily Asian (47 percent) and Hispanic (42 percent). There was great distrust and frequent conflict between these ethnic communities with many fights and gang confrontations that involved racial issues. However, there were also two mixed racial neighborhoods where the interaction between neighbors appeared unaffected by the ethnic diversity. This appeared to be the situation in both Northside and Parkview. In Northside, both white and Hispanic residents spoke positively about the importance of living in a mixed ethnic neighborhood, had relatively effective informal networks and high levels of normative and value consensus. In Parkview, there were few references to any racial tension in the neighborhood, although there were comments about racial conflicts and tensions *at school*. Several residents also noted that two of three gangs operating in the neighborhood had recently been "pushed out," indicating some effective social control in this neighborhood. There was still a fairly high level of exposure to violence, gangs, and conflict here, but there did not appear to be any racial or ethnic overtones to these activities or groups.

There are several extenuating circumstances in Northside and Parkview that might account for this situation, which appears atypical of the entire sample of neighborhoods. First, both neighborhoods were better off economically than Allenspark and the other neighborhoods in the study where there were high levels of racial/ethnic mix and weak organizations and cultures. Both were classified as moderately Disadvantaged Neighborhoods. Second, in Northside, the Hispanics identified with a larger surrounding community made up of multiple neighborhoods in which Hispanics were the dominant cultural group. This may account for the higher level of normative and value consensus in this neighborhood than in Allenspark. Finally, it may be that the disruptive effect of ethnic diversity on informal networks is largely limited to more seriously disadvantaged neighborhoods with serious gang, violence, and drug problems. In any case, it is clear that high levels of ethnic diversity are not always linked to weak informal networks, although that is the general tendency.

NEIGHBORHOOD ORGANIZATION AND YOUTH
DEVELOPMENT OUTCOMES

Having demonstrated that a neighborhood's physical condition and socioeconomic disadvantage are related to the quality of neighborhood organization and culture, we now consider how these organizational and cultural characteristics are related to neighborhood-level youth development outcomes. We will also estimate the combined effects of physical, compositional and organizational/cultural characteristics on success outcomes. If our full model of neighborhood effects as presented in Chapter 5 is correct, organizational and cultural effects mediate the influences of socioeconomic disadvantage and physical conditions on youth development and we should see a significant improvement in our ability to predict successful outcomes over that found in Chapter 4 where we considered only the effects of disadvantage and deterioration. We begin with an analysis using the general classification of neighborhoods, a classification that combines both organizational and cultural features of the neighborhood. Figure 6.3 illustrates differences in youth development outcomes for neighborhoods grouped by organization types.

Living in an Organized compared to a Disorganized Neighborhood does have a significant impact on average developmental outcomes for youth in that neighborhood. While the effects are stronger for some outcomes than others, neighborhood organization has a significant influence on *each* of these success outcomes in each city. Organization effects are relatively strong on average levels of Personal Competence (Denver) and the pattern of differences by types of neighborhood is consistent with our thinking about neighborhood effects. A typical (average) adolescent from an Organized Neighborhood has the highest level of Personal Competence, followed in order by those living in Regular, Weak and Disorganized Neighborhoods. And there is almost no overlap in the range of competence outcomes between Organized and either Weak or Disorganized Neighborhoods. Regular Neighborhoods have a similar range, but a considerably lower level of Personal Competence, than Organized Neighborhoods. Weak and Disorganized Neighborhoods appear to be similar, with a slightly smaller range of variation in Disorganized Neighborhoods and levels of Personal Competence are much lower in both. Type of neighborhood organization accounts for about half (53 percent) of the variation in typical levels of Personal Competence.

For Prosocial Behavior (Denver), success rates again decrease for each neighborhood type as we move from Organized to Disorganized Neighborhoods. However, differences in the level of Prosocial Behavior for Regular, Weak, and Disorganized Neighborhoods are very small. The major difference is between these types of neighborhoods and Organized

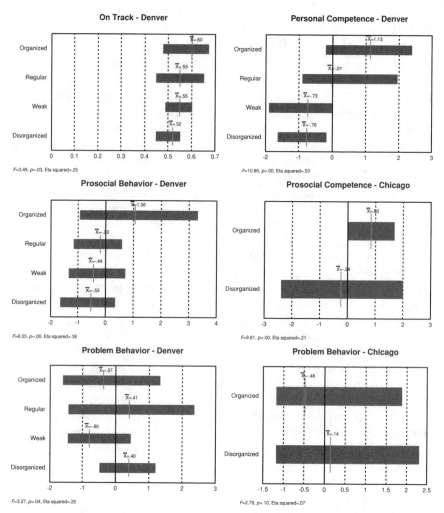

FIGURE 6.3. Neighborhood Adolescent Outcomes by Level of Organization

Neighborhoods where the level of Prosocial Behavior is substantially higher than that for any of the other organizational types. Neighborhood organization accounts for about a third (38 percent) of the variation in Prosocial Behavior across neighborhoods.

The strength of neighborhood organizational influence on the other success outcomes is smaller but the pattern of differences is the same – the most favorable outcomes are always found in Organized Neighborhoods and the least favorable in Disorganized Neighborhoods (there is one exception). Type of neighborhood organization accounts for 21 percent of the variation in Prosocial Competence (Chicago). For the On Track measure (Denver), youth in Regular and Weak Neighborhoods have the same probability (55 percent) of being On Track for successful adulthood, slightly higher than Disorganized (52 percent) and lower than Organized Neighborhoods (60 percent). Neighborhood organization type accounts for 25 percent of the variation in being On Track. For Problem Behavior outcomes in Chicago, type of neighborhood organization accounts for only seven percent of the variance between neighborhoods.

Problem Behavior in Denver suggests a more complex pattern. Adolescents in Organized Neighborhoods have lower rates of Problem Behavior than those in Regular Neighborhoods, and adolescents in Weak Neighborhoods have lower rates of Problem Behavior than those in Disorganized Neighborhoods. However, adolescents in Weak Neighborhoods have the lowest levels of Problem Behavior and those in Regular Neighborhoods have levels nearly identical to those in Disorganized Neighborhoods.

This is close to the pattern of differences in rates of Problem Behavior we expected, based on our discussion of the particular organizational characteristics of Weak and Regular Neighborhoods and our theoretical expectation that the conditions that lead to high rates of Problem Behavior do not always impede a successful course of development. We predicted that rates of Problem Behavior would be similar for Disorganized and Regular Neighborhoods and that they would be lower in Weak than Disorganized Neighborhoods. But we did not expect that the rates would be lower or similar in Weak as compared to Organized Neighborhoods. We also predicted that there would be relatively small differences in success outcomes between Weak and Disorganized Neighborhoods and this is the pattern we found for Personal Competence. The pattern is less clear for Prosocial Behavior and On Track.

Taken together, these results provide good support for the proposed model of neighborhood effects: Average youth development outcomes are clearly related to type of neighborhood organization.[15] Youth living in neighborhoods characterized as Organized clearly have the best rates of Personal Competence, Prosocial Behavior, Prosocial Competence, being On Track for successful adulthood, and lower rates of Problem Behavior (Chicago only). Disorganized Neighborhoods also have the lowest levels of success. The pattern of differences in Problem Behavior across neighborhoods was more complex in Denver, and only partly supported our model of neighborhood effects.

Neighborhoods with Weak Organization have a limited capacity for promoting success but appear to be trying hard to control involvement in Problem Behavior. These neighborhoods have few institutional connections or resources, few success role models, weak informal networks, and low levels of normative consensus. These neighborhoods also have low levels of Personal Competence (the lowest minimum levels of all the neighborhoods), low levels of Prosocial Behavior (only slightly better than

Disorganized Neighborhoods), but also the lowest levels of Problem Behavior. And their probabilities of being On Track are comparable to Regular Neighborhoods (same average level, but smaller range).

An important point illustrated here is that not all Disadvantaged Neighborhoods are alike. They have different levels of social organization and types of cultures and these differences contribute to important differences in youth development outcomes.

TESTING THE FULL NEIGHBORHOOD MODEL: EFFECTS ON
SUCCESSFUL DEVELOPMENT

In Chapter 4, we found that neighborhood physical Deterioration and socioeconomic Disadvantage explained 6–58 percent of the variance in neighborhood-level youth development outcomes. In the analysis presented above, measures of neighborhood organization accounted for a very similar level of explained variance (7–53 percent).[16] The question is, are Deterioration and Disadvantage accounting for the same variation as indicators of organization and culture? Or are these different features of the neighborhood accounting for different parts of the variation in success outcomes across neighborhoods? Here, we examine the full neighborhood model, that is, the combined impact of physical Deterioration, Disadvantage, and neighborhood General Organization on success outcomes and how much of this effect can be attributed to each type of neighborhood influence. We begin with an analysis of these effects at the neighborhood level, that is, on the neighborhood *rates* of successful development or on the effects for a typical (*average*) youth living in the neighborhood.

Neighborhood-Level Effects on Rates of Successful Development

Table 6.4 shows the percent of explained variance for (a) Disadvantage and Deterioration, (b) Disadvantage, Deterioration, and General Organization, all taken together, and (c) the resulting increase in explained variance attributable to General Organization.[17] In this analysis, the increase in explained variance is a very conservative, minimum estimate of the effect of General Organization. Even where there is little change, it may be the case that General Organization is responsible for *most* of the explained variance in the combined model. We do expect measures of organization and culture to be the strongest predictors, but at this stage of the model-building process, we will not attempt to measure the unique effects of each of the different predictors because we expect these effects to change as we add family, school and peer group influences to the model in subsequent chapters. We will establish the unique influences of each predictor in the model when the model is complete. At this point, we can note that later analyses will show that neighborhood organization and culture do in fact account

TABLE 6.4. *Neighborhood Level Percent Explained Variance in Youth Development Outcomes: Deterioration, Disadvantage, and General Organization as Predictors*

Dependent Variable	Personal Competence (Denver)	Prosocial Behavior (Denver)	Prosocial Competence (Chicago)	Problem Behavior (Denver)	Problem Behavior (Chicago)	On Track (Denver)
Percent Explained Variance (R^2):						
Disadvantage and Deterioration	58	45	19	6	19	32
Disadvantage, Deterioration, and Organization	78	65	33	33	29	51
Increase Attributable to Organization	20	20	14	27	10	19

for most of the neighborhood effect on developmental outcomes and in this sense mediate the effects of composition and physical environment.[18] Precise estimates of these unique effects will be presented in a later chapter.

As Table 6.4 indicates, at the neighborhood level, the addition of General Organization increases the level of explained variance substantially for all youth development outcome variables, about 20 percent for Personal Competence, Prosocial Behavior, and On Track, and nearly 30 percent for Problem Behavior in Denver, and 14 percent for Prosocial Competence, and 10 percent for Problem Behavior in Chicago. For all of the success measures, but most especially for Problem Behavior in Denver, knowing the organizational characteristics of a neighborhood substantially improves our ability to predict rates of youth success. Although the overall level of predictability is lower in Chicago, the *proportional* increase in explained variance attributable to General Organization is larger. For Problem Behavior, the total explained variance in Denver and Chicago is similar (33 and 29 percent, respectively), but Neighborhood Organization appears more important in Denver than in Chicago.

Neighborhood Effects on Individual-Level Success

In the preceding section, we looked at differences *between* neighborhoods in *aggregated rates* or average levels of successful development for youth living in each neighborhood. Here, we shift focus once again to differences between *individuals* in successful youth development outcomes. Again, we use neighborhood physical environment (Deterioration), demographic composition (Disadvantage), and the summary measure of neighborhood organization as predictors.[19] Table 6.5 shows the percent of explained variance attributable: (1) to Disadvantage, Deterioration and General Organization separately, (2) to the set of individual attributes (age, gender, race/ethnicity, socioeconomic status, and length of residence in the neighborhood), (3) to the interactions among these predictors (how one changes or modifies the effect of another), and (4) that shared among the predictors (not uniquely attributable to any one of them or their interaction). Both Denver and Chicago results are presented in Table 6.5.

As in Chapter 4, we are not as successful in predicting individual success outcomes as we are neighborhood rates or outcomes for typical youth (averages) living in different types of neighborhoods. For example, when all neighborhood and individual characteristics are considered, physical Deterioration, by itself, accounts for no more than one percent of the individual variation in Prosocial Behavior and Problem Behavior in Denver. It contributes nothing to the explanation of Personal Competence or being On Track in Denver. And it accounts for none of the variance on either outcome in Chicago. Disadvantage appears to have no significant influence on individual outcomes. Its apparent unique effect is zero for all of the youth development outcome variables in both cities.

TABLE 6.5. *Individual Level Percent Explained Variance in Youth Development Outcomes: Deterioration, Disadvantage, and General Organization as Predictors*

	Personal Competence (Denver)	Prosocial Behavior (Denver)	Prosocial Competence (Chicago)	Problem Behavior (Denver)	Problem Behavior (Chicago)	On Track (Denver)
Unique Deterioration	0	1	0	1	0	0
Unique Disadvantage	0	0	0	0	0	0
Unique Organization	1	0	1	0	0	0
Unique Individual	2	18	11	13	8	4
Unique Interaction	2	2	1	1	2	2
Shared Effects	10	5	8	0	2	3
Total Explained Variance[a]	15	26	21	14	13	9

[a] Totals may differ from sum of column values due to rounding.

151

In the full model, General Organization fares little better, uniquely explaining no more than one percent of the variance (Personal Competence in Denver and Prosocial Competence in Chicago). Overall, the *unique* effect of the neighborhood context on individual youth development outcome variables is very small, accounting for no more than a total of 1 percent of the variance for any of these success measures. The unique interaction effects are also small, only 1 or 2 percent for any of the outcome variables. Again, it is worth remembering that the unique contribution to explained variance is a very conservative estimate of the impact of a variable, and is likely to understate its true impact.

The largest contribution to explained variance comes, as it did in Chapter 4 (with only physical Deterioration and socioeconomic Disadvantage in the model), from the sociodemographic characteristics of individuals and from shared effects of all the variables in the model. Except for Personal Competence in Denver, the largest contribution to explained variance comes from the individual sociodemographic characteristics: 18 percent for Prosocial Behavior (Denver), 11 percent for Prosocial Competence (Chicago), 13 percent (Denver) and 8 percent (Chicago) for Problem Behavior, and 4 percent for On Track, but only 2 percent for Personal Competence.

Shared effects contribute nothing to Problem Behavior for Denver, and only 2 percent to Problem Behavior for Chicago and 3 percent for On Track in Denver. However, the contributions to Personal Competence (10 percent in Denver), Prosocial Behavior (5 percent in Denver), and Prosocial Competence (8 percent in Chicago) are more substantial. The full neighborhood model (Table 6.5) provides only a small improvement over the model incorporating only Disadvantage and Deterioration: an absolute increase of 2 percent in explained variance for Prosocial Competence (Chicago), 1 percent for Personal Competence (Denver) and Problem Behavior (Denver and Chicago), and no increase for Prosocial Behavior[20] or On Track (both in Denver). Overall, at this stage in the process of building a model that can explain why some youth have a successful course of development while others do not, individual level youth development outcomes are best explained by individual level characteristics and by the shared effects of individual and neighborhood-level variables.

SUMMARY AND DISCUSSION

Does the full neighborhood model that includes organization and culture do a better job of accounting for differences in youth development outcomes? At the neighborhood level, the answer is clearly "yes." At the individual level, the answer is "not much."

Average successful development outcomes are higher in Organized than Disorganized Neighborhoods and this effect holds for both "good" and "bad" neighborhoods as defined by levels of Disadvantage and

Deterioration. This means there were Disadvantaged and Deteriorated Neighborhoods where residents reported a supportive culture and organization and relatively high rates of successful youth development. Residents of Poor, Disadvantaged, and Deteriorated Neighborhoods *can* create a reasonably well-organized neighborhood that promotes positive outcomes for children and youth, but such neighborhoods are relatively rare. It also indicates that living in an Advantaged Neighborhood, by itself, does not guarantee a good neighborhood organization or a successful course of youth development.

There was clear support for this finding from the qualitative study. Residents living in the two study neighborhoods with Modest levels of Disadvantage, both ethnically mixed neighborhoods, had very different perceptions about their neighborhood organization and culture and their children's chances for success. There appeared to be more effective Informal Networks and higher levels of Neighborhood Bonding/Control in Northside than Parkview. Northside parents reported high levels of Normative and Value Consensus, particularly with respect to their children's behavior and the value of education; high levels of participation in formal organizations (e.g., PTA and church); and they were heavily involved in their children's education. This neighborhood with Modest levels of disadvantage appeared to have a relatively good organization and culture.

Few Parkview parents seemed actively involved in their children's education or formal organizations. Adults and youth reported no gangs and little crime or drugs, in Northside. All three were present in Parkview. When asked about these influences, Northside adults saw them as problems their children sometimes encountered at school or the influence of outsiders. They believed they could control these activities. Parkview adults did not. Youth in Parkview were preoccupied with the gangs, tagging, crime, drugs, and violence in the neighborhood. Youth in Northside acknowledged having to manage some of these problems at school but not in the neighborhood.

With respect to average success outcomes as measured in the survey, youth in Northside reported average levels of Personal Competence, above average levels of Prosocial Behavior, and the lowest levels of Problem Behavior in our qualitative study neighborhoods (including the two high Disadvantaged Neighborhoods, Allenspark and Martin Park). In comparison, Parkview youth reported the lowest average levels of Personal Competence and Prosocial Behavior, and the highest levels of Problem Behavior. Youth living in Parkview reported lower average levels of success than youth living in Martin Park. These two neighborhoods illustrate how the emerging quality of organization and culture in a neighborhood can vary even when the levels of socioeconomic Disadvantage are quite similar.

There were also major differences in the social organization and cultures of Broadmore and Westside, our two Advantaged Neighborhoods. Broadmore had very active and efficacious informal networks; neighbors enjoyed frequent walks, coffee breaks, and dinners together; and attended frequent block parties and neighborhood organization meetings. Adults spent a lot of time coordinating their children's activities and this contributed to the building of informal relationships. Adults in Broadmore also had the highest levels of involvement in formal community organizations of the six neighborhoods studied: community sports teams, PTA, neighborhood watch, political organizations, churches, etc. There were high levels of normative and value consensus, particularly on the quality of education desired for their children and neighborhood safety. Youth took school seriously, focused on getting good grades and getting into the "best" colleges and universities. There was very little crime, violence or drug use in the neighborhood, apart from an occasional drinking party at a neighborhood home while parents were away. Drugs and violence were encountered primarily at school. The peer network was primarily a neighborhood network – these youth had less involvement in school organizations, work, or recreational organizations than those in Northside, and were much more likely to be found just "hanging out" in the neighborhood.

Westside was an older neighborhood in the sense that there was a large number of residents who were retired and had lived there for a long time. While residents were relatively affluent, the culture here was quite different from that in Broadmore. The informal networks were much less active and effective. There was a fair degree of normative consensus, but the dominant norm was "mind your own business" with a high value placed on individualism and privacy. Interaction between neighbors and between adults and youth was more restricted and involvement in formal organizations was minimal. There were relatively few teens living in this neighborhood and they typically described the neighborhood as safe but boring. There was little youth activity in the neighborhood, the action was at the school, and this was the one place in the neighborhood with the greatest exposure to drugs and violence and the potential for trouble. Youth networks were more typically school-based than neighborhood-based. Although, there was little exposure to dysfunctional lifestyles and problem behavior in the neighborhood, there were also weak adult ties to the school and community.

Survey results indicate that youth in Westside report average levels of Personal Competence, low levels of Prosocial Behavior, and relatively high levels of Problem Behavior. Youth living in Broadmore report the highest levels of Personal Competence and Prosocial Behavior and low levels of Problem Behavior. The affluence of Westside together with relatively low levels of exposure to drugs, crime, and violence in the neighborhood did not provide either a uniformly positive course of development or a protection from involvement in dysfunctional behavior for the children and youth living there.

Both the survey and qualitative findings indicate that neighborhood success rates do not depend heavily upon the financial resources available to residents living in a neighborhood. At the same time, relatively few Disadvantaged and Deteriorated neighborhoods actually develop an effective organization and culture. Poverty, residential instability, cultural diversity and large numbers of single parent families make it hard for neighbors to have sustained positive interactions, to develop shared goals and norms and to provide positive role models and experiences for their children. However, an intervention that focuses on encouraging informal interaction among neighbors, on developing informal networks, common goals and norms and on using their collective influence to ensure that institutions provide effective services to their children, should increase the rates of successful development in that neighborhood. This may be a more effective strategy than trying to change the composition of the neighborhood because we know that most of the effects of Disadvantage and Deterioration actually work through the type of organization and culture that emerges in the neighborhood. Changing the composition of the neighborhood does not guarantee that an effective organization and culture will emerge, although it will increase the chances that this will happen.

Our qualitative study also suggests that it is not enough just to have *consensus* on norms and goals. We found at least one neighborhood where there was an effective culture and informal network organized around drugs, and we found a consensus in Westside around privacy and individualism, neither of which facilitated a successful course of development. The content of culture matters.

There are two important differences in neighborhood-level effects between Denver and Chicago. First, our model of neighborhood effects works better in Denver than in Chicago; that is, Disadvantage, Deterioration and General Organization do a better job of accounting for differences in neighborhood success rates in Denver than Chicago. There are several possible explanations for this difference. First, it might be the result of using Poverty as the measure of composition in Chicago while Disadvantage was used in Denver. Second, it might be explained by the differences in the sample of neighborhoods in these two cities. Recall that Disadvantage is a better predictor of both neighborhood organization and youth success outcomes than is Poverty in Denver.[21] However, this is not the explanation for the better prediction of success rates in Denver. If we used Poverty as our measure of composition in Denver, we still get better predictability of success outcomes. Poverty is a much stronger predictor of Prosocial Competence in Denver than Chicago.[22] This represents a true city difference, not a measure difference.

The Denver sample is a representative sample of the entire city and county of Denver and includes the full range of racial/ethnic and socioeconomic neighborhoods, whereas the Chicago sample is limited to predominantly African American neighborhoods and has relatively lower representation of neighborhoods with average- or middle-income levels. It may be that living in predominantly black neighborhoods limits the range of outcomes and there is less variability in average levels of competence across neighborhoods in Chicago. However, when we looked into this possibility, our analysis indicated that this is not the case. It turns out that there are no city differences in the amount of variation between neighborhoods, no differences in the amount of neighborhood variation to explain.[23] It is also possible that these characteristics of the neighborhood just do not do as good a job of explaining different rates of success in predominantly African American neighborhoods as in predominantly Hispanic, white or mixed Hispanic/white neighborhoods. That seems unlikely. Unfortunately, we can not check out this possibility. We are left with the conclusion that this model of neighborhood effects does not work as well in Chicago as in Denver, but do not know why.

The addition of organization and culture to our original neighborhood model provides only a small increase (0–2 percent) in our ability to account for *individual* differences in success outcomes. This small increase in explanatory power was as much an increase in the shared effect as a unique added contribution of organization/culture. With these small effects, it is impossible to formally test our hypothesis that organization and culture mediate the effects of disadvantage and deterioration.

It seems clear that conditions that are unique to the neighborhood do not account for much of the variation in individual success outcomes. However, we will demonstrate later that neighborhood effects are greater than the unique effects estimated here because they contribute to both the interaction and shared effects shown in Table 6.5. But even if we sum all of these separate effects, which certainly over-estimates the contribution of neighborhood influences, they are still quite modest (5–13 percent). In fact, the Full Neighborhood Model, which includes individual-level characteristics as well as neighborhood-level characteristics, does not do a very good job in accounting for individual-level differences in success (9–26 percent).

As an explanatory model for individual differences in successful development, this model is incomplete. From the outset, we proposed to build a comprehensive model that included features of the family, school, and peer contexts as well as the neighborhood. We turn now to consider each of these contexts, adding them to our model. The final Multiple Contextual Model will do a much better job of explaining individual differences. But it is already clear that neighborhood effects on individual success outcomes are quite modest.

Notes

1. The potentials and pitfalls of using cross-sectional data to infer causal relationships are well known (e.g., Menard, 2002:5–22,50–57) and need not be discussed in detail here. Our empirical results consist of cross-sectional differences among neighborhoods, which may or may not be consistent with our theoretical framework of the (causal) impact of the neighborhood on youth development outcomes. To the extent that these cross-sectional differences are consistent with the predictions of the theory, we interpret them as evidence (but not proof) for the causal relationships suggested by the theory.

2. The construction of neighborhood organization and culture measures involved the same process described earlier for success measures: the construction of individual indicators, a principal components analysis, and a confirmatory factor analysis. Indicators were identified for each of the four components of neighborhood social organization identified in Chapter 5 (Figure 5.1): institutional resources and opportunities, informal promotion and control structures, normative and value consensus, and illegitimate opportunities. A total of 21 indicators were identified, using data from parent and youth interviews about the characteristics of the neighborhoods in which these parents and youth lived, aggregated to the neighborhood level. Four indicators were dropped because they appeared to be poor indicators of the concepts they were being used to measure (Public Networks, Positive Models, Mutual Respect, and Parent Attitudes toward Deviance). Furthermore, the principal components analysis indicated that the indicators for the informal promotion/control and illegitimate opportunities concepts represented two dimensions rather than a single dimension.

3. Examination of the relationship between Illegal Performance and the other organization/culture variables in Denver indicated that the relationships were nonlinear, first increasing, then leveling off or even decreasing slightly. For this reason, both in constructing the composite measure of neighborhood organization and in the aggregate analyses involving illegal behavior, we use squared Illegal Performance (illegal performance multiplied by itself) either instead of or in addition to Illegal Performance as originally scaled. General Organization is statistically significantly correlated with all organization and culture measures, including squared Illegal Performance ($r = .377$, $p = .031$). There was no evidence of nonlinearity in relationships involving Illegal Performance in Chicago. All of these relationships were in the expected direction and statistically significant, except for the relationship with Informal Networks. For Chicago, the original Illegal Performance measure is retained without transformation throughout the analysis.

4. This set of composites was based on the results from the final confirmatory factor analysis. Both the principal components and the confirmatory factor analysis were used only to verify and, for the first two composite variables, to make slight modifications to the list of which indicators should be used to construct each of the composite variables. To construct the composite variables, each indicator was standardized, and the indicators were then added together. Each indicator is therefore treated as equally important in the construction of

the composite variables. Scale reliabilities are not available ("n/a") for scales involving a single item or simple numerical counts. See Note 7 in Chapter 4 for a more detailed explanation.

5. Standardization involves subtracting the mean and dividing by the standard deviation. Standardized scores can be interpreted as how many standard deviations each case is above (for positive values) or below (for negative values) the average (the mean). An alternative procedure would have been to weight each indicator by its *factor score coefficient*, assuming that (1) different variables are more or less important in constructing each of the composite variables and (2) the factor score coefficients and the factor loadings from which they were derived, are reasonably precise and stable indicators of the relative importance of each indicator. The first assumption is reasonable, but we regard the second assumption as questionable, especially when we consider replication beyond the original Chicago and Denver samples. Factor scales can be difficult to replicate with any precision in independent samples. By simply adding standardized indicator scores, we produce composite variables that should be comparatively easy to replicate, and are potentially less likely to capitalize on chance variation than the weighted factor scores.

6. For this purpose, we used *cluster analysis* (Aldenderfer and Blashfield, 1984; Everitt, 1980), a statistical technique designed to identify groups of neighborhoods or other units of analysis based on their similarity on scores for a set of variables.

7. The four types of neighborhoods and their average values on the neighborhood organization and culture variables are summarized in Appendix A, Table A6.1. As indicated by the values of η^2 in Table A6.1, the neighborhood organization clusters do a fairly good job of differentiating between types of neighborhoods with regard to neighborhood organization for Denver. For Chicago, there is good differentiation on all of the neighborhood organization variables except for Informal Networks, but even for this variable, the relationships are in the expected direction.

8. This classification of neighborhoods was empirically derived from a cluster analysis, we did not force this distinction on the classification.

9. The physical condition of the neighborhood accounts for 58 percent of the variance in Denver ($\eta^2 = .58, p = .00$) and 33 percent of the variance in Chicago ($\eta^2 = .33, p = .00$).

10. There is one exception to the above generalizations in each city. When examining separate measures of organization and culture, there is no significant difference in Illegal Performance Opportunities between neighborhoods classified on either demographic composition or physical environment in Denver. Both Modest and Disadvantaged Neighborhoods tended to have higher levels of illegal opportunities than Advantaged Neighborhoods. In Chicago, there is no significant difference in Informal Networks by either neighborhood classification. If anything, Informal Networks tend to be larger in more Disadvantaged Neighborhoods (opposite to Denver) *and* in more socially organized neighborhoods (similar to Denver).

11. These findings were replicated in an analysis of the bivariate correlations for our continuous measures of organization and culture with Disadvantage and

Deterioration. See Table A6.2 in Appendix A for these results. The strength of these relationships is greater than observed with the classification data. In Denver, the correlations range from .36 to .90, excluding Illegal Performance ($r = .26$) which was not statistically significant. In Chicago they range from .35 to .87, excluding Informal Networks ($r = .03$, NS).

12. Based on either or both of η^2 and the absence of overlap in the range of organization scores.

13. See Agresti and Finlay, (1986); Berry and Feldman, (1985); and Ryan, (1997).

14. The correlation between racial mix and the general measure of organization was $-.59$. Racial mix was also correlated negatively to Institutional Effectiveness ($-.51$), Informal Networks $-.44$), Neighborhood Bonding/Control ($-.54$), Normative/Value Consensus ($-.47$), and positively to Illegal Models (.50), and Illegal Performance Opportunities (.27). Although our neighborhood model focused on the effect of cultural differences on the formation of informal networks, it appears that it is adversely related to all organizational features measured.

15. Each measure of organization and culture is significantly correlated with each measure of success in the expected direction. Two thirds of these r values are above .50.

16. The simple bivariate relationship (Pearson correlation) between the General Organizational composite and the developmental outcomes was substantially greater than the Eta Squared estimates presented in Figure 6.3. based upon the organizational typology. They range from a $-.30$ for Problem Behavior to .85 for Personal Competence. See Table A6.4 in Appendix A.

17. Here we refer to absolute increase (explained variance with General Organization minus explained variance without General Organization) to describe the absolute impact of General Organization on the dependent variable. An alternative would be to use the proportional increase in explained variance, which would be the absolute increase divided by the explained variance without General Organization. The preference for absolute increase is because proportional increases can appear to be quite large when the explained variance is small to begin with, and this can be misleading for practical applications. The absolute increase is a more useful measure when the desire is to indicate the practical utility of interventions aimed at changing a particular independent variable.

18. Because neighborhood organization variables are so highly correlated with one another, it is necessary at this stage of the model building process to employ a ridge regression analysis. Ridge regression is very much like multiple linear regression but it helps us to get better estimates of the effects of highly correlated predictors (see Ryan, 1997 and Hoerl and Kennard, 1970). The percent explained variance in Table 6.4 for the combined Deterioration–Disadvantage–Organization model is based on ridge regression analysis, and tends to be slightly smaller than the percent explained variance that we would get using multiple linear regression.

19. The measures of neighborhood organization and culture are so highly correlated that their use as separate variables in the analysis of individual outcomes using hierarchical linear modeling (HLM) proved problematic. In order to

perform the analysis, it was necessary to use the General Organization measure. The technical problem with using very highly correlated predictors in a
hierarchical linear model (HLM) is *collinearity* (Agresti and Finlay 1986; Berry
and Feldman 1985), which makes it impossible to clearly separate the influence
of one variable from the influences of the others. In the neighborhood level
analysis, it is possible to reduce the impact of collinearity by using a technique
called Ridge regression (Hoerl and Kennard, 1970; Ryan, 1997), but this option
is not presently available for the HLM models used to analyze the individual
level data.

20. In multiple linear regression using ordinary least squares estimation we obtain
    a closed form solution, and R^2 cannot decrease when we add a variable to the
    model. In hierarchical linear modeling (HLM) using maximum likelihood esti-
    mation, we use an iterative process to estimate the solution, and it is possible for
    the estimate of R^2 to decrease, but this probably does not reflect a true decrease
    in the explained variance; instead, it is most likely a combination of rounding
    error and error in estimation. This accounts for the apparent decrease in R^2 for
    Prosocial Behavior when we add General Organization to the model. Using
    a precision of five digits instead of two, the reduction in explained variance
    is a substantively insignificant $0.26673 - 0.26326 = 0.00347$ or three-tenths
    of one percent, which is not statistically significant ($\chi^2 = 0.10557$ with one
    degree of freedom, $p = .75$). The most reasonable conclusion from this is that
    General Organization simply does not add to the explained variance for Proso-
    cial Behavior.

21. Based upon a comparison of these two predictors in Denver. This may not be
    the case for Chicago. Given the sample in Chicago, it is not possible to test this
    claim there, but this is a viable hypothesis.

22. The correlation between Poverty and neighborhood rates of Prosocial Compe-
    tence is $-.633$ in Denver and $-.173$ in Chicago.

23. The between neighborhood variation on Prosocial Competence in Denver and
    Chicago is identical and small (0.41).

Family Influences
Managing Disadvantage and Promoting Success

SYNOPSIS

The family is added to our model of contextual effects and we estimate the power of this new, multilevel contextual model to account for neighborhood-level and individual-level rates of successful youth development. Parents are assumed to play the dominant role in socialization and development, particularly in early childhood. Some are very skilled and effective in directing the developmental progress of their children; others are not. Our concern in this chapter is to understand how the neighborhood influences the form and quality of parenting, how it shapes parenting practices and supplements or limits the type and quality of resources available to the family, and how it structures the experiences and events in the lives of both parents and children. Moreover, we test the widely held idea that a strong, effective family can buffer youth from the effects of neighborhood Disadvantage, physical deterioration and disorganization; and its corollary, that the combination of a bad neighborhood and a dysfunctional, ineffective family have particularly disastrous effects on youth development.

We focus on four characteristics of families: (1) family social and economic resources, (2) family dysfunction, (3) parenting practices, and (4) the normative and value climate in the family. Families living in Disadvantaged and/or Deteriorated Neighborhoods had fewer resources (Income and Support Networks) and poorer Parenting Practices than families living in more Advantaged and Well-Kept Neighborhoods, and these two features of the family context were the strongest predictors of successful youth development outcomes at the neighborhood level. However, the neighborhood-level analysis indicates it was not Disadvantage, but rather the emergent social organization and culture of the neighborhood that predicted differences in these family characteristics across neighborhoods. A positive family context is related to the presence and effectiveness of Informal Support Networks, high levels of Bonding and Control, Institutional Effectiveness, and an absence of Illegal Performance Opportunities in the neighborhood – on both the opportunities and risks present in the neighborhood. Parenting Practices were even *better* in high- than low-Poverty Neighborhoods, when these neighborhoods were well organized (Chicago).

While neighborhood Organization and Culture do a good job of explaining neighborhood-level variation in family characteristics, they do not account for much of the variation at the individual level, once individual characteristics (socioeconomic status, age, gender, race/ethnicity, family structure and length of residence) are taken into account. This suggests that observed differences in individual family characteristics by level of neighborhood Disadvantage is, at least in part, a selection effect; the result of the type of families that choose or are relegated to particular neighborhoods.

The combination of family and neighborhood contexts does a good job of explaining neighborhood rates of Personal Competence, Prosocial Behavior, and being On Track for a successful transition into adulthood (62–90 percent). Levels of explained variance for problem behavior are lower (44–54 percent). At the individual level, this combination of neighborhood and family factors also provides a better explanation of successful development than neighborhood factors alone (15–39 percent). However, it is clear that it is the family characteristics that account for most of the variance in individual success outcomes; neighborhood factors contribute little unique explanatory power. Family effects are also typically greater than effects of individual characteristics, but shared effects (neighborhood, individual, and family) are often quite large. Finally, we found few significant interaction effects. The commonly held idea that minority youth or youth from poor families are particularly vulnerable to the effects of neighborhood disadvantage is not supported.

7

Family Influences

Managing Disadvantage and Promoting Success

Martin Park Parent: It's not like, you know, it used to be when I was a kid, we used to be able to go anywhere. But now, I think parents are just more strict, watching what their kids are doing – I know I am. I mean, tell me where you are going? Where is that? I'll pick you up, you know.

Interviewer: And why is that?

Martin Park Parent: Because times have changed. There's lots of violence now. I mean, these kids, they'll just be walking up the street and somebody'll, you know, it's really spooky.

INTRODUCTION

In this chapter, we add the family context to our model of contextual effects on youth development, and consider how features of this more immediate socialization setting influence a successful course of youth development. As noted earlier, Shaw and McKay argued that the organization and culture of the neighborhood directly influenced family socialization processes and the structure and normative orientation of peer groups (gangs) in the neighborhood. Yet there have been relatively few studies of the relationship between neighborhood organization and culture and specific family socialization resources and parenting practices.[1] Because of the interest in gangs, there is a more extensive body of research on neighborhood disadvantage and peer group structure, norms, and behavior,[2] a context we will explore in the next chapter.

Parents are assumed to play the dominant role in socialization and development, particularly during early childhood. There are parents who are very skilled and effective in directing the developmental progress of their children and there are parents who are neither skilled nor effective in their parenting. Our concern here is to understand how the neighborhood impacts the form and quality of parenting, how it shapes parenting styles and influences the type and quality of resources available to the family, and how it structures the experiences and events in the lives of both parents and youth that will determine a particular youth's developmental trajectory. Because families are situated within neighborhoods, they may both influence and be influenced by the physical conditions, socioeconomic composition, and social organization and culture of their neighborhood. In this respect, families living in a particular neighborhood are expected to be similar to one another, both because of selection processes in finding a place to live and because of their shared neighborhood environment once in the neighborhood. They are also expected to be different from families in other neighborhoods, to the extent that the environment of their particular neighborhood is different from the environment in other neighborhoods. At the same time, within each neighborhood, families will differ in their structure (single or dual parent family, number of children), socioeconomic status, their beliefs, attitudes, and values, and in the patterns of interaction between parents and children. We thus expect that family characteristics, socialization practices, and parenting styles will have an effect on youth development outcomes that is partly a result of the type of neighborhood the family lives in and partly unique family-level and individual effects that are not dependent on the neighborhood. However, what goes on inside families is, at least in part, the result of outside neighborhood influences.

Of equal importance is the question of whether and how particular family structures and processes operate to protect youth from the risks and adversity encountered in disorganized neighborhoods and how they promote a successful course of development. Because the family is considered by most to play the dominant role in early youth development, it is widely believed that a strong, effective family can buffer children from the effects of neighborhood disadvantage and disorganization.[3] By the same token, a disorganized or dysfunctional family could exacerbate the risks and danger to youth living in disorganized neighborhoods. Youth experiencing both neighborhood and family disorganization should be at particularly high risk for a failure to complete a successful course of development.[4]

In this chapter, we examine several issues: (1) the extent to which neighborhood physical conditions, socioeconomic composition, organization and culture influence family resources for parenting, parenting competency and styles, and the family culture in which children are raised; (2) the extent to which these family characteristics and practices add to our ability to predict youth development outcomes, above and beyond our ability to predict those outcomes from neighborhood characteristics alone; and (3) whether family differences related to neighborhoods are true generative effects of the neighborhood or simply the result of individual differences and the process by which families select or end up in a particular neighborhood.

FAMILY INFLUENCES ON YOUTH DEVELOPMENT

Our view of how the family environment influences youth development focuses on four characteristics of families: (1) family resources (economic and social), (2) family dysfunction (disruption and problem behavior), (3) parenting practices, and (4) the normative/value climate of the family. In a general sense, these contextual characteristics parallel those we have identified as organizational and cultural features of the neighborhood context. Families, like neighborhoods, vary by the types and levels of resources they can commit to their child-rearing efforts. Families also differ in the type of normative and value climate they develop and maintain in the home, and by levels of dysfunctional behavior and lifestyles to which they expose their children – behaviors that can impede or compromise a healthy course of development. There is also a neighborhood parallel for parenting practices, involving the modeling, teaching, and monitoring of children that typically occurs in the informal networks of adults and children that emerge in the neighborhood. We thus described these informal neighborhood networks as promotion and control structures – as having a teaching, monitoring and reinforcing role in the socialization and development of children. However, we believe these neighborhood socializing experiences are less direct, less intimate, and largely mediated by the parenting practices employed in individual families. It is in the family that children encounter the most immediate, intimate, and direct forms of teaching, nurturing, modeling, supervising, and disciplining, particularly during the early years. Figure 7.1 presents our model of neighborhood and family effects. We will consider each of these characteristics and processes in turn.

Family Resources

Family resources refer to both the economic and social assets available to the family in their child rearing efforts.[5] There is an extensive body of research documenting the relationship between family income (poverty) and youth development outcomes such as school achievement,[6] dropout,[7] delinquency and substance abuse,[8] conduct disorder,[9] child abuse and neglect,[10] nonmarital childbearing,[11] physical and mental health,[12] and employment.[13] Duncan et al. (1998), identify several general conclusions about this body of research: (1) family income effects vary by the developmental outcome considered; (2) for achievement outcomes like grades, school completion and early work success, family income effects are consistently significant (statistically) but effect sizes are quite variable; and (3) the failure to take into account potential confounding variables (unmeasured

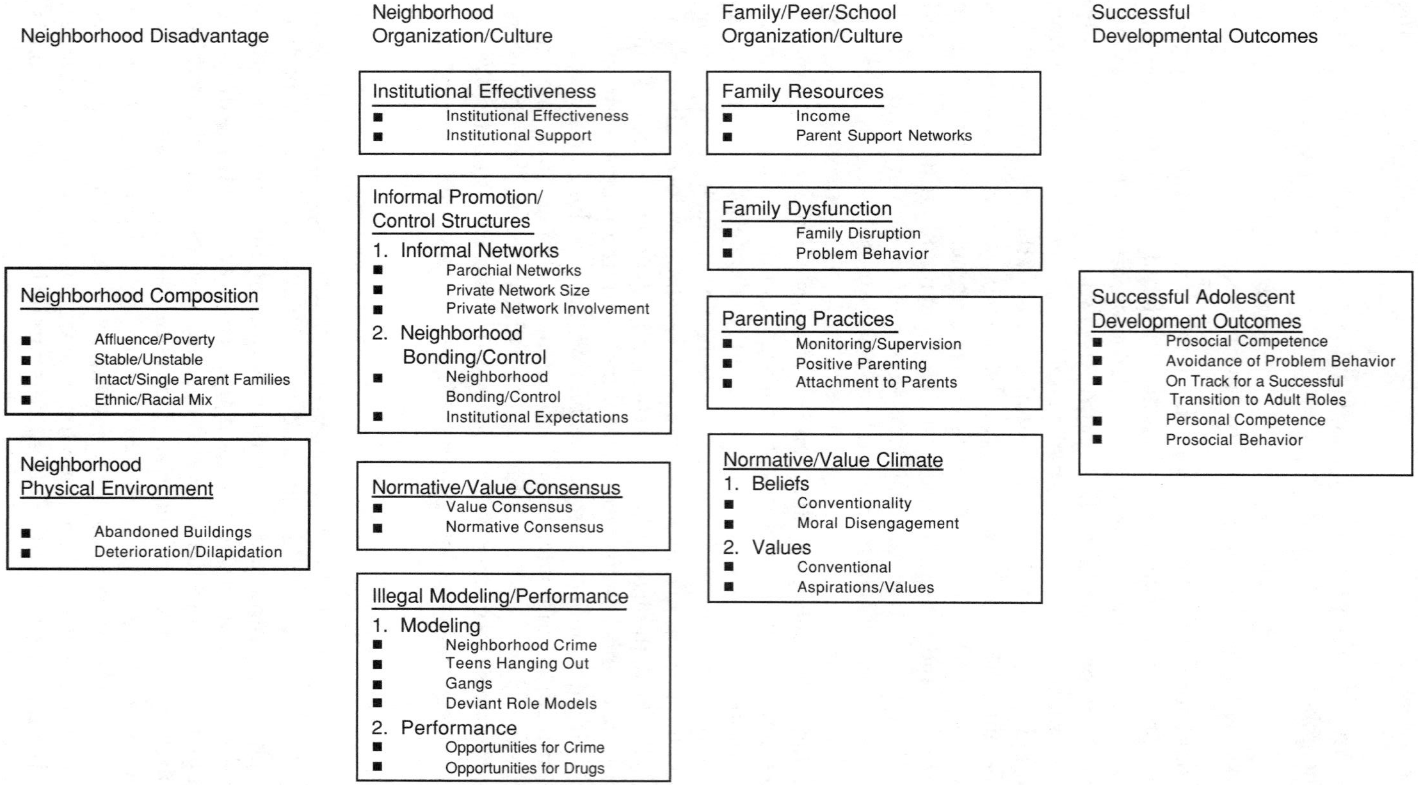

Neighborhood Disadvantage

Neighborhood Organization/Culture

Family/Peer/School Organization/Culture

Successful Developmental Outcomes

Neighborhood Composition
- Affluence/Poverty
- Stable/Unstable
- Intact/Single Parent Families
- Ethnic/Racial Mix

Neighborhood Physical Environment
- Abandoned Buildings
- Deterioration/Dilapidation

Institutional Effectiveness
- Institutional Effectiveness
- Institutional Support

Informal Promotion/ Control Structures
1. Informal Networks
   - Parochial Networks
   - Private Network Size
   - Private Network Involvement
2. Neighborhood Bonding/Control
   - Neighborhood Bonding/Control
   - Institutional Expectations

Normative/Value Consensus
- Value Consensus
- Normative Consensus

Illegal Modeling/Performance
1. Modeling
   - Neighborhood Crime
   - Teens Hanging Out
   - Gangs
   - Deviant Role Models
2. Performance
   - Opportunities for Crime
   - Opportunities for Drugs

Family Resources
- Income
- Parent Support Networks

Family Dysfunction
- Family Disruption
- Problem Behavior

Parenting Practices
- Monitoring/Supervision
- Positive Parenting
- Attachment to Parents

Normative/Value Climate
1. Beliefs
   - Conventionality
   - Moral Disengagement
2. Values
   - Conventional
   - Aspirations/Values

Successful Adolescent Development Outcomes
- Prosocial Competence
- Avoidance of Problem Behavior
- On Track for a Successful Transition to Adult Roles
- Personal Competence
- Prosocial Behavior

FIGURE 7.1. The Neighborhood and Family Model

parental and neighborhood effects, age of children) leaves the "mostly modest" effects of family income uncertain. Duncan et al., conclude that family income is predictive of children's competence and achievement, but not their behavior or health. The evidence also indicates that family income effects are stronger during early and middle childhood than during adolescence or early adulthood, and the failure to consider the timing of these effects accounts for some of the differences in findings noted by Duncan et al.[14] As children age, other contextual factors become more important (peers and school), and family income has less influence on achievement and behavior.

Several different processes or mechanisms have been suggested to account for the influence of family income on child development outcomes. Furstenberg et al. (1999) suggest that parents use their financial resources to move into neighborhoods that are safer, have better schools and recreation facilities, and more neighbors who share their values and expectations. In this sense, family income is used to select neighborhoods and neighbors who will function as cosocializers with the parents. It has also been suggested that income is related to the quality of the physical and learning environment established in the home.[15] Others have argued that a poverty-level income, as compared to a higher level of income, leads to high and sustained levels of psychological stress resulting from difficulties in providing the basic food, shelter, health, and educational needs of the family. An unrelenting high level of stress comes to impair a parent's sense of efficacy, their ability to effectively manage their children, and to provide a safe, healthy, nurturing environment for them.[16] Finally, it has been suggested that poverty leads to social isolation and few social (family and friends) resources to facilitate and support the parent's socialization and management of children, weakening their effectiveness.[17] In one sense, this represents a failure to find or develop a set of cosocializers in the neighborhood.

Family social resources include parental education and social status, which are typically included with income as indicators of the families' social class or socioeconomic status (SES) in the research on child and youth development. Many of the income studies cited already also document the influence of education or SES on the same developmental outcomes. There is some evidence that education may have an even stronger influence on child development than income, particularly on educational performance and the quality of the learning environment established in the home.[18] There is also evidence that parents' education is linked to positive child development through increased feelings of personal efficacy which can offset some of the stress of economic hardship and improve the quality of parenting.[19]

Social resources also include informal social relationships, friends, and family that support parent efforts to establish a good learning environment, teach positive skills and attitudes, and promote the internalization of family norms and values. They also include interpersonal institutional connections (e.g., school, church, work, and service agencies) developed by parents that serve to encourage and reinforce their children's participation and access to opportunities in these settings. Research has demonstrated that these social supports are linked to positive youth development outcomes by reducing the levels of stress associated with economic hardship (e.g., sharing of resources), encouraging better parenting practices, and providing cosocializing agents.[20] These social relationships, sometimes referred to as "social capital,"[21] together with financial capital, constitute the primary family-level (contextual) resources available to the family in their socialization efforts. These social resources may be more important than the financial resources for facilitating a positive course of development for children, but it is more difficult to design and implement programs to improve these social as compared to financial resources.[22]

Family Dysfunction

There are two conceptual components to this contextual feature of families, family disruption and parental involvement in problem behavior. The first involves experiences and conditions that occur within the family that may disrupt the normal socialization processes and quality of caregiving, such as parental depression, prolonged illness or unemployment, chronic arguments and fights, and separation or divorce. The second component includes parental involvement in various forms of problem behavior such as criminal activity, drunkenness, drug use, cheating, and lying.

Family conflict, separation, divorce, unemployment, and mental health problems (specifically maternal depression) have consistently been linked to poor developmental outcomes for children.[23] Marital conflict, when it occurs in front of the children is also predictive of negative developmental outcomes for children and adolescents.[24] For some specific outcomes, for example, educational achievement, the evidence is mixed[25] and relationships often become weaker or disappear when family resources are held constant.[26] There is also evidence that the effect of family disruptions and conflict on developmental outcomes decreases with children's age, and is strongest in early childhood.[27] Still, families experiencing these types of conditions are at elevated risk for poor developmental outcomes for their children. Parent involvement in criminal activity, illicit drug use, alcohol abuse, and other forms of problem behavior is one of the best predictors of children's involvement in these same behaviors as well as other dysfunctional developmental outcomes.[28] Together, they have the potential to seriously impede or undermine the family's ability to promote a healthy, positive course of development for their children.

For the most part, the effects of family disruption on child development are thought to be indirect, operating primarily through their influence on family functioning and the quality of parenting. Parents in disrupted families are experiencing greater levels of stress, are less resourceful, less efficacious, have more mental health problems, and are particularly vulnerable to the effects of economic adversity and neighborhood disadvantage.[29] These conditions limit the quality and effectiveness of their parenting which in turn has adverse effects on their children's development. The effects of parental involvement in problem behavior are considered more direct modeling effects.[30]

Good Parenting Practices

The traditional work on parenting practices focused on discipline and emotional support (Maccoby and Martin, 1983) and Baumrind's, (1966, 1991) typology based on these two dimensions of parenting. There is considerable support for the view that an authoritative parenting style, as compared to an authoritarian or permissive style, results in better developmental outcomes in childhood – better school performance, higher self-esteem, greater personal competence, and less antisocial behavior.[31] There are clear negative effects associated with a rejecting, neglecting style.[32] Unfortunately, most of this work involves preschool and elementary-school children from middle class neighborhoods. We would expect parenting practices to undergo some change during the adolescent years in response to children's increasing competence and independence and their participation in a wider range of social contexts, and there may well be racial and ethnic differences in parenting styles involving different cultural norms.

Recent work has focused on parenting strategies for adolescent children and for children from a broader range of socioeconomic and racial/ethnic backgrounds. Four primary dimensions of adolescent parenting emerged from this body of research: (1) the provision of consistent guidelines, expectations, rules and discipline; (2) support for autonomy; (3) warmth and a positive affective climate; and (4) parental involvement. Providing a clear set of rules and consequences for violating them, together with an effective monitoring and supervision of activities leads to strong internal controls and the development of self-regulating mechanisms.[33] While much of the earlier research focused on internal dynamics within the home, to dyadic relationships between parents and children,[34] our focus is equally on parent monitoring and supervision as a means of managing youth involvement in activities outside the home, in encouraging positive peer relationships, involvement in recreational activities, and healthy work experiences. Support for autonomy involves including youth in family decision making and problem solving, and encouraging their assuming new responsibilities and renegotiating the parent–child relationship, all of which contribute to a sense of autonomy and personal independence.[35] Warm and supportive parenting creates an affective bond between the parent and adolescent and has been linked to high self esteem, academic and social competence, individual autonomy, better mental health adjustments, and a commitment to conventional behavior.[36] Parent involvement, the final component of an effective parenting style, predicts school achievement, good self-control, and low levels of problem behavior.[37]

These four dimensions of parenting have both promoting and controlling/protective effects on youth development. Just as the informal networks in a neighborhood operate to promote certain developmental outcomes and constrain or discourage others, so parenting practices operate to promote or control potential outcomes.

Family Normative/Value Climate

Every group that has sustained interaction develops a set of rules, expectations and values that regulate their behavior. We included the normative value climate of the neighborhood as an important dimension of that social context and there is a parallel dimension in the family context. In large part, family norms and values are passed on from one generation to another. These norms and values define the "right" or approved way of doing things and deviations from these expectations are often punished. Parental values and normative expectations have a significant influence on the behavior of children and adolescents and are particularly important because these norms and values provide a form of regulation or control that extends into other contexts in which children participate. For example, when adolescent girls think their parents disapprove of their involvement in sexual activity, they are less likely to engage in this behavior or become pregnant.[38] This is also true for involvement with drugs and alcohol, and involvement in other forms of problem behavior.[39]

To the extent parent values and norms are consistent with those found in the school, peer networks, neighborhood, workplace, and larger community, and children get the same normative messages and are held to the same standards of behavior in these settings, these norms become legitimized and more powerful influences on their behavior. When there are inconsistencies or differences in normative messages across these contexts, parental values and norms are less effective in regulating children's behavior.[40] In this case, the consistency of normative standards of behavior in the family and the neighborhood, which we are examining in this chapter, may have particularly positive or adverse effects on developmental outcomes. In sum, when parents hold conventional values and norms, their children are more likely to develop prosocial values and avoid involvement in problem behavior.

MEASURES OF FAMILY CHARACTERISTICS

Some family characteristics have already been included in our measures of neighborhood disadvantage, organization and culture.[41] But these measures were all aggregated to the neighborhood level; they reflected, for example, the *percentage* of families in poverty, the *proportion* of families living in a different house in 1985, the *proportion* of families headed by a single parent, the *average size* of family (parent) informal networks, and the *average level* of perceived consensus on values, in each neighborhood. What was described in each case was a particular neighborhood characteristic.

In this chapter, family characteristics are all measured at the individual level. The measures all reflect family conditions experienced by each youth in the study. For measures obtained from parent interviews, like estimates of family income, each child in the family was given the same score on that measure; all children in the family were influenced by that level of family income. For measures obtained from youth interviews, like the level of parental monitoring experienced, each child received a unique score, reflecting his or her own perceived level of parental monitoring.

As outlined above, our measures of the family environment focus on four characteristics that roughly parallel those identified as neighborhood conditions and processes: family resources, parenting practices, normative and value climate, and family dysfunction. The parallels should not be overdrawn, however; family measures are measured at a different (individual) level, are based entirely on survey data, and in most instances rely on different survey questions than those used for neighborhood measures. The family measures are listed with their reliabilities in Table 7.1.[42]

A combination of factor analysis and additive scaling was used to construct the family measures. With the exception of family income (a single item), all family measures were constructed by adding standardized scale scores and then standardizing the result, as in previous chapters. We describe the family measures as developed for the Denver site first.

Family Resources consists of two scales, measured at the individual level using data from the parent interview. Family Income is a total household income measure that includes income from all sources, including work, child support, food stamps, AFDC, and Social Security payments. It represents the financial resources available to the family. Parental Network Size is the same variable used as a component of the informal networks measure at the neighborhood level, but is an individual-level measure here. It includes questions about how many of their friends and family members live in the neighborhood, how many adults in the neighborhood they talk to on a regular basis, and how many children or teenagers in the neighborhood they know by name. It is an indicator of the interpersonal, nonfinancial resources or social capital[43] available to the family. Parental Network Size and Family Income are used as separate but related indicators

TABLE 7.1. *Family Measures*

	Number of Items Or Scales		Reliability (Cronbach's Alpha)	
	Chicago	Denver	Chicago	Denver
Family Resources				
1. Family Income	1	1	n/a	n/a
2. Parental Network Size	4	4	n/a	n/a
Family Dysfunction	1	3	n/a	n/a
1. Parental Crime	–	16		n/a
2. Parental Alcohol & Drug Problems	2	3	n/a	n/a
a. Illicit Drug Use (Denver)	–	3		n/a
b. Alcohol Problems (Denver)	–	11		n/a
c. Drug Problems (Denver)	–	11		n/a
d. Alcohol Use (Chicago)	1	–	n/a	
e. Illicit Drug Use (Chicago)	1	–	n/a	
3. Family Disruption	–	2		n/a
a. Sought Help for Children	–	13		n/a
b. Sought Help for Self/Spouse	–	12		n/a
Parenting Practices	4	3	.73	.65
1. Parental Monitoring	1	7	n/a	.69
2. Positive Parenting (Denver)	–	6	n/a	.73
3. Attachment to Parents	1	7	n/a	.80
4. Curfew (Chicago)	2	–	.75	n/a
5. Involvement (Chicago)	4	–	.62	n/a
Normative/Value Climate				
1. Parental Moral Beliefs	14	14	.86	.79
2. Parental Conventional Values	13	13	.91	.85

of Family Resources. Although, within the same conceptual domain, factor analysis indicates that the two should not be combined into a single measure.

Family Dysfunction includes three subscales. These include: Parental Crime (prevalence of offending on 16 offenses), Parental Alcohol and Drug Problems (prevalence of illicit drug use, seeking help for alcohol problems, and seeking help for drug problems), and Family Disruption (prevalence of seeking help for oneself, one's spouse, or one's children, as a result of problems in family relationships).[44]

Measures of Parenting Practices include Parental Monitoring, (whether parents know where their children are and have rules about being at home by a certain time on weekday and weekend nights), Positive Parenting (how often parents express approval of good behavior), and Attachment to Parents (positive involvement and interactions between parents and children). Two separate measures of Normative and Value Climate in the family were developed. Parental Moral Beliefs is a 14-item scale indicating how wrong parents think it is for someone their child's age to commit different illegal or deviant acts. *Parental Conventional Values* is a 13-item scale indicating how important parents think it is in life to achieve several financial, educational, and personal goals. Family Dysfunction and Parenting Practices were each confirmed as a single dimension by factor analysis, then constructed by adding their standardized scale scores and standardizing (subtracting the mean and dividing by the standard deviation) the result.

While the family measures for Chicago and Denver are conceptually similar, the specific items and subscales used to construct them vary somewhat. This is partly because Chicago had fewer family-related items, and partly because of cross-site differences in relationships that affect the validity and reliability of scales. Family Income and Parental Network Size are similarly measured for Denver and Chicago. For the Family Dysfunction scale, the Chicago survey had several items related to alcohol and drug use that differed somewhat from the Denver items, but none that indicated whether help had been sought for alcohol, drug, or family problems. As a result, the Family Dysfunction measure for Chicago is limited to alcohol use (the number of times in the past month the respondent had two or more drinks) and illegal drug use (the number of times in the past year the respondent has used various illegal drugs). Most of the items used to construct the sub-scales for Chicago's Parenting Practices scale differ from Denver's, although the subscales are conceptually similar. The Parental Monitoring subscale, in particular, is similar to Denver's, but the remaining subscales for Chicago are Curfew (part of the monitoring subscale for Denver), Involvement (the sum of different types of parent–child activities respondents participated in during the previous four weeks), and Attachment, a single item asking whether the child was close to the parent at age 10. Finally, the Parental Moral Beliefs and Parental Conventional Values measures are replicated across the two sites.

In previous chapters, we classified neighborhoods into types based on Deterioration, Disadvantage, and General Organization (hereafter simply Organization). We do not make a parallel classification of families into a simple typology for two reasons. First, the neighborhood constitutes a separate level of analysis, where each neighborhood is represented by multiple cases (respondents and parents) at the individual level. Analytically, we do not treat families as separate units of analysis, and for any given family, we may have no more than two observations (a parent and her or his child), limiting the reliability of measures of differences between families. Second, we have measured many of our neighborhood characteristics directly, using census data or aggregate measures such as means or medians that are inapplicable at the individual level. In contrast, nearly all of our family scales are measured for *individuals* in the family, rather than for the family itself. For example, Family Income and Family Disruption (one component of Family Dysfunction) are measured for the family as a whole, but Parental Network Size, two of the three components of Family Dysfunction,

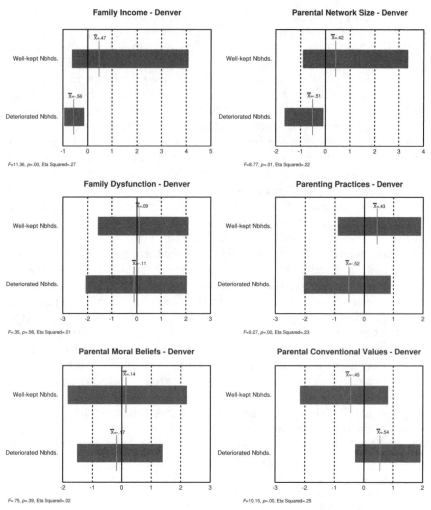

FIGURE 7.2. Neighborhood Family Characteristics by Level of Physical Deterioration

Parenting Practices, and Parental Moral Beliefs are all based on data from a single individual (parent or child) in the family.

With one exception for Denver, these measures of family characteristics and processes are all related to one another as expected – each is related negatively to Family Dysfunction and positively to other measures (see Table A7.1 in Appendix A for bivariate correlations). Not all of the inter-correlations are statistically significant, although the vast majority are. In Denver, those that are significant range from 0.06 to 0.16; they are typically larger in Chicago, ranging from 0.10 to 0.43. The one exception in Denver involved Parental Conventional Values, which was negatively related

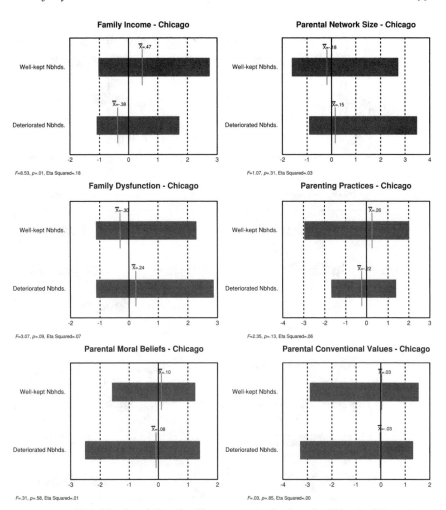

FIGURE 7.2. Neighborhood Family Characteristics by Level of Physical Deterioration (*continued*)

to Family Income, Parental Support Network, and Parenting Practices, although only the relationship with Family Income was statistically significant ($r = -.16$). It is not clear why those parents with greater financial resources should report lower levels of commitment to conventional values. We will pick up on this unexpected finding later when we consider how these family measures are related to types of neighborhoods and successful youth development outcomes. One thing is clear, however. These measures of Family Resources, Family Dysfunction, Normative Value Climate, and Parenting Practices are fairly independent of one another and appear to capture different features of the family context.

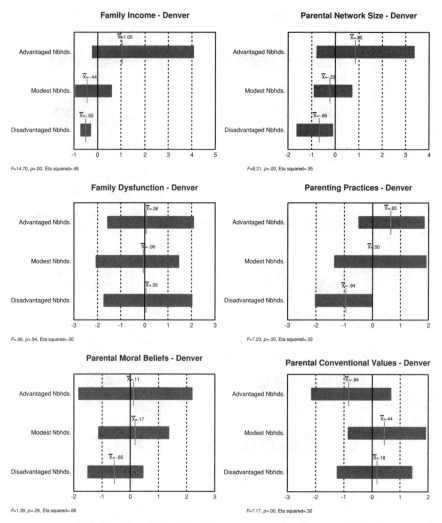

FIGURE 7.3. Neighborhood Family Characteristics by Level of Disadvantage/ Poverty

FAMILY CHARACTERISTICS BY TYPE OF NEIGHBORHOOD

Do families living in Disadvantaged, Deteriorated, and Disorganized Neighborhoods, on average, look different from those living in Advantaged, Well-Kept, Organized Neighborhoods? Do parents in these different types of neighborhoods use different parenting styles and resources? The answer to this question differs somewhat for Denver and Chicago (see Figures 7.2–7.4). In Denver, the answer is yes, they look different.

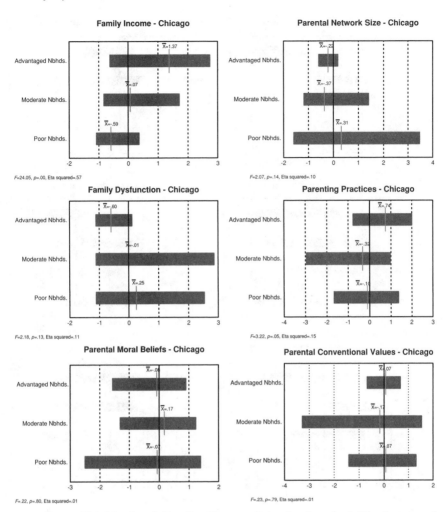

FIGURE 7.3. Neighborhood Family Characteristics by Level of Disadvantage/ Poverty (*continued*)

In Denver, average Family Income levels are substantially lower, informal support networks are smaller, and Parenting Practices are not as good in Disadvantaged, Deteriorated, and Disorganized Neighborhoods. Some of these differences are fairly dramatic. For example, average income levels and support networks are much larger and the upper ranges are much greater in better neighborhoods, but there are no statistically significant differences across types of neighborhoods on average levels of Family Dysfunction or Parental Moral Beliefs. Not surprisingly, rates of dysfunctional behavior are higher in neighborhoods with opportunities for involvement

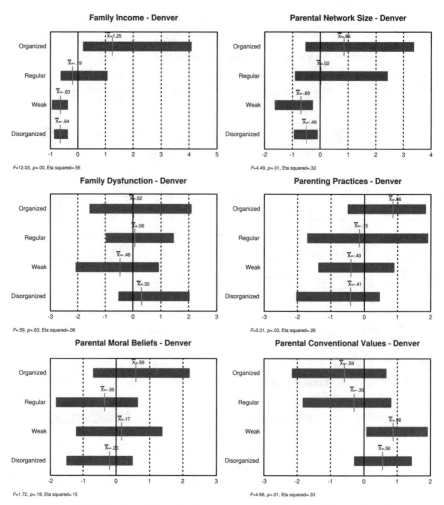

FIGURE 7.4. Neighborhood Family Characteristics by Level of Organization

in criminal and drug-related activities (Illegal Performance Opportunities subscale, Table A7.1 in Appendix A), but it is not significantly related to the overall measure of neighborhood organization.

Conventional Values are positively related to Deterioration and Disadvantage and negatively related to Organization. Families living in Deteriorated and Modest Neighborhoods had higher average endorsement levels of conventional values than those in Well-Kept, Advantaged Neighborhoods. Moreover, families with strong conventional values are more likely to be found in neighborhoods that have weak organizational characteristics: low levels of Institutional Effectiveness, weak Informal

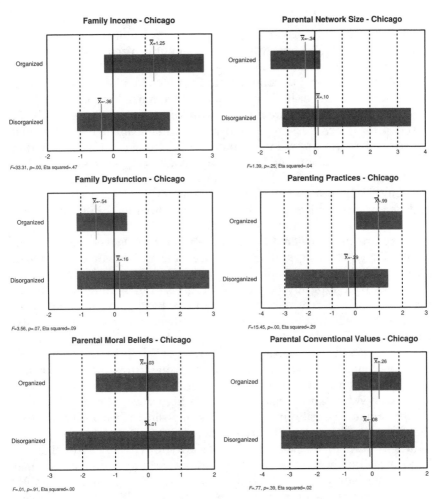

FIGURE 7.4. Neighborhood Family Characteristics by Level of Organization (*continued*)

Networks, low levels of Bonding and Control, and higher levels of Illegal Modeling (see Table A7.1 in Appendix A). Why families living in some of the worst neighborhoods should, on average, have a higher commitment to conventional values is puzzling. We will speculate on this set of unexpected relationships later, after we have considered them at the individual level.

For Denver, these results indicate that physical neighborhood Deterioration, neighborhood Disadvantage, and neighborhood Organization are each fairly good predictors of Family Resources, Parenting Practices, and Parent Conventional Values (in an unexpected direction); but not of Family Moral Beliefs or Family Dysfunction.

Family differences across Chicago neighborhoods are less consistent and weaker than those in Denver (see Figures 7.2–7.4). Family Income is consistently higher in Well-Kept, Advantaged, and Organized Neighborhoods. Family Dysfunction is lower in Well-Kept and Organized Neighborhoods, but not in Advantaged as compared to Poor Neighborhoods; and Parenting Practices are better in Advantaged and Organized but not Well-Kept Neighborhoods. There were no significant differences by types of neighborhood for either measure of Normative/Value Climate or for Parental Network Size. Not surprisingly, a moderately strong relationship is found between Family Income and level of Poverty ($\eta^2 = .57$; see Figure 7.3). The other statistically significant relationships are all weaker than those found for Denver.[45] In sum, average Family Income, level of Family Dysfunction, and Parenting Practices differ by type of neighborhood in Chicago; but Parental Network Size and Normative/Value Climate do not.

There are three major differences between the Denver and Chicago results. First, parent support networks are typically larger in Chicago than Denver. Recall that in Chapter 6 we noted that neighborhood Informal Networks were typically larger in Chicago, so this finding is not unexpected. Second, Parent Network Size differs by type of neighborhoods and has different relationships to other family characteristics in each city. Chicago neighborhoods in which families tend to have larger support networks are *more* likely to also have higher rates of Family Dysfunction, more exposure to persons involved in crime and using drugs, more opportunities to participate in these activities, less effective social institutions, weaker levels of bonding and social control, and higher rates of neighborhood Disadvantage. The pattern is close to the opposite in Denver. Third, with the exception of support network size noted above, Parental Conventional Values in Chicago are significantly related to other family and neighborhood measures in the manner expected; values are more conventional when other family and neighborhood characteristics are more favorable. Again, the pattern is quite different in Denver. We will return to these city differences in the Discussion Section.

PREDICTING FAMILY CHARACTERISTICS AND PRACTICES:
COMBINED NEIGHBORHOOD MEASURES

In general, we have shown that better neighborhoods tend to have, on average, better family resources, less family dysfunction, better parenting practices, and more conventional Normative/Value Climates (Chicago only). But the earlier analysis considered each of our neighborhood characteristics separately. How well do these neighborhood measures predict average family characteristics when taken together? Do our measures of Deterioration, Disadvantage, and Organization, when combined, provide a good explanation for variation in family characteristics and practices across neighborhoods? The results of this multivariate analysis[46] are presented in Figure 7.5. We used neighborhood Disadvantage,

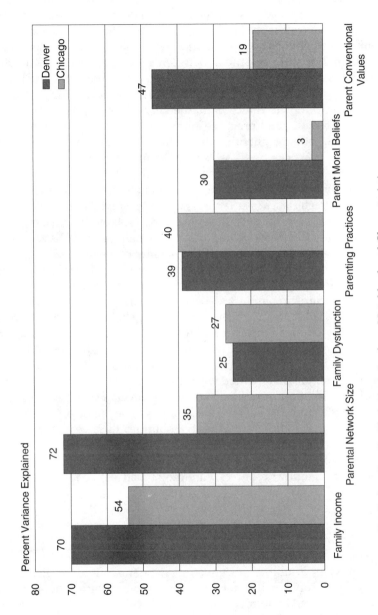

FIGURE 7.5. Predicting Family Characteristics from Neighborhood Characteristics

Deterioration, and the six measures of social organization in this neighborhood-level analysis.

Neighborhood characteristics do a good job of predicting Family Resources in Denver. They also do a good job in predicting Family Income, one of the resource measures, in Chicago. For the other family characteristics (with two exceptions in Chicago), the levels of prediction are not exceptionally high, but still substantial, between 25 and 54 percent. Knowing neighborhood characteristics in Chicago does not improve the prediction of Parental Moral Beliefs much, and only weakly improves the prediction of Parent Conventional Values. Still, the general finding is that average family characteristics and practices are predicted by neighborhood characteristics. The better neighborhoods tend to have better Family Resources and Parenting Practices, and less Family Dysfunction than more Deteriorated, Disadvantaged, and Disorganized Neighborhoods.

When looking at the particular neighborhood features that predict average family characteristics (see Table A7.2 in Appendix A), they are almost exclusively indicators of social organization. Notable by their absence as predictors are Illegal Modeling (Denver), neighborhood Disadvantage (Denver) and physical condition of the neighborhood (both Denver and Chicago), none of which has a statistically significant direct influence on any of the neighborhood-level family characteristics when the other neighborhood characteristics are included as predictors. It might be surprising to some that Disadvantage, which is conceptually linked to Family Income, and was fairly strongly correlated to it ($r = -0.462$) is not necessary for predicting income, or any of the other family characteristics. But this finding is consistent with our conceptual model of neighborhood effects presented in earlier chapters where we argued that the effects of disadvantage and deterioration would be mediated by level of social organization in the neighborhood. For Denver, this appears to be the case; for Chicago, it holds for Deterioration, but Poverty continues to have a direct effect on family characteristics. It is important to note that it is the more emergent features of neighborhood collective life that are associated with the development of Family Resources, Parenting Practices and levels of Family Dysfunction.

There are several specific findings in this analysis that deserve comment. First, Illegal Performance Opportunities is a predictor of Family Dysfunction in both Denver and Chicago. There was evidence of a nonlinear pattern in the relationship between Family Dysfunction and Illegal Performance Opportunities in Denver, so a nonlinear term for Illegal Performance Opportunities (Illegal Performance Opportunities squared) was included in the prediction model for Family Dysfunction. As it turns out (see Table A7.2 in Appendix A), the nonlinear form of Illegal Performance Opportunities (Illegal Performance Opportunities plus Illegal Performance Opportunities squared) is the only statistically significant predictor of

Family Dysfunction for Denver, probably reflecting the crime and drug use components of both Illegal Performance Opportunities in the neighborhood and Family Dysfunction in the family context.[47] As illegal activities and opportunities in the neighborhood increase, Family Dysfunction also increases up to a point, then levels off and may even decline.

Given the unexpected finding in Denver that family endorsement of conventional values was highest in Deteriorated and Modest/Disadvantaged Neighborhoods, it is important to examine what organizational features predict this family characteristic. Parent commitment to conventional values appears strongest in neighborhoods with low levels of Bonding and Control, low levels of Institutional Effectiveness, and high levels of Normative and Value Consensus – a curious mixture of neighborhood organizational features. In Chicago, Parental Conventional Values is stronger in neighborhoods with effective Informal Networks and low levels of Illegal Activities.

We cannot, of course, make causal interpretations of these findings, given the limitations of this study. While average neighborhood Family Income in Denver is related to neighborhood organizational characteristics, it is unlikely that living in neighborhoods characterized by high levels of Bonding and Control, Normative Consensus, and strong Informal Networks will lead to higher Family Incomes. Rather the process is likely one in which individuals with higher incomes are able to select neighborhoods that have these characteristics, neighborhoods that also happen to have low levels of Disadvantage and Deterioration (Chapter 6). Still, by attracting families with higher incomes, these neighborhoods might generate a type of organization and culture that enhances family resources and good parenting practices in the neighborhood. We think both processes are probably at work, but we cannot demonstrate their independent effects.

NEIGHBORHOOD AND FAMILY CHARACTERISTICS AT THE INDIVIDUAL LEVEL

When we consider variation in individual-level family characteristics, rather than in neighborhood averages, the picture changes somewhat. First, levels of explained variance for individual variables are typically smaller than levels of explained variance for neighborhood variables (we have already seen this for the youth development outcomes in Chapters 4 and 6) because it is easier to predict neighborhood averages than individual outcomes.

Second, in addition to the neighborhood variables (Deterioration, Disadvantage, and Organization), we have individual-level variables (age, gender, socioeconomic status, family structure, length of residence, and ethnicity (Denver only) as predictors of family characteristics. This allows us to separate individual- and neighborhood-level influences on family characteristics; to separate emergent effects of living in a particular type of neighborhood from the effects of particular types of persons choosing to live in particular types of neighborhoods (selection effects). In comparing the results for Chicago and Denver, bear in mind that the Denver sample is ethnically diverse, and ethnicity is included as a predictor, while the Chicago sample is quite ethnically homogeneous (predominantly African American) and ethnicity is therefore not included as a predictor for that sample.

The detailed results of this analysis (HLM) are found in Table A7.3 in Appendix A. These results are simplified for presentation in Table 7.2. Here you can see which variables had statistically significant influences on each family characteristic for Denver, Chicago, and for both cities. Table 7.2 also indicates whether that influence was positive or negative, as indicated by the sign that precedes each variable. It is immediately evident from Table 7.2 that Denver and Chicago do not produce identical results for predicting family characteristics. Note, however, that except for Parenting Practices, for which there are no significant predictors, ethnicity is a statistically significant predictor for all other family characteristics in Denver. Because Race/Ethnicity is not available for use as a predictor for Chicago, differences between Denver and Chicago results should be viewed with some caution; the replication across sites is less than perfect, and there is evidence that sampling differences, in particular, may be responsible for some of the differences.

The predictors of individual Family Income are primarily individual factors rather than neighborhood characteristics – parents socioeconomic status, two-parent families, residential stability and majority race/ethnicity (Denver). This is not surprising; occupation and education are two of the best predictors of individual earnings, and single parent families, particularly mother-only families, are well known to have lower average income than two-parent families. In Denver, both Hispanic and African American families have significantly lower incomes than white families, and families that have lived longer in their study neighborhoods had higher incomes. In addition to these individual characteristics, neighborhood Organization (Denver) and neighborhood Poverty (Chicago), predicted Family Income. Recall that at the neighborhood level, neighborhood Organization was a predictor of average individual Family Income in both Denver and Chicago.

Having good support networks is positively related to Length of Residence for both Denver and Chicago; the longer a family has lived in one place, the more likely they are to have developed a more extensive informal network of friends and acquaintances. For Chicago, neighborhood Poverty is once again a statistically significant predictor, but perhaps contrary to expectations, people living in impoverished neighborhoods tend to have more extensive and active social networks,[48] a phenomenon loosely

TABLE 7.2. *Statistically Significant Predictors of Individual Family Characteristics: Denver and Chicago*

Sample Family Characteristic	Statistically Significant Predictors		
	Denver Only	Chicago Only	Both Denver and Chicago
Family Income R^2 Denver = .52 Chicago = .27	+ NH Organization − Minority ethnicity + Length of residence	− Poverty	+ Socioeconomic status + Intact family structure
Parental Network Size R^2 Denver = .15 Chicago = .09	− Age − Minority ethnicity − Socioeconomic status + Intact family structure	+ Poverty	+ Length of residence
Family Dysfunction R^2 Denver = .05 Chicago = .04	− Physical Deterioration − Minority ethnicity (− NH Organization)	− Socioeconomic status	− Intact family structure
Parenting Practices R^2 Denver = .05 Chicago = .17	(none)	+ Poverty + NH Organization − Gender (male) + Socioeconomic status + Intact family structure	− Age
Parental Moral Beliefs R^2 Denver = .12 Chicago = .03	− Age + Minority ethnicity	− Gender (male) + Socioeconomic status + Intact family structure + Length of residence	(none)
Parental Conventional Values R^2 Denver = .13 Chicago = .05	− Gender (male) + Minority ethnicity − Socioeconomic status	+ NH Organization + Intact family structure + Socioeconomic status	+ Age

paralleled in Denver with the finding that people with lower socioeconomic status tend to have more extensive social networks. For Denver, people of majority ethnic status, people with younger children, and those in intact families also tend to have larger and more active informal social networks. There are no statistically significant neighborhood predictors of Parent Network Size in Denver. This dimension of family resources appears to be a function of individual attributes and characteristics.

Family Dysfunction is more characteristic of single-parent families than of intact families in both Denver and Chicago. Once again, we may question which is cause and which is effect. Are individuals who engage in problem behavior, or with children or spouses whose behavior is problematic (family disruption) more susceptible to family dissolution through divorce, separation, or desertion, or do the pressures associated with single parenthood increase the likelihood of dysfunctional behavior in parents and children? In all likelihood, both explanations are at least partially valid, and the relationship should be regarded as predictive, but not necessarily as a cause-and-effect relationship. For Chicago, lower socioeconomic status is also predictive of Family Dysfunction. For Denver, there are two neighborhood predictors and one additional individual predictor. The combination of predictors is a little unexpected. Dysfunctional families tend to be white families, living in Disorganized Neighborhoods,[49] and Well-Kept Neighborhoods. In part, this may reflect the frequently observed finding that there is *less* illicit drug use among minority groups than among majority group members (for example, Johnston, O'Malley, and Bachman, 2000a,b; Elliott et al., 1989); and that whites, on average, are more affluent and able to afford alcohol and both licit and illicit drugs. It may also reflect ethnic differences in the likelihood of seeking outside help for family problems.

The findings for socioeconomic status in Chicago may appear inconsistent with the above finding in Denver; they suggest that Family Dysfunction is more likely for less advantaged black families in Chicago and for white, (generally more advantaged) families, in Denver. But these are also Denver families living primarily in Disorganized Neighborhoods and we can not make racial/ethnic comparisons with the Chicago sample. The apparent contradiction may be attributable to sample differences or to differences between Denver and Chicago in the measurement of Family Dysfunction.

In both Denver and Chicago, Parenting Practices are better for families with younger children, a finding consistent with research cited earlier. With the transition from childhood to adolescence, youth rely less on parents for advice and support, parental monitoring becomes more difficult and less effective, and there is more direct contact with other adults and peers in the neighborhood. In Chicago, Parenting Practices are also better for families living in *high* poverty and in *better* Organized neighborhoods, families with female children, higher family socioeconomic status, and intact families. The only real surprise here is that Parenting Practices are better in high-poverty neighborhoods, perhaps reflecting a response to increased risks in those neighborhoods. In some sense this may seem contradictory with the result for neighborhood Organization (better parenting practices in more Organized neighborhoods), but in a way this makes sense; it suggests that parenting styles are best in well organized, High-Poverty Neighborhoods (where both the need and the means may be present). This interpretation would be consistent with the fact that the positive relationship between Poverty and Parenting Practices in Chicago occurs only when neighborhood Organization is taken into account.[50] The better Parenting Practices for female children is consistent with research cited earlier, which suggest that girls are more likely to receive intensive supervision than boys. The association of Parenting Practices with higher socioeconomic status and intact families may represent, among other things, the presence of better resources to monitor children.[51]

Strong Parental Moral Beliefs that it is wrong to violate the law are associated with having younger children and with ethnic minority status in Denver. The first finding is unsurprising; some behaviors are more likely to be tolerated in older adolescents than in younger children. The finding regarding ethnic minority status may be surprising to some, but it is consistent with past research that indicates that ethnic minorities often are less tolerant of deviance (this may be especially true for minority group members who perceive themselves as having access to legitimate opportunities; see Menard,1995). For Chicago, parents are more intolerant of deviance if they have female children, higher socioeconomic status, intact families, and longer residential stability.

Parental Conventional Values are more likely for families with older children (educational attainment and occupational success become more relevant at later ages; see for example Sullivan 1989 and Menard 1995) in both Denver and Chicago. In the most direct contradiction between the Denver and Chicago findings, socioeconomic status is *positively associated* with Parental Conventional Values in Chicago, but *negatively associated* with Parental Conventional Values in Denver. This pattern for Denver was noted earlier in the discussion of the neighborhood level results; the Chicago results are more consistent with our general expectations. In Denver, Parental Conventional Values are also more likely for parents with female children, and for ethnic minority parents (paralleling the findings for Parental Moral Beliefs for minority group members, as described earlier). For Chicago, Parental Conventional Values were more likely in intact families and Well Organized Neighborhoods.

In summary, the results for Denver and Chicago are sometimes similar, sometimes inconsistent. The inconsistencies may be attributable to differences in sampling and measurement, but it is also possible that they reflect different patterns in different geographic (and social) locations. Ethnic differences, which are not measurable for the Chicago study, are prominent in the Denver results. Ethnicity and age are the two predictors most likely to be statistically significant for Denver. For Chicago, neighborhood Poverty, socioeconomic status, and intact family structure emerge repeatedly as predictors of family characteristics. It is speculative, but not unreasonable, to suggest that these may be important predictors of family characteristics *within a single ethnic group*, but we are left with the question of whether the results would have been substantially different had the Chicago sample been more ethnically diverse. Finally, with the exception of Family Income, which is well explained in both the Denver and Chicago samples, levels of explained variance for individual family characteristics are modest in both samples.

In a final analysis of neighborhood effects on family characteristics and practices, the explained variance is broken out for neighborhood and individual level components in Table 7.3. This allows us to estimate what percentage of the variation in individual family characteristics and practices can be uniquely attributed to neighborhood contextual effects (concentration and emergent effects) when individual attributes and characteristics associated with selection processes are taken into account (controlled).

Overall, the neighborhood level variables contribute little in the way of a unique explanation for variation in family characteristics when we control for individual characteristics. Furstenberg et al. (1999) report a similar finding for the MacArthur Network Study in Philadelphia which focused on family influences on youth development. Variation in Family Resources, Parenting Practices, Family Dysfunction and Normative/Value Climate, are more uniquely a function of individual than neighborhood characteristics.

There are reasons for viewing these results as more positive evidence that living in particular types of neighborhoods has some effect on individual family resources and practices. First, for some specific family characteristics, neighborhood features account for as much or more variation than individual characteristics: for Family Dysfunction and Family Income in Denver and for Parental Network Size and Parental Conventional Values in Chicago. In most cases, it is primarily neighborhood organization that is influencing family characteristics. Second, estimates of the unique influence of these separate components are very conservative estimates. Shared effects, that is, effects that involve both neighborhood and individual characteristics that can not be uniquely attributed to either, are often quite large. For example, this is the largest effect for Family Income. There is thus some evidence which is consistent with the claim of emergent neighborhood influences. Neighborhood influences on Family Income with this model are somewhere between 5 and 49 percent. Third, except for Family Income, our model of neighborhood and individual effects account for a relatively small part (4 to 17 percent) of the observed variation in Family Resources and Parenting Practices. Neighborhoods do have some influence on Family Resources, Family Dysfunction, family Parenting Practices and family Normative/Value Climate, even when individual characteristics are taken into account, on how families function and the culture in which they raise their children. However, except for Family Income, these effects are quite modest.

TABLE 7.3. *Neighborhood Contributions to Explained Variance of Family Characteristics*

Family Variables Predictors	Family Income		Parental Network Size		Family Dysfunction		Parenting Practices		Parent Moral Beliefs		Parental Conventional Values	
	Chi	Den	Chi	Den	Chi	Den	Chi	Den	Chi	Den	CHI	Den
Deterioration	0	0	0	0	0	2	0	0	n/a	0	0	0
Disadvantage	1	0	5	0	0	0	1	0	n/a	0	1	0
Organization	0	5	0	0	0	1	3	0	n/a	0	3	0
Individual	12	5	5	14	1	3	8	3	n/a	12	2	9
Shared	14	44	0	1	4	0	5	2	n/a	0	0	5
TOTAL**	27	52	9	15	4	5	17	5	3*	12	5	13

* Not statistically significant.
** Totals may differ from sum of columns due to rounding.

189

THE INFLUENCE OF NEIGHBORHOODS AND FAMILIES
ON SUCCESSFUL YOUTH DEVELOPMENT

We turn now to a different set of questions. Are good family resources, low levels of dysfunction, positive parenting practices and a supportive family climate or culture important for a successful course of youth development? We learned above that these family characteristics vary somewhat by the type of neighborhood in which the family lives. Are family influences and neighborhood influences independent, that is, does each have a unique influence on development? How strong are their separate effects? Are the combined effects substantially better than the effects we observed for neighborhood characteristics alone in Chapter 6?

Family Influences on Successful Development – Neighborhood Level

Let's begin by considering the relationships between our family characteristics and successful developmental outcomes at the neighborhood level – do youth from neighborhoods with good family characteristics have higher rates of successful development? In general, they do, but the strength of this positive relationship between good family characteristic and high rates of success, varies by which outcome is being considered. Neighborhoods characterized by high levels of Family Resources (high income and large support networks) and good Parenting Practices have high rates of Personal Competence and Prosocial Behavior in Denver. These two family characteristics are very strong predictors of these forms of successful development (rs in the .60 to .80 range; see Table A7.4 in Appendix A). They are also predictive of being On Track in Denver, but the relationships are not as strong. In Chicago, all of the family characteristics with the exception of Family Network Size are predictive of Prosocial Competence, with Parenting Practices ($r = .71$) and Family Dysfunction ($r = -.66$) being particularly strong predictors. Surprisingly, Family Dysfunction is not predictive of either Personal Competence or Prosocial Behavior in Denver, although it is related to being On Track. Neighborhoods with poor Parenting Practices and high levels of Family Dysfunction have the highest rates of Problem Behavior in both Denver and Chicago; in addition, neighborhoods with low levels of Family Income and low levels of Parental Moral Beliefs have high rates of Problem Behavior in Chicago.

Overall, the most consistent predictor of success outcomes at the neighborhood level is good Parenting Practices, followed by high levels of Family Income. Neighborhoods with these two characteristics have good rates of successful development on every outcome measured. The two measures of family culture work pretty much as expected for Chicago, particularly strong for promoting Prosocial Competence. However, except for a relationship with rates of Prosocial Behavior, Parental Moral Beliefs is not predictive of any other success outcome and Parental Conventional Values is

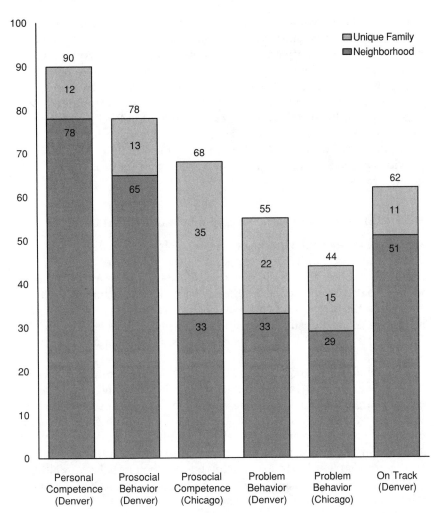

FIGURE 7.6. Cumulative Explained Variance in Youth Development Outcomes: Neighborhood and Family Predictors–Neighborhood Level

associated with *lower* levels of Personal Competence and being On Track in Denver. Although not what we expected in our model of neighborhood and family effects, there is general consistency in this finding regarding a high endorsement of conventional values.

Does adding the family context to our model improve our ability to predict neighborhood rates of successful adolescent development? It clearly does. As shown in Figure 7.6, the addition of family variables adds 11–13 percent to the explained variance for Personal Competence, Prosocial Behavior, and On Track in Denver, 35 percent to the explained variance for Prosocial Competence in Chicago, and 15 percent (Chicago) to 22 percent

(Denver) to the explained variance for Problem Behavior. Knowing family characteristics adds substantially to our ability to predict neighborhood rates of youth development outcomes (see Table A7.5 in Appendix A).[52] Moreover, this combined model does very well in accounting for variation in Personal Competence and Prosocial Behavior across Denver neighborhoods, 90 and 78 percent, respectively. It is also substantial for the other success outcomes: Prosocial Competence, 68 percent, On Track, 62 percent, and Problem Behavior, 55 percent (Denver), and 44 percent (Chicago). Overall, a model including both neighborhood and family context measures provides a good explanation for the variation in rates of success across neighborhoods.

Family Influences on Youth Development – Individual Level

We turn now to consider these same relationships at the individual level. Do youth with good family characteristics have better success outcomes than those with poorer family characteristics? Again, the answer is generally yes. The patterns are similar to those observed at the neighborhood level, and while the strength of the relationships is not as great, more of the relationships are statistically significant and in the expected direction (see Table A7.4 in Appendix A). The evidence for our explanatory model is thus *better* at the individual level.

In general, those youth in families with good Parenting Practices, better Family Resources (income and support networks), and a high commitment to Parental Moral Beliefs, are more successful. Again, good Parenting Practices provide the most consistent and strongest influence on successful development. The simple correlations with the competence measures and the On Track measure range from 0.38 to 0.50. Youth with good parenting are also less likely to be involved in Problem Behavior, although the relationships are weaker ($r = -.13$ and $-.24$). Family Dysfunction was related only to Prosocial Competence (negatively) and to Problem Behavior. There was thus some evidence that parental involvement in crime and substance abuse interfered with the development of Prosocial Competence in their children, at least in Chicago, and predicted the involvement of their children in Problem Behavior in both cities.

Parental Conventional Values is related negatively to Problem Behavior (both cities) and positively to Prosocial Competence (Chicago). This dimension of family culture is not related to Personal Competence or being On Track, and it is negatively related to Prosocial Behavior (Denver). The other dimension of family culture, Parental Moral Beliefs, is related to success outcomes as expected; having parents with strong moral beliefs is related to the successful development of individual competencies, positive behavior, being On Track, and avoidance of Problem Behavior.

Table 7.4 shows the variance explained in individual youth development outcomes, separated into components attributable to Deterioration,

TABLE 7.4. *Explained Variance in Youth Development Outcomes: Individual Level*

	Personal Competence (Denver)	Prosocial Behavior (Denver)	Prosocial Competence (Chicago)	Problem Behavior (Denver)	Problem Behavior (Chicago)	On Track (Denver)
Unique Deterioration	0	1	0	1	0	0
Unique Disadvantage	0	0	0	0	0	0
Unique Organization	1	0	0	0	0	0
Unique Family	21	9	17	1	4	8
Unique Individual	3	11	3	9	5	4
Unique Interaction	0	1	0	0	2	2
Shared Effects	11	13	18	5	4	5
Total Explained Variance*	36	35	39	15	16	17

* Totals may differ from sum of columns due to rounding.

Disadvantage, Organization, family characteristics, individual characteristics, interaction effects, and shared effects. Comparing Table 7.4 with
Table 6.4, we find that the individual level explained variance has also
increased with the addition of the family characteristics as predictors:
only slightly for Problem Behavior (from 14 to 15 percent for Denver, and
from 13 to 16 percent for Chicago), substantially for Prosocial Behavior
in Denver (from 26 to 35 percent), and the explained variance is approximately doubled for Personal Competence in Denver (from 15 to 36 percent),
Prosocial Competence in Chicago (from 21 to 39 percent), and On Track in
Denver (from 9 to 17 percent). Knowing family characteristics substantially
improves our ability to predict all of the individual-level youth development outcomes except Problem Behavior.

A second point to notice is that, in absolute terms, neighborhood characteristics continue to play a very small unique role in explaining individual-
level youth development outcomes; in relative terms, given the increase in
explained variance attributable to family characteristics, the unique contribution of neighborhood characteristics is even smaller than estimated in
Chapter 6. The addition of family characteristics produces little change
in the unique contribution of the interaction effects[53] or in the unique
individual effects for Personal Competence in Denver (an increase from
2 to 3 percent) or On Track in Denver (no change). With family characteristics in the model, however, the unique contribution of individual
characteristics is somewhat reduced for Problem Behavior in Chicago
(from 8 to 5 percent) and Denver (from 13 to 9 percent), and substantially reduced for Prosocial Behavior in Denver (from 18 to 11 percent) and
Prosocial Competence in Chicago (from 11 to 36 percent). The contribution
of shared effects increases slightly for Personal Competence in Denver
(from 10 to 11 percent), On Track in Denver (from 3 to 5 percent), and
Problem Behavior in Denver (from zero to 5 percent) and Chicago (from
2 to 4 percent), and more than doubles for Prosocial Behavior in Denver
(from 5 to 13 percent) and Prosocial Competence in Chicago (from 8 to
18 percent).

The overall effect of adding the family variables to the models is to
(1) increase the overall explained variance, (2) reduce the unique contribution attributable to individual characteristics, (3) increase the contribution attributable to shared effects, and (4) include a unique contribution of family characteristics to each of the youth development outcomes.
For Personal Competence in Denver, Prosocial Competence in Chicago,
and On Track in Denver, family and shared effects are the major components of explained variance; for Prosocial Behavior in Denver and Problem Behavior in Chicago, family and shared effects plus individual effects
account for most of the variance explained. Only for Problem Behavior
in Denver, which is explained primarily by individual and shared effects,

does the addition of family characteristics to the model fail to result in a substantial proportion of the explained variance being attributable to family characteristics.

QUALITATIVE STUDY FINDINGS

Our in-depth comparisons of disadvantaged and advantaged neighborhoods with different success rates revealed many of the same differences in family resources and parenting practices found in the survey responses. Differences in parenting styles appeared to be related to levels of perceived threats in the neighborhood and the need to protect children. Parents living in neighborhoods with high rates of crime, drug use and delinquent gangs, were focused almost exclusively on how to protect their children from these dangers and they relied heavily on restrictive, isolating practices such as grounding, chaperoning, threats, corporal punishment, and loss of freedom to be with friends.[54] Both Jarrett, (1997) and Furstenberg et al. (1999) report a similar finding. In highly disadvantaged and deteriorated neighborhoods, there appeared to be a threshold of increasing control and restrictiveness, at which the accelerating demands of monitoring and supervision appeared to become overwhelming for the parent, and they essentially gave up, abandoning their efforts at supervision and monitoring. This was interpreted by adolescents and neighborhood adults as a lack of caring by these parents.

There were clear differences in parent awareness of outside resources and opportunities available to families and youth by type of neighborhood. But the use of whatever resources and positive supervised activities were available, depended on family financial and/or social resources, parent time to manage their children's involvement in these activities, plus nonrestrictive/noncontrolling parenting styles that gave more freedom and choice to adolescent children. These conditions tended to be related to neighborhood advantage, but also varied within both advantaged and disadvantaged neighborhoods. This appeared to be a factor in the low success rates for youth living in Westside, one of our more affluent study neighborhoods. But this also appeared to explain the good success rates for adolescents in Northside, a Modest Disadvantaged Neighborhood.

In sum, the poor development outcomes in three of the six study neighborhoods appeared to be associated with: (1) higher levels of authoritarian/restrictive parenting styles (controlling, restrictive, frequent use of corporal punishment) which tended to increase with increased fear and contextual risk or danger, (2) neglect, which was perceived by teens as a lack of caring by parents/caregivers, and (3) limited access to both informal positive networks and formal organizations which was associated with parental restrictiveness, limited awareness of opportunities, lack of family resources and time to manage these types of involvement. None of these dimensions of family context appeared to be related to the race/ethnicity of parents.

DISCUSSION

There were several findings that deserve some further discussion. First, the in-depth focus group discussions revealed that *all* parents in our study neighborhoods expressed hope for their adolescent children's success,[55] but it was clear that parenting is more challenging in disadvantaged neighborhoods, as has been reported in other studies.[56] Virtually all parents living in study neighborhoods where there were gangs, widespread use of drugs, and high rates of crime, were concerned about protecting their children from these neighborhood risks, and their parenting strategies focused heavily on restricting their teens activities and time spent on neighborhood streets and hangouts. These families, often headed by single parents, spent less time with their teens and typically with other adults in the neighborhood. And they tended to have relatively low expectations for their children. In more affluent neighborhoods, danger was not a focal concern. Parents were quite relaxed about control and restrictiveness, gave their children increasing freedom as they entered adolescence, expressed high expectations for success and were much more likely to be personally involved with both their children and other adults in the neighborhood.

It was also the case that the use of restrictive parenting in highly disadvantaged, dangerous neighborhoods did not always occur without warmth and parent involvement, that is, these features of parenting which are more typical in advantaged neighborhoods were not uncommon to parents using a restrictiveness strategy. Moreover, on the few occasions where some potential danger appeared in more advantaged neighborhoods, where parents were typically warm, involved, less restrictive and more consistent in their monitoring and supervision, they were quick to use the same type of restrictive practices used more frequently in disadvantaged neighborhoods. In general then, parenting practices reflected the specific circumstances present in the neighborhood rather than single uniform parenting strategy or style used uniformly under all conditions.

In some ways, our survey findings are quite consistent with these qualitative findings, but are also unable to confirm others. First, we did find that families living in Disadvantaged and/or Deteriorated Neighborhoods had fewer resources (lower incomes, smaller support networks) and poorer parenting practices than families living in more Advantaged/Well-Kept Neighborhoods and that these two features of the family context were the strongest predictors of successful developmental outcomes at both the neighborhood and individual levels. However, our analysis also suggests an important qualifier: it was not neighborhood Disadvantage per se that accounted for the differences in neighborhood-level resources and parenting practices, but rather, the emergent social organization and culture of the neighborhood. A positive family context thus depends on the presence and effectiveness of the informal support structures, levels of bonding and control, institutional effectiveness, and illegal performance structures – on both the opportunities and risks present in the neighborhood.

Furstenberg et al. (1999), in the MacArthur study focusing on family effects on youth development in Philadelphia, report that, on average, parenting practices were better in high-poverty than low-poverty neighborhoods. In Chicago, we replicated this neighborhood-level finding, but *only* when the level of neighborhood social organization was controlled. Parents living in poor neighborhoods appear to have good parenting practices when there is a greater institutional presence and effectiveness, better levels of bonding and control, and more consensus on values and norms (see Figure 7.5). Overall, in both Chicago and Denver, parenting practices were better in Organized than Disorganized Neighborhoods, and it was this feature of the neighborhood rather than Poverty or Disadvantage, that predicted a better quality of parenting.

Second, our survey measure of Parenting Practices did not include a restrictiveness component that would allow us to look specifically at this practice. However, the finding that a specific practice like restrictiveness may be appropriate and functional under some neighborhood conditions and not others, is consistent with prior research.[57] Furstenberg et al. (1999:119) also report that restrictiveness was used by parents in both advantaged and disadvantaged neighborhoods; by lower educated parents in disadvantaged and more highly educated parents in advantaged neighborhoods. There was no evidence, however, that restrictiveness was an effective strategy for youth development outcomes; it was not related to any success outcomes.

When individual characteristics (socioeconomic status, age, race/ethnicity, family structure and length of residence) were taken into account, neighborhood effects on individual family features were very small, uniquely accounting for zero to 5 percent of the explained variance. Considering shared effects as potential neighborhood effects, the maximum potential effects range from zero to 15 percent.[58] With one exception,[59] individual family characteristics accounted for as much or more variation in family contextual features as neighborhood characteristics. This finding is consistent with that of other studies.[60] It is also noteworthy that for some family characteristics, there are substantial shared effects, that is, effects that can not be uniquely assigned to either individual or neighborhood factors, although there were some exceptions to this general conclusion which were detailed earlier. While neighborhood organization and culture do a reasonably good job of explaining neighborhood-level variation in family characteristics, they do not account for much of the variation at the individual level. This suggests that some, maybe most of the apparent effect of neighborhood factors on family characteristics is a selection effect; the result of the types of individuals and families that choose or are relegated to particular neighborhoods. These results challenge the idea that family norms and parenting practices are strongly influenced by the type of neighborhood.[61]

We noted above that the relationship between the family's socioeconomic status and their endorsement of conventional values is different in Denver and Chicago. More advantaged families in Chicago had more conventional values whereas the less advantaged families in Denver had the more conventional values. In Denver, we also found that African American and Hispanic families tended to have more conventional values as compared to whites. Given that the Chicago sample is predominantly black and the Denver sample is predominantly white, and that minority families tend to be less advantaged, this could explain some of this city difference. However, among African Americans in Denver, more advantaged families had more conventional values, so there is still a city difference that involves some complex interaction between socioeconomic status and race/ethnicity.

The combination of family and neighborhood characteristics does a relatively good job of predicting neighborhood rates of successful developmental outcomes, accounting for 44–90 percent of the variation in neighborhood rates. At the individual level, this combination of family and neighborhood factors also provides a better explanation of successful development than the neighborhood factors alone (15–39 percent of the variance). However, it is clear that it is the family characteristics that account for most of the variance in success outcomes; neighborhood factors typically contribute no unique explanatory power. Family effects are also greater than the effects of individual characteristics, in most instances. Shared effects are also substantial for some outcomes.

Finally, interaction effects are rare and when they are present, they account for a very small part of the variance. This was a surprise. There is a common belief that minority youth from poor families, or youth with little parental support and monitoring, might be particularly vulnerable to the effects of neighborhood disadvantage. This does not appear to be the case, and the interactions that do exist have a very small influence on success outcomes.[62] We will consider these small interactions after the complete model, which includes school and peer group effects, is examined. We turn next to an examination of the influence of schools and peer groups and the full model of contextual effects on a successful course of youth development.

Notes

1. See Belsky, 1984; Bronfenbrenner, 1986; Stern and Smith, 1995; and Furstenberg et al., 1999.
2. See Klein, 1995.
3. Dumka et al., 1995; Masten et al., 1990; Werner and Smith, 1992; Garmezy, 1985; Baldwin et al., 1990.
4. Bronfenbrenner, 1986 and Massey, 2001. Massey notes, "The total disadvantage of experiencing both at the same time is much greater than their simple sum (2001:46)."
5. See Schmitz et al., 1995; Furstenberg, 1996; Figueira-McDonough, 1992.
6. For general reviews see Duncan et al., 1998; Corcoran, 1995; Haveman and Wolf, 1995; Mayer, 1997.
7. Elliott and Voss, 1974; Luster and McAdoo, 1996; Braddock and McPartland, 1992.
8. Farrington, 1993; Loeber et al., 1995; Hawkins et al., 1998.
9. Myers and King, 1983; Loeber et al., 1995.
10. Kruttschnitt, McLeod, and Dornfeld, 1994; McLoyd, 1990; Gelles, 1973, 1992; Maden and Wrench, 1977; Garbarino, and Ganzel, 2000; Baumrind, 1994.
11. Duncan, Brooks-Gunn, Yeung, and Smith, 1998.
12. Hofferth et al., 1998; Gibbs, 1986; Lempers et al., 1989; McLoyd, 1990; NICHD, 2005.
13. Caspi, Moffit, Wright, and Silva, 1998.
14. Duncan et al., 1998; Sim and Vuchinich, 1996; Haveman and Wolf, 1995.
15. Caspi et al., 1998; McLanahan, 1985; Klebanov et al., 1994.
16. McLoyd, 1990; McLoyd and Wilson, 1991; Garbarino, 1976; Klebanov, Brooks-Gunn, and Duncan, 1994; Elder et al., 1995.
17. Wilson, 1991; Klebanov, Brooks-Gunn, and Duncan, 1994; Taylor, 1996.
18. Reynolds and Gil, 1994; Kao and Tienda, 1998; Klebanov, Brooks-Gunn, and Duncan, 1994.
19. Bandura, 1995; Eccles et al., 1997; Furstenberg et al., 1999.
20. Taylor and Covington, 1993; Taylor et al., 1993; Taylor and Roberts, 1995; McAdoo, 1982; McLoyd, 1990; Furstenberg and Crawford, 1978; Hetherington, Cox and Cox, 1978; Kellam, Ensminger, and Turner, 1977; Stack, 1974.
21. Coleman, 1988; Sampson, 1992; Furstenberg et al., 1999.
22. Duncan, Brooks-Gunn, Yeung and Smith, 1998.
23. Furstenberg et al., 1999; Elder et al., 1995; Sampson and Laub, 1993; Sampson and Lauritsen, 1994; Shihadeh and Steffensmeier, 1994; Murray, 1996; Adlaf and Iris, 1996; Chase-Lansdale, Cherlin, and Kiernan, 1995; Hetherington, 1989; Sim and Vuchinich, 1996; Patterson, Reid and Dishon, 1992; Knight et al., 1998; Neighbors, Forehand, and Bau, 1997; Coley, 1998; Astone and McLanahan, 1991; David et al., 1996; McLoyd and Wilson, 1991; Caspi et al., 1998. A few studies found no significant relationship between broken homes and delinquency (Loeber and Stouthamer-Loeber, 1986; Sampson, 1992; Furstenberg and Tietler, 1994; McCord, 1991) or educational achievement (Battle, 1997).
24. See David et. al., 1996.
25. See Battle, 1997 for a review.

26. Schmitz et al., 1995; Battle, 1997; Chase-Lansdale et al. 1995.
27. Sim and Vuchinich, 1996. For an important exception, see Chase-Lansdale et al. (1995) who report that there is a delayed effect on mental health problems that does not emerge until early adulthood.
28. For recent reviews see U.S. Surgeon General, 2001; Hawkins et al., 1998; Lipsey and Derzon, 1998.
29. Furstenberg et al., 1999; Elder et al., 1995; Hetherington, 1989; Sim and Vuchinich, 1996; Sampson and Lauritsen, 1994; Klebanov et al., 1994; Guerra et al., 1995; Prior-Brown and Cowen, 1989; Cowen and Work, 1988.
30. Herrenkohl el al., 2000; Hawkins et al., 1998; Patterson et al., 1992.
31. Hill, 1980; Dornbusch et al.,1987, 1991; Steinberg et al., 1989, 1991, 1992; Buri, 1989; Hirschi, 1969; Hirsh, 1983; Eccles et al., 1993; Maccoby and Martin, 1983.
32. Garbarino, 1976; Baumrind, 1991, 1994: Conger and Elder, 1994; Widom, 1994.
33. Loeber and Stouthamer-Loeber, 1986; Baumrind, 1989; Bank et al., 1993; Maccoby and Martin, 1983; Hawkins et al., 1999; Sampson, 1993; Laub and Sampson, 1988; Curran and Chassin, 1996; Patterson, 1982, 1992; Patterson and Bank, 1987; Windle, 1994; Peeples and Loeber, 1994; Melby and Conger, 1996; Chilcoat and Anthony, 1996; Gorman-Smith et al., 1996; Sokol-Katz, Dunham, and Zimmerman, 1997; Steinberg, 2001; Jackson and Davis, 2000; Roth and Brooks-Gunn, 2000. However, there are several longitudinal studies that found no predictive effects for these parenting variables on specific developmental outcomes (Dishion et al., 1991; Jessor and Jessor, 1975; Curran and Chassin, 1996; Herrenkohl et al., 2000).
34. Furstenberg et al., 1999.
35. Eccles et al., 1993; Leahy, 1981; Epstein and McPartland, 1977; Herman et al., 1997.
36. Hirschi, 1969; Baumrind, 1991; Ryan and Lynch, 1989; Lamborn and Steinberg, 1993; Klebanov et al., 1994; Eccles et al., 1993; Rice, Cunningham and Young, 1997; Furstenberg et al., 1999; Furstenberg and Harris, 1993; Blum and Rhinehart, 1997; Delaney, 1996; Grotevant, 1998; Steinberg, 2001; Eccles and Gootman, 2002.
37. Maccoby and Martin, 1983; Elliott et al., 1989; Comer and Haynes, 1991; Grolick and Ryan, 1989.
38. Blum and Rhinehart, 1997.
39. Elliott and Voss, 1974; Elliott, Huizinga, and Menard, 1989; Jessor et al., 1991; Elder and Conger, 2000; Eccles and Gootman, 2002.
40. Small and Supple, 2001.
41. One family measure (youth involvement in family activities) was used in our measure of Prosocial Behavior, an individual-level youth development outcome measure. No other individual-level family measures were used as youth development outcomes and family involvement is not used in any of our family predictors of youth development outcomes.
42. The reliabilities of some scales could not be calcuated, as indicated by "n/a." See Note 7 in Chapter 4 for a detailed explanation.
43. See Coleman, 1988; Putnam, 1995; and Sampson, 1992.
44. Since the Family Dysfunction indicators are frequencies referring to related but distinct behaviors, calculation of an internal consistency measure of reliability is inappropriate for this scale and its subscales.

45. There is more consistency in the expected relationships in the bivariate correlation analysis found in Table A7.1, in Appendix A. For example, the correlations between types of neighborhood and Family Dysfunction are all significant (and weak) and in the expected direction whereas they were nonsignificant in the ANOVA analysis; for Chicago, Family Dysfunction, and Parenting Practices are significantly correlated in the expected direction to *all* of the neighborhood types, not just some of them.

46. Ridge regression (see Chapter 6, Endnote 17) is used once again because of the collinearity among the neighborhood Organization, Disadvantage, and Deterioration measures. Figure 7.5 is based on the regression presented in full in Table A7.2, in Appendix A. We have eliminated predictors whose effects were not statistically significant through a technique called *backward elimination* (Ryan 1997:222). In Table A7.2, the usual 0.10 cutoff for statistical significance is used. The advantage to using backward elimination to get rid of predictors whose effects are not statistically significant is that it reduces "clutter" in two ways, technically, by reducing the standard error and thus improving the statistical significance of the coefficients, and in terms of presentation, by removing predictors that have no apparent effect on, or are not particularly useful in predicting, the outcome variable. The original model, with all of the predictors, is called the *full* model, and the model produced at the end of the backward elimination process is called the *reduced* model. Table A7.2 presents the results for the reduced models for the family variables at the neighborhood level. There are also disadvantages with this procedure, as discussed by Berry and Feldman (1985) and Ryan (1997). In the present analysis, the results for the reduced models (after using backward elimination) and the results for the full models are substantively identical, suggesting the same variables as important influences on the dependent variable, with the exception that two variables that would otherwise not have been included as influences on conventional values based on the full model are included in the reduced model.

47. These are independent measures. The neighborhood measure is based on responses from the youth interview about opportunities to get drugs and engage in crime. The parent measure is based on parent interview questions about drug use, criminal behavior, and seeking help for emotional, behavioral, alcohol, and other behavioral problems.

48. This is consistent with findings reported by Klebanov et al. (1994, 1997) who note that having affluent neighbors is associated with less social support.

49. This relationship is only marginally significant ($p = .10$), but should probably not be ignored.

50. The bivariate correlation between Poverty and Parenting Practices is statistically significant and *negative* ($r = -.15, p = .000$), as we would expect based on our model of neighborhood effects on family characteristics and practices.

51. Some studies find no relationship between SES and parenting practices, for example, Furstenberg et al. (1999).

52. Once again, ridge regression with a ridge constant of 0.25 is used to calculate the model. The results in Table A7.5 refer to the full model, with all predictors; reduced models will be considered in Chapter 9.

53. A reduction from 2 percent to zero for Personal Competence in Denver, a reduction from 2 to 1 percent for Prosocial Behavior in Denver, a reduction from

1 percent to zero for Prosocial Competence in Chicago and for Problem Behavior in Denver, and no change for Problem Behavior in Chicago or On Track in Denver.

54. Wright-Atkinson, 1995.

55. See Wright-Atkinson, 1995.

56. Wilson, 1991; Klebanov et al., 1994, 1997; Peeples and Loeber, 1994; Stern and Smith, 1995; Chase-Landsdale et al., 1997; Leventhal et al., 1997.

57. Steinberg et al., 1981, 1992; Jarrett, 1997; Battle, 1997; Sampson and Morenoff, 1997; Furstenberg et al., 1999; Roth and Brooks-Gunn, 2000.

58. In Denver, the shared effect for Family Income was very large, 44 percent. For this one case, the maximum neighborhood effect would be 49 percent. However, this is clearly an exception to the more modest range between unique (minimum) and maximum effect sizes for all other family variables across the two sites.

59. The only exception involved parental endorsement of conventional values in Chicago, but the combined effect of individual and neighborhood factors for this family feature accounted for only five percent of the variation.

60. Chase-Landsdale et al., 1997; Spencer et al., 1997; Jarrett, 1995, 1997.

61. Furstenberg et al. (1999) report a similar conclusion.

62. For a similar finding, see Gerard and Buehler, 1999; Halpern-Flesher et al., 1997.

School Climate and Types of Peer Groups

SYNOPSIS

After early childhood, the school and the peer group begin to compete with the family and neighborhood as primary socializing contexts. Schools provide important training and opportunities for the development of both social and academic competencies. However, they are also contexts in which youth are exposed to different lifestyles, to drugs, violent or aggressive behavior of other students, and a new status system with its own unique performance demands. Good schools facilitate a successful course of development and bad schools undermine this type of success. The characteristics of the neighborhood immediately surrounding the school, the neighborhoods from which the school draws its students, and the characteristics of the families of those students, all combine to influence the school's social and academic environment. In this chapter, we identify two dimensions of the school context: the learning environment which we refer to as a Positive School Environment, and the level of safety or risk of violence in the school referred to as School Violence/Safety. Mechanisms linking features of the neighborhood and family contexts to the school environment and, in turn, characteristics of the school climate to successful developmental outcomes, are identified.

With the onset of puberty, the peer group emerges as the most influential interactional setting for patterns of adolescent behavior and an important influence on other dimensions of successful development. The neighborhood and the school are the two primary contexts in which peer groups are formed and interact, largely in response to characteristics of these two social settings. Families also influence peer groups directly and indirectly by their parenting styles: by their encouraging certain relationships and regulating activities in which their children may or may not participate. Peer group influences on successful development may be either positive or negative, although most parents see these influences as potentially more negative, and there is some evidence to support this view. Our measure of this context, Positive Peer Group Environment, reflects the balance of prosocial behavior and deviant behavior in the group, the level of individual commitment to the group, and the amount of time spent in high-risk group activities.

With the addition of the school and peer contexts, our model of successful youth development is complete. Each new context added to the model improves our prediction of successful developmental outcomes. The overall accuracy of prediction is much greater for differences between neighborhoods (45–89 percent) than between individuals (17–43 percent). At both the neighborhood and individual levels, it is evident that neighborhood and family characteristics have important influences on school and peer group environments. Parenting Practices and age (individual level) are the most consistent predictors of school and peer group characteristics for both Denver and Chicago. As expected, youth living in better neighborhoods and families, attending better schools, and involved in more prosocial peer groups, had the best developmental outcomes.

Some specific findings include:

1. Good schools are found primarily in neighborhoods where families have good Parenting Practices, Parental Conventional Values, and low levels of Family Dysfunction (Chicago);
2. Violent, unsafe schools are found disproportionately in Disorganized Neighborhoods and neighborhoods with poor Parenting Practices and limited Family Resources;
3. Positive peer climates are found in Well Organized Neighborhoods where families have good Parenting Practices and Conventional Values;
4. Females and younger youth have more positive peer groups;
5. The strongest predictor for all individual level success outcomes is a shared effect involving all contexts;
6. For individual levels of competence, the family effect is very strong, but school and individual effects are also significant;
7. Family, school, neighborhood, and individual characteristics all contribute equally to Prosocial Behavior;
8. Family, school and individual effects contribute equally to being On Track; and
9. The peer group is the dominant predictor of involvement in Problem Behavior.

Most of the findings are consistent with the proposed model of successful development, but there are some unexpected findings. These are discussed along with some observed differences between cities.

8

School Climate and Types of Peer Groups

Interviewer: What are some of the other things that are in their lives right now that can really help them be successful?

Martin Park Parent: School. School and they need to set some kind of goal. I know that. And then, kind of take it from there and just work toward that, you know, if they have to do it through school, you know. Or other activities. It's so hard to find any, you know. I really don't know where to go for activities for my kids. Really I don't. I just – they – it's just school, you know, as far as I know. School and but like neighborhood things. I don't know where to go for that for my kids. But they do need a goal and I figure school will help them that way, you know.

Interviewer: Okay. What kinds of things are you afraid might get in the way of them being successful?

Martin Park Parent: What kinds of things. Well, things violent and getting hooked up with the wrong crowd. I worry about that even at school. I think, you know, well, I just hope they don't hook up with the wrong crowd, start ditching school and you know, going out, you know. I don't know what I'd do if I got a call like that. You know, she hasn't been in school all day here, you know. Well, where has she been all day, you know? That's just the crowd, I think, the wrong crowd.

INTRODUCTION

The views expressed by this parent who lives in Martin Park, a mixed-ethnic, Disadvantaged Neighborhood, are typical of parental views of school and peer groups in the qualitative study of neighborhoods. In all of the neighborhoods, schools are viewed both as sources of opportunity for success, and as contexts in which there are potential risks from the violent or aggressive behavior of other students (and sometimes teachers) and from poor quality education. Respondents did not view all schools the same, but instead made clear distinctions between what they considered to be good and bad schools. In contrast to their mixed views of the schools, both parents and adolescents viewed the peer group primarily in a negative light, as a risk factor for success in adolescence and in the transition from adolescence to adulthood. In five of our six focus neighborhoods, comments about the peer group emphasized the negative impact, both potential and actual, of being in with the "wrong crowd" or hanging out with friends who were frequently involved in a wide range of problem behavior, ranging from vandalism to violence. Only in Broadmore, an Advantaged Neighborhood with high levels of neighborhood Organization, and generally good youth development outcomes, was the peer group viewed in a positive light. In this neighborhood, respondents mentioned the peer group as a context in which competition to do well in school was encouraged. This is also the neighborhood in which respondents reported the most favorable overall view of the schools. Parents in the focus group just assumed all neighborhood children would be going to college, the question was whether or not they could get accepted at Harvard, Yale, or the University of California, Berkeley. Along with parenting practices, school and peer group were frequently mentioned when respondents were asked what led to success or failure in their neighborhoods.

In this chapter, we finish the process of building our multicontextual model of successful youth development by adding the last set of predictors – school and peer group characteristics. These two contexts are represented in the bottom two blocks in the second-to-last column of Figure 8.1. We continue with the format of previous chapters, focusing on the impact of other variables in the model on the variables introduced in this chapter, and on the overall impact of school and peer group variables (rather than effects of specific variables) on the youth development outcomes. More detailed examination of the effects of individual predictors on the youth development outcomes will be presented in the next chapter.

EXPANDING SOCIAL CONTEXTS IN CHILDHOOD AND ADOLESCENCE: THE SCHOOL AND THE PEER GROUP

The earliest social relationships form in the context of the family, and typically involve individuals who are related genetically or by marriage. Individuals have little or no choice about their membership in a particular family context in early childhood, and the family is usually (homeless families are an exception) firmly embedded in the physical neighborhood, in the sense that the family resides at a specific address for some ascertainable period of time. Once the individual's social horizon expands beyond the family, the neighborhood is one of the earliest contexts in which intimate personal relationships are likely to be formed.

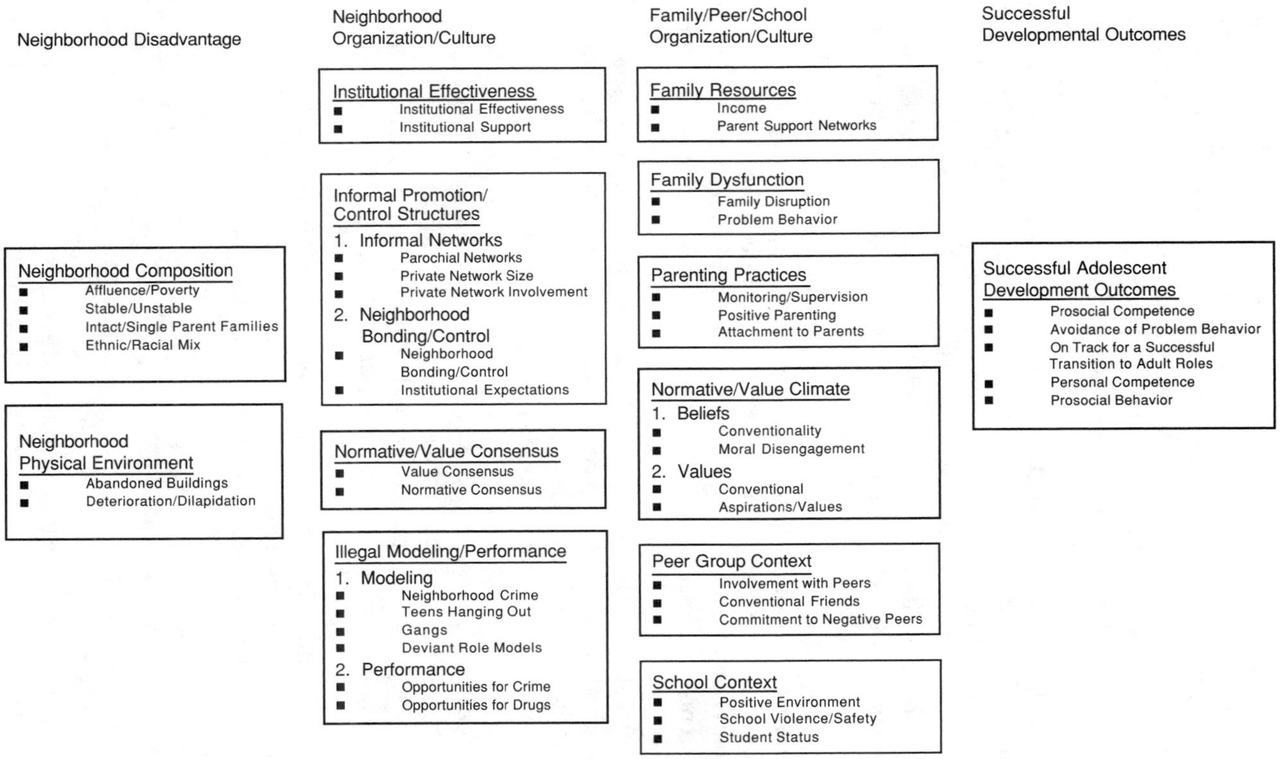

FIGURE 8.1. The Full Multicontextual Model

When we move beyond early childhood, we begin to expand the number of contexts in which we interact with other people and experience the structural and cultural conditions unique to that context. Although we continue to interact in the family context, the time spent in the family is rivaled first by the time we spend in school, and beginning at about the same time but with a more gradually increasing time commitment, in the peer group. For children, the school is also a context over which they may have little or no choice, but which is often not embedded exclusively in a single physical neighborhood from which it draws its students. Schools may effectively define their own physical neighborhood (the "school neighborhood" or the area immediately adjacent to the school) and draw students from many, possibly very different, physical neighborhoods.[1] This is especially true in lower-density suburban areas, and where students are transported by bus to schools well outside their neighborhoods, often considerably farther away than the closest school, as a result of efforts to achieve racial integration or balance in the schools.[2]

At about the same time that one begins to attend school, and increasingly from childhood through late adolescence, the peer group context also becomes an important arena for interpersonal interaction. With the onset of puberty and the beginning of the move toward independence in early adolescence, adolescents begin to disengage from parents and the peer group becomes the dominant social context for establishing one's identity and social status.[3] Unlike the school and the family, the peer group context is largely a matter of choice, and may be embedded in the school or neighborhood or may transcend both.

It is important to recognize that the neighborhood is not the only context in which peer group formation is likely to take place. Preschool introduces individuals to age mates who may not live in their neighborhood, and elementary school typically mixes unrelated individuals from several different physical neighborhoods. In middle school and high school, youth experience the greatest exposure to other adolescents with different backgrounds, values, and behavior patterns. Although the school climate may have some influence on the relative frequency of different types of peer groups,[4] most schools, particularly in urban areas, will have sufficiently large numbers of students that the nature of the school context is unlikely to limit the characteristics or the variety of informal friendship groups that emerge in that context. Athletic teams and other social organizations may also be contexts for peer group formation and continuity. Such social organizations may draw their participants primarily from the immediate physical neighborhood or from the school, but often include individuals from several different neighborhoods or schools, or perhaps from the entire city (especially in the case of sports activities that appeal to a more limited clientele, such as gymnastics and hockey). These friendships may be further reinforced in other contexts, for example participation in a church or school choir.

NEIGHBORHOOD AND FAMILY INFLUENCES
ON THE SCHOOL CONTEXT

Schools are not typically embedded within a single physical neighborhood, but instead draw their students (and teachers) from multiple physical neighborhoods. Different schools, moreover, may draw students from the same physical neighborhood, especially in situations where school integration policies have led to the busing of students to schools outside the school attendance area they live in to achieve racial balance, or where legislatively mandated school choice allows parents to choose to send their children to a school outside (and possibly far from) their immediate neighborhood. The characteristics of the neighborhood immediately surrounding the school, the neighborhoods from which the school draws its students, and the characteristics of the families of those students, all combine to influence the environment of the school.

For this study, the school environment is broadly described in terms of two elements, the learning environment in the school or school climate, and the level of safety or risk of violence in the school. School climate includes the level of intellectual demand or challenge imposed on students by teachers, the degree to which students are respected by their teachers, the extent to which students are encouraged to participate, and the general perception of fairness in grading and treatment in the classroom. School safety or violence includes the extent to which individuals are victimized or know others who are victimized by violent crimes (including personal assaults and gang fights), and the extent to which they fear being victimized at school.

The extent of violence in and around schools has been extensively studied and documented.[5] Generally, the findings indicate that although there appear to be changes in the forms of violence at school (more use of guns and multiple victims), rates of school violence have been relatively stable for a decade or more.[6] Outside the school, rates of serious violence by youth increased substantially in the decade between 1984 and 1994, and homicide rates in particular increased dramatically during this period. Since the mid-1990s the rates have declined, particularly the homicide rate which in 2003 was below the 1984 level.[7] The increase in youth homicide rates in the late 1980s and early 1990s has been attributed to a combination of expanding drug markets during this period, particularly for "crack" cocaine, and to the increased carrying of and use of firearms for protection on the part of dealers. This led to a more general increase in the carrying of firearms by adolescents for a combination of self-protection and status in the neighborhood.[8]

Both school climate[9] and school violence[10] tend to be worse in disadvantaged, socially disorganized neighborhoods. For example, Blankston and Caldas (1998), in a study of 18,000 10th graders in Louisiana, found that being surrounded at school with peers from female-headed households,

resulted in lower levels of academic achievement. Moreover, neighborhood crime rates and measures of community disorganization are among
the best predictors of school violence.[11] This suggests that the correlation
between school climate and school violence could represent a causal relationship (better school climate reduces school violence, or school violence
diminishes the quality of the school climate), or that the relationship simply
indicates that the two are results of the same causes, for example, neighborhood disadvantage and social disorganization.[12]

Family influences on the school context are less direct and appear to be
smaller in magnitude. Although families whose parenting practices produce or tolerate aggressive or violent behavior in their children might be
expected to influence school violence at least indirectly, much of the violence in and around schools, particularly gun-related violence, appears to
be gang related or involve persons who are not students at the time.[13] Students and teachers see it differently, however. According to the Metropolitan Life Survey of the American Teacher (1993), students and teachers
perceive lack of parental supervision at home and lack of family involvement with the school as the two most important factors contributing to
school violence, followed by exposure to media violence.[14] Loeber and
Stouthamer-Loeber's (1998) review of aggression in the school and family
contexts suggests that school and family violence are indeed linked, but
the relationship is not strong.

The influence of family resources on the school's educational climate
is noted by the National Research Council (1993). Families with greater
financial and political resources are less likely to allow their children to
attend schools that they perceive as being inferior. Options include political
action to improve the conditions in the school, sending their children to
other schools (public, private, or parochial schools where the school climate
is thought to be better), working for legally mandated school choice, and
home schooling their children. These different family strategies, and the
differences between residents of wealthier and poorer neighborhoods in
the ability to pursue them, are reflected in the ethnographic data from our
focus neighborhoods. One parent in Martin Park, a mixed Disadvantaged
Neighborhood, contrasted her experiences with private and public schools
as follows (italics added for emphasis):

INTERVIEWER: What's different about what they're doing at the private
school?
PARENT: I think it's the fact that they've got the one on one. Their classes
aren't over-crowded. You know? They don't shuffle 'em through.
they actually come out and tell the kids, "Hey! This is the way it IS.
You either bring your grades up, and you keep 'em up on level, you
work hard at it, or you're out the door!" ... He went to [public school]

seventh and eighth grade, he pulled Ds and Fs. . . . Excuse ME, but this kid's failing and you're passin' him into high school. Why?! "Because come next year, we don't have space for him because of the other kids comin' up." ExCUSE me.

That's not the whole thing of it. He had a learning disorder that Denver Public Schools could not pick up on. We pulled him out of ninth grade, held him back a year and put him in a private school. Private school teacher that he had assessed him. . . . found out he had a learning disorder, and needed special education classes. Private schools can't offer that. The only place that has it IS public school. So we put him back in public schools, but he ended up having more problems, which he'd had off and on all of his life. So he ended up in a treatment facility at [institution]. . . . He is now 19 years old. . . . He got out of that – out of the treatment facility, finished his high school education at [institution] in the [program], and today has his diploma. So, you know, if it hadn't been for sending him to that private school for that year, he wouldn't have his diploma, he wouldn't be anywhere. And I'm sorry to say it, but I really don't think the public schools anymore have what it takes to teach the kids to – to detect, you know, or even – most of the teachers don't even care. I think a lotta times – I mean, I've seen a few that don' care except for that paycheck each month. You know? And that hurts the rest of 'em, you know?

. . . my oldest boy was also assaulted by one of the teachers at [school], and nothing was ever done. The teacher was moved to another school. And I objected and I tried to take it beyond that, but they wouldn't let it go on any further. I even took it to, um, the superintendent. I don't know what HIS name is. My husband and him got into a big argument. They won't do nothin' about it. They just moved the guy to another school, and I said, "Look," I said, "if he did it to him he could do it to another student," I says, "and next time," I said, "that other student might not be lucky that there are other kids standin' around." But that was all they would do! And, you know, I mean, AFTER going through things like that with your kids, with the public schools, you lose faith.

INTERVIEWER: Right. Since most of your – you think most of your neighbors agree with you, the public school system is screwed up, to put it mildly, why do you think they're, um, still sending their kids there? Is it a money thing?

PARENT: Because they can't – YEAH. I mean, how many people can – I mean, like I was saying, my husband and I both work. . . . school for [child's name] right now runs us $200 a month . . . Okay? So, and this is for a small, a small school. Now [other private school] is more in the neighborhood of $200 to $300 a month, for one child to go there. Okay, people have two children of school age, you're gonna pay a fortune. People can't afford that. You know? So if they need – their kid's got have an education, so what are they gonna do? They don't have no choice.

School quality was not considered a major problem in the two less dis-advantaged neighborhoods. In the more organized of the two low Dis-advantage Neighborhoods, most (80 percent) of the parents interviewed mentioned closely monitoring children's teachers, school administrators, and the general quality of education, in addition to being moderately-to-heavily involved with their children's extracurricular activities. In this neighborhood, failure to participate in school activities, was sharply criti-cized by one of the mothers:

PARENT: So you know, where are these other parents? They're the par-ents that need to be there. Their kids need them there and they're not there and that's hard, but at the same time it's nice to see parents are really involved and that these teachers started coming up. They're setting a good example.

NEIGHBORHOOD AND FAMILY INFLUENCES ON PEER GROUPS

In describing the role of the neighborhood as a context for the forma-tion, maintenance, and change of peer groups, it may be useful to make the distinction made by Wellman and Leighton (1979) between the phys-ical neighborhood and the broader concepts of the community and social networks. Briefly, while the neighborhood refers to a physical location, "community" is a broader concept that refers to a pattern of social relation-ships, similar to our description of neighborhood organization and culture, but (for Wellman and Leighton) not limited to the geographical neighbor-hood as such. The social networks that define an individual's "community" generally, or one's peer group (one component of "community") more specifically, may arise in the context of the neighborhood, or in other con-texts including the school, formal and informal social and athletic asso-ciations, churches, the internet, or some combination of these contexts. Increased access to transportation (automobiles and public transportation) and communication (cellphones and e-mail) in the general population may have broadened the scope of potential contacts, so that for adolescents, the physical neighborhood is less important than it was in the past.

Nonetheless, the neighborhood is one context in which the peer group may emerge, act, and persist, and neighborhood characteristics consti-tute one potential set of influences on the nature of the peer group. Although the neighborhood is not the only context for peer groups, it is potentially important. Neighborhood characteristics (disadvantage, physical condition, organization, and culture) may have substantial influence on the types of peer groups that arise within its boundaries, and may form the basis for involvement in other contexts in which peer group activity takes place. The influence of the neighborhood on the peer group is most extensively described in work on informal neighborhood-based friendship groups, and on neighborhood subcultures and gangs. Cloward and Ohlin (1960) theorized that disadvantaged neighborhoods do not all have the same level or type of neighborhood organization and culture, and as a result, disadvantaged neighborhoods with different levels of social disorganization produce different types of peer groups, gangs, or delinquent subcultures. Specifically, in disadvantaged but more organized neighborhoods, gangs, groups, and subcultures involved in crimes for profit (innovative or criminal subcultures) may be more likely to emerge, while in other disadvantaged but more disorganized neighborhoods, the gangs, groups, and subcultures may be more involved in violence (violent subculture) or illicit drug use (retreatist subcultures). Empirical evidence supports the hypothesis that social disorganization is related to the extent of delinquent or deviant peer groups in the neighborhood.[15] There is also evidence, primarily observational, that there are different types of gangs or subcultures, including very informal, loosely organized "social" gangs as well as the more specialized types described by Cloward and Ohlin.[16] The evidence is not as clear, however, on whether the gang types are as clearly associated with neighborhood types as suggested by Cloward and Ohlin.

Families may influence the peer group by allowing their children more or less access to certain activities. For example, poorer families may be less likely to allow their children to participate in sports activities that require expensive equipment (e.g., hockey) or extensive (paid) instruction (e.g., gymnastics). Parents who more closely monitor their children may be more likely to try to encourage them to participate in prosocial contexts (e.g., church youth groups) and to avoid extensive contact with other children whom the parents regard as likely to get themselves and other children into trouble.[17]

Families in which the children are more attached to the parents may be less likely to rebel against their wishes, and more likely to try to maintain friendships of which they know their parents would approve. The research literature generally indicates that families can have a substantial influence on the peer groups in which their children are involved, and particularly in whether children become involved in delinquent as opposed to prosocial peer groups. Several dimensions of family relationships have been found to increase the involvement of children and adolescents in prosocial rather than antisocial or delinquent peer groups, including involvement in family activities, quality of parenting, parental disciplinary practices, and especially parental supervision or monitoring.[18]

SCHOOL CONTEXT INFLUENCES ON
YOUTH DEVELOPMENT OUTCOMES

The importance of the school context and the problematic nature of the school climate in disadvantaged neighborhoods is highlighted by the National Research Council (1993:102):

> Education is widely viewed in the United States as the means by which individuals from economically or socially disadvantaged backgrounds can build the skills and credentials needed for successful adult roles in mainstream American life. For many students, however, schools do not now work this way, despite two decades of public debate and reform.
>
> ... Because of residential stratification, most of these adolescents [from low income families and neighborhoods] attend schools with the fewest material resources and the least well-trained teachers. Their schools use instructional methods that are not conducive to learning challenging tasks. Compounding these disadvantages are generally lower expectations for student achievement.

Education has long been recognized as an important influence on occupational status and, through occupational status, income.[19] As documented by Wilson (1997), the labor market increasingly demands more educated workers, workers with better skills, particularly language skills (reading ability, ability to speak articulately) which may be used as criteria for screening potential employees. High-paying industrial jobs with low educational demands are being replaced in the modern economy by a combination of low-paying jobs (with low educational demands) in the service sector, and high paying jobs that often require a college education or more, particularly in the high technology and information processing industries. Extensive research[20] suggests that school climate can play an important part not only in eventual educational attainment, but also in the acquisition of basic skills that have become necessary in the modern labor market for an individual to be hired, retained, and promoted in her or his chosen line of work.

The influence of the school climate on educational attainment and the acquisition of skills is only one aspect of the impact of the school environment on developmental outcomes. School climate may also affect involvement in prosocial or problem behavior. The belief that a good school environment leads to a reduction in violence and social disorder and an increase in good citizenship goes back at least[21] as far as 1846 and persists to the present day.[22] Learning-focused school settings have lower rates of general deviance and several specific types of problem behavior, even controlling for peer group influences.[23] Having a sense of community in the school is predictive of lower levels of drug use and delinquency.[24] School safety as opposed to school violence increases personal competence, prosocial behavior, physical and mental well-being, and reduces problem behavior.[25]

It appears, then, that school climate and school violence may be attributable to a common set of causes and may influence a broad range of youth development outcomes, including not only competence and aspirations but also the extent of prosocial behavior and problem behavior, both during the school years and afterward.

PEER CONTEXT INFLUENCES ON YOUTH DEVELOPMENT OUTCOMES

As indicated above, we expect the school climate and school safety/ violence to have a broad impact on youth development outcomes. The impact of the peer context is expected to be narrower, but more intense, primarily influencing involvement in prosocial and problem behavior. While the great bulk of research focuses on the negative impact of peer groups on delinquency, drug use, and other forms of problem behavior, there is also evidence that peers have a positive influence on conventional types of behavior and successful developmental outcomes (graduating, college aspirations, excelling in sports).[26] The type of peer group in which one participates can either facilitate or impede the development of personal competence and the potential for adult success. For example, in *Growing Up Poor*, an ethnographic study of young people growing up in high poverty neighborhoods, Williams and Kornblum describe how peer groups and the "street culture" often work against academic achievement and the successful completion of school:

Many of the achievers in this age group (that is, those in junior high school) appear to be hovering between careers that could lead them toward further schooling or work, or toward the faster life of street hustles. They are most at risk of failure at school because of negative peer influences and the distractions of puberty. (1985:28)

The influence of the peer group on orientations to competence and success, particularly academic achievement and competence, has been noted by others as well,[27] but it generally appears from this body of research that family and school influences are at least as important as peer group influences on competence and academic success. Sebald (1989), for instance, found that while social activities were predominantly peer oriented, educational, career, and financial concerns were more parent oriented, that is, influenced more by parents than by peers. Our respondents attest to the importance of the peer group as an influence on success and failure:

INTERVIEWER: What kind of trouble do you think they get into?
PARENT: Well, a lot of them get into, I guess, the gang activity. A lot of them get into partying with the wrong groups or they go to parties that's really not their age appropriate. But they have no other place to go (Latina – Allenspark).

INTERVIEWER: Would you say as a teenager growing up in this neighborhood, what were some of the things that might have gotten in your way, of making it, of being successful?

TEEN 1: Probably the influence of my friends would be the biggest. 'Cause I let them influence me (laugh) really good (female, aged 18, Martin Park).

INTERVIEWER: So you think when you were younger, there were any things that got in the way of you of you doing something you might now looking back, you might have wanted to do? Like were there things that got in the way of making it for you?

TEEN 2: Yes, I think mainly just hanging out with friends. It always seemed to be more important to me than anything else. And now it's just like I could have done stuff. I mean I had opportunities to do some pretty sweet stuff that I passed up, 'cause I just, all I wanted to do was hang out with my buddies (male, aged 17, Martin Park).

The peer group can also provide a positive influence:

INTERVIEWER: And, uh, we were talking... about what you like about your kids' schools.

PARENT: Right. And that peer group is there that expects them to do well.

When it comes to involvement in problem behavior, the evidence indicates that the effect of the peer group outweighs neighborhood, family, and school influences.[28] Moreover, the overall influence of peers appears to be negative on adolescent behavior. Virtually all youth have some exposure to delinquent peers during adolescence and some pressure to engage in antisocial forms of behavior, but it is not until delinquent peers become the dominant influence in the peer group that this pressure becomes strong and the risk for delinquency, drug use and precocious sexual behavior becomes high.[29] While there are differences of opinion about the explanation for this relationship, the evidence suggests that the relationship between delinquent or deviant associations and delinquent or deviant behavior is in some measure reciprocal, but the predominant effect is one of delinquent or deviant associations influencing delinquent or deviant behavior.[30] In particular, the *initiation* of delinquent friendships usually precedes initiation of delinquent behavior,[31] and, once initiated, the influence of peer associations on behavior appears to be stronger than the influence of behavior on associations.[32] There is also some evidence that the influence of deviant friends on problem behavior increases with age during adolescence.[33] Further evidence for the socialization hypothesis comes from research on juvenile and adolescent gangs. Although there is some disagreement over whether gang members are,[34] or are not,[35] more delinquent than other at-risk youths before they join the gang, there is solid longitudinal evidence from several independent studies that once individuals join gangs, their illegal behavior is higher than it was before they joined the gang, and higher than it will be once they leave.[36]

As noted earlier (Chapter 4), short-term involvement in problem behavior may or may not interfere with the acquisition of personal competence, commitment to conventional goals, and access to institutional resources. While generally encouraging some involvement in antisocial behavior, particularly early exploration of types of behavior considered appropriate only for adults (sex, alcohol, and drugs), peer influence can also encourage positive goals, academic achievement and the development of social skills. There is some evidence that peer influence on these positive outcomes may be as strong their influence on problem behavior.[37]

NEIGHBORHOOD, FAMILY, SCHOOL, AND PEER GROUP: THE MULTIPLE CONTEXTS OF ADOLESCENCE

With the introduction of the school and peer group contexts, our model becomes more complex, and more consistent with the complexity of the real world of multiple relationships in multiple physical and social settings. As Elliott, Williams, and Hamburg (1998:379) conclude, neighborhood, family, peer group, and school are interconnected. These social contexts, and their influences on individuals, overlap. With respect to youth development outcomes, we may expect some influence from all four contexts, but there likely are differences in the relative strength of those relationships for different outcomes. We would expect that the inclusion of school climate and school violence, and to a lesser extent the inclusion of prosocial peer group climate, would improve our ability to predict competence and general success outcomes, possibly with some decrease in the apparent direct effect of family variables. For prosocial behavior and even more for problem behavior, we would expect the influence of the peer group to predominate. In prior research there is mixed evidence on whether neighborhood, family, and school characteristics have any direct impact on prosocial and problem behavior once peer group characteristics have been controlled.[38] Prior studies also suggest the impact of the family on problem behavior is substantially diminished in the presence of controls for the peer group climate,[39] but the impact of the school on problem and prosocial behavior appears to persist even when peer group climate is included in the model.[40]

MEASURES OF SCHOOL AND PEER GROUP VARIABLES

The school and peer group measures are summarized in Table 8.1. Technically, individuals who are not enrolled in school are not directly exposed to a school environment, although the school environment they experienced in the past may at least indirectly affect their present environment and

TABLE 8.1. School and Peer Group Measures

	Number of Items		Reliability (Cronbach's alpha)	
	Chicago	Denver	Chicago	Denver
Student Status	–	1	n/a	n/a
Positive School Environment	2	4	.35	.68
1. Teacher Respect	2	3	.58	.59
2. Ease of Participation	–	5	n/a	.49
3. Rules and Fairness	–	4	n/a	.67
4. Positive Learning Environment	6	5	.91	.73
School Violence/Safety	3	13	.57	.87
Positive Peer Group Environment	3	3	.41	.63
1. Conventional Friends	2	2	.51	.65
a. Prosocial Friends	5	5	.79	.64
b. Delinquent Peers	3	5	.59	.68
2. Commitment to Troublesome Peers	1	3	n/a	.83
3. Involvement in Potentially Negative Group Situations	1	4	n/a	n/a

behavior. Whether an individual is enrolled in school, however, may be important, especially for respondents in the ages we are studying. Being in school is one indication that the individual is still on what most would consider an appropriate trajectory, engaging in age-appropriate behavior, whether the school in question is middle school or junior high school, high school, or college.

For ages 10–12, being in an age-appropriate grade in school is one component of the On Track youth development outcome measure; enrollment is not a component of On Track for the other ages, but grade point average, which is only available for respondents enrolled in school, is. Grades in school and involvement in school athletics or activities, all presupposing enrollment in school, are also elements of Prosocial Behavior, another youth development outcome measure. Attachment to school and educational expectations (not dependent on, but almost certainly influenced by, school enrollment) are components of Personal Competence, a third youth development outcome. Thus to some extent, school enrollment is used not only as a predictor, but also as a part of three of our four youth development outcome measures. Problem Behavior is the only youth development outcome measure that is operationally (i.e., in terms of measurement) independent of school enrollment. Of all the Denver respondents, 67 (8.2 percent) were not enrolled in school at the time of the interview. Of the 67 not in school, 29 reported that they had graduated from high school or received their GED, 35 reported that they had not yet graduated, and of these, 33 reported that they had dropped out of school. An additional eight respondents reported being in school *and* having received their GED or graduated. These students were presumably enrolled in vocational or higher education programs. Comparisons among students, graduates, and dropouts[41] indicated that graduates were not systematically or consistently different from students, but both graduates and students were consistently and statistically significantly different from dropouts with respect to Personal Competence, On Track, neighborhood Deterioration, neighborhood Disadvantage, neighborhood Organization, and Family Income. For this reason, in examining the impact of not being in school on the youth development outcome variables, graduates are treated as being essentially the same as enrolled students, but dropouts are considered distinct from both, and form a separate group. For Chicago, based on information about enrollment in the previous academic year, there were only seven children (0.84 percent of the total sample) who were not attending school in the previous year, a number too small for any meaningful analysis as a separate group.

While it is necessary to consider the impact of school enrollment on youth development outcome variables, because most (92 percent) of our sample is in school, we focus on the impact of school climate, and on the subsample of students who are enrolled, through most of the analysis. This effectively eliminates the potential circularity between school and youth development outcome variables. Originally, school environment was considered as a single conceptual domain, but factor analysis indicated that one of the six components of school environment, School Violence and Safety Concerns (hereafter, School Violence/Safety), constituted a separate dimension. As indicated in Table 8.1, therefore, there are three school measures for Denver: Student Status (whether the individual has dropped out of school, as opposed to being either enrolled, graduated, or a recipient of a GED), Positive School Environment, and School Violence/Safety. Student Status is a simple yes–no dichotomy, available for Denver but not for Chicago (as noted above), which is used separately from Positive School Environment and School Violence/Safety because the latter two measures have no data for dropouts (or for individuals who are no longer in school because they have graduated or received their GED). Positive School Environment for Denver reflects the extent to which teachers respect students, students find it easy to participate in school activities and decision making, rules and their enforcement are perceived as fair, and teachers provide an environment conducive to learning, all based on responses from students. For Chicago, data were not available on ease of participation or rules and fairness in school, so the Chicago index of Positive School Environment is based on the remaining two components, teacher Respect and

Positive Learning Environment. School Violence/Safety indicates how safe or threatened students feel in and around school, and the extent to which there is violence and conflict (including gang fighting and ethnic conflict) at school. A high score indicates a high level of violence and concerns about safety.

Positive Peer Group Environment indicates the extent to which an individual's friends are involved in Prosocial Behavior or (negatively) illegal behavior, the willingness or unwillingness of the individual to continue to hang out with friends who were getting into trouble with family, school, or the criminal justice system, and the amount of time spent in group situations potentially conducive to illegal or deviant behavior (time in groups where adults are not present, including mixed-sex groups and groups where alcohol or drugs are available).

Bivariate relationships among the school and peer group variables, and between the school and peer group variables and other variables in the model, can be found in Table A8.1 in Appendix A. Being in school (Denver) is associated with having a more Positive Peer Group Environment ($r = .264$). The relationships between the other Denver school and peer group measures are all statistically significant and in the expected direction (correlations range from .27 to .49). For Chicago, all of the correlations are statistically significant and in the expected direction. School Violence/Safety is negatively related to Positive School Environment ($r = -.248$) and to Positive Peer Group Environment ($r = -.440$), and Positive School Environment and Positive Peer Group Environment are positively related to each other ($r = .277$).

SCHOOL AND PEER GROUP CHARACTERISTICS
BY TYPE OF NEIGHBORHOOD

Figures 8.2, 8.3, and 8.4 show the averages, minimums, and maximums for the school and peer group characteristics for different types of neighborhoods as defined by neighborhood physical Deterioration, Disadvantage, and Organization. In Denver, there is no statistically significant difference between physically better and worse neighborhoods with respect to school environment or peer group climate. There are differences, however, in School Enrollment and School Violence/Safety. In Well-Kept Neighborhoods, an average of 99 percent of the respondents are either in school or graduated, compared with an average of 93 percent in Deteriorated Neighborhoods. Perhaps more informative is the fact that in all of the Well-Kept Neighborhoods, over 90 percent of the respondents are in school or have graduated, while the lowest rate of in school/graduation for Deteriorated Neighborhoods drops almost as low as 80 percent. School Violence/Safety is higher in Deteriorated Neighborhoods, and the minimum level of School Violence/Safety in these Deteriorated Neighborhoods is higher than the average for Well-Kept Neighborhoods. Schools in Deteriorated

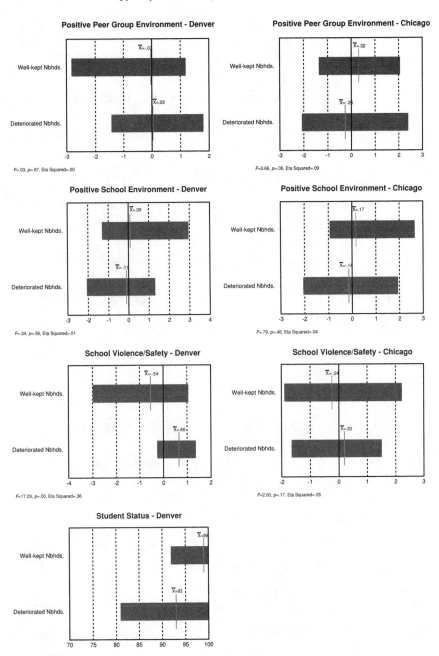

FIGURE 8.2. Neighborhood Peer Group and School Characteristics by Level of Physical Deterioration

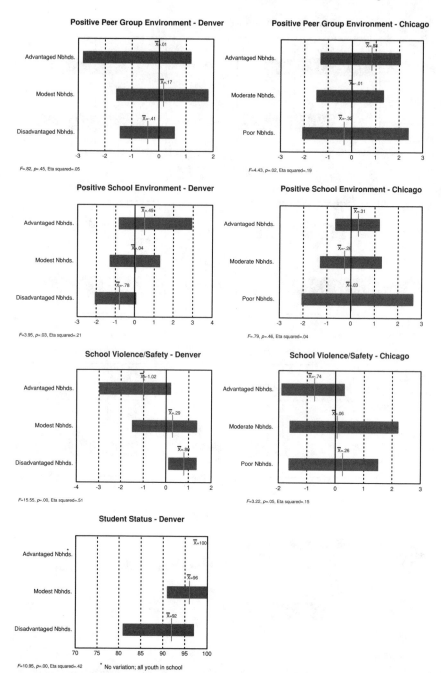

FIGURE 8.3. Neighborhood Peer Group and School Characteristics by Level of Disadvantage/Poverty

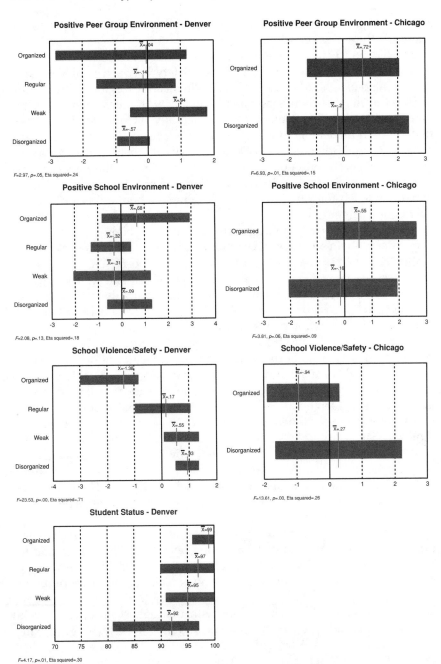

FIGURE 8.4. Neighborhood Peer Group and School Characteristics by Level of Organization

Neighborhoods are quite uniformly seen as violent, unsafe places by youth attending these Denver schools.

In Chicago, there is no statistically significant difference in Positive School Environment or School Violence/Safety between Well-Kept and Deteriorated Neighborhoods. Differences in mean scores for the two types of physical neighborhoods are small, and there is much overlap in the ranges. The Well-Kept Neighborhoods actually include neighborhoods that are both higher *and* lower on School Violence/Safety than the Deteriorated Neighborhoods. As in Denver, physically better neighborhoods have better peer group environments on average, but the range for the Deteriorated Neighborhoods includes both lower minimum and higher maximum levels than are found in Well-Kept Neighborhoods for Positive Peer Group Environment.

In Denver's socioeconomically Advantaged Neighborhoods, *all* of the respondents are in school or have graduated; 96 percent in Modest Neighborhoods and 92 percent in Disadvantaged Neighborhoods are in school or have graduated. Again, the minimum rates of being in school or graduated may be even more informative: 100 percent for Advantaged Neighborhoods, a little over 90 percent for Modest Neighborhoods, and just over 80 percent for Disadvantaged Neighborhoods.

Positive School Environment and School Violence/Safety both vary systematically by neighborhood Disadvantage. Nearly all of the Disadvantaged Neighborhoods have below average scores on Positive School Environment, while the best school environments are found, predictably, in Advantaged Neighborhoods. For School Violence/Safety, the differences among types of neighborhoods are even more striking. School Violence/Safety is always high (above the mean) in Disadvantaged Neighborhoods, and almost always low (below the mean) in Advantaged Neighborhoods, with little or no overlap in levels of School Violence/Safety between Advantaged and Disadvantaged Neighborhoods. There is no statistically significant difference among more and less advantaged neighborhoods on Positive Peer Group Environment.[42]

In Chicago, in contrast to Denver, there was no statistically significant difference among Advantaged, Moderate, and Poor Neighborhoods in school environment. For School Violence/Safety, the Chicago results are more consistent with the results for Denver. Neighborhoods at different levels of poverty have different levels of School Violence/Safety, with similar minimum levels of violence, but with the highest maximum levels of violence in Moderate Neighborhoods, and the lowest levels in Advantaged Neighborhoods. Average levels of School Violence/Safety follow the expected pattern of being lowest in Advantaged Neighborhoods and highest in Poor Neighborhoods. The sharpest distinction appears to be between the Advantaged Neighborhoods and the other two types, with *maximum* levels of school violence in Advantaged Neighborhoods reaching levels near the *average* levels of school violence found in the other two types of neighborhoods. In a second contrast with Denver, Positive Peer Group Environment was statistically significantly related to neighborhood Poverty in Chicago, with the expected pattern that, on average, the most favorable peer group climate occurs in Advantaged Neighborhoods, and the least favorable in Poor Neighborhoods. Poor Neighborhoods include both the highest and the lowest levels of Positive Peer Group Environment, while Moderate Neighborhoods have the narrowest range on Positive Peer Group Environment.

In neighborhoods with good Organization in Denver, an average of 99 percent and a minimum of 95 percent of respondents are in school or graduated. For both Regular and Weak (organized) Neighborhoods, the minimum percent in school or graduated is about 90 percent, and the averages of 97 percent for Regular Neighborhoods and 95 percent for Weak Neighborhoods are not very different. The biggest difference is between Disorganized Neighborhoods and the other three neighborhood organization types; 92 percent are in school or graduated, the minimum percent in school or graduated is just above 80 percent, and none of the Disorganized Neighborhoods has 100 percent of its respondents in school or graduated. There is no statistically significant difference between neighborhood organization types for Positive School Environment in Denver, but there are sharp differences among neighborhood types for School Violence/Safety. Disorganized Neighborhoods have the highest levels of school violence, consistently above the average for Denver. Even more significant, the lowest levels of School Violence/Safety in Disorganized Neighborhoods are substantially higher than the highest levels found in Organized Neighborhoods; these are huge differences. School Violence/Safety varies directly by level of neighborhood Organization and this relationship is quite strong, with type of organization accounting for more than 70 percent of the variance in levels of School Violence/Safety. In Chicago, both Positive School Environment and School Violence/Safety are statistically significantly related to type of neighborhood organization, which does the best job of the three neighborhood-level variables in capturing differences by neighborhoods. Positive School Environment and School Violence/Safety are both better in Organized Neighborhoods.

Finally, in contrast to the results for types of deteriorated and disadvantaged neighborhoods in Denver, type of neighborhood organization is significantly related to Positive Peer Group Environment, explaining 24 percent of the variance. The best peer group climates, in terms of averages, minimums, and maximums, are surprisingly found in Weak Neighborhoods. Disorganized Neighborhoods consistently have Positive Peer Group Environments that are worse than average, but based on minimum levels of Positive Peer Group Environment, the worst peer environments occur, remarkably, in Organized Neighborhoods, followed by Regular Neighborhoods. Balancing this is the fact that Organized and Regular Neighborhoods also have higher maximum and average levels of Positive

Peer Group Environment than Disorganized Neighborhoods. For Chicago, we also find a significant relationship between type of neighborhood organization and Positive Peer Group Environment, with the expected pattern that average peer climate is better in Organized than in Disorganized Neighborhoods. Type of neighborhood organization explains 15 percent of the variance in Positive Peer Group Environment for Chicago and 24 percent in Denver.[43]

In summary, the most consistent results are the absence of any relationship between Positive School Environment and physical Deterioration, the strong relationship of School Violence/Safety to Disadvantage and Disorganization, and the unexpected relationship of Positive Peer Group Environment to neighborhood Disorganization in Denver.

SCHOOL, PEER GROUP, AND FAMILY CHARACTERISTICS

How are the characteristics of families within the neighborhood related to the characteristics of schools and peer groups in which neighborhood adolescents are involved? Because our measures of family context are individual-level measures and we were not able to develop a single summary classification for the family context, the number of relationships to examine is too large to use the same approach we have used to examine neighborhood effects on school and peer group characteristics. Instead, we calculated the correlation between each of the family characteristics and the school and peer group characteristics, *all aggregated to the neighborhood level*. These correlations are found in Table 8.2. For Denver only, Table 8.2 also includes an estimate of the combined effect of all family characteristics on school and peer group characteristics (R^2 in the table). The R^2 value indicates the overall strength of the relationship of all of the family variables (combined) to each of the school and peer group context measures, *if* we ignore the effects of the neighborhood (and other) variables.[44] Here the focus is only on the relationship of neighborhood-level family characteristics to school and peer group characteristics; a more complete description of the relationship of the school and peer group contexts to the neighborhood and family contexts will be presented later.

For Student Status in Denver, Family Dysfunction and Parental Conventional Values are not statistically significant predictors, but family Income, Parental Network Size, Parenting Practices, and Parental Moral Beliefs are all associated with higher neighborhood rates of graduating or being in school. Neighborhood Family Income and Parental Network Size have relatively weak effects, however, and average Parenting Practices and Parental Moral Beliefs are the only neighborhood-level variables that we would consider to be related to Student Status rates strongly enough to have any practical significance (in other words, an intervention focusing on these variables might actually make a difference) or substantive

TABLE 8.2. *School and Peer Group with Family Characteristics: Neighborhood-Level Bivariate and Multiple Correlations*

Cell Entries: Pearson's r (p) Except Last Row, R^2 (p)	Student Status (non-Dropout) Denver Only	Positive School Environment		School Violence and Safety		Positive Peer Group Environment	
	Den	Chi	Den	Chi	Den	Chi	Den
Family Income	.085 (.021)	.088 (.014)	.039 (.305)	-.180 (.000)	-.309 (.000)	.228 (.000)	-.024 (.530)
Parental Network Size	.087 (.017)	.051 (.155)	.046 (.223)	.072 (.043)	-.076 (.044)	-.084 (.020)	.067 (.071)
Family Dysfunction	.004 (.906)	-.229 (.000)	.063 (.096)	.139 (.000)	.005 (.887)	-.158 (.000)	-.052 (.160)
Parenting Practices	.250 (.000)	.285 (.000)	.388 (.000)	-.181 (.000)	-.259 (.000)	.359 (.000)	.324 (.000)
Parental Moral Beliefs	.107 (.003)	.239 (.000)	.037 (.330)	-.151 (.000)	.028 (.451)	.218 (.000)	.241 (.000)
Family Conventional Values	-.053 (.143)	.291 (.000)	.035 (.347)	-.008 (.814)	.081 (.030)	.055 (.130)	.081 (.028)
All Family Measures: R^2 (p):	.439 (.010)	.425 (.000)	.442 (.006)	.492 (.000)	.863 (.000)	.482 (.001)	.389 (.020)

significance (in other words, our prediction of an individual's student status might actually be more accurate if we knew about the family's parenting styles and moral beliefs).

For Chicago, all of the neighborhood-level family variables except Parental Network Size are predictive of Positive School Environment, and all in the expected direction (all positive except Family Dysfunction, which is associated with poorer school environments). Family Income and Parental Network Size, however, are weak predictors (not practically or substantively significant). For Denver, the only statistically and substantively significant neighborhood predictor of Positive School Environment is Parenting Practices, in the positive direction as expected.

For School Violence/Safety in Chicago, all of the neighborhood-level family context predictors are statistically significant except for Parental Conventional Values, and all except Parental Network Size are in the expected direction. The effect of Parental Network Size is weak, however, indicating a relationship with little or no practical significance. For Denver, Family Dysfunction and Parental Moral Beliefs are not statistically significant predictors of neighborhood rates of School Violence/Safety. The relationship between Parental Conventional Values and School Violence/Safety is unexpectedly positive, but neither it nor the relationship between Parental Network Size and School Violence/Safety is strong enough to be considered substantively or practically significant. Family Income and Parenting Practices, however, are strongly associated with School Violence/Safety and in the expected (negative) direction.

In Chicago, neighborhood-level Family Income, Family Dysfunction, Parenting Practices and Parental Moral Beliefs are all significantly associated with the neighborhood's Positive Peer Group Environment. Parental Network Size is unexpectedly negatively associated with Positive Peer Group Environment, but once again is too weak to be of practical significance. For Denver, Family Income and Family Dysfunction are not statistically significantly associated with a Positive Peer Group Environment in the neighborhood. The other four family context variables are statistically significantly related to Positive Peer Group Environment, and in the expected direction, but only Parenting Practices and Parental Moral Beliefs are sufficiently strongly related to Positive Peer Group Environment to be considered practically significant.

Taken all together, family variables explain over 40 percent of the variance in Student Status and Positive School Environment, a little over a third of the variance in Positive Peer Group Environment, and over 85 percent of the variance in School Violence/Safety, at the neighborhood level. All of the correlations that are both (1) statistically significant, and (2) substantively or practically significant are consistent with our expectations, based on the model in Figure 8.1. Bear in mind, however, that these results ignore the contribution of the neighborhood variables to the explanation of

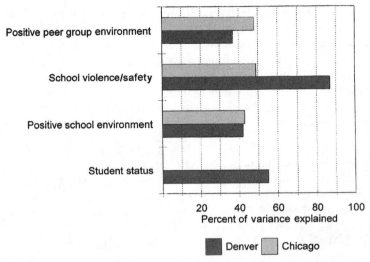

FIGURE 8.5. School and Peer Group Characteristics: Neighborhood Level

the school and peer group contexts, and that the inclusion of the neighborhood variables may (in fact, will) lead us to modify some of the tentative conclusions reached on the basis of these simple, bivariate correlations.

COMBINED NEIGHBORHOOD AND FAMILY EFFECTS ON SCHOOL AND PEER GROUP CHARACTERISTICS

Neighborhood Level Effects

Figure 8.5 shows how well we are able to explain the differences among neighborhoods in their average levels of Student Status, Positive School Environment, School Violence/Safety, and Positive Peer Group Environmet. At the neighborhood level, we are able to explain about half of the variance in Student Status for Denver, and a little over 40 percent of the variance in Positive School Environment for both Chicago and Denver.[45] About half of neighborhood-level School Violence/Safety in Chicago, and nearly 90 percent in Denver, is explained by differences between neighborhoods in neighborhood Disadvantage, neighborhood Organization, and family variables. Between one-third (Denver) and one-half (Chicago) of the variance in Positive Peer Group Environment is also explained by the neighborhood and family variables in the model.

Detailed results for individual predictors of school and peer group characteristics, including Student Status, are presented in Table A8.2, in Appendix A. With three exceptions,[46] the results are in the direction we would anticipate from our model. Although neighborhood Deterioration and Disadvantage appeared to have little or no effect on family characteristics at the neighborhood level (see Table 7.3 in Chapter 7), they re-emerge as important influences on school variables for Denver in the present context. It is also worth noting that, in contrast to Denver's results, neighborhood Poverty and Deterioration had no direct effect on any school or peer measure in Chicago. It appears that neighborhood effects on school and peer characteristics in Chicago work through social organizational factors. To summarize:

1. For Denver, Student Status is related primarily to neighborhood Deterioration, Disadvantage, and Organization.
2. For both Denver and Chicago, Positive School Environment is related primarily to positive family environments, particularly to Parenting Practices and Parental Conventional Values in both cities, and to Family Dysfunction (negatively) in Chicago.
3. For both Denver and Chicago, School Violence/Safety is related to neighborhood Organization and family characteristics at the neighborhood level, particularly to Parenting Practices and Illegal Performance and Illegal Modeling in both cities, and to Parental Network Size and Family Income in Denver, and for Denver, School Violence/Safety is also related to Neighborhood Bonding/Control and neighborhood Disadvantage.
4. For both Denver and Chicago, Positive Peer Group Climate is related to a positive family environment, including Parenting Practices and Parental Conventional Values in both cities, and Family Income in Chicago; and for Chicago, Positive Peer Group Environment is also related to neighborhood Organization, particularly Illegal Performance, Illegal Modeling, and Normative/Value Consensus.

THE EFFECTS OF NEIGHBORHOOD AND FAMILY ON SCHOOL AND PEER GROUP CHARACTERISTICS

Individual Level Effects

Table 8.3 shows the explained variance in individual school and peer group characteristics attributable to neighborhood physical Deterioration, Disadvantage, and Organization, and to family, individual, and shared effects. Student Status is not included in this table for technical reasons.[47] The explained variance is substantially lower than that observed for the neighborhood level and slightly higher for Denver than Chicago. Three quite different patterns emerge for explaining Positive School Environment, School Violence/Safety, and Positive Peer Group Environment.

For Positive School Environment, family characteristics are clearly the strongest predictors. For School Violence/Safety, most of the explained

TABLE 8.3. *Contributions to Explained Variance of School and Peer Group Characteristics*

School and Peer Group Variables Predictors	Positive School Environment		School Violence and Safety		Positive Peer Group Environment	
	Chicago	Denver	Chicago	Denver	Chicago	Denver
Deterioration	0	0	0	0	0	1
Disadvantage	1	1	0	0	0	0
Organization	1	0	1	0	0	0
Family	10	14	2	4	6	5
Individual	0	7	4	2	5	14
Shared	4	1	8	11	14	9
TOTAL*	15	23	14	18	26	29

* Total may differ from sum of column due to rounding.

variance is attributable to the shared effects of the neighborhood and family contexts (11 percent in Denver, 8 percent in Chicago). In Denver, individual effects predominate in the explanation of the type of peer group climate, followed by shared effects and unique family effects, with only 1 percent uniquely attributable to physical Deterioration (and that in a direction contrary to what we would expect). In Chicago, individual, shared, and family effects are again the major predictors of Positive Peer Group Environment, but their contributions to the explained variance are approximately equal, and none of the neighborhood variables makes any unique contribution. Together, unique family effects, unique individual effects, and shared effects account for most of the explained variance in the school and peer group characteristics, but their importance relative to each other differs, depending on which of the school and peer group characteristics is being considered and, to a lesser extent, on which city is being examined. Neighborhood Deterioration, Disadvantage, and Organization appear to have little or no unique effect on the individual level school and peer group characteristics.

More detailed results for individual predictors are presented in Table A8.3 in Appendix A. To summarize:

1. Younger adolescents (school attendance is mandatory until age 16) living in Well-Kept Neighborhoods, in families with higher income and good Parenting Practices were more likely to be attending or to have graduated from school (Denver). African American adolescents are more likely to be attending or to have graduated from school than whites, when these (and other) variables are controlled.[48]
2. For both Denver and Chicago, Positive School Environment at the individual level was better for adolescents from families with better Parenting Practices and stronger Parental Conventional Values.

Except for these two relationships, however, the Denver and Chicago results were different from one another and in three instances different from what we would have expected. In Denver, Positive School Environment was better for adolescents from Advantaged Neighborhoods, families with Larger Parental Networks, younger adolescents, Hispanics, and (anomalously) for adolescents from families with *higher* levels of Family Dysfunction and *weaker* Parental Moral Beliefs. For Chicago, Positive School Environment was better for adolescents from better Organized Neighborhoods, *lower* levels of Family Dysfunction and *stronger* Parental Conventional Values (both directly opposite to the Denver findings), longer residence, and (both anomalously and contrary to the findings for Disadvantage in Denver) *more* impoverished neighborhoods.[49]

3. For both Denver and Chicago, younger respondents reported less school violence, possibly reflecting a difference between levels of violence in middle schools and high schools. All of the other results for School Violence/Safety were consistent with the theoretical model, but not consistent across the two sites. Lower Family Income and poorer Parenting Practices emerge as statistically significant predictors in Denver, as they did at the neighborhood level. In addition, students with lower socioeconomic status and those from ethnic minority groups report higher levels of School Violence/Safety. In Chicago, poor neighborhood Organization, weak Parental Moral Beliefs, and (anomalously) strong Parental Conventional Values are associated with higher levels of School Violence/Safety.[50]

4. In both Chicago and Denver, younger, female adolescents from families with good Parenting Practices were more likely to have Positive Peer Group Environments. In Denver, intact Family Structure, Strong Parental Conventional Values, and (anomalously) higher levels of physical Deterioration were also predictive of better peer group climates. In Chicago, stronger Parental Moral Beliefs but also (contrary to our expectations) smaller Parental Network Size and (contrary to Denver) weaker Parental Conventional Values[51] were predictive of more Positive Peer Group Environments. We will attempt to make sense of these mixed findings in the next chapter.

PREDICTING YOUTH DEVELOPMENT OUTCOMES
WITH THE FULL MODEL: NEIGHBORHOOD LEVEL

Table 8.4 shows the explained variance for each of the youth development outcomes once we add the school and peer group characteristics to our explanatory model.[52] At the neighborhood level, average Positive School Environment and average School Violence/Safety, together with percentages of students enrolled or graduated, can be calculated and included in

TABLE 8.4. *Explained Variance in Youth Development Outcomes: Neighborhood Level*

Percent Explained Variance (R²):	Predictors:					
	Personal Competence (Denver)	Prosocial Behavior (Denver)	Prosocial Competence (Chicago)	On Track (Denver)	Problem Behavior (Denver)	Problem Behavior (Chicago)
Disadvantage and Deterioration	58	45	19	32	6	19
Disadvantage, Deterioration, and Organization (Separate Measures)	78	65	33	51	33	29
Disadvantage, Deterioration, Organization, and Family Characteristics	86	78	68	62	55	44
Disadvantage, Deterioration, Organization, Family Characteristics, and School and Peer Group Characteristics	89	88	71	73	73	45
Increase Attributable to School and Peer Group Characteristics	3	10	3	11	18	1

our explanatory model. For Denver, school and peer group characteristics add little, only 3 percent, to the variance explained in Personal Competence (perhaps not surprising because the explained variance was so high to begin with). The results for Prosocial Competence in Chicago are comparable, producing an increase in explained variance of 3 percent, from 68 to 71 percent. For Prosocial Behavior and On Track, the increase to explained variance is more substantial, 10 percent for Prosocial Behavior and 11 percent for On Track, bringing the total explained variance to 88 percent for Prosocial Behavior and 73 percent for On Track. The largest increase in explained variance in the Denver data occurs for Problem Behavior, which increases by 18 percent, from 55 to 73 percent. By contrast, the addition of the school and peer group variables to the model for Problem Behavior in Chicago increases the explained variance by only 1 percent, from 44 to 45 percent.

Having started with just neighborhood Deterioration and Disadvantage in the model, then adding neighborhood Organization, family, school, and peer group characteristics, we have gone

1. from 58 to 89 percent explained variance in Personal Competence in Denver;
2. from 45 to 88 percent (nearly double) for Prosocial Behavior in Denver,
3. from 19 to 71 percent (nearly quadruple) for Prosocial Competence in Chicago;
4. from 32 to 73 percent (more than double) for On Track in Denver;
5. from only 6 to 73 percent (a factor of 9) for Problem Behavior in Denver; and
6. from 19 to 45 percent (more than double) for Problem Behavior in Chicago

At each step of the process, the addition of variables from the new contextual domain has reduced the error in predicting youth development outcomes at the neighborhood level, substantially in most cases. With the full model, we are able to predict average neighborhood levels of Personal Competence and Prosocial Behavior in Denver with almost 90 percent accuracy; Prosocial Competence in Chicago, On Track in Denver, and Problem Behavior in Denver with 71–73 percent accuracy (in other words, reducing the error in prediction by nearly three-fourths); and Problem Behavior for Chicago with 45 percent accuracy (a reduction in error of nearly half).

PREDICTING YOUTH DEVELOPMENT OUTCOMES
WITH THE FULL MODEL: INDIVIDUAL LEVEL

At the individual level, we cannot include Student Status in the same model with Positive School Environment and School Violence/Safety, because individuals who are not in school cannot report on the environment and levels of violence/safety of schools they are not in; or to put it another way, individuals who are not enrolled in school have missing data on school environment and school violence. We therefore focus here on the model which excludes School Status and includes School Violence/Safety and Positive School Environment. This model is limited to individuals in Denver who are enrolled in school.[53]

Table 8.5 shows the explained variance in individual-level youth development outcomes. With one exception, the addition of the school and peer group context characteristics has improved the explanatory power of our model of successful adolescent development. The increases in explained variance range from 4 to 16 percent. The exception involves the On Track outcome in Denver for which there is no increase in the total explained variance above that found in the earlier model (Chapter 7). However, the addition of school and peer context variables did decrease the levels of explained variance attributable to family and individual variables, indicating some unique effect of the school context and an increase in the shared effect.

For Personal Competence and Prosocial Competence, the shared effects and the unique family effects dominate, but school and individual effects are also evident. For Prosocial Behavior, shared effects are again strongest, but with about equal unique contributions (5 percent each) from family, peer group, and individual characteristics. For On Track, shared effects dominate, with equal unique contributions (3 percent each) from family, school, and individual characteristics. For Problem Behavior, shared effects and peer group climate dominate. The net effect of adding the school and peer group characteristics to the model, when comparing the results in Table 8.5 with the results in Table 7.4 in Chapter 7, has been (a) no change in the variance attributable to neighborhood Deterioration, Disadvantage, or Organization (it remains very small, zero to 3 percent); (b) an increase in the variance attributable to shared effects, approximately tripling the variance attributable to shared effects for Problem Behavior in both Denver and Chicago, doubling it for On Track and Personal Competence, and increasing it from 13 to 18 percent for Prosocial Behavior and from 18 to 24 percent for Prosocial Competence; (c) reducing the variance uniquely attributable to family characteristics by about half for Personal Competence and Prosocial Behavior; and (d) reducing the unique contribution of individual characteristics to Prosocial Behavior from 11 to 5 percent and Problem Behavior from 9 to 2 percent in Denver, and from 5 to 1 percent in Chicago.

SUMMARY

With the addition of the school and peer group variables to the model, we have completed the process of model building begun in Chapter 3. In

TABLE 8.5. *Explained Variance in Youth Development Outcomes: Individual Level*

	Personal Competence (Denver)	Prosocial Behavior (Denver)	Prosocial Competence (Chicago)	On Track (Denver)	Problem Behavior (Denver)	Problem Behavior (Chicago)
Unique Deterioration	0	3	0	0	0	0
Unique Disadvantage	0	0	0	0	0	0
Unique Organization	1	0	0	0	0	0
Unique Family	10	5	13	3	1	0
Unique School	5	0	3	3	0	1
Unique Peer Group	1	5	0	0	13	9
Unique Individual	4	5	3	3	2	1
Unique Interaction	0	1	1	0	0	2
Shared Effects	23	18	24	9	15	15
Total Explained Variance* (increase from school and peer group variables)	43 (+7)	39 (+4)	43 (+4)	17 (+0)	31 (+16)	29 (+13)

* Total may differ from sum of column due to rounding.

the next chapter, we will focus more closely on the effects of individual predictors on youth development outcomes, seeing *which* of the neighborhood, family, school, and peer group characteristics are the most important predictors for each outcome, and which might provide the best clues for developing effective interventions aimed at improving youth development outcomes.

Except for a few anomalous findings, none of them replicated across the two sites, the results from Denver and Chicago are generally consistent with the theoretical model. As we move from neighborhood characteristics to add contexts theoretically more closely related to these youth development outcomes, our predictions improve. The overall accuracy of prediction is much more impressive for differences among neighborhoods than for differences among individuals. This is a typical result when comparing aggregate and individual level findings; as noted earlier, neighborhood (or group) averages in attitudes or behavior are usually easier to predict than individual attitudes or behaviors. At both the neighborhood and individual levels, it is evident that neighborhood and family characteristics have important influences on school and peer group environments. Looking at results that show fairly consistent patterns, age at the individual level, and Parenting Practices at both the neighborhood and individual levels, are particularly consistent as significant predictors of school and peer group characteristics for both Denver and Chicago. Ethnicity at the individual level in Denver is also a consistent predictor of school context characteristics. At the neighborhood level, Illegal Modeling, and Illegal Performance Opportunities are predictive of School Violence/Safety and, in Chicago, Positive Peer Group Environment. These results are consistent with the theoretical model and with past research.

Along with better neighborhood and family characteristics, better peer group and school environments, including lower levels of school violence and better safety, increase the chances of success in adolescence. In the next chapter, we consider in more detail specifically which of the predictors from the neighborhood, family, school, and peer group contexts are most important in influencing successful adolescent development. We also will consider whether these general influences on successful youth development are any different for adolescents in Disadvantaged as opposed to Advantaged Neighborhoods.

Notes

1. Laub and Lauritsen, 1998.
2. Despite the perception by some people that this practice began with the Civil Rights movement in the 1960s, busing has a long history in the United States. One of the authors clearly remembers being bused past the nearest public elementary school to another public elementary school almost twice as far away, not as a tool of *integration*, but to maintain school *segregation* between African American and white students in the rural South of the 1950s.

3. Havighurst, 1953; Larson et al., 1996; Steinberg and Silverberg, 1986; Hauser et al., 1991; Elliott et al., 1989.
4. Laub and Lauritsen, 1998.
5. Elliott et al., 1998, Felson et al., 1994; Kaufman et al., 2000; Anderson, 2001; Ryan-Arredondo et al., 2001; OJJDP, 2001; Metropolitan Life Insurance Company, 1993.
6. There is some preliminary evidence that the rate of school-related deaths increased substantially in the 2003–2004 school year compared to rates since 1998–1999 (Trump, 2004).
7. U. S. Department of Health and Human Services, 2001; Snyder, 2005.
8. Blumstein, 1995; Elliott et al., 1998.
9. National Research Council, 1993; Wilson, 1987.
10. Laub and Lauritsen, 1998.
11. Laub and Lauritsen, 1998.
12. Arnette and Walsleben, 1998; Gaziel, 1997; Laub and Lauritsen, 1998.
13. Laub and Lauritsen, 1998.
14. A minority of teacher and student respondents identify (in descending order of importance) boredom or lack of motivation to learn, gang or peer group influences, poverty, student achievement levels, racial or ethnic background, involvement with drugs or alcohol, and overcrowding or lack of supervision in school as sources of school violence (Metropolitan Life Insurance Company 1993).
15. McCarthy and Hagan, 1995; Menard, 1997; Sampson and Groves, 1989; Simcha-Fagan and Schwartz, 1986.
16. Covey et al., 1997.
17. This strategy was explicitly mentioned by some of the parents in the focus neighborhoods.
18. Aseltine, 1995; Curtner-Smith and MacKinnon-Lewis, 1994; Elliott et al., 1989; Masten and Coatsworth, 1998; Patterson and Dishion, 1985; Simons et al., 1996; Brown, 1990.
19. Blau and Duncan, 1967; Jencks et al., 1972.
20. Wilson, 1997; see also Wilson, 1987, Anderson and Keith, 1997, and the National Research Council, 1993.
21. Anderson, 1998.
22. Hawkins et al., 1998.
23. Kasen et al., 1998.
24. Battistich and Hom, 1997.
25. Arnette and Walsleben (1998:11) note that the consequences of school violence range from debilitating anxiety to personal injury, and to a disassociation from school "that restricts individual options and limits the development of academic and life skills." Lorion (1998:302) lists potential consequences of exposure to violence including negative physical and cognitive consequences, low social competence, difficulty attending to schoolwork, mental health problems (depression, anxiety, anger, stress, low self-esteem, posttraumatic stress disorder), and other problem behaviors (truancy, conduct disorder, perpetration of violence).
26. Brown, 1990; Scales and Leffer, 1999; Steinberg, 2001.
27. Entwisle, 1990; Goodenow and Grady, 1993; Masten and Coatsworth, 1998; Winiarski-Jones, 1988: Fordham and Ogbu, 1986; Luthar, 1995.

28. Elliott, Huizinga and Menard, 1989; Beyers, Loeber, Wikstrom and Stouthamer-Loeber , 2001; Beyers et al., 2003.
29. Elliott and Menard, 1996; Haynie, 2002.
30. Thornberry et al., 1994; Elliott and Menard, 1996. For studies using multivariate models, with controls for sociodemographic and other variables that demonstrate this relationship is not spurious, see Aseltine (1995); Curran et al., (1997); Duncan et al. (1995); Elliott et al. (1989); Fletcher et al. (1995); Heimer (1997); Keenan et al. (1995); Menard (1997); Menard and Elliott (1994); and Reinarman and Fagan (1988). For an exception, see Coie et al. (1995). Although some studies have indicated that the sole or primary causal path is from involvement in problem behavior to having deviant or delinquent friends (Cairns et al., 1988, 1995; Cohen, 1977; Jussim and Osgood, 1989; Kandel, 1996; Matsueda and Anderson, 1998), much of this research is plagued with methodological problems, including reliance on officially recorded as opposed to self-reported problem behavior, or relying on nonprobability samples of incarcerated criminals or delinquents, or the use of cross-sectional instead of longitudinal data, or the use of one or two "best friends" instead of the whole peer group context. Matsueda and Anderson (1998) are an exception to this generalization, but even their conclusions may be questioned based on the exclusion from their analysis of variables found to be important in other studies.
31. Elliott and Menard, 1996.
32. Aseltine, 1995; Elliott and Menard, 1996; Fletcher et al., 1995; Menard and Elliott, 1994.
33. Menard, 1997; O'Brien and Bierman, 1988.
34. Esbensen and Huizinga, 1993.
35. Thornberry et al., 1993.
36. Battin et al., 1998; Esbensen and Huizinga, 1993; Huff, 1998; Thornberry et al., 1993.
37. Brown, 1990; Scales and Leffert, 1999; Steinberg, 2001.
38. Evidence from Reinarman and Fagan (1988), Simcha-Fagan and Schwartz (1986), and Simons et al. (1996) suggests that community effects on problem behavior are weak or disappear when the delinquent or deviant peer group is included in the model, but Menard (1997) found that social disorganization affected problem behavior even controlling for delinquent or deviant peer group.
39. Aseltine, 1995; Elliott et al., 1989.
40. Anderson and Keith, 1997; Battistich and Hom, 1997; Kasen et al., 1998.
41. We used *t*-tests for differences in means with youth development outcomes and all predictors except school environment.
42. Cattarello (2000) reports that neighborhood disadvantage predicted delinquent peer associations and peer associations predicted marijuana use.
43. See Table A8.1 in Appendix A for the correlations between specific neighborhood measures and school and peer group measures.
44. For consistency with later analyses, ridge regression was used to calculate the explained variance (R^2) in Table 8.2.
45. Ridge regression with backward elimination was used to obtain the best set of predictors for each of the school and peer group outcomes (see Table A8.2 in Appendix A). Notice that the standardized and unstandardized coefficients are identical for Positive School Environment, School Violence/Safety, and

Positive Peer Group Environment, but not for school enrollment. This is because school enrollment is not standardized, but is instead a percentage (the percent who are either enrolled in school or who have graduated high school).

46. The single exception for Denver is the positive effect of Illegal Modeling on being in school or having graduated high school. The exceptions for Chicago are the positive impact of Informal Networks on School Violence/Safety and the negative impact of Parental Conventional Values on Positive Peer Group Environment. It is tempting to attach some special significance to these findings, but it is entirely possible that they are statistical artifacts, a result of random variation. The positive relationship between Informal Networks and School Violence/Safety is, however, consistent with our earlier finding that Informal Networks appear to be associated with worse neighborhood conditions in Chicago. For present purposes, it is best to admit that we do not really understand why we get this relationship, or the other two anomalous relationships, and to suggest that unless they are replicated elsewhere, they have no practical policy implications.

47. Because Student Status is a dichotomous variable, instead of the standard linear model, we used a nonlinear Bernoulli model for Student Status. Design weights cannot be used with the Bernoulli model, so the analysis was run unweighted. Additionally, there is limited variation in the outcome; fewer than 5 percent of the respondents neither were enrolled nor had graduated from high school. Many of the neighborhoods had no within-neighborhood variation because all of the respondents in the neighborhood either were enrolled in school or had graduated. The simple analysis of variance model would not converge, and the reliability of the Level-1 coefficient β_0 was close to zero, indicating that the sample neighborhood means are highly unreliable estimates of the true mean. The full model, however, did converge, albeit still with low reliability. These considerations raise concerns about the interpretation of results involving student Status, but in general, the results for student Status were consistent with the theory and with the results for the other school variables.

48. It may seem surprising that being African American would be positively associated with school enrollment, but bear in mind that this is controlling for family Income and Parenting Practices. This finding is actually consistent with results from other studies that indicate higher educational aspirations among minority group members who perceive their chances for educational attainment as good (Menard 1995).

49. The results with respect to Parental Moral Beliefs and Family Dysfunction in Denver and Poverty in Chicago are completely unexpected, and there is no clear, sensible explanation for them; we suspect that this may be a statistical artifact, a result of random sampling variation, but we cannot be sure. The positive relationship between Poverty and Positive School Environment in Chicago is only apparent when other controls are present and the bivariate relationship between Poverty and Positive School Environment is negative (although quite small and not statistically significant). It is highly unlikely that school environments, in general, are better in poorer neighborhoods. The fact that the anomalous findings are not replicated and in fact are contradicted when we compare the two cities confirm that these findings are not readily generalizable to other cities.

50. This anomalous finding is one of several involving our measure of Parental Conventional Values.
51. See Note 43 above.
52. As in Chapter 5, ridge regression analysis with the full model is used to calculate the explained variance. Because there are multiple respondents in each neighborhood, it is possible to include Student Status in the same model with Positive School Environment and School Violence/Safety for Denver, despite the fact that individuals who are not enrolled in school cannot report on their school environment.
53. We did examine a model which included Student Status and excluded Positive School Environment and School Violence/Safety as predictors, and the results were very similar to those reported for the model described in the text. The model that included student Status did produce slightly higher levels of explained variance for On Track (32 percent) and Prosocial Behavior (42 percent), but this is likely the result of the conceptual and operational overlap between these measures and School Status. The levels of explained variance for Personal Competence (38 percent) and Problem Behavior (23 percent) were slightly lower.

What Matters Most for Successful Youth Development?

SYNOPSIS

In earlier chapters we focused on critical features of the neighborhood, family, school, and peer group and the unique and overall contribution of each context to our success outcomes. Now with the full model explicated, we can specify *which* variables in each context are most important for predicting and understanding successful development. And we can address the major questions posed in Chapter 1 – What factors contribute to a successful course of development in disadvantaged, poor neighborhoods? Are the conditions and processes that account for success in disadvantaged neighborhoods the same or different from those that account for success in advantaged neighborhoods? To answer these questions, we estimate the *directly explained variance* (d) for each contextual characteristic and each overall context, assigning the large shared variance effect from our earlier analyses to specific factors and contexts.

As predicted in Chapter 5, neighborhood Disadvantage per se, has no negative effect on youth development outcomes at the neighborhood level. Its influence is mediated entirely by the type of neighborhood Organization, and to some extent by the quality of the school. However, a deteriorated, run-down neighborhood does have a negative effect on neighborhood success rates, at least for some outcomes. Organized Neighborhoods make a substantial contribution to a successful course of development, as does a good family context (particularly Parenting Practices and Family Resources), a safe school with a positive climate, and a positive peer group. With the exception of Problem Behavior in Chicago ($d = 36$ percent), the full model accounts for 62–88 percent of the variance in all neighborhood-level success outcomes with multiple social contexts each contributing some independent additive effect on rates of success.

Individual-level success is also influenced by multiple contexts and individual characteristics. Personal and Prosocial Competence is highest for youth in families with good Parenting Practices and Parental Conventional Values, in schools with good environments and low levels of violence, and Organized Neighborhoods. Disadvantage and Deterioration have no direct effects. Prosocial Behavior is most likely among younger youth in positive peer groups, living in Well-Kept Neighborhoods, and in families with good Parenting Practices. Attending good schools may also contribute to higher levels of Prosocial Behavior. Neighborhood Organization appears to have no direct or indirect effects on positive behavior. Youth who are on track for a successful course of development are attending schools with low levels of violence, and living in families with good Parenting Practices. Gender and ethnicity also make a difference. There are no direct effects from neighborhood factors or peer group climate. Finally, avoiding involvement in Problem Behavior is primarily a matter of the type of peer context a youth is in. Family and school (Chicago only) contexts, gender, and age each add a little to our ability to predict Problem Behavior. The full multicontextual model accounts for 18–43 percent of the variance in individual success.

The determinants of success are a little different for youth living in Disadvantaged Neighborhoods. Good Parenting Practices is the strongest factor associated with high levels of Personal Competence, and this family influence is greater in Disadvantaged than Advantaged Neighborhoods. Both a positive school climate and low school violence and perceived danger also facilitate Personal Competence, but the negative effect of a violent, unsafe school is greater in Advantaged than Disadvantaged Neighborhoods. Living in an Organized Neighborhood also has a positive effect. Going to a good school has the greatest positive influence on Prosocial Behavior, with involvement in a Positive Peer Group Environment, living in a Well-Kept Neighborhood and good Parenting Practices also facilitating Prosocial Behavior. In Chicago, youth in families with good Parenting Practices and Parental Conventional Values were most likely to develop Prosocial Competence. The avoidance of Problem Behavior is facilitated by a Positive Peer Group Environment, good Parenting Practices, and good schools. In Chicago, living in Disadvantaged and Deteriorated Neighborhoods both increased the likelihood of Problem Behavior. Finally, in Disadvantaged Neighborhoods, males, younger children, and nonminority youth are more likely to be "on track." Attending violent, unsafe schools has a negative influence, (particularly for males) and good parenting has a positive effect (only for older youth) on this measure of success.

Overall, the determinants of success vary by the level of explanation, by success outcome, and by type of neighborhood. In most cases, multiple social contexts are involved and their effects are independent and additive.

9

What Matters Most for Successful Youth Development?

INTRODUCTION

In Chapters 3–8, we gradually built a model of successful youth development that included neighborhood, family, school, and peer group contextual characteristics, and individual characteristics. Up to this point, we have focused on relationships between critical features of these four social contexts, and the overall contribution of each context to youth development. We did not go into detail to indicate *which* variables in each context are most important for predicting success. This is because the estimates of effects for specific contextual variables change as we add more variables to the model. With all of the variables in the model, we can now consider the influences of particular variables in each context on successful development.

It is also evident, particularly from Table 8.5 in the last chapter, that about half of the explained variance in each of the youth development outcomes is accounted for by "shared" effects, effects that cannot be uniquely attributed to any one variable or social context, at least not using the analysis of variance (ANOVA) or partial correlational approaches we have been using up to now. There are, however, other statistical techniques for sorting out how much of the explained variance can reasonably be attributed to each variable and context. This involves dividing up the shared effects, roughly in proportion to the direct effect of each variable on the success outcome. The result is the direct contribution that each variable makes to the explained variance, or *directly explained variance* (*d*). This measure has been used in prior studies in demography[1] and criminology.[2] A brief technical description of this measure is provided in Appendix B. In this chapter, we use this measure to estimate the direct influence of each variable and the combined influence of each set of contextual variables on successful developmental outcomes.

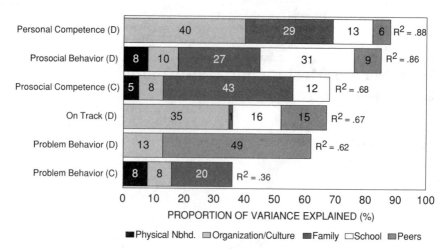

FIGURE 9.1. Contextual Effects on Rates of Successful Development: Direct Contributions to Explained Variance – Neighborhood Level

For clarity in presenting findings in this chapter and the next, we will use the term neighborhood Disadvantage to describe the neighborhood ecology measure used in Denver and the term neighborhood Poverty to describe the measure used in Chicago. These two measures only partially overlap and it will facilitate understanding to remember the difference between them. This distinction will also help to differentiate findings for Chicago from those for Denver.

EXPLAINING SUCCESSFUL DEVELOPMENT
AT THE NEIGHBORHOOD LEVEL

What accounts for the differences in average rates of successful development across neighborhoods? Why do youth living in certain neighborhoods seem to have better youth development outcomes than those living in other neighborhoods? Estimates of the total explained variance that is directly attributable to each context are presented in Figure 9.1. The contributions of specific measures within each context are presented in Table 9.1.[3] In Table 9.1, only the predictors with directly explained variances greater than zero are included (from Tables A9.1 and A9.2 in Appendix A). The predictors are listed in order, from largest to smallest directly explained variance contributions, and divided into more and less important predictors, with the more important predictors in **boldface** type. This division is somewhat subjective, but it does have the advantage of simplifying the findings and clarifying the parallels and contrasts between the important predictors at the neighborhood and individual levels. It also provides a relative rank ordering of the predictors for each of the youth development outcomes in each city. The plus or minus sign in the parentheses after each predictor indicates the direction of the relationship for that predictor.

As expected, in this full model *neither neighborhood Disadvantage nor neighborhood Poverty has a direct effect on any of the youth development outcomes at the neighborhood level.* This is not to say that neighborhood ecology has no effect whatsoever. Rather, its effects are indirect, operating primarily through neighborhood Organization, Student Status and School Violence/ Safety.

Physical Deterioration, does have some significant direct effects in both cities. It has a direct negative effect on both Prosocial Behavior and Prosocial Competence. Moreover, in Chapter 5 we found physical Deterioration had a negative relationship to Institutional Effectiveness (Chicago). Together, these findings suggest support for anecdotal accounts relating poor developmental outcomes to the lack of adequate facilities in physically deteriorated neighborhoods. In what might seem a contradiction to this interpretation, we reported earlier (Chapter 6) that Allenspark, a Disadvantaged Neighborhood, had relatively good physical facilities and yet very low rates of success in the development of Prosocial Behavior. But the residents of this neighborhood reported low levels of Institutional Effectiveness in spite of these facilities and youth reported that they rarely used them. This suggests that the physical presence of facilities in a neighborhood does not guarantee that they will be utilized to facilitate a positive course of development; that there can be an institutional presence without institutional effectiveness. Physical Deterioration also has a direct positive effect on rates of Problem Behavior in Chicago but not in Denver. It also has a negative effect on other youth development outcomes indirectly, through its influence on several components of neighborhood Organization and Student Status.

As predicted, *Neighborhood Organization has a direct effect on all of the success outcomes.* The evidence suggests this effect is weaker for behavioral measures of success than personal attitude and cognitive competency measures. As for specific variables, Normative Consensus is the primary predictor for three of the four success outcomes in Denver. It is the cultural climate of neighborhoods that has the strongest overall influence on success outcomes. For the one exception, Prosocial Behavior, it is neighborhood social networks that account for the neighborhood effect. In Chicago, it is Institutional Effectiveness (Prosocial Competence) and Illegal Performance Opportunities that account for the neighborhood Organizational effect (see Table 9.1). Overall, neighborhood organizational/cultural characteristics account for 8–40 percent of the variance in success rates across neighborhoods. Neighborhood Organization also has indirect effects through family, school, and peer group characteristics, but the direct effects alone are impressive.

Family variables are the dominant predictors of success in Chicago and strong predictors for some outcomes in Denver. It is primarily good Parenting

TABLE 9.1. *Most Important Variables for Explaining Youth Development Outcomes*

Dependent Variable	Neighborhood Level: Predictor	d %	Individual Level: Predictor	d %
Personal Competence (Denver)	**Bonding and control (+)**	**25**	**Parenting practices (+)**	**16**
	Household income (+)	**18**	**School environment (+)**	**7**
	Normative consensus (+)	**13**	**School violence (−)**	**6**
	School violence (−)	**13**	**Neigh Organization (+)**	**4**
	Parenting practices (+)	**11**	Ethnicity (Hispanic) (−)	2
	Positive peer group environment (+)	6	Socioeconomic status (+)	2
	Illegal performance (+)	2	Positive peer group environment (+)	2
			Residential stability (+)	1
			Parent network size (+)	1
			Age (+)	1
Prosocial Behavior (Denver)	School violence (−)	12	**Positive peer group environment (+)**	**9**
	School environment (+)	11	**Physical deterioration (−)**	**5**
	Parenting practices (+)	10	**Parenting practices (+)**	**5**
	Informal networks (+)	10	Age (−)	4
	Positive peer group environment (+)	9	Intact family structure (+)	3
	Student status (+)	8	Conventional values (−)	2
	Physical deterioration (−)	8	School violence (−)	2
	Parent Moral Beliefs (+)	5	Gender × Disadvantage (+)	2
	Household income (+)	5	Ethnicity (Other) (−)	2
			Household income (+)	1
			Neighborhood disadvantage (−)	1
			Socioeconomic status (−)	1
			Residential stability (+)	1
			Family dysfunction (+)	1

TABLE 9.1 (*continued*)

Dependent Variable	Neighborhood Level: Predictor	d %	Individual Level: Predictor	d %
Prosocial Competence (Chicago)	**Parenting practices (+)**	**19**	**Parenting practices (+)**	**11**
	Family dysfunction (−)	**14**	**Family conventional values (+)**	**8**
	School environment (+)	**12**	**School environment (+)**	**7**
	Family conventional values (+)	**10**	**Socioeconomic status (+)**	**6**
	Institutional effectiveness (+)	**8**	**Household income (+)**	**5**
	Physical deterioration (−)	**5**	Gender (−)	2
			Gender × organization (+)	2
			Neighborhood organization (+)	1
			Parental network size (+)	1
Problem Behavior (Denver)	**Positive peer group environment (−)**	**49**	**Positive peer group environment (−)**	**25**
	Normative consensus (−)	**13**	Parental moral beliefs (−)	2
			Gender (+)	2
			Age (+)	2
			Conventional values (−)	1
Problem Behavior (Chicago)	**Family income (−)**	**13**	**Positive peer group environment (−)**	**17**
	Illegal performance structures (+)	**8**	Age (+)	3
	Physical deterioration (+)	**8**	School environment (−)	2
	Parental moral beliefs (−)	**7**	School violence/safety (−)	2
			Parenting practices (−)	2
			Age × Organization (−)	2
			Family dysfunction (+)	1
On Track (Denver)	**Normative consensus (+)**	**22**	**School violence safety (−)**	**7**
	Student status (+)	**16**	**Parenting practices (+)**	**5**
	Positive peer group environment (+)	**15**	Ethnicity (−)	3
	Bonding and control (+)	**13**	Gender (−)	2
	Parental moral beliefs (−)	1	Age × Disadvantage (−)	1

Practices and higher Family Income that account for the family effect on success in Denver. The family effect on Prosocial Competence in Chicago is largely attributable to the combination of good Parenting Practices, low levels of Family Dysfunction in the family and Parental Conventional Values. Also in Chicago, it is primarily higher household income that accounts for the protective family effect on Problem Behavior. Family variables do not appear to have a direct influence on Problem Behavior or being On Track in Denver, but they do appear to operate indirectly on these outcomes via Positive Peer Group Environment.

The school context provides the greatest direct contribution to the explanation of Prosocial Behavior and together with the family context, features of these two contexts account for about two-thirds of the variance explained. All three school variables are significant predictors of Prosocial Behavior. School context variables also account for significant variation in On Track, Personal Competence, and Prosocial Competence. School variables have no direct impact on average neighborhood levels of Problem Behavior, once we control for Positive Peer Group Environment and neighborhood Organization in Denver and neighborhood and family variables in Chicago.

Positive Peer Group Environment is the predominant factor accounting for Problem Behavior in Denver. Moreover, Positive Peer Group Environment contributes some direct explained variance to all four youth development outcomes in Denver. However, in Chicago, it does not appear to have a direct effect at the neighborhood level on either of the youth development outcomes. Positive Peer Group Environment did not differ much across Chicago neighborhoods (Chapter 8).

To summarize, if we focus on the direct impact of the contextual predictors on average neighborhood levels of successful development:

1. Positive Peer Group Environment matters for everything in Denver, and is by far the most important predictor of Problem Behavior; but it does not appear to be important in Chicago. This may be a result of differences between Denver and Chicago measures of Positive Peer Group Environment, or it may reflect real differences in the social processes in the two cities or differences related to the racial/ethnic populations represented in these samples.
2. Neighborhood Organization also matters for all success outcomes in both cities, and is the most important predictor of On Track and Personal Competence (Denver).
3. Positive School Environment (Denver and Chicago) and Student Status (Denver) are statistically significant predictors for everything except Problem Behavior, and are the most important predictors of Prosocial Behavior (Denver).
4. Family characteristics are important predictors of Personal Competence, Prosocial Behavior, and Prosocial Competence, and are nearly

as important as school variables for predicting Prosocial Behavior. Family characteristics are also important predictors of Problem Behavior in Chicago but not in Denver. Taking this result in combination with the results regarding the influence of the peer group, it may be that peer group is more important in Denver and family is more important in Chicago. City differences will be considered in more detail in the next chapter.

5. Neighborhood Disadvantage or Poverty has no direct effect on neighborhood success rates. Deterioration has a direct effect only on Prosocial Behavior in Denver, but appears to be an important predictor of both youth development outcomes in Chicago.

6. Neighborhood Disadvantage/Poverty, Deterioration, and family characteristics also have indirect effects on these youth development outcomes, via neighborhood Organization and Positive Peer Group Environment for Disadvantage, Poverty, and Deterioration, and via Positive Peer Group Environment for family characteristics.

Our full model of contextual effects on youth development outcomes works quite well at the neighborhood level, except perhaps for rates of Problem Behavior in Chicago. For all of the other outcome measures, the model accounts for 62–88 percent of the variance. Again, with the exception of Problem Behavior, four to five separate contexts have contributed independent effects to these success outcomes; no single context captures a majority of the variance to be explained. Moreover, the influence of any particular context changes considerably with the specific outcome being considered: for example, neighborhood Organization has a strong influence on Personal Competence and On Track, but a relatively modest influence on the other success outcomes. Only for Problem Behavior in Denver does a single context (the peer group) truly dominate a success outcome.

EXPLAINING INDIVIDUAL LEVEL YOUTH DEVELOPMENT OUTCOMES

How much does the neighborhood contribute to an individual's course of youth development? Which social context is most powerful in explaining individual differences in developmental success and how does this compare with the influence of individual characteristics? The direct contributions to explained variance for each context and the set of individual characteristics is presented in Figure 9.2.[4] Direct contributions to explained variance for individual predictors within each context and the set of individual characteristics (Age, Sex, Family SES, Ethnicity, Family Structure, Residential Stability) are also presented in Table 9.1. These estimates are all derived from an HLM analysis of the full multicontextual model. Because the Denver sample involved a multistage cluster design and current HLM

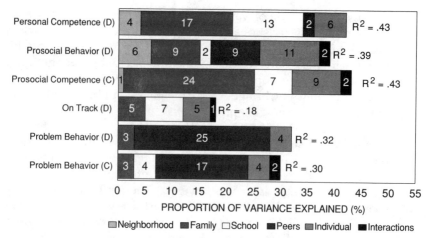

FIGURE 9.2. Contextual and Individual Effects on Successful Development: Direct Contributions to Explained Variance–Individual Level

programs do not control for potential clustering effects, a balanced repeated replication (BRR) analysis was also completed for the Denver site. There were few substantive differences in findings from the two analyses, and these differences are noted in the text.

For Personal Competence, the best single predictor is the measure of Parenting Practices, and the family context has the strongest contextual direct effect on this outcome. The school environment is the second most important context. Together, these two contexts account for most of the variance explained in Personal Competence. Individual sociodemographic characteristics, neighborhood and peer contexts each contribute some explanatory power in the HLM analysis, but these effects are relatively small. In the BRR analysis, the Positive Peer Group Environment predictor was not statistically significant and the neighborhood Organization predictor was marginally significant ($p = .107$).[5] In general then, individual levels of Personal Competence are highest for youths in families with good parenting practices and attending good schools. This is not a surprise. Living in neighborhoods with a good organization/culture also may facilitate this form of success. Individual characteristics also help – being older, having higher socioeconomic status and residential stability, and *not* being Hispanic. Other variables, for all practical purposes, have no significant direct effects.

For Prosocial Behavior, Positive Peer Group Environment is the strongest single predictor. Its positive effect is greater than the combined effects of all family context measures. Parenting Practices account for over half of the aggregated influence of the family context. The neighborhood effect (Deterioration) is similar to the effect of Parenting Practices and greater than the effect of the school.[6] Individual sociodemographic characteristics, when combined, account for about the same percent of explained variance as the family and peer contexts with age and Family Structure the primary individual predictors.

To summarize, having a positive peer group climate, a neighborhood that is in relatively good physical condition, a family with good parenting practices, an intact family structure, and being younger, all predict higher involvement in positive forms of behavior. Being in a school with low levels of violence may also help. Having higher individual socioeconomic status, parents with more conventional values and lower levels of family dysfunction, all appear to *reduce* levels of Prosocial Behavior, contrary to what we would have expected.

The unexpected negative roles of conventional values and socioeconomic status and the positive effect of Family Dysfunction on Prosocial Behavior are small (in total accounting for 4 percent of the total variance) and not readily explicable. We might speculate that family dysfunction leads some adolescents to seek activities outside the family context, in school or in the community, but this could as easily involve antisocial (e.g., gang involvement) as prosocial activity. It is also possible that participation in school and community athletics and other activities (components of our Prosocial Behavior measure) are to some extent discouraged by families with conventional values and higher socioeconomic status, who may instead place a greater emphasis on academic school work, but this would presumably be reflected in other components of the Prosocial Behavior measure (e.g., school grades). Another possibility is that these apparent negative effects on Prosocial Behavior are statistical artifacts, resulting from random variation in the sample, and unlikely to be replicated in other studies. For now, these findings remain puzzling, but in view of the low levels of explained variance involved and the counterintuitive direction of the findings, they suggest neither direct policy intervention with the variables involved nor modification of intervention strategies suggested by other relationships in the model. Despite these findings, it seems appropriate to suggest policies that would improve the peer group climate, parenting practices, and the physical condition of the neighborhood as the primary interventions for improving participation in Prosocial Behavior at the individual level.

The results for Prosocial Competence in Chicago are similar to the results for Personal Competence in Denver. Family environment, particularly Parenting Practices and Parental Conventional Values, are the most important predictors. Taken altogether, the family context accounts for over half of the total variance explained. Individual characteristics, primarily socioeconomic status, account for about nine percent of the variance, followed closely by Positive School Environment, which explains about seven percent of the variance. Again, neighborhood has a very small direct influence but interacts with Gender. This interaction effect is small and indicates that individual levels of Prosocial Competence are lower for males than females in Well Organized Neighborhoods and that they do even worse in more Disorganized Neighborhoods. High individual socioeconomic status and high Family Income also make significant contributions to the prediction of Prosocial Competence.

As at the neighborhood level, Positive Peer Group Environment dominates the explanation of Problem Behavior in Denver, directly accounting for over three-fourths of the variance explained. Although the peer context was not predictive of Problem Behavior at the neighborhood level in Chicago, it is the dominant predictor at the individual level, accounting for over half of the variance explained. In both cities, aggregated family and individual characteristics account for similar small portions of the variance. No other individual predictors account for more than three percent of the variance.[7] The explanation for Problem Behavior is thus quite similar for both cities at the individual level. The only substantive difference is that school variables contribute to the explanation in Chicago but not in Denver. It is primarily older, male (Denver) respondents who are most likely to be involved in Problem Behavior. Ethnicity is a negligible factor (Denver). The same is true for intact family structure in both cities. In short, being in a Positive Peer Group Environment substantially reduces the likelihood for involvement in Problem Behavior in both Denver and Chicago. Having a generally good family (Chicago), being younger and female (Denver), also appear to be beneficial for avoiding Problem Behavior.

Being On Track for a successful transition from adolescence to adulthood depends primarily on the school and family contexts. More specifically, lower School Violence/Safety and better Parenting Practices, lead to higher probabilities of being On Track. There are small effects of being a male or an ethnic minority that slightly reduce the probability of being On Track.[8]

The major findings regarding the explanation for individual differences in successful adolescent development can be summarized as follows:

1. Personal and Prosocial competence are highest for youth in families with good Parenting Practices, Parental Conventional Values (Chicago), in schools with good environments and low levels of violence/perceived danger, and good neighborhoods (particularly females in Chicago). Individual sociodemographic characteristics are also important, but neighborhood Disadvantage, Poverty and Deterioration have no direct effects.

2. Prosocial Behavior is most likely among younger youth in Positive Peer Group Environments, living in Well-Kept Neighborhoods, and in families with good Parenting Practices. Neighborhood Organization appears to have no direct or indirect effects on good behavior in Denver.

3. Youth who are on track for a successful course of development and transition into adult roles are attending schools with low levels of violence/perceived danger, and living in families with good Parenting Practices. Gender and ethnicity also make a difference. There are no direct effects from neighborhood Organization, Disadvantage, or Deterioration, or Positive Peer Group Environment.

4. Avoiding involvement in Problem Behavior is primarily a matter of the type of peer context a youth is in. Family and school (Chicago only) contexts, gender, and age each add a little to our ability to predict Problem Behavior.

COMPARING NEIGHBORHOOD- AND INDIVIDUAL-LEVEL MODELS

While the set of individual predictors differs considerably by specific success outcome and level of prediction, there is more consistency across neighborhood- and individual-levels in the relative importance of general contexts. Moreover, if we consider success more generally, aggregating across all success outcomes, there is some consistency in the individual predictors that account for most of the variance in success at both the neighborhood and individual levels. Summing across all success outcomes does ignore differences by developmental outcome and city, and because there are more measures of success for Denver, this puts more weight on the Denver results. The advantage is that it provides a clearer picture of which contexts and predictors are most important in accounting for these indicators of developmental success. Although it is important to know that different developmental outcomes have somewhat different configurations of specific predictors, interventions are rarely so narrowly targeted. The question more typically is what intervention strategies will work best to improve the widest range of developmental outcomes.

Considering our multiple contexts and averaging across all outcomes, the family is the strongest context for both neighborhood and individual levels of success. At the neighborhood level, the neighborhood context is the second strongest predictor of success followed by the peer group and then the school context. *The neighborhood is clearly the weakest context for individual success, and this is a major difference in the prediction of success at these two levels.* Once again, neighborhoods have very limited direct effects on individual-level success. However, if we eliminate the neighborhood context, the ordering of remaining contexts by their average effect size on success is the same at both levels: family, followed by peer group, and then school contexts. At the neighborhood level, family characteristics are substantially stronger predictors than peer group characteristics, but at the individual level, the differences between all three contexts are smaller. *This is a second important difference by level of explanation: family, peer group, and school factors all make important and nearly equal contributions to success at the individual level.*

The strongest and most consistent **individual** predictors across levels of explanation are Positive Peer Group Environment and Parenting Practices. Positive Peer Group Environment was a significant predictor for four different success outcomes at each level of explanation; Parenting Practices was a significant predictor for three neighborhood and five individual level success outcomes. The average effect size was greater for Positive Peer Group Environment (0.09–0.13) than Parenting Practices (0.06 at both levels), but no other individual predictor was as strong or consistent as these two predictors.[9] Parenting Practices is the stronger predictor for the nonbehavioral success outcomes, and Positive Peer Group Environment is the strongest for the behavioral outcomes at each level. The latter's greater overall average effect size is largely due to the prediction of Problem Behavior. As noted earlier, *a third major difference in our ability to predict success at these two levels is that our predictors account for a much greater portion of the variance in neighborhood-level success rates than in individual success outcomes.*

The differences between the most important predictors identified for the neighborhood and individual levels highlights the importance of being specific about intervention goals. If we are planning to intervene at the individual level, then Peer Group Environment and Parenting Practices may be our most important targets for intervention. If, on the other hand, our goal is to change aggregate levels or rates of behavior, with a focus on improving outcomes at the neighborhood level, then neighborhood organizational deficiencies are equally important as parenting practices as targets for intervention.

SUCCESS IN DISADVANTAGED NEIGHBORHOODS

In this and previous chapters, we presented a model of successful youth development for all respondents – male and female, all ethnic groups, whether they were living in more or less disadvantaged neighborhoods. We wanted to know to what extent neighborhood advantage led to improvements in the likelihood of a successful course of adolescent development. Here, we refine that analysis further by asking whether the individual-level *process* of successful adolescent development is different for youth living in highly disadvantaged neighborhoods as compared to neighborhoods that are more advantaged; whether the effects of neighborhood organization, family context, peer group context, and school context depend on whether we are looking at youth living in disadvantaged or more advantaged neighborhoods. Age, gender, and ethnic interactions are included in this analysis.

For this analysis, we dichotomized neighborhoods. The first group we refer to as Disadvantaged Neighborhoods and the second as Advantaged Neighborhoods. Disadvantaged Neighborhoods include those classified as

Disadvantaged in Denver and Poor in Chicago. Advantaged Neighborhoods include those classified as Modest, or Advantaged in Denver and Moderate or Advantaged in Chicago.[10] Those neighborhoods included in the Disadvantaged group are thus restricted to the most disadvantaged or highest poverty neighborhoods in our samples. Neighborhood Disadvantage was coded in a way that allows for the interpretation of all of the relationships, except for those involving interactions with Disadvantage, as predictors of success outcomes for youth living in Disadvantaged neighborhoods.[11] Interactions between Disadvantage and other predictors indicate how relationships between the predictors and the youth development outcomes in Disadvantaged Neighborhoods are *different* from the same relationships in Advantaged Neighborhoods. The details of this analysis are found in Tables 9.3A–F in Appendix A.[12] Our discussion here highlights only the major findings, in this case only those statistically significant predictors and relationships that account for five percent or more of the individual-level variance in a given success outcome. Moreover, *we focus primarily on those processes that appear unique or substantially different in Disadvantaged as compared to Advantaged Neighborhoods (interactions in the analysis) or as compared to neighborhoods generally.* A comparison of these predictors for the general analysis (Figure 9.2) and in this specific analysis of Disadvantaged Neighborhoods is summarized in Figure 9.3.

Personal Competence, Prosocial Behavior, and On Track in Disadvantaged Neighborhoods

Here we are considering the three forms of positive development in Denver. For all three of these success outcomes, the levels of explained variance are higher in Disadvantaged Neighborhoods as compared to all neighborhoods. The increase is substantial for On Track, but not for Personal Competence or Prosocial Behavior. The processes in our explanatory model appear to work as well or better in Disadvantaged Neighborhoods as compared to all neighborhoods in general.

There appear to be four important differences in what determines success on these three outcomes for youth living in Disadvantaged Neighborhoods.

1. Exposure to School Violence/Safety is a significant predictor for lower Personal Competence and a lower probability of being On Track in the general analysis; it does not have a significant effect on these success outcomes for youth living in Disadvantaged Neighborhoods.

2. The school plays a more important role and the family a lesser role in the promotion of positive behavior.

All Neighborhoods	Disadvantaged Neighborhoods
Personal Competence (Denver) $R^2 = .43$	$R^2 = .48$
• Parenting Practices (+)	• Parenting Practices (+)
• School Environment (+)	• School Environment (+)
• School Violence/Safety (−)	• Ethnicity × Age[b]
• Neighborhood Organization (+)	• Residential Stability (+)
	• Neighborhood Organization (+)
Prosocial Behavior (Denver) $R^2 = .39$	$R^2 = .42$
• Positive Peer Environment (+)	• School Violence/Safety × Age (−)
• Physical Deterioration (−)	• School Environment (+)
• Parenting Practices (+)	• Ethnicity (Hispanic) × Gender[b]
	• School Violence/Safety (+)
	• Positive Peer Environment (+)
	• Ethnicity (Hispanic & Other) (−)
Prosocial Competence (Chicago) $R^2 = .43$	$R^2 = .45$
• Parenting Practices (+)	• Family Conventional Values (+)
• Family Conventional Values (+)	• Parenting Practices (+)
• School Environment (+)	
• Socioeconomic Status (+)	
• Family Income (+)	
On Track (Denver) $R^2 = .18$	$R^2 = .27$
• School Violence (−)	• Parenting Practices × Age[b]
• Parenting Practices (+)	• Family Income (−)
	• Family Income × Age[b]
	• SES × Age[b]
	• Gender (−)
	• Ethnicity (African American) × Age[b]
	• Parent Network Size (−)
Problem Behavior (Denver) $R^2 = .32$	$R^2 = .35$
• Positive Peer Environment (−)	• Family Income × Disadvantage[b]
	• Positive Peer Environment × Age[b]
	• Ethnicity (Other) × Age[b]
Problem Behavior (Chicago) $R^2 = .30$	$R^2 = .43$
• Positive Peer Environment (−)	• Positive Peer Environment × Age[b]
	• School Environment × Age[b]

[a] Statistically significant predictors accounting for 5% or more variance in the success outcome.

[b] Complex interaction. See text for interpretation.

FIGURE 9.3. Important[a] Predictors of Success in All Neighborhoods and Disadvantaged Neighborhoods

3. The development of Personal Competence is more strongly linked to good Parenting Practices for youth living in Disadvantaged as compared to Advantaged Neighborhoods.

4. Individual characteristics (ethnicity, gender, and age) appear to play a more important role in achieving these forms of success in Disadvantaged Neighborhoods.

We noted earlier that the quality of parenting was better in Disadvantaged Neighborhoods when other conditions were taken into account

(Chapter 7). In this analysis, we found a weak but significant Parenting Practices by Disadvantage interaction (not shown) that indicates a stronger role for parenting in Disadvantaged than Advantaged Neighborhoods for building Personal Competence. At the same time, it appears that good parenting has less of an impact on the promotion of Prosocial Behavior; this outcome is predicted by peer and school climates to a greater degree in Disadvantaged Neighborhoods. In sum, parenting effects in Denver Disadvantaged Neighborhoods appear to be stronger but more limited to nonbehavioral outcomes.

For On Track, the impact of good parenting practices, while a main effect in the general analysis, depends on age in Disadvantaged Neighborhoods; it has little or no association with the probability of being On Track for the youngest respondents, but has a strong positive effect for the oldest youth. The role of Family Income in being On Track is complex. Essentially, for older youth, income increases the probability of being On Track and high SES decreases it, the latter effect experienced particularly for youth in Disadvantaged Neighborhoods.

Why should higher SES youth approaching adulthood and living in Disadvantaged Neighborhoods have *lower* probabilities of being On Track? In what way might neighborhood disadvantage *reverse* the expected effect of SES on successful development? There was some evidence from earlier general analyses that SES does not have much of an effect on success once the other contextual conditions are taken into account. This analysis suggests that its effect, once the other contextual conditions are taken into account, depends on the level of disadvantage in the neighborhood, and may be negative in Disadvantaged Neighborhoods and positive in Advantaged Neighborhoods. Why do we not see this same effect for income? One possible explanation is that high SES in Disadvantaged Neighborhoods may be a marker for a lack of success in parlaying occupation and education into better (neighborhood) living conditions for one's family, and the realization of that failure could result in a sense of status deprivation, which may be deleterious to developmental success. High family income, on the other hand, is not necessarily related to high education and occupational status, and may provide resources that offer some protection for youth from the limited resources associated with living in a disadvantaged neighborhood. This form of protection may become even more important as youth enter adolescence, accounting for the observed-age effect. It is hard to dismiss these findings as they are relatively strong effects, but the anomalous findings suggest that there is some danger that the model is overfitted, and the conclusions should be interpreted with caution. We will discuss the general relationship of SES and income with success outcomes in the next chapter.

The different role of the school in Disadvantaged Neighborhoods is also complex, related differently to different success outcomes. Recall that schools serving youth from Denver Disadvantaged Neighborhoods, on average, have substantially higher levels of School Violence/Safety than found in Advantaged Neighborhoods (see Figure 8.3). School violence thus appears to be more normative for youth living in these neighborhoods. Perhaps there is a desensitization effect occurring here. In any case, the negative effect of school violence on the development of competence and being on track is largely limited to youth living in Advantaged Neighborhoods. Although, School Violence/Safety is predictive of less involvement in Prosocial Behavior, particularly for older males in Disadvantaged Neighborhoods, it has no effect on the development of Personal Competencies, being On Track, or of involvement in Problem Behavior. In Advantaged Neighborhoods, it has all of these negative effects. It is also possible that the effect of School Violence/Safety on Prosocial Behavior is a general dampening effect on participation in any activities because of safety concerns. The general climate of the school also has a more positive influence in Disadvantaged than Advantaged Neighborhoods, particularly for younger youth. It predicts an increase in Prosocial Behavior that is not found in neighborhoods generally.

In the general analysis, ethnicity appeared to have a weak direct effect on competence, with Hispanic respondents having, on average, lower Personal Competence than whites (when other conditions are taken into account). In Disadvantaged Neighborhoods, it appears that the primary role of Ethnicity is to mitigate the effect of Age on the development of Personal Competence. For white youth, Personal Competence increases with Age. For respondents from all three minority ethnic groups, there is a statistically significant *decline* in Personal Competence with Age, relative to whites. Although being a minority ethnic group member is associated with *higher* Personal Competence at age 10 (statistically significant for African American and Other), by age 18, being a member of any ethnic minority group is associated with lower levels of Personal Competence. It appears that the rate of acquiring personal competencies begins to slow down for minority youth living in Disadvantaged Neighborhoods as they approach late adolescence. It is likely that they encounter more opposition and barriers to success as they get older and experience the effects of neighborhood and larger community conditions more directly.[13] The earlier finding that neighborhood effects grow stronger with age appears to be particularly true for minorities living in Disadvantaged Neighborhoods.

Prosocial Competence in Disadvantaged Chicago Neighborhoods

For Prosocial Competence in Chicago, there is only a small increase in the explained variance, likely the result of adding the interaction effects to the model. The strongest predictors of Prosocial Competence in Disadvantaged Neighborhoods are quite similar to those for neighborhoods in general: Good Parenting Practices and Parental Conventional Values.

However in Disadvantaged Neighborhoods, these are the only important predictors for Prosocial Competence. The role of the school environment and individual SES and Family Income, important predictors in the general analysis, are not important predictors in Chicago Disadvantaged Neighborhoods. It is particularly surprising that neither Positive School Environment nor School Violence/Safety is a predictor in Disadvantaged Neighborhoods. Once again, it appears that the family is the dominant context in Chicago, even more so in Disadvantaged Neighborhoods than in neighborhoods more generally.

Problem Behavior in Disadvantaged Neighborhoods (Denver and Chicago)

Positive Peer Group Environment, the dominant predictor of Problem Behavior in both Denver and Chicago in the general analysis, remains one of the most important predictors for Disadvantaged Neighborhoods. However, in Disadvantaged Neighborhoods in Denver and Chicago, this relationship appears to be conditional on age. The negative relationship between positive peer groups and Problem Behavior is strongest for older youth in both cities. In Denver, there is also a weak peer group by gender interaction indicating the relationship is strongest for males, moderately strong for older females and the younger males, and practically zero for younger females. It is likely that the strength of this relationship is in part attributable to a feedback loop, a reciprocal influence from problem behavior to the composition of the peer group. Prior research[14] strongly suggests that *initiation* of delinquency and drug use, in particular, are preceded by entry into more delinquent or deviant peer groups, and that the predominant influence is from peer group to problem behavior. Once involved in delinquency or drug use, there is a reciprocal relationship between type of peer group and behavior; those engaging in delinquency tend to choose others who are engaging in the same behavior as friends, and as the peer group becomes more homogeneously delinquent, members become more frequently and seriously involved in delinquent activity. It is the case that many individuals are substantially involved in problem behavior before they enter the *most* deviant or delinquent peer groups. Research on gang membership and illegal behavior[15] reinforces this point: individuals who become members of gangs are already more involved in illegal behavior than their counterparts who do not become gang members, but their involvement in illegal behavior while in the gang is much higher than their involvement in illegal behavior either before they became gang members or after they leave the gang.

   In Denver, two other predictors are important for Disadvantaged Neighborhoods that were not significant predictors in the general analysis – ethnicity and Family Income. The relationship between ethnicity and

Problem Behavior is not statistically significant for the youngest (age 10) respondents, but being a member of an ethnic minority group is positively related to Problem Behavior for the oldest (age 18) respondents. There is an interaction with Disadvantaged Neighborhoods for the relationship between Family Income and Problem Behavior. The interaction indicates that for youth living in Advantaged as compared to Disadvantaged Neighborhoods, High Family income is associated with *more* Problem Behavior. This may reflect a difference primarily in drug use as youth from higher income families have greater resources for acquiring illicit drugs, but it is not clear why this potential is more likely to materialize in Advantaged than Disadvantaged Neighborhoods. More likely, it reflects the greater commitment to conventional values found in Disadvantaged Neighborhoods.

For Chicago, adding the interactions to the model for Problem Behavior in Disadvantaged Neighborhoods substantially increases the explained variance, from 29 percent in the general analysis to 43 percent in this analysis. In addition to the Positive Peer Group Environment by age interaction, the school environment is now a major predictor for involvement in Problem Behavior, and School Violence/Safety is a weak predictor (not shown). Neither school measure was a predictor in the general analysis. For each of these predictors, the strongest effect on Problem Behavior is the interaction with age. One way to interpret this is that the positive relationship between age and Problem Behavior is reduced and even reversed in Disadvantaged (high poverty) Neighborhoods as a result of being in schools with good school climate and higher levels of school safety, and by being in prosocially oriented peer groups. In this sense, good schools and positive peer groups are protective factors for youth living in Disadvantaged Neighborhoods. To put it another way, the beneficial effects of good and safe schools and good peer groups in Disadvantaged Neighborhoods are stronger for older than for younger respondents. For school environment and school safety, this effect is reduced and may even be reversed in Advantaged Neighborhoods (see Table A9.3F). This apparent reversal for Advantaged Neighborhoods is unexpected, not replicated in the Denver results, and should be viewed with caution until further research is done to clarify this relationship. As noted earlier, for Positive Peer Group Environment, it appears that both being older and being male amplify the potential of good schools for reducing Problem Behavior.

PREDICTORS OF SUCCESS IN DISADVANTAGED
NEIGHBORHOODS − SUMMARY

Overall, the multicontextual explanatory model for successful development worked as well or better in Disadvantaged/High Poverty neighborhoods as in Advantaged Neighborhoods. The improvements in explained variance may well be the result of including age, gender, and ethnic interactions in the model. Many of these interactions did not account for five percent or more of the variance and were thus excluded from our overview of the findings. Interactions involving important predictors that did meet the five percent threshold were most often discussed, even if the interaction term did not meet that threshold. However, these models for Disadvantaged Neighborhoods are often quite complex, and Tables A9.3A–F in Appendix A should be reviewed for a more detailed presentation of all significant relationships.

A PERSON-FOCUSED ANALYSIS OF THE EFFECTS OF DISADVANTAGE

All of the analyses to this point have been variable-focused analyses, estimating the influence of specific measures and combinations of measures that reflect individual attributes and characteristics of social contexts on successful development outcomes; on how much variance in success is explained by these predictors. Here we turn to a person-focused analysis (Magnusson, 1988), an analysis where persons are classified as being essentially on or not on a successful course of development. We are not looking at variation in how much success, but whether a person can be considered successful or not. The question is then how many youth are succeeding in various combinations or clusters of good and bad social contexts, again classifying each of their contexts as being primarily favorable or unfavorable for development. We use the On Track measure available for the Denver sample to classify youth. Those having a score of 50 percent or better are considered to be On Track for this analysis. That means the predictive model we use for determining this measure indicates the probability they will make a successful transition into adulthood is 50 percent or better. These are considered to be youth that will make it, those with a successful course of development. We look at success rates for persons in three different types of neighborhoods: Disadvantaged, Average, and Advantaged. Within each neighborhood, the success rate is determined for youth in good families (above the mean on Parenting Practices), good schools (above the mean on Positive School Environment) and good peer groups (above the mean on Positive Peer Group Environment). There is no control for individual characteristics in this analysis; we are considering only the effects of particular clusters of social contexts on individual success rates.[16] The results of this analysis are presented in Table 9.2.

Among those youth who are in good families, 70 percent of those living in Disadvantaged Neighborhoods, 77 percent of those in Average Neighborhoods and 80 percent of those in Advantaged Neighborhoods appear to be on track for a successful course of development. This same pattern of increasing rates of success by type of neighborhood is observed for youth

TABLE 9.2. *Percent Youth "On Track" by Quality of Combined Neighborhood, Family, School, and Peer Contexts in Denver*

Context*	Disadvantaged Neighborhoods			Average Neighborhoods			Advantaged Neighborhoods		
	% On Track	% in Context	N	% On Track	% in Context	N	% On Track	% in Context	N
Good Family	70.0	46.7	84	77.0	53.3	264	80.1	72.4	87
Good School	68.5	50.0	82	77.5	51.4	240	90.3	53.7	63
Good Peer Group	68.6	54.9	97	76.7	63.3	304	89.6	55.7	64
None of the above	45.8	23.2	39	32.0	15.0	67	38.7	14.8	17
One of the above	64.1	23.2	37	55.2	28.0	121	55.2	23.5	27
Two of the above	69.4	26.2	44	73.3	27.7	124	65.6	27.8	32
All of the above	71.0	27.4	44	86.5	29.3	130	98.0	33.9	39

* Each context based on a dichotomy at the mean score. For Good Family, the measure of Parenting Practices was used; for Good School, the Positive School Environment measure was used. Individual characteristics are not controlled in this analysis.

attending good schools and participating in good peer groups. In essence, living in an Advantaged as compared to Disadvantaged Neighborhood results in a 14 percent increase in success rates for those with good families, a 32 percent increase in success for those attending good schools and a 31 percent increase in success rate for those involved with good peer groups. This represents a substantial neighborhood effect on successful development, controlling for the other social contexts, one at a time.

About half of youth in each type of neighborhood are in good schools. However, the proportion in good families is substantially higher in Advantaged Neighborhoods; less than half in Disadvantaged compared to nearly three-quarters in Advantaged Neighborhoods. Good peer groups are found disproportionately in Average Neighborhoods. Youth living in Disadvantaged Neighborhoods are thus at double risk: they are less likely to be in good families and peer groups and those that are in good families, schools and peer groups are less likely to be on track for success than those living in Advantaged Neighborhoods.

By looking at one context at a time, the above analysis does not take into consideration any clustering of the family, school, and peer contexts. The bottom half of Table 9.2 indicates how the *number* of favorable contexts is related to the proportion of youth on track. There does not appear to be any major clustering of these three contexts by type of neighborhood. More than 27 percent of youth living in Disadvantaged Neighborhoods have good families, schools, and peer groups. The percentage for those living in Advantaged Neighborhoods (33.9 percent) is slightly higher, but the difference is not statistically significant. While significantly fewer youth in Advantaged Neighborhoods have *no* favorable contexts, the proportions with one, two or three favorable contexts are roughly similar. *In this analysis, there is little evidence that good families, schools or peer groups tend to cluster in Advantaged Neighborhoods.*

For youth living in Disadvantaged Neighborhoods, about one in four have *no* favorable family, school, or peer contexts and less than half (45.8 percent) of these youth are On Track. Only 15 percent of youth in Average and Advantaged Neighborhoods are in this situation, but the effect of being in unfavorable family, school and peer contexts appears to be more deleterious on their development with only 32–39 percent being on track.[17] Being in all three favorable contexts results in substantially (and statistically significantly) higher rates of being On Track, but here again, the effect of multiple favorable contexts is much stronger for youth living in Advantaged Neighborhoods: nearly all (98 percent) such youth in Advantaged Neighborhoods are On Track compared to 71 percent of those from Disadvantaged neighborhoods ($p = .001$). Again even when youth are in good families, schools, and peers groups, success rates are 38 percent higher in Advantaged as compared to Disadvantaged Neighborhoods.

For youth in Disadvantaged Neighborhoods, the greatest change in the proportion being On Track is the change from no favorable contexts to one favorable context, irrespective of which context is involved ($p = .035$). The success rate for youth in two or three favorable contexts is not statistically significantly different from that for those in one favorable context. The situation is quite different for those living in Average and Advantaged Neighborhoods. There is a substantial and statistically significant increase in the proportion On Track with each additional favorable context.[18] For youth living in Disadvantaged Neighborhoods, the expected gain in successful development associated with growing up in more than one favorable learning environment does not appear to occur. *Contextual effects do not appear to be additive in Disadvantaged neighborhoods; they clearly are in Average and Advantaged Neighborhoods.* This is a critical potential qualifier to the general finding that the chances of a successful course of development are directly related to the number of favorable social contexts or protective factors and inversely related to the number of unfavorable contexts and risk factors.[19] In this analysis, the expected effects of living in more than one favorable family, school, or peer context appears to be seriously attenuated in Disadvantaged Neighborhoods.

SUMMARY

Accounting for Successful Youth Development Outcomes

Our model of contextual effects does a good job of explaining differences in rates of successful development between neighborhoods. As predicted, neighborhood Disadvantage or Poverty has no direct effect on any of our success outcomes, but this does not mean that neighborhood Disadvantage/Poverty is unimportant for success, as there is clear evidence that it has indirect effects; that its influence operates primarily through the emergent social organization and culture in the neighborhood, and to some extent through the kinds of schools and peer groups typically found there. When these conditions are taken into account, neighborhood Disadvantage or Poverty have no additional influence.

Neighborhood organization, culture, and physical environments are important predictors for each success outcome at the neighborhood level. At least two of these three characteristics are strong predictors for each outcome except Problem Behavior in Denver. Although their contribution to our explanation for success varies considerably by the success outcome considered, they are the strongest predictors of neighborhood rates of Personal Competence and being On Track. The school context is the strongest predictor for Prosocial Behavior, the peer group for Problem Behavior in Denver, and the family for Problem Behavior in Chicago. Averaging across success outcomes, the direct contributions to explained variance are about the same for neighborhood and family predictors; school and peer group contexts each account for slightly over half as much as neighborhood and family characteristics. In general, the neighborhood context is the most important in Denver and the family context in Chicago.

For individual level success, there are no statistically significant direct effects of Disadvantage/Poverty; all observed effects were indirect. More importantly, the total set of neighborhood characteristics accounts for only a modest amount of the difference between individuals' success outcomes, and then only for Personal Competence and Prosocial Behavior. Again, features of different contexts play a central role in predicting different individual success outcomes: The family and school are the critical contexts for the two competence outcomes; family and peer contexts contribute the strongest predictors for Prosocial Behavior; the peer context is the dominant predictor for Problem Behavior; and the family and school contexts are the strongest predictors for being On Track. Except for Problem Behavior, the family appears to be the most important context for influencing individual success. However, multiple contexts have significant effects on every success outcome and these effects appear to be independent and additive. In general, individual characteristics and attributes account for a relatively modest level of variation in outcomes compared to that attributable to social context characteristics. The specific contextual predictors that account for most of these contextual effects are: good Parenting Practices and Parent Conventional Values; both Positive School Environment and School Violence/Safety; Positive Peer Group Environment; and neighborhood Organization and neighborhood Deterioration.

Does Neighborhood Disadvantage/Poverty Matter?

The simple answer to this question is yes, it matters. We have established that most of the effects normally attributed to neighborhood Disadvantage/Poverty are not the direct result of compositional characteristics but rather neighborhood organization and culture, the emergent products of the social interaction among residents that does or does not take place in the neighborhood. Living in Well-Organized, Well-Kept neighborhoods clearly contributes to a positive development at both the neighborhood and individual levels. With that understanding, this study demonstrates that growing up in Disadvantaged Neighborhoods has real consequences for the course of youth development. There is some evidence that growing up in the more adverse conditions encountered in these neighborhoods requires greater effort and may produce higher levels of Personal Competence (controlling for other factors), a necessity if one is to succeed, or perhaps even survive here. This finding is similar to that reported by Elder in his study of children raised during the Great Depression (Elder, 1974). But in general, youth living in these neighborhoods had poorer developmental outcomes and greater exposure to unhealthy lifestyles and activities.

We also found that the developmental process is somewhat different in Disadvantaged or Poor Neighborhoods as compared to all neighborhoods or Advantaged Neighborhoods.[20] Both the family and school environments appear to play a stronger role in development for youth living in Disadvantaged as compared to Advantaged Neighborhoods. For example, good schools (and positive peer groups) appear to buffer youth in Disadvantaged Neighborhoods from the general tendency for involvement in Problem Behavior to increase with age; schools have a stronger positive relationship with involvement in Prosocial Behavior for youth in Disadvantaged Neighborhoods. Likewise, good Parenting Practices have a stronger impact on the development of competence and reductions in Problem Behavior in Disadvantaged Neighborhoods, a differential neighborhood effect that erodes as youth get older; having an intact family is positively related to being On Track in Disadvantaged Neighborhoods but not in Advantaged Neighborhoods; and higher Family Income reduces the risk of Problem Behavior in Disadvantaged but not Advantaged Neighborhoods.

However, with a few important exceptions, being in positive peer groups does not appear to be as important in Disadvantaged Neighborhoods. Apart from its strong role in reducing the risk for involvement in problem behavior, the peer group climate does not appear to provide much support for developing competencies. Positive Peer Group Environment had essentially no effect on Personal Competence in Disadvantaged Neighborhoods whereas it had a significant positive effect in Advantaged Neighborhoods; it was unrelated to Prosocial Competence in both types of neighborhoods.

Moreover, the effect of Positive Peer Group Environment on both Prosocial and Problem Behavior (Denver) was substantially weaker in Disadvantaged Neighborhoods than neighborhoods in general. We also found that the expected negative effect of attending violent, unsafe schools on the development of Personal Competence is not as great in Disadvantaged as in Advantaged Neighborhoods.

It also appears that ethnicity has a more negative influence on developmental processes in Disadvantaged Neighborhoods as compared to all neighborhoods. Minorities in Disadvantaged Neighborhoods experienced a decline in levels of Personal Competence with increasing age whereas the general trend in neighborhoods generally was for Personal Competence to increase with age; the tendency for minorities to be less involved in Prosocial Behavior, more involved in Problem Behavior, and not On Track, were also stronger in Disadvantaged Neighborhoods as compared to all neighborhoods.

The results from the "person" analysis with our On Track measure suggests stronger negative effects of living in Disadvantaged Neighborhoods for this success outcome. The cumulative effects of multiple contexts is not as great in Disadvantaged as Advantaged Neighborhoods: both the positive effects of multiple favorable contexts and the negative effects of multiple negative contexts are substantially weaker in Disadvantaged Neighborhoods. For youth living in Disadvantaged Neighborhoods, being in *any one* of these favorable contexts greatly improved the chances for success, but there was little added advantage from multiple favorable contexts for this success outcome. While there were relatively few youth in Advantaged Neighborhoods with *no* favorable family, school or peer group environments, this clustering of conditions had a greater negative impact on youth in Advantaged than Disadvantaged Neighborhoods. This is consistent with a relative deprivation argument; in neighborhoods where there are more good families, schools and peer groups, having none of these advantages has a more deleterious effect on development than that experienced by youth with the same family, school and peer conditions living in Disadvantaged Neighborhoods. Having good families, schools and peer groups, however, does not provide the same level of advantage for youth living in Disadvantaged Neighborhoods; those with these contextual conditions in Advantaged Neighborhoods were 38 percent more likely to be On Track. Neighborhood Disadvantage somehow limits the cumulative effectiveness of good families, schools and peers on the liklihood of being On Track. While we tend to place less confidence in this analysis because it involves classifying contexts as either good or bad and ignores the within-context variation that we know exists, it does suggest some relationships that were not found in the variable-oriented analysis. The finding that there is a relatively weak clustering of these contexts in Disadvantaged Neighborhoods is consistent with the findings from the earlier regression-based analyses and strengthens our confidence in this finding.

WHAT DETERMINES SUCCESS IN DISADVANTAGED NEIGHBORHOODS?

Although we have noted some differences in the processes linked to a successful course of development in Advantaged and Disadvantaged Neighborhoods, those conditions and personal traits that predict success in Disadvantaged Neighborhoods are pretty much the same as what predicts success in Advantaged Neighborhoods. The primary difference involves the variation in the *strength* of particular relationships. Still, the most important predictors are different for behavioral and nonbehavioral indicators of developmental success. For the development of competence and being On Track, good Parenting Practices is the most consistent and generally the strongest predictor. In each case, the positive effect of good parenting is conditioned by age: Its relationship to youth competency levels declines with age whereas its effect on the prediction of future success as an adult is strongest for older youth. This suggests that the influence of Parenting Practices on children's social and academic competence diminishes as they approach their adult years, but remains a good predictor of their eventual success as an adult. In Chicago, Parental Conventional Values is a slightly stronger predictor of competence than Parenting Practices, and like Parenting Practices, its effect declines with age.

For behavioral success outcomes, it is the peer group that is the most consistent predictor. For involvement in Problem Behavior, the peer group is the dominant predictor in both cities; for involvement in conventional behavior, the peer group effect is not as strong as that of the two school predictors, but is still substantial. As was the case with Parenting Practices, the positive influence of a good school environment appears to be strongest on younger youth's Prosocial Behavior; in contrast, the negative effect of attending a violent, unsafe school is greatest on older youth's conventional behavior. Minority ethnic status is also a consistent predictor of behavioral success outcomes: Hispanic and other minority females have lower levels of involvement in conventional behavior while Hispanic males have higher levels of involvement; and older, but not younger, minority youth, have higher levels of involvement in Problem Behavior than white youth.

There are several interesting findings regarding Family Income and SES. Income is related to lower levels of involvement in Problem Behavior for youth in Disadvantaged Neighborhoods, but not for youth in Advantaged Neighborhoods. It is thus a protective factor for disadvantaged youth, buffering them from the potential negative effects of living in Disadvantaged Neighborhoods. It has no effect for youth in Advantaged Neighborhoods. Income is also related to a higher probability of being On Track for a successful transition into adulthood. However, SES is negatively related to On Track for older youth. One interpretation of this combination of effects is that for youth living in Disadvantaged Neighborhoods and approaching their adulthood, it is not their parents' education and occupation that predicts their early success as an adult, but their parents' income. When income is taken into account, the effects of education and occupational status appear to reduce one's chances for being On Track.

The fact that ethnicity is related to higher levels of involvement in Problem Behavior for older but not younger youth parallels the finding that as youth grow older, Personal Competence declines for minority youth while it increases for white youth. In Disadvantaged Neighborhoods, minority youth have higher levels of Personal Competence than whites and similar levels of involvement in Problem Behavior at age 10; but by age 18, their level of Personal Competence is lower and their involvement in Problem Behavior is significantly higher. We also know that the influence of good Parenting Practices and good school environments on the development of competence diminishes as youth grow older, and that the influence of peer groups and attending unsafe schools on Problem Behavior becomes stronger with age. But it is not clear why these age effects are experienced differently for minority and white youth. Perhaps this is a reflection of the fact that during the later adolescent years, the awareness of personal competence depends less and less on interactions with parents and schools, and more and more on peer groups and other adults and institutions in the community, and these encounters are more positive for whites than minority youth. In any event, for both Personal Competence and Problem Behavior, it appears that minority and white youth living in Disadvantaged Neighborhoods are on different age-graded trajectories as they pass through their adolescent years.

The implications of these findings are similar to the implications to be drawn from the findings in the general analysis. The most promising interventions for improving personal or prosocial competence in disadvantaged neighborhoods would focus on the family, especially promoting good parenting practices and on the school, including both reducing school violence and improving the general climate of the school. Increasing neighborhood organization in Denver and family resources (household income; also socioeconomic status) in Chicago would also promote the development of competence. For increasing levels of involvement in conventional behavior, the intervention implications are similar, however; the results here suggest adding the school context to the family, peer group, and physical neighborhood contexts as targets for intervention. The school and family contexts remain the most important contexts for predicting On Track, and the intervention implications, to reduce school violence and improve parenting practices, remain largely the same as in the general analysis. For avoiding dysfunctional, unhealthy forms of behavior, a positive peer group climate remains the most important factor. This is one of the most consistent findings in the study of illegal behavior and drug use, and its support here, regardless of the level of analysis or the specific variables included in the model, comes as no surprise.[21]

The principal intervention implication from the general analysis, to focus on the peer group context to reduce involvement in problematic behavior, remains the same, and school-based interventions also appear to hold some promise. The results for Disadvantaged Neighborhoods, however hint that family intervention may be more useful than the general analysis results suggested. Interventions to improve parenting practices for pre-teens and younger adolescents may be beneficial for reducing problem behavior and increasing personal competence, and may also be beneficial or at least do no harm for promoting prosocial behavior and for being on track for a successful to transition adulthood.

In our general analysis, whether in disadvantaged or affluent neighborhoods, the conditions and social processes occurring in multiple social contexts combine to influence the course of development for youth. These contextual and individual effects appear to be largely independent and additive. For some success outcomes, all five contexts considered here make some significant and substantive contribution; for all outcomes, the family and school play a significant role, and in all but one (Prosocial Competence), the peer group plays a role. In four of the six outcomes, the neighborhood plays a significant role. No one of these contexts dominates all developmental outcomes we have considered.

Our person-level analysis with the On Track measure confirmed this cumulative effect of multiple favorable contexts for youth living in Advantaged Neighborhoods. However, there is little evidence of this cumulative effect for youth living in Disadvantaged Neighborhoods. While the general analysis of the On Track outcome found no statistically significant neighborhood effect on this success outcome, the person-level analysis found a substantial effect – taking into account being in good families, schools and peer groups, youth living in Disadvantaged Neighborhoods were nearly 40 percent less likely to be On Track.

Notes

1. Menard, 1985,1986,1987a.
2. Elliott, Huizinga and Menard, 1989; Menard and Morse, 1984; Menard and Covey, 1987.
3. Table A9.1 in Appendix A presents in detail the results of using ridge regression to estimate the effects of each of the predictors on neighborhood averages for the youth development outcomes. As in previous chapters, backward elimination is used to eliminate predictors whose unstandardized coefficients are not statistically significant at the .10 level (p less than 10 percent that the results are attributable to random sample variation).

4. At the end of the last chapter we noted several problems associated with using the full Denver sample, including school dropouts, for individual-level analyses. For these reasons, we restrict the analysis of individual differences in youth development outcomes in Denver to the 92 percent of the sample who were enrolled in school at the time of the survey. Table A9.2 in Appendix A provides a detailed examination of individual differences in youth development outcomes for both Denver and Chicago. We will only summarize these analyses in the text.

    The direct explained variance presented in Figure 9.2 is for reduced models. Estimates for these models are approximately the same as for the full models. The simplified models allow us to focus on only those variables that appear to have some effect on the outcomes, without any loss in our ability to predict the outcomes.

5. Parent Network Size also had a significant effect in the HLM analysis but was not statistically significant in the BRR analysis.

6. The effect of Disadvantage and the male-by-Disadvantage interaction were not statistically significant in the BRR analysis and the effect of School Violence/Safety was marginally significant.

7. Parental Moral Beliefs and Parental Conventional Values were both statistically significant in the HLM analysis with very small effect sizes in Denver, but neither was statistically significant in the BRR analysis.

8. The HLM analysis produced a significant but very small effect of an age by Disadvantage interaction, which was not replicated in the BRR analysis.

9. These are average effect sizes across all six success outcomes.

10. In most of our earlier analyses involving the neighborhood disadvantage or poverty typologies, this was the critical difference, i.e., the biggest differences were between Disadvantaged/high Poverty and Moderate/low Poverty Neighborhoods.

11. Disadvantaged neighborhoods were coded as zero and Advantaged neighborhoods as one.

12. In the Table in Appendix A (A9.3-F), predictors are grouped by context, with individual and interaction terms, respectively, grouped together. Whenever an interaction between two variables is statistically significant, both variables are retained in the model, a practice consistent with hierarchical model building using interaction effects in regression and analysis of variance (e.g., Agresti and Finlay, 1986). We used the same HLM procedures with backward elimination of statistically nonsignificant effects as in earlier analyses.

13. See Kao and Tienda (1998) for a discussion of how different socialization processes may account for this difference.

14. Elliott and Menard, 1996; Menard and Elliott, 1990; Thornberry, 1998.

15. Esbensen and Huizinga, 1993; Hill et al., 1999; Thornberry, 1998. This finding is not supported by Thornberry et al. (1993).

16. For a discussion of this type of analysis, see Magnusson, 1988 and Haapsalo et al., 2000.

17. The difference between those in Disadvantaged and Average Neighborhoods (45.8 vs. 32.0) is statistically significant ($p = .025$) but the difference between Disadvantaged and Advantaged (45.8 vs. 38.7) is nonsignificant.

18. Of the 12 binomial tests (two-tailed) involved, two were nonsignificant: none to one and one to two favorable contexts in Advantaged Neighborhoods.
19. See Rutter, 1979; Furstenberg et al., 1999; Sameroff et al., 1987, 1993; Hawkins et al., 2001.
20. Stouthamer-Loeber, et al. (2002) report that although youth in disadvantaged neighborhoods were exposed to higher levels of risk than those in more advantaged neighborhoods, the relationships between these risks and involvement in serious delinquency were similar across these neighborhoods. We find some differences in these relationships by level of neighborhood disadvantage.
21. For example, see Elliott et al., 1985, 1989; Simcha-Fagan and Schwartz, 1986.

10

Successful Development in Disadvantaged Neighborhoods

We have invested millions of dollars to hire researchers to conduct failure studies of the poor. These researchers take their notebooks into low-income communities and tally how many people are on drugs and in prison, how many young girls are pregnant and how many youths have dropped out of school. They do not look for models of success – families that, in spite of similar circumstances, have raised children who have refused the lures of drugs and gangs, who have stayed in school, have not had babies out of wedlock.... Scholars on both the left and right make comfortable livings detailing the pathologies of the poor without ever talking with a single poor person.

(Woodson, *The Triumphs of Joseph*, 1998:10)

INTRODUCTION

In this chapter we will look backward and forward: back to the questions we raised when we initiated this study on successful development in poor, disadvantaged neighborhoods, and forward to the program and policy implications of our findings. We do not provide a detailed summary of findings here (see the Synopsis and Discussion Sections of the individual chapters), but rather a broad overview of findings and a discussion of the general issues they raise for present and future policy and programs designed to improve youth development outcomes for those living in disadvantaged neighborhoods. Some of the more unusual or unexpected findings are also considered in more detail here. Finally, some suggestions for future research on neighborhood effects and the development and testing of multicontextual models of successful youth development are presented.

As we review and integrate these findings, we need to be careful not to present an over-socialized view of youth and their development. We found good support for our explanatory model, but there is ample room for personal agency on the part of youth and their parents as they interact in neighborhoods, families, schools, and peer groups. Much of the unexplained variance, particularly at the individual level of analysis should properly be attributed to personal choice.

In this broad overview, there are several keys to differentiate findings that apply uniquely to Denver or Chicago. First, the social compositional characteristic of the neighborhood is referred to as neighborhood Poverty in Chicago and Disadvantage in Denver. Although Poverty is common to both measures, the composite measure for Denver is substantially different and this difference may well account for some of the city differences in findings. When generalizations can be made to both cities' neighborhood compositions, we will use the term neighborhood Disadvantage/Poverty. Second, whenever the outcome is Prosocial Competence, the finding is specific to Chicago; when it is to Personal Competence, Prosocial Behavior, or On Track, it is specific to Denver. The Problem Behavior outcome is common to both cities and when findings differ by city, this will be indicated in the text. A section of this chapter is devoted to discussing differences in findings by city.

BROAD OVERVIEW

How Important are Neighborhoods?

The primary focus of this study was on the role of the neighborhood as a socialization context for the development of youth. We started with the hypothesis that some neighborhoods are better than others in supporting the lives and maximizing the potential of those who live there; more specifically, that advantaged/low-poverty neighborhoods were better than disadvantaged/high-poverty neighborhoods at promoting a positive course of youth development and protecting youth from health compromising, dysfunctional behavior. The evidence clearly supports this hypothesis. *On average*, Advantaged Neighborhoods have more supportive social networks, better institutional resources and connections, cultures that promote conventional norms and values, and less exposure to crime, drugs, violence, and other health-compromising, dysfunctional behavior. As a result, children living in Advantaged as compared to Disadvantaged/High-Poverty Neighborhoods have greater chances of developing the competencies, positive identities, and value commitments necessary for functioning as responsible adults in today's world while avoiding involvement in delinquent behavior, drug use, and other problem behaviors that can derail a successful course of development. Rates of successful development *are* higher in more Advantaged Neighborhoods.

In one sense, this finding is not new. In their recent review of neighborhood studies, Leventhal and Brooks-Gunn (2000) report that most nonexperimental neighborhood studies report significant neighborhood effects on youth development. However, unlike much of the earlier work, the present study also provides direct evidence for the contextual *mechanisms* or *processes* that link type of neighborhood to rates of successful development. Few of the earlier studies cited considered or measured these hypothesized emergent structures and processes. This represents an important extension of our understanding of neighborhood effects. Our findings shed light on *how* neighborhoods influence youth development.

However, the finding that neighborhood characteristics are related to *rates* of successful development is only half of the story about possible neighborhood effects, and perhaps the less significant half at that. While differences in compositional, organizational, and cultural characteristics of neighborhoods account for most of the differences in developmental success rates between neighborhoods, the vast majority (typically 90 percent or more) of the *individual* variation in success outcomes occurs *within*, not between neighborhoods. We (along with others) are quite successful in accounting for the small part of the variation in success outcomes that lies between neighborhoods. However, for any given *individual*, the practical advantage of living in an Advantaged, as compared to a Disadvantaged neighborhood, appears to be quite modest.[1] There is simply much more variation in the quality of families, schools, peer groups, and community agencies than suggested by high-poverty neighborhood ethnographies and conventional wisdom about the inner-city poor.[2] Simply living in a bad neighborhood, by itself, is unlikely to produce incompetent, poorly-adjusted, deviant, or dysfunctional youth, who are unprepared to assume responsible adult roles.[3] Likewise, living in an advantaged or even an affluent neighborhood is no guarantee for success. The explanation for any individual child being successful or unsuccessful depends on the *combined* influences of their neighborhood, family, school, and peer group, together with their own personal attributes, characteristics, and personal choices.

While there is some clustering of favorable family, peer and school contexts within Advantaged Neighborhoods and unfavorable family, peer and school contexts in Disadvantaged/High-Poverty Neighborhoods, the degree of clustering also is relatively modest. Overall, relative to the direct influences of family, school and peer contexts, direct neighborhood influences on individual success are typically small. There are some indirect effects of the neighborhood, primarily through family contextual characteristics, but even the combined direct and indirect effects on individual success are modest. It is important to note, however, that these effects do increase with age and are substantially stronger for youth in their later adolescent years. For 16- to 18-year-old youth, neighborhood effects are often as strong as family, peer, or school effects.

Characteristics of "Good" Neighborhoods – Neighborhoods That Promote Success

While our findings indicate that neighborhoods are not the most power-ful contextual determinants of children's developmental success or fail-ure, they still play a significant role and that role is more important for some developmental outcomes than others (see Figure 9.2). What have we learned about neighborhood characteristics that promote positive youth development? What makes a neighborhood a good neighborhood for rais-ing children? The evidence was quite consistent with our theoretical model. As predicted, it is not primarily the level of socioeconomic advantage or poverty in the neighborhood that accounts for the observed differences in neighborhood or individual success rates. The effects of neighborhood advantage or poverty on success are mediated almost totally by the effec-tiveness of the emergent social organization and culture of the neighbor-hood. In our full multicontextual models, concentrated Poverty or Disad-vantage never account for more than a tiny part of any success outcome at the individual or the neighborhood level. It is the social organization and culture that largely determine the quality of the neighborhood as a socialization context and these emergent properties account for nearly all of the neighborhood effect on development.

Neighborhood organization and culture do not mediate all of the effects of the *physical environment* of the neighborhood, however. This feature of neighborhoods accounts for as much as 8 percent of the direct influence on success at the neighborhood level and 5 percent at the individual level. Physically Deteriorated neighborhoods have higher rates of delinquency, drug use, and other problem behaviors (Chicago) and Well-Kept Neigh-borhoods have higher rates of positive behavior (Denver and Chicago), controlling for other features of the neighborhood.

Good neighborhoods are thus neighborhoods with good social organiza-tion, a conventional normative culture, and a relatively well-kept physical environment. It is worth noting which specific organizational and cultural characteristics appear most important in promoting success. In our full models, with all of the social contextual predictors included, the strongest and most consistent neighborhood predictor was Normative/Value Cli-mate, a cultural dimension of neighborhoods, followed closely by Neigh-borhood Bonding and Control, and Institutional Effectiveness. These are also the strongest bivariate predictors. Elements of both organizational structure and a supportive culture characterize those neighborhoods that promote successful development.

While neighborhood organization and culture tend to be better in more affluent neighborhoods and worse in Disadvantaged, Poor neighbor-hoods, there are important exceptions. Poverty and Disadvantage do not *determine* Organization and Culture. In Chicago, it is not Poverty but Deterioration that is more strongly associated with neighborhood Organization in predominantly black neighborhoods. Even when Poverty and Deterioration are combined, they are not strong determinants of neighborhood Organization in Chicago. In Denver, Disadvantage and Deterioration are stronger predictors than in Chicago, but it is primarily Disadvantage that predicts neighborhood Organization. In neither city is the relationship of Disadvantage/Poverty and Deterioration to the normative culture exceptionally strong (mean $r = .46$). Moreover, in both Chicago and Denver we found High-Poverty/Disadvantaged neighborhoods with above average levels of Organization and positive Normative/Value Climate. For example, nearly four out of ten Poor Neighborhoods in Denver had average or better consensus on conventional norms and values. High-Poverty or Disadvantaged neighborhoods are not always bad neighborhoods for raising children; and more affluent neighborhoods are not necessarily good neighborhoods. It depends on their organizational, cultural and physical characteristics. *The quality of the neighborhood is not fixed or determined by its level of socioeconomic advantage or disadvantage/poverty.*

The racial mix in a neighborhood is also an indicator of compositional disadvantage in Denver. The sampling design precluded our analysis of this relationship in Chicago. Racial mix clustered strongly with poverty, single-parent families, and residential instability in our measure of Disadvantage and, on average, neighborhoods with a high racial/ethnic mix were more Disorganized, had lower levels of consensus on conventional norms, and lower rates of successful youth development than neighborhoods with a predominant racial/ethnic composition. This finding remained even when the other indicators of Disadvantage were held constant. Similar findings have been reported by others.[4] Following Shaw and McKay, we theorized that the underlying causal process involves cultural conflict and normative ambiguity, a situation where no single set of cultural norms is established in the neighborhood and exposure to multiple cultural groups creates normative ambiguity for youth living in these neighborhoods. The relatively high correlation between racial mix and level of consensus on conventional values and norms in Denver is consistent with this hypothesis. We saw this situation in Allenspark, one of our ethnographic sites with a high racial/ethnic mix. Here interaction patterns of both adults and children were largely restricted to one's own ethnic group and there was distrust and fear of other groups, heavy ethnic gang activity and high levels of crime, violence and drug use. However, we found other neighborhoods with a high racial/ethnic mix that had average to high levels of normative consensus and predominantly white neighborhoods with low levels of normative consensus. A high racial/ethnic mix does not consistently result in low normative consensus and its potential negative influence appears to depend on whether it impedes social interaction and the emergence of common values and norms or not. In any event, *the relationship between compositional and emergent properties of the neighborhood are not exceptionally strong.* The quality of the neighborhood as a place to raise children is predominantly a function of the collective life that emerges as neighbors interact, the levels of bonding and control, links to conventional institutions, and consensus on values and norms, rather than the socioeconomic status, racial/ethnic mix, or other compositional factors.

In general then, neighborhood demographic composition has a relatively weak influence on youth development and these effects are largely indirect, mediated almost entirely by the emergent social organization and culture of the neighborhood. This finding has important implications for social policies and programs designed to improve the quality of neighborhoods and rates of successful youth development, issues discussed next.

The Clustering and Cumulative Effects of Neighborhood, Family, School, and Peer Contexts

Why is it that most urban scholars initially expected neighborhood poverty and disadvantage to have much stronger deleterious effects on individual success outcomes? In part, this expectation was based on early neighborhood-level studies which found relatively strong relationships between disadvantage/poverty and youth development outcomes.[5] It was also based on the rich ethnographic studies of life in disadvantaged neighborhoods which suggested a strong relationship. From both sets of studies we came to believe that adverse socialization contexts were tightly clustered, that most families in disadvantaged/poor neighborhoods were dysfunctional, most schools grossly inadequate, most peer groups delinquent, drug using gangs. It was assumed that adverse social contexts were inextricably linked to each other and a direct result of or response to the level of disadvantage and deterioration in the neighborhood.

This is a myth. We did not find these contexts to be tightly clustered in either Advantaged or Disadvantaged Neighborhoods. The range and variation in effective parenting, school quality, and peer group orientations is much greater within neighborhoods than between them; and the direct effects of the neighborhood on each of these contexts is relatively modest. This finding is essentially replicated in the other MacArthur Network on Successful Adolescent Development sites in Philadelphia and Prince Georges County.[6] Almost a third of youth living in Disadvantaged Denver neighborhoods were in families with better than average parenting practices, attending better than average schools and participating in primarily prosocial peer groups. The proportion of youth attending better than average schools and involved in better than average peers groups was only slightly higher in Advantaged than Disadvantaged Neighborhoods; the primary difference by type of neighborhood involved the proportion of youth living in above-average quality families (Table 9.2). In this study, these socializing contexts are only weakly linked to each other and to types of neighborhoods.

Characteristics of a "Good" Family

All of the parents we interviewed in our focus groups wanted to be good parents and expressed hope for their children's success. However, it was clear that some were better prepared than others for their parenting role and that there were different demands on and resources available to those living in affluent and poor neighborhoods, particularly those living in neighborhoods with organized gangs and illicit economies. Effective parenting did appear much more difficult in Disadvantaged, high-Poverty Neighborhoods.

The family characteristic most strongly and consistently tied to youth success outcomes at both the neighborhood and individual level is effective Parenting Practices, which includes high levels of parental monitoring, personal warmth, and children's strong attachments to their parents. There is less consistency for other family characteristics, but in the full multicontextual models, the family's Normative and Value Climate, Family Income and Family Dysfunction were also important predictors, depending on the particular success outcome involved. Together with effective Parenting Practices, these account for most of the family influence on success outcomes.

It is interesting that Family Income was a strong predictor of success only at the neighborhood level. Those neighborhoods with high average Family Incomes and better Parenting Practices typically had better youth development success rates. This was certainly expected. But with one exception, Family Income was *not* a significant predictor of success at the individual level when all family characteristics were included in the model. In the one exception (Prosocial Competence in Chicago), Family Income accounted for a relatively small percent of the directly explained variance. In general then, having good financial resources in the family does not appear to be necessary for the family's positive influence on their children's success. *Having a good family, one that promotes a successful course of development, does not depend on a high level of family income.* At the same time, living in a relatively high-income neighborhood does appear to improve one's chances of success slightly, a finding reported earlier.[7]

To what extent does the type of neighborhood constrain and shape these family characteristics? Are good families found overwhelmingly in good neighborhoods and rarely in bad neighborhoods? The evidence indicates that, on average, good families *are* more likely to be found in good neighborhoods – neighborhoods with effective informal support networks, high levels of bonding and control, high consensus on conventional norms and values, effective ties to local institutions, and few illegal role models or illegitimate opportunities. In particular, families in good neighborhoods typically have more resources (personal income, social support networks, and access to institutions) and better Parenting Practices, than families living in Disorganized Neighborhoods with unsupportive cultures. These are the two family characteristics most strongly linked to neighborhood rates of successful youth development.

When neighborhood Organization was controlled, there was no relationship between Poverty (Disadvantage) and average family characteristics across neighborhoods. It is neighborhood organization and culture that most directly account for observed differences in Parenting Practices and Family Resources, not Disadvantage, Poverty or affluence. In fact, *Parenting Practices were slightly better in High-Poverty than Advantaged black neighborhoods when the level of neighborhood organization and culture were taken into account* (Chicago). Furstenberg et al. (1999) also report that parent management practices were, on average, better in high poverty than affluent study neighborhoods in Philadelphia. Our findings suggest an important qualifier to this finding – this relationship is most likely to occur when these neighborhoods have a similar type of organization and culture.

Our ethnographic data suggest that parenting practices are, at least in part, a response to specific circumstances encountered in the neighborhood, school, and surrounding areas (Chapter 7). When living in a dangerous neighborhood, parenting practices are dominated by the need to protect children from these very real dangers. There was clear survey evidence in Chicago, that the presence of illegal activities in the neighborhood influenced the type of parenting practices adopted. The survey data in Denver provided weaker confirmation than found in Chicago, but the ethnographic data certainly suggest it. In Chicago, there appears to be an increased level of monitoring in Disadvantaged as compared to Advantaged Neighborhoods, when there is organizational and cultural support for good parenting. The ethnographic findings in Denver highlight the extent to which a concern over "trouble" and the dangers in Disadvantaged Neighborhoods dominated parent concerns for their children and increased monitoring was one strategy frequently used to address this concern. Physical danger was not a dominant concern for parents in more affluent neighborhoods and they were less likely to use this strategy.

A different picture emerged at the individual level. When individual attributes (Age, Gender, Socioeconomic Status, Race/Ethnicity, etc.) were taken into account, unique neighborhood effects on family contextual features were relatively small. In most cases, these individual family attributes accounted for as much or more variation in family context characteristics as did type of neighborhood. Stated simply, for any individual, living in a good neighborhood improves the quality of parenting, family resources and other contextual characteristics, but this effect is relatively weak.

There are several implications of this finding. First, good families are not tightly clustered in good neighborhoods. There is some clustering, which accounts for the neighborhood-level findings, but it is relatively modest (see Table 9.2). Knowing the type of neighborhood one lives in does not provide strong clues about her or his family's Parenting Practices, social support networks, or other family contextual characteristics. Second, the observed neighborhood-level differences in family Parenting Practices and Family Resources noted earlier, may be in part the result of a selection process; good parents select good neighborhoods to live in, and poor parents frequently have no option but to live in bad neighborhoods. Differences in neighborhood level Family Resources, in particular, are likely to be the result of selection rather than neighborhood effects (Furstenberg et al., 1999). At the same time, we have established that the major source of variation in Parenting Practices lies within neighborhoods and have introduced controls for a number of family background characteristics that are associated with both parenting and neighborhood selection processes. This gives us some confidence that our finding is not purely a selection effect[8]. There do appear to be direct neighborhood effects on other family characteristics but they are small. We can not rule out the possibility that the direction of any causal relationship between neighborhood and family contexts goes in the opposite direction we have postulated; that good families living in the neighborhood increase the likelihood that social networks, institutional connections and a supportive culture will emerge. We can not untangle the causal direction here and recognize this is a possibility.[9] Still, there is both survey and ethnographic evidence that parenting practices are at least partly a direct response to the dangers and opportunities in the neighborhood and the presence or absence of a supportive organization and culture. Although these effects may be small, they are likely to be true neighborhood effects.

Characteristics of "Good" Schools and Peer Groups

In all of our focus group interviews, parents made clear distinctions between good and bad schools and viewed these institutional settings as both places of opportunity for success and as contexts with real risks for drugs, violence, and other unhealthy behavior. Some saw schools as good places for their children's successful development and others thought the quality of education was low and the risks far outweighed the benefits for their children. In contrast to these mixed views of schools, both adolescents and their parents uniformly viewed the peer groups emerging in early adolescence as *negative* influences on a successful course of development. Most parents, regardless of the affluence or poverty of their neighborhood, expressed concern over their children falling in with the "wrong crowd" and fears of serious adverse consequences from these peer relationships. Only in Broadmore, our most affluent ethnographic study neighborhood, was the peer group viewed in a positive light, specifically because it encouraged competition to do well in school. Overall, when parents were asked what led to success or failure for the children in their neighborhoods, the most frequent responses were the effectiveness of parenting practices, the quality of schools, and type of peer group.

Those neighborhoods with youth attending good schools,[10] i.e., those considered both safe and having a positive learning environment, do have better rates of successful development (excluding Problem Behavior) at the neighborhood level. At the individual level, attending good schools substantially increases an individual's chances for *all* success outcomes examined. Both the quality of the learning environment and the safety of the school contribute to better success. Moreover, being in school or successfully completing school is also related to all dimensions of success except for Problem Behavior at the neighborhood level (see Table A8.4). In the full multicontextual models, one or both of these school measures made some direct contribution to all success outcomes except Problem Behavior. Good schools play an important role in a successful course of youth development.

Peers are also important for successful development. In our full models, Positive Peer Group Environment[11] makes some direct contribution to explained variance for all success outcomes in Denver (but not Chicago) at the neighborhood level, and all individual level outcomes except Prosocial Competence (Chicago) and being On Track (Denver).

Are good schools and positive peer groups tightly clustered within Disadvantaged or High-Poverty Neighborhoods? On average, the best schools are those attended by Denver youth from Well-Kept and Advantaged Neighborhoods. All youth in these neighborhoods are in school or have graduated, whereas in some Disadvantaged Neighborhoods, only 80 percent are in school or graduated. Moreover, youth living in Deteriorated and Disadvantaged Neighborhoods almost uniformly report that their schools are relatively unsafe, violent schools. The perceived quality of peer contexts did not differ much by neighborhood Disadvantage or Deterioration. This probably reflects a school-based perception; there are prosocial and antisocial peer groups in every school and little basis for individual respondents knowing how these groups differ across schools.

In Chicago, there were no differences in the quality of the school's learning environment by neighborhood Poverty or Advantage; there were differences in reported school violence, with the highest rates of violence in Moderate-Poverty Neighborhoods and the lowest in Advantaged Neighborhoods. The most positive peer contexts were found in Advantaged Neighborhoods.

Essentially this same set of findings characterizes school and peer context differences by level of neighborhood organization and culture. There is some clustering of good schools and peer groups by level of Disadvantage and Poverty, or level of organization and culture, but it is quite modest. The variation in the quality of these socializing contexts is much greater within neighborhoods than between them. *Overall, the clustering of good or bad neighborhoods, families, peer groups and school contexts in Denver and Chicago is weak; knowing that one lives in a Disadvantaged or Poor Neighborhood does not help us much to predict what kind of family, school, or peer group they are likely to have.*

Cumulative Effects across Multiple Contexts

The weak relationship between neighborhood, family, school, and peer contexts helps explain the relatively modest effects of living in Disadvantaged or High-Poverty Neighborhoods on individual success. It also accounts for the finding that the effects of these different socialization contexts are for the most part independent, additive, and modest (Chapter 9). A good family has a positive effect on youth development that is essentially the same whether that family lives in a good or bad neighborhood and, depending on the success outcome, accounts for 9–56 percent of the variance in our full models. There are only two success outcomes where a single context accounts for more than half of the variance explained – the family influence on Prosocial Competence in Chicago (56 percent) and the peer group influence on Problem Behavior (78 percent Denver; 57 percent Chicago). *It is the combined effects of these separate socialization contexts that produces a truly large effect on the chances for a successful course of youth development.* All four contexts, neighborhood, family, school, and peer group, made some contribution to the individual level explained variance for Personal Competence and Prosocial Behavior; three contexts contributed to the explanation of Prosocial Competence and Problem Behavior (Chicago), and two contexts contributed to the explained variance in On Track and Problem Behavior (Denver). Individual attributes contributed to *each* success outcome (12–28 percent).

The influence of any specific context varies substantially with the success outcome being considered. The family has the strongest relative influence on Personal and Prosocial Competence, the school on the predicted chances for a successful adult life (On Track), the peer group on involvement in Problem Behavior, and the family, peer group and individual attributes have about equal influences on Prosocial Behavior. Overall, assuming each of these success outcomes is equally important, the family and peer group have the most influence on success, followed by individual attributes and the school, and then the neighborhood.

Success in Disadvantaged Neighborhoods

In some respects, success for youth living in Disadvantaged Neighborhoods is even more dependent on the above relationships and processes

than for youth living in Advantaged Neighborhoods. Our model of multicontextual effects works better in Disadvantaged Neighborhoods; levels
of explained variance are uniformly higher in Disadvantaged than Advantaged Neighborhoods. In particular, *there appears to be a greater payoff for good
parenting, neighborhood support, and good schools in Disadvantaged Neighborhoods.* Moreover, some hypothesized effects occur *only* in Disadvantaged
Neighborhoods. For example, the longer one lives in a Disadvantaged
Neighborhood the lower one's level of Prosocial Competence (other factors taken into account). Length of residence has no effect on competence
in Advantaged Neighborhoods. This does not appear to be a simple age
effect, but rather a length of exposure effect that influences a successful
course of development only in Disadvantaged Neighborhoods.[12] Having
an intact family increases the chances of success and decreases the chances
of delinquency and drug use for youth living in Denver Disadvantaged
Neighborhoods, but does not appear to have these positive effects for youth
living in Advantaged Neighborhoods. Stated differently, *single parenting in
Denver Disadvantaged Neighborhoods appears to have negative implications for
youth development that are not associated with single parenting in more Advantaged Neighborhoods.* An intact family is either a protective factor for youth
living in Disadvantaged Neighborhoods, buffering them from other risk
conditions in the neighborhood, or a condition that simply presents less
family-based risk for poor developmental outcomes. In either case, it does
not serve this positive function in Advantaged Neighborhoods. Finally, in
Poor Neighborhoods in Chicago, attending good schools and involvement
with positive peer groups appeared to protect youth from the expected
increase in Problem Behavior with age. This effect was not observed in
Advantaged Neighborhoods.

SES, Race, and Ethnic Effects on Success

In the general analysis, we found that youth from families with more
education, white-collar/professional occupations and higher incomes had
slightly higher levels of individual competence, regardless of the type of
neighborhood in which they lived. High SES provided no advantage for
any other success outcome in neighborhoods generally or in Disadvantaged Neighborhoods specifically. Apart from this relatively small effect
on individual competence, differences in social class have little to do with
who is and is not successful in Disadvantaged Neighborhoods, once all
of the other personal and contextual factors are taken into account. In
Advantaged Neighborhoods, youth from low SES families had especially
poor chances for being On Track – a relationship not found in Disadvantaged Neighborhoods (see Chapter 4 and Table A9.3D). There is thus
some evidence that SES matters more in Advantaged than Disadvantaged
Neighborhoods, a finding also reported by Furstenberg et al. (1999) in
their Philadelphia study. Overall, SES does not have a strong influence on

youth development once the other conditions in our model are controlled. Furstenberg et al. (1999) report a similar finding for education; its effect was primarily on outcomes for youth living in more advantaged neighborhoods.

In the general analysis, minority youth tend to have slightly poorer success outcomes than majority youth when other factors are taken into account, but again these differences are small; Race/ethnicity accounts for zero to 3 percent of the directly explained variance in these individual success outcomes. However, minority status has a stronger association with negative outcomes for youth living in Disadvantaged Neighborhoods. In these neighborhoods, minority youth appear to be on a different trajectory than white youth. For several developmental outcomes (Personal Competence, On Track, Problem Behavior), there are no ethnic or racial differences in early adolescence, but by age 18, minority youth have significantly poorer outcomes than white youth. For example, without controls for age, racial/ethnic identity was unrelated to involvement in delinquency and drug use, but ethnic differences in these behaviors increased with age. By age 18, minority youth had significantly higher involvement in Problem Behavior than whites. Moreover, even stronger race and ethnic differences were found for the more positive types of development for older youth. For example, at younger ages, minority youth in Disadvantaged Neighborhoods had higher levels of Personal Competence than white youth, but by age 18, their levels were lower than those of white youth. Minorities also tend to have lower involvement in Prosocial Behavior, more typically for females than males and for Hispanics and other minorities than African Americans. Minorities are also less likely to be On Track than whites and to fall further behind with increasing age. Further, the observed decline in positive influences of family and school with age noted earlier is more accentuated for minority youth. In sum, it appears that *minority youth living in disadvantaged neighborhoods are on a trajectory that puts them at increasing risk for poor developmental outcomes as they approach their adult years.* This effect is not found in early adolescence and is largely obscured when effects are averaged across age.

Age and Gender Effects on Success

As might be expected, age is a critical variable for development. Some significant age effects have already been noted above. In general, Personal/Prosocial Competence increases, Prosocial Behavior declines and Problem Behavior increases with age throughout the adolescent years. Moreover, the positive effects of good parenting, good schools, intact families and residential stability on success typically decline with age.[13] However, there are some counter trends in Disadvantaged Neighborhoods. As noted above, Personal Competence *declines* with age for minority relative to white youth – a negative outcome for minority youth. But we also found some positive age effects in Disadvantaged Neighborhoods. For example, Prosocial Behavior *increases* with age for youth from higher-income families and those with longer-term residence in the neighborhood. In Chicago neighborhoods, stable residence and family income were associated with *increases* in Prosocial Behavior for older youth and good schools and involvement in prosocial peer groups *decreased* the likelihood of involvement in Problem Behavior for older youth. There are thus some contextual conditions that appear to mitigate the general decline in success outcomes for youth living in Disadvantaged Neighborhoods as they grow older, but the overall effect of growing older is to reduce the influence of the family and school, and both the quality of peer associations and peer influence on success outcomes.

Unexpectedly, we found SES to be *negatively* related to Prosocial Behavior and being On Track (Denver) in the general analysis. This may have been the result of an SES-by-age interaction observed for youth living in Disadvantaged Neighborhoods. In these neighborhoods, SES was essentially unrelated to Prosocial Behavior and being On Track for younger youth, but with increasing age, youth from higher SES families reported lower levels of success for these outcomes. This is one more indicator of a general finding – that the negative effects of living in a Disadvantaged Neighborhood become stronger as youth approach adulthood. It also suggests that higher family SES is not always an advantage for youth living in Disadvantaged Neighborhoods.

Overall, there are neither strong nor consistent gender effects. In the general neighborhood analyses, males typically had lower success rates than females for those success outcomes where there were significant gender effects. However, gender effects are sometimes reversed in Disadvantaged Neighborhoods, with males having better success rates than females. For example, in Denver Disadvantaged Neighborhoods, male rates of Personal Competence are slightly higher than female rates, and good schools have a more positive effect on Prosocial Competence for males than females. In Poor Neighborhoods in Chicago, males benefitted more than females from living in better-organized neighborhoods. Other gender effects were similar to those found for neighborhoods in general. However the general conclusion is that *living in a disadvantaged neighborhood typically reduces the relative chances of success for females more than that for males.*

COMPARING DENVER AND CHICAGO

At the neighborhood level, the model we developed and tested fits Denver better than Chicago. The levels of explained variance for similar neighborhood outcomes (the competence and Problem Behavior measures) were nearly always higher for Denver than Chicago. At the individual level, however, there were few substantial differences by city. Moreover, the model appears to work equally well in both cities when applied to Disadvantaged/High-Poverty Neighborhoods.

There were several potentially important neighborhood-level city differences. This involved the relationship between Poverty and neighborhood Organizational characteristics, and Poverty's effect on family characteristics once neighborhood Organization was taken into account. Poverty was *not* a good predictor of neighborhood Organization in Chicago, whereas it was in Denver. However, neighborhood Poverty *was* a predictor of several family characteristics in Chicago (but not Denver) after the organizational characteristics of the neighborhood were controlled. Thus Poverty's effect on youth success outcome rates was relatively small and indirect in Chicago, operating primarily through its effect on family characteristics. In Denver, its effect (and that of Disadvantage) on success rates is stronger but again largely indirectly through its effect on neighborhood organizational characteristics.

Why this difference in how neighborhood poverty appears to influence youth development rates in these two cities – primarily through the family in Chicago and neighborhood organization in Denver? It is possible that this reflects a difference in the racial/ethnic composition and cultures of the samples in these two cities. In general, the family played a more important role in Chicago success outcomes at both the neighborhood and individual-levels than in Denver, where neighborhood organization effects were typically stronger than in Chicago. The neighborhood ecology in these two cities was quite different. In Denver, high poverty neighborhoods were also neighborhoods with a high racial-mix and high rates of mobility, and single parent households. This was not the case in Chicago; poverty was not linked to racial mix or mobility. This city difference may also involve a cultural difference reflecting specific African American experiences and practices. The size of the informal networks was larger in Chicago than Denver and this could easily reflect a large extended family in Chicago. It is also possible that the general failure to find neighborhood organization effects on youth development outcomes in Chicago is a result of using census tracts as neighborhoods. Neighborhood units in Denver involved smaller numbers of persons and families where face-to-face interaction was more likely. Perhaps these smaller neighborhood units generate more accurate and reliable measures of emergent organizational characteristics, hence stronger relationships to success outcomes.

Informal parental networks, conceptualized as a social resource or "social capital," operated quite differently in Chicago and Denver. In Chicago, larger parent networks were associated with more family dysfunction, less effective local institutions, lower levels of neighborhood bonding and control, and more exposure to antisocial role models and illegal activities. In sum, larger parent networks in Chicago were found disproportionately in Poor, Disorganized Neighborhoods and had no effect on Prosocial Competence levels and rates of Problem Behavior (see Chapter 6).[14] These relationships are the reverse of what was theoretically predicted and found in Denver.

It is possible that families in Poor/Disorganized Chicago Neighborhoods have relatively higher levels of local neighboring (social interaction) while being isolated from contacts in the broader mainstream society, and having little control over their immediate environment, including the environment's negative influence on their children. Although, their parents have more contact with other neighborhood parents, these children remain at elevated risk because of the limited social controls present in their neighborhoods, the interaction between neighbors provides little support for conventional success goals (academic success, prosocial behavior, and employment in the formal labor market, etc.) and often provides encouragement and opportunities for illegal or antisocial activities. In our ethnographic study of selected Denver neighborhoods, we found some relatively large informal networks actually organized around drug dealing and unconventional or antisocial norms (gangs are informal networks – often very effective ones). This highlights the need to consider the normative orientation of informal groups, not just their efficacy, size, or frequency of interaction.

It is not clear why the larger parent networks in Chicago were more likely to be found in high poverty, poorly organized neighborhoods. Parent Network Size was not related to either the family's endorsement of conventional values and norms or the level of consensus in the neighborhood about norms and values. We did not get an assessment of the normative/value orientation of the *network*, but suspect these larger networks in Chicago may be less conventional and more antisocial than those in Denver.

Given these city differences and the finding that the demographic indicators used in our Denver measure of neighborhood Disadvantage did not hang together in Chicago, generalizations from one city to another or to cities in the United States must be made with caution. While some of these city differences may be attributed to differences in sampling design and measurement, it does not appear that this accounts for all of the observed differences. In those instances where we could check for sample and measure differences, we did not find that controls for these factors eliminated the city differences.

THEORETICAL ISSUES

Type of Success Outcome

In general, our model of multicontextual effects worked quite well. However, our findings did raise several theoretical issues in addition to those addressed above. First, our decision to split the general measure of

Prosocial Competence into a positive behavioral subscale (Prosocial Behavior) and a subscale reflecting conventional attitudes and expectations, values, and academic skills (Personal Competence) proved important.[15] For both behavioral indicators of success (Prosocial Behavior and Problem Behavior), the peer group appears to be the critical context for a favorable individual-level development that facilitates involvement in positive activities and avoids involvement in negative health compromising behaviors.[16] In contrast, the family is the more important context for the development of positive (prosocial) attitudes, values, and skills. It appears that the environmental determinants of *behavior* may be different from those related to the development of Personal Competence (skills, attitudes and expectations). This was not a distinction anticipated in our theoretical model.

The Role of Socioeconomic Class

Second, as noted above for youth living in Disadvantaged Neighborhoods, differences in individual-level socioeconomic status typically was *not* an important factor in determining success. This was not an unexpected finding because we postulated that the effects of individual SES would be largely mediated by the quality of parenting, neighborhood organization, and other contextual conditions. However, there was one important exception to this general finding involving a complex interaction between SES, Age, and Disadvantaged Neighborhoods in Denver. For older youth, lower socioeconomic status predicted a higher involvement in conventional behavior and being On Track. How is it that higher SES would function to reduce involvement in positive behavior and one's chances of being On Track for youth living in Disadvantaged Neighborhoods? The picture is further complicated by the finding that Family Income is positively related to being On Track for older youth. We did not expect to find this negative effect of SES in Disadvantaged Neighborhoods. This effect was not consistent across all outcomes and may be an anomaly. Perhaps this reflects a form of relative deprivation, higher level of frustration, anger, hopelessness, and status incongruence on the part of those youth with better educational and occupational backgrounds who increasingly see their opportunities limited by their social contexts as they approach adulthood. It may also be linked to minority status and identity, with higher SES black youth reacting to peer presser not to be "white," labeled an "Oreo" – black on the outside and white on the inside. The search for a more authentic minority identity may cause some higher SES kids to embrace an oppositional culture that is deleterious to successful development.

Family Dysfunction and Moral Beliefs

Surprisingly, there were no differences in average levels of Family Dysfunction or Parental Moral Beliefs by type of neighborhood. Moreover, in

Denver (but not Chicago), average family endorsement of conventional values and norms was slightly higher in Disadvantaged than Advantaged Neighborhoods. At least in part, this may be a result of a racial/ethnic difference in endorsing conventional values and beliefs. In Denver, we found that black and Hispanic families, in general, tend to have more conventional values than whites. Given that minority families tend to live in more disadvantaged neighborhoods, race and ethnic differences may account for at least some of this apparent city difference. It is also possible that the effects of disadvantage are primarily on the family's ability to realize outcomes consistent with these values or to enforce conventional norms, not on their endorsement of them. At the same time, families in more affluent neighborhoods who have the means to realize these outcomes and enforce these norms, are not as idealistic about them; they are not as abstract, and they are more likely view them as conditional or relative. In any event, more work on this characteristic of the family context is needed to explicate its relationship to neighborhood characteristics.

Poverty and Crime

Our findings indicate that neighborhood Disadvantage/Poverty and criminal behavior are not related in Denver and only weakly related in Chicago. This finding appears at odds with a large body of research indicating a relatively strong neighborhood-level relationship. There are several potential explanations for this difference in findings. First, the bulk of the prior evidence for this neighborhood finding involves the use of official agency-generated data, most frequently Uniform Crime Reports or local police arrest reports.[17] Studies relying on self-reported measures of crime, particularly youth crime, as is the case in this study, typically report little or no relationship between neighborhood poverty and rates of delinquent or criminal behavior.[18] There is general agreement that most criminal behavior, even serious felony crimes, do not result in an arrest. Arrests represent a relatively small fraction of all criminal events that occur in the neighborhood.[19] Moreover, the probability of arrest is related to the race, gender, and social class of the offender, as well as the type of neighborhood where the crime occurs.[20] At least some of the neighborhood differences in arrest rates may be the result of compositional differences and not a true neighborhood effect. Although the evidence indicates that police surveillance and official arrest rates differ by type of neighborhood, it also suggests that neighborhood differences in rates of criminal *behavior* are much smaller and often not substantively significant. Self-reported arrests in Denver were significantly (marginally) higher in Disadvantaged than Advantaged Neighborhoods, although the rates of self-reported Delinquent Behavior or Problem Behavior were not. In fact, the highest rates of Problem Behavior were found in Moderately

Disadvantaged, not highly Disadvantaged Neighborhoods in Denver, a finding reported earlier by Seidman et al. (1998).

Second, official arrest rates are an index of the reported crimes that occurred in a neighborhood; persons arrested may or may not be neighborhood residents.[21] This distinction between where the crime occurred and where the offender lives may be an important one. Several recent studies have found that making this distinction leads to different conclusions about the relationship between type of neighborhood or housing and criminal behavior.[22]

A comparison of our findings and those of Sampson et al. (1998) is also relevant to this issue. Sampson et al. report that it is primarily the variation in neighborhood collective efficacy that accounts for variation in official rates of crime between Chicago neighborhoods.[23] Our measure of Neighborhood Bonding/Control, although not identical, is similar to their measure of collective efficacy. Our measures of crime involve self-reports of delinquency, arrest and problem behavior whereas their measure was an official arrest measure reflecting crimes of both adults and juveniles. Their sample is a representative sample of all Chicago neighborhoods while ours is a representative sample of Denver neighborhoods and predominantly African American neighborhoods in Chicago. Although the comparison is thus crude, it does suggest a somewhat different pattern of relationships between neighborhood characteristics and criminal behavior that may be a function of the measure of criminal behavior used. The strongest neighborhood predictors of delinquency and problem behavior rates in this self-report study were the measures of neighborhood consensus on norms and values, and exposure to illegal role models and activities. Neighborhood Bonding/Control was not a significant predictor in Denver although it was a weak predictor in Chicago. At the individual level, living in a Denver neighborhood characterized by high levels of bonding and control was unrelated to involvement in Problem Behavior; the strongest neighborhood predictor was again the level of Illegal Activity in the neighborhood. In Chicago, Neighborhood Bonding/Control was associated with levels of Problem Behavior, but again, the strongest relationships involved Illegal Modeling and Illegal Performance Opportunities. It thus appears possible that different neighborhood characteristics are associated with variation in self-reported delinquency and problem behavior as compared to officially recorded arrests.

FACILITATING SUCCESS IN DISADVANTAGED NEIGHBORHOODS:
PROGRAM AND POLICY IMPLICATIONS

In general, the design of programs and interventions to improve the success rates of children and youth living in disadvantaged, high-poverty neighborhoods should be grounded in a body of research with a high level of scientific consensus about the mechanisms that facilitate or impede a successful course of development. From this perspective, this study has a number of important limitations – cross-sectional data, a relatively small number of neighborhood units in each city, the use of census-defined boundaries of neighborhoods, a limited set of individual characteristics – that demand caution in recommending programs or policies based solely on our findings. To the extent these findings contribute to a general consensus, we have more confidence in recommendations based on these findings. Some of our most interesting findings lack confirmation from other studies, and therefore must be considered tentative. It is with this reservation and caution, that we offer some suggestions for social interventions and policies designed to improve the developmental success outcomes for children and youth living in high poverty, disadvantaged neighborhoods.

First, it is important to remember that a majority of children and youth from Disadvantaged Neighborhoods in this study appear to be doing OK. There is now sufficient evidence from multiple studies to conclude that growing up in a high-poverty, disadvantaged neighborhood by itself, has relatively modest effects on youth development. Likewise, growing up in a wealthy, advantaged neighborhood does not guarantee success (as we have conceptualized it); it provides a very modest advantage at best.

Second, the cumulative effects of growing up in multiple dysfunctional, impoverished social contexts are much more serious and this makes the task of facilitating a successful course of youth development much more difficult. Effective interventions must be multicontextual, they must address the structure and dynamics of families, schools and peer groups, as well as neighborhoods, if they are to have strong, robust effects on the course of development. We found that these socialization contexts have a slight tendency to cluster, although not as much as generally believed. This weak clustering also makes the task of effectively intervening in these multiple settings more difficult: The need for effective parenting is not limited to disadvantaged neighborhoods, antisocial peer groups are found in all types of neighborhoods, and providing schools that are safe and effective learning environments is problematic in many communities that are not poor. However, the fact that there is some clustering suggests that our initial targeting of these multiple contexts should be in our most disadvantaged neighborhoods. Moreover, these neighborhoods have the most limited within-neighborhood resources and may be least able to initiate these interventions without some help.

Third, the effects of the neighborhood on development appear to be stronger for older teens than for children and those in their early teens. In contrast, the effects of family and schools tend to diminish with age. Contextual influences are thus not constant over the course of development and this needs to be taken into account when developing interventions.

Within this multicontextual, developmental approach, there are some neighborhood-level interventions that can be recommended. Neighborhoods with more effective informal social organizations and conventional cultures do have better success rates. This, coupled with the finding that neighborhood organization and culture are not tightly linked to Poverty and Disadvantage, suggests that direct neighborhood-level organizational interventions hold promise for improving the developmental success rates for children living in high-poverty or disadvantaged neighborhoods. In general, bringing neighbors together, whether for encouraging mutual support, sharing resources, working on common problems, building a sense of empowerment, or just for fun and leisure activities, should promote a more effective neighborhood social organization and better developmental outcomes. Specifically, neighborhood interventions should focus on building neighborhood consensus on appropriate behavior and shared values, improving expectations for youth completing school and getting a reasonable job, increasing the willingness of adults to intervene if they see neighborhood children in trouble, improving the availability and effectiveness of services provided by local institutions; and addressing any signs of physical deterioration in the neighborhood. These are the characteristics of neighborhood ecology, organization and culture we found to be most predictive of better neighborhood success outcomes.[24]

There is a long history of neighborhood organizational and empowerment (mobilization) interventions.[25] Unfortunately, few of these interventions have been rigorously evaluated with respect to their effect on youth development outcomes and those that have considered these outcomes report either no significant effects or small, mixed effects.[26] On the one hand, this should not be a surprise, given the relatively modest effects that recent studies, including this one, have found for neighborhood effects on individual-level developmental outcomes. Moreover, it is hard to detect small or even moderate effects with the research designs employed in most of these neighborhood- and community-level studies when the outcomes involve children rather than older adolescents. Second, the planned intervention is often unsuccessful in achieving the targeted change in organizational structure or functioning. For example, establishing neighborhood "block watches" has proved difficult in disadvantaged neighborhoods.[27] It is also difficult to get adults in high-poverty neighborhoods, particularly those with active gangs, to intervene with neighborhood children and teens when they see or encounter inappropriate behavior and attitudes (establish neighborhood controls or collective efficacy).[28] Not only is there is a general belief that neighbors "should mind their own business," but in these neighborhoods there is a genuine fear of retaliation from youth and/or their parents.[29] We saw this concern with retaliation very clearly in Allenspark. The failure to find consistent effects in neighborhood mobilization or organizational change studies may thus represent ineffective programs and interventions rather than a failure of the postulated effect of better organization on developmental success rates.[30]

Given this history, we believe interventions designed to improve the effectiveness of the informal organization and culture in disadvantaged neighborhoods may still be viable strategies to improve the developmental success of children and youth. But we should not expect that these interventions by themselves will have dramatic effects and we must develop more effective, utilitarian interventions, i.e., strategies that have higher implementation success rates and demonstrated effectiveness in changing organizational structures and cultures.[31]

Interventions that are likely to have more dramatic effects on youth development must involve a multicontextual, comprehensive intervention strategy that addresses specific features of the family, school, peer group, and neighborhood contexts. There is now sufficient evidence to conclude that each of these contexts plays an independent role in promoting a successful course of development.[32] Effective interventions will need to facilitate the integration and coordination of neighborhood, family, and school programs, focusing on achieving greater consistency in the normative expectations and socialization practices employed in *each* of these contexts. This strategy involves working with indigenous adults responsible for what takes place in these settings to establish positive patterns of interaction, effective communication and a shared set of goals. Eccles and Gootman (2002) recently reviewed existing community programs that promote youth development and note that effective programs have this multicontextual, integrative approach: Principals and teachers need to be talking with parents; parents need to know what is going on at school; parents and teachers need to know what is happening in the peer networks; and parents, teachers and adults in the neighborhood need to be promoting and enforcing the same set of standards for appropriate behavior and worthwhile goals. School and community/neighborhood programs that are effective in increasing individual academic performance, social skills, work-related skills and reducing the risk for involvement in problem behavior have been identified.[33] Moreover, some of the school programs have demonstrated the ability to change the school's normative context with substantial reductions in the rates of problem behavior and improved social development outcomes. The evidence suggests that these contextual change programs are more successful in promoting positive developmental outcomes and reducing problem behavior than are individual treatment oriented programs.[34] What is lacking is the coordination and integration of these efforts across contexts. There are virtually no truly comprehensive interventions that have been successfully implemented and carefully evaluated.

Our findings suggest that when a specific developmental outcome is targeted for change, e.g., improving personal competence levels or reducing involvement in problem behavior, different types of interventions addressing different stages of development may be required. For example, interventions designed to improve personal competencies will need to target different contexts and specific contextual features than those designed to reduce unhealthy, dysfunctional, and illegal behavior. The latter involve older youth and the peer context almost exclusively; the former typically involve children and are primarily related to parenting practices, conventional values, school climate, and family income (Chicago). In general, the predictors of behavioral success are different from predictors of success involving cognitive skills, attitudes, beliefs, and future expectations.

Third, there is now considerable consensus across numerous studies about the importance of good parenting practices for a successful course of early development. This may be the most significant single contextual characteristic to target for improving individual and aggregated youth success outcomes. Fortunately, there are several family-based interventions, e.g., the *Nurse-Family Partnership, Multisystemic Family Therapy,* and *Functional Family Therapy,* that teach effective parenting practices and have demonstrated good success in improving youths' academic performance, positive peer relationships, and reducing involvement in problem behavior.[35] The cost and practicality of implementing family-based clinical interventions on a wide scale in disadvantaged neighborhoods would certainly be problematic. But our findings suggest that a relatively low proportion of families in disadvantaged neighborhoods would require an intense clinical intervention.

There are some effective alternatives to clinical interventions. We noted earlier that disrupted families and single parenting in Disadvantaged, Poor neighborhoods appeared to have particularly negative effects on youth development. These conditions did not have the same negative effects in Advantaged Neighborhoods. The visiting nurse program (*Nurse – Family Partnership*) has demonstrated remarkable success in working with single, at risk, first-pregnancy mothers in reducing rates of child abuse, welfare dependency, and alcohol and drug problems for these mothers and improving positive developmental outcomes and lower involvement in problem behavior for their children. The effects of this program have been demonstrated to extend into the later adolescent years. While this is primarily a family-based intervention, it also has some more general community-level components as well, working to establish a supportive network of fathers, grandparents, friends and neighbors for these mothers. Neighbors can play an important co-parenting or extended family role.[36] The other two programs target the families of adolescents and are clearly multicontextual, teaching parents how to manage their adolescent's school involvement and monitor their peer activities.

For established families with less serious presenting problems, basic educational approaches such as parenting classes offered during the evening hours at local schools, would cost less and may be effective for most parents. Unfortunately, there are few rigorous scientific evaluations of these short-term educational programs, and they do not yet have credible evidence of their effectiveness. We need to conduct some good experimental studies of parent effectiveness classes to determine the specific content, delivery and dosage required to achieve significant improvements in parenting practices.

Finally, any effort to address youth involvement in problem behavior must deal with the formation of gangs and antisocial peer groups in our neighborhoods and schools, the presence of illegal opportunity structures (e.g., drug distribution, theft rings, organized crime, organized scams) and highly visible adult role models for illegal behavior in the neighborhood. Exposure to positive peer groups is far and away the most important factor in limiting involvement in problem behavior in both Denver and Chicago. Currently, there are relatively few formal programs or interventions that attempt to redirect or disband gangs and antisocial peer groups. There are a few current gang intervention programs, but almost no programs directed toward less formal antisocial peer groups. Moreover, none of these interventions have yet demonstrated their effectiveness in clinical trials or rigorous evaluations.[37] Effective gang and antisocial peer group interventions are sorely needed and federal and state funding for these programs should be a high priority.

There is some hope for developing interventions that would prove effective in reducing problem behavior in disadvantaged neighborhoods that do not directly involve peer group programs. Family Parenting Practices (and Family Income) had an important influence on youth involvement in problem behavior and we have had some success with parent effectiveness training programs, as noted above. A key feature of these parenting programs is teaching parents how to monitor their children's friends and peer activities, and to facilitate prosocial peer relationships. They thus impact peer group membership indirectly. Moreover, good schools and positive peer groups were shown to function as protective factors for disadvantaged neighborhood youth, offsetting the normal trend toward increasing problem behavior as youth move into the late adolescent years. In the absence of effective gang and antisocial peer interventions, programs that improve parenting practices and provide better quality schools, should reduce levels of involvement in problem behavior in disadvantaged neighborhoods. Our findings clearly lend support to the often heard policy refrain: (1) invest in schools to improve the quality of education and the safety of students, and (2) provide youth with better nonschool and after-school activities that will provide adult supervision and promote the formation of prosocial peer groups.

RECOMMENDED DIRECTIONS FOR FUTURE RESEARCH

Future neighborhood research needs to address several conceptual and operational measurement issues. First, the conceptualization of the "neighborhood" and the delineation of neighborhood boundaries remain critical issues. It is still common, even in our most ambitious, well funded studies (e.g., Sampson et al., 1997) to use multiple census tracts as the unit of neighborhood or community. Our construct validity analysis (Chapter 2) raises potentially serious questions about this practice. This study, along with others, finds that neighborhoods, as perceived by residents, are substantially smaller than census tracts.[38] Sampson (2001) reports much larger perceived neighborhoods, but frames the definition of neighborhood to include places residents shop, business districts, churches or synagogues attended, and other institutions visited.[39] Moreover, the census boundaries for tracts or block groups do not coincide very well with residents' perceptions of neighborhood boundaries. It is hard to imagine socially meaningful neighborhoods of 4,000–6,000 residents, where they can know one another by name and interact on a face-to-face level to develop the shared understandings, neighborhood cohesion, and other features of emergent social organization we attribute to neighborhoods. Census-level measures typically lack face validity as measures of these theoretical constructs. However, even in Denver where neighborhoods were block groups, the overall neighborhood effect on successful development, particularly at the individual level, is smaller than one might expect from the ethnographic studies of neighborhoods.[40] Out of convenience we used census units. But theory, not convenience should drive our definitions of what constitutes a neighborhood. More conceptually appropriate units may generate stronger evidence of neighborhood organizational effects on youth development. It is time to seriously explore other definitions of neighborhood.

A related problem is that the cognitive maps of residents are somewhat flexible. Individual residents tend to expand their notion of neighborhood boundaries when asked about the presence and effectiveness of institutions serving their neighborhood, compared to boundaries identified for friendship networks, neighborhood-sponsored activities, and feelings of attachment to their neighborhood. This flexibility in boundary definition was related to resident's socioeconomic status, race and type of neighborhood with more consistent (less flexible) boundary identification for lower SES minority residents in disadvantaged neighborhoods. It may well be that the physical and functional neighborhood may be essentially the same for those in disadvantaged neighborhoods with less overlap between physical and functional neighborhoods in more affluent neighborhoods. This is similar to the argument McCahey (1986) makes, asserting that many affluent suburbs or central city districts do not have extensive informal networks, social cohesion, or voluntary organizations, and they somehow have low rates of street crime with an effective organizational structure. The meaning and definition of "neighborhood" may be different for those living in advantaged as compared to disadvantaged neighborhoods. We also found that the cognitive maps of teenagers were substantially larger than those of adults – teen-perceived neighborhoods encompass areas not considered as "within the neighborhood" by their parents. This is another form of Burton's (2001) claim that teens live in multiple neighborhoods, and that the meaning of neighborhood is different for adults and adolescents.

Second, our findings clearly indicate that the critical sources of disadvantage for children involve more than poverty levels in the neighborhood, yet this continues to be the almost exclusive focus of neighborhood studies (e.g., Brooks-Gunn et al., 1997a and 1997b). This represents an example of the omitted-variable bias problem (Duncan and Raudenbush, 2001); poverty is but one indicator of ecological disadvantage. In this study, residential instability (mobility) is an equally important and largely independent compositional indicator (negative) of social organization and culture, which, in turn, are the critical features of neighborhoods that promote a successful course of development. Each of the other two indicators of neighborhood Disadvantage were also independently linked to social disorganization. There are probably other ecological features that would cluster with this particular set of ecological characteristics as well. The composite measure in Denver was clearly more predictive of success outcomes and the mediating effects of social organization than poverty alone. Moreover, physical Deterioration in the neighborhood was a stronger predictor than Poverty for neighborhood-level success outcomes in Chicago.

While our conceptualization of neighborhood characteristics and mechanisms that influence youth development was a relatively complex, multi faceted one, our failure to find anything, but small effects on individual-level outcomes raises questions about the adequacy of our conceptualization and measurement of these neighborhood effects. This is a common problem in neighborhood research (Duncan and Raudenbush, 2001). Perhaps we have not captured the dynamic impact of differences in the institutional resource base in Advantaged and Disadvantaged Neighborhoods, as we relied on resident descriptions of these resources and their perceived usefulness rather than some independent, more objective measure. We did find significant differences in perceived presence and effectiveness of institutional resources by type of neighborhood, but these neighborhood differences appeared to have relatively little influence on individual-level developmental outcomes.

We did not measure some of the more subtle, indirect structural factors identified by others, for example, the flow of information into poor inner-city neighborhoods that restricts their access to reliable information concerning labor markets, schools, apprenticeship programs, and financial markets (Wilson, 1997); the fluidity of family structure over time in disadvantaged neighborhoods (Burton, 2001); or the distinction between residential instability resulting from the conversion of owner occupied to rental units, as compared to instability from the addition of new owner occupied units or conversion from rental to owner-occupied units (Korbin, 2001). Nor did we assess some of the indirect cultural factors, such as prolonged exposure to subcultural norms and behavior patterns that are the products of racial exclusion that can impede successful maneuvering in the larger community, or different developmental trajectories and the "adultification" of teens that often occurs in disadvantaged neighborhoods (Burton, 2001). There is always a need for developing a better understanding of the social processes and physical conditions operating in the neighborhood that have the potential for influencing youth development outcomes and obtaining good measures of these neighborhood characteristics.

It is possible that there is a differential susceptibility to neighborhood influences that is related to type of neighborhood. Certain families and children may be more susceptible to – or immune to – the influences of neighborhood ecology, organization, and culture. We only began to explore this issue with the various interaction models we tested. Future research should examine this possibility and include additional individual characteristics that might be related to a differential susceptibility. The research on resilience suggests that personality, temperament, and other psychological characteristics may play an important role in suppressing or amplifying the effects of contextual risk.

Another theoretical issue that needs to be explicated is the relationship between neighborhoods and schools. Although we conceptualized schools as embedded in neighborhoods, the connection is often quite loose. Schools, particularly secondary schools, draw from several different neighborhoods. We know that in our samples, some youth attended schools that were not only outside their neighborhood, but outside neighborhoods that were immediately adjacent to their neighborhood. This also confounds the assumed embeddedness of peer groups, as schools play an important role in the formation of peer groups. Some youth have both neighborhood friends and school friends, and there may be little overlap in these group memberships. It may prove important to make this distinction. We suspect that as youth enter later adolescence, having positive school peers may protect them from the influence of gangs or antisocial peer groups that operate in the neighborhood. Neighborhood characteristics may predict neighborhood peer-group quality, but not school peer-group quality.

While our conceptual model and measures of neighborhood processes and conditions is fairly complex and sophisticated compared to that used in most earlier neighborhood studies, there is still important work to be done in this area. The social contexts of work and leisure activities were not considered, and these are important contexts influencing youth development.

The role of neighborhood culture is remains seriously underdeveloped (Kubrin and Weitzer, 2003). We have demonstrated that each social context adds to the explained variance in youth outcomes, that some contexts are more influential than others, and that the size of their effect depends on the outcome considered. We have also argued that to some extent, contextual disadvantage clusters and their effects are cumulative. However, with the exception of a few interaction tests and the "person-level" analysis, we have operated under the assumption that the effects of various contexts are linear. Further research should consider the limits imposed by this assumption. Neighborhood effects may be non-linear. There may be important "tipping points" or threshold effects. Further, our estimates of the effect of various configurations of contexts in the person-level analysis, while informative, was only a beginning approach to this question. The simple counting up of contextual risks assumes that any combination of equal number has the same effect, which may not be the case if particular combinations of contextual risk interact. A rigorous multivariate testing of this issue is called for.

It is also critical that future studies consider the direction of causal influences and the possibility of reciprocal or simultaneous influences between individuals and their social contexts. The task of separating selection effects and emergent effects in the neighborhood is a difficult one. The negative relationship between Family Income and neighborhood Disadvantage, for example, is more likely a result of families with low income levels choosing to live in Poor Neighborhoods because they have no other choice (a selection effect), rather than a neighborhood influence on family Income (emergent effect). However the causal relationship between type of neighborhood and type of parenting practices employed by families living in these neighborhoods is more difficult to sort out. It could involve the influence of the neighborhood on family practices – a response to the very real physical danger in the neighborhood, the support or lack of support from informal networks and institutions operating in the neighborhood, and the culture that evolves in the neighborhood; or it could represent good parents selecting neighborhoods where their values and parenting styles would be encouraged and supported; or it could involve both selection and emerging effects. The cross-sectional design of this study precluded our establishing the causal sequence. Our only grounds for interpreting the direction of relationships or influences from neighborhood ecology to neighborhood organization and culture, to family, schools, and peer groups, to individual success outcomes, is the theoretical formulation of our model of multicontextual effects and the specification of the expected causal mechanisms involved. This does not provide a strong argument for the direction of causal influences. We cautioned readers on several occasions that the direction of influence might be the opposite of that suggested by the model. Future research would greatly enhance our level of confidence in estimates of neighborhood effects if they adopt longitudinal design and establish the direction(s) of contextual and individual influences.

Addressing the above issues will add significantly to our understanding of how the neighborhood ecology, organization, and culture influence a successful course of youth development. There are also other developmental outcomes that need to be considered, like personal autonomy, intimacy, and social and sexual identity. However, we would not be surprised to find that even with improved conceptualization, measurement, and study design, unique neighborhood effects on successful development will prove to be quite modest compared to those of family, schools, peers, and individual traits.

Finally, the established finding that neighborhood effects differ by stage of development,[41] and during the adolescent years do not appear substantial until ages 16–18, has implications for the design of future neighborhood studies. First, we know a lot about neighborhood effects on children, less about effects on early adolescents, and almost nothing about effects during late adolescence and early adulthood. Our neighborhood research on effects by developmental stage and age is quite truncated. Second, many of the most serious dysfunctional and health compromising problems emerge or peak in the 16–25 age range, but we know little about how neighborhood disadvantage, social organization and culture influence the onset, developmental course or termination of these problems. This is the age population that has the greatest negative impact on our neighborhood conditions – crime, violence, drugs, unprotected sex, AIDs, teenage parenting – and we know little about how the neighborhood influences their behavior. Third, this is the period in the life course when the adolescent – adult transition normally occurs, when we can study the effects of child and adolescent development on the entry (or failed entry) into adult roles. Conceivably, neighborhood effects might be greatest for this stage of the life course.

Notes

1. Leventhal and Brooks-Gunn (2003) compared neighborhood effects from experimental and nonexperimental studies and report substantially larger effect estimates from experimental studies. They argue that nonexperimental studies, like this one, underestimate neighborhood effects.
2. Newman (1999) and Alex-Assensoh (1995) come to a similar conclusion, challenging the conventional wisdom about the inner-city poor.
3. Stewart et al. (2002), Costa et al. (2003), and Cook et al. (1997) all make this same argument.
4. Suttles, 1968; Lee and Campbell, 1998; Merry, 1981a,b; Sampson and Lauritsen, 1994; Bellair, 1997; Lee, 2001.
5. For a summary of major findings from these studies, see Leventhal and Brooks-Gunn (2000, 2003).

6. See Furstenberg et al., 1999 and Cook et al., 1997.
7. Brooks-Gunn et al., 1993; Leventhal and Brooks-Gunn, 2003; Korbin, 2001.
8. Sampson et al. (2002:474) recommend caution in treating selection bias "... as an individual trait and a nuisance to be controlled." They call for research to better understand the relationships between selection decisions, structural characteristics and social interactions.
9. Leventhal and Brooks-Gunn (2003) note that untangling these effects is very difficult and few studies have done this successfully.
10. These are schools that residents of a given neighborhood attend; the school may or may not be physically located in the neighborhood.
11. Peer groups may or may not involve friends living in the neighborhood. Many of these groups are formed at school and involve youth from different neighborhoods.
12. See Jencks and Mayer (1990) and Tienda (1991) for similar findings.
13. O'Donnell, Hawkins and Abbott, 1995; Duncan, Duncan, and Hops, 1994.
14. Parent Network Size was related to individual levels of Prosocial Competence in Chicago, as predicted theoretically. This relationship was substantially weaker than that found for Personal Competence and Prosocial Behavior in Denver.
15. Brooks-Gunn et al. (1997) also report stronger neighborhood effects for cognitive and achievement indicators than behavioral indicators of development.
16. See Duncan et al. (1994) and O'Donnell et al. (1995) for a similar finding.
17. See Shaw and McKay, 1969; Bursik and Grasmick, 1993; Sampson, 2001, 1992.
18. See Ireland, Thornberry and Loeber (2003) and Simcha-Fagan and Schwartz (1986). Simcha-Fagan and Schwartz used both self-report and official measures of delinquency and note that neighborhood disadvantage was weakly related to self-reported delinquency but more strongly related to officially recorded delinquency.
19. Gottfredson, McNeil and Gottfredson, 1991; Hindelang, 1976; Skogan, 1986; Laub and Lauritsen, 1997.
20. Elliott, 1995; Farrington, 2000; Geerken, 1994; Huizinga and Elliott, 1986; Elliott and Ageton, 1980; Elliott and Huizinga, 1983.
21. See Weatherburn et al., 1999 and Ireland et al., 2003. Victimization rates also fail to make this important distinction between where the crime occurs and where the offender lives.
22. See Ireland et al., 2003 and Dunworth and Saiger, 1994.
23. Duncan et al., 2003 report no relationship between their measure of neighborhood ecology (mobility, percent white, and poverty) and perceived collective efficacy. Also see Morenoff et al., 2001.
24. These are the neighborhood characteristics included in our measures of Normative and Value Consensus, Neighborhood Bonding and Control, and Institutional Effectiveness.
25. See Shaw and McKay, 1969; Miller, 1962; Helfgot, 1981; Sorrentino, 1977; Cunningham and Kotler, 1983; Eccles and Gootman, 2002; Garofalo and McLeod, 1988; Fisher and Romanofsky, 1981.
26. Bursik and Grasmick, 1993; Lundman, 1993; Sampson, 1995; Sherman et al., 1997.

27. Garofalo and McLeod, 1988.
28. This is one of our indicators in the Neighborhood Bonding and Control measure. It is also identified as a predictor of success by Sampson et al. (1998) and Korbin (2001).
29. Adults in all of our focus groups expressed the belief that today's adults were much less likely to intervene with children and youth in their neighborhood, and even with other adults, than in the neighborhoods in which they were raised. Also, see Korbin (2001) who also reports this finding.
30. Bursik and Grasmick, 1993; Helfgot, 1981; McCahey, 1986.
31. Taylor (2001), after reviewing the effectiveness of the currently popular "crime fighting" approach, expresses caution that this neighborhood-level approach will "turn around" a neighborhood.
32. Furstenberg et al., 1999; Elder and Conger, 2000; Cook et al., 1997; Cook et al., 2002; Eccles and Gootman, 2002.
33. See Elliott and Tolan, 1999, Elliott, Hamburg and Williams, 1998a and U.S. Department of Health and Human Services, 2001 for a review of these programs.
34. Gottfredson, 2001.
35. Olds et al., 1997; Henggeler et al., 2001; Alexander et al., 2000; Mihalic et al., 2001.
36. Furstenberg et al., 1999.
37. See Elliott and Tolan, 1999; Elliott, 1998 and U.S. Department of Health and Human Services, 2001 for reviews of prevention programs. See Ellis, 1992 and Klein and Maxon, In press for reviews of gang-suppression programs.
38. See Coulton, et al., 1997.
39. Sampson, 2001.
40. Anderson, 1994; Williams and Kornblum, 1985, 1994; Burton, Allison, and Obeidallah, 1995; Suarez, 1999; Spencer, 2001. Leventhal and Brooks-Gunn, 2003 claim that experimental studies typically report stronger neighborhood effects than nonexperimental studies.
41. For a review of the effects of neighborhood poverty on developmental outcomes by age and developmental stage, see Brooks-Gunn et al., 1997a.

Appendix A

TABLE A4.1. *Bivariate Correlations: Youth Outcomes*

Cell entries: Pearson's r (p)	Personal Competence (Denver)	Prosocial Behavior (Denver)	On Track (Denver)	Prosocial Competence (Chicago)
Neighborhood Level:				
Prosocial Behavior (Denver)	.796 (.000)			
On Track (Denver)	.730 (.000)	.606 (.000)		
Problem Behavior (Denver)	−.378 (.030)	−.504 (.003)	−.572 (.001)	
Problem Behavior (Chicago)				−.333 (.036)
Individual Level:				
Prosocial Behavior (Denver)	.394 (.000)			
On Track (Denver)	.455 (.000)	.389 (.000)		
Problem Behavior (Denver)	−.167 (.000)	−.317 (.000)	−.297 (.000)	
Problem Behavior (Chicago)				−.192 (.000)

TABLE A4.2. *Mean Adolescent Developmental Outcomes by Predominant Racial Group of Neighborhood and Individual Ethnicity, Controlling for Individual Socioeconomic Status*

Denver Full Sample

Predominant Racial Group	Personal Competence (sd = .68) Individual Ethnicity			Prosocial Behavior (sd = .63) Individual Ethnicity			Problem Behavior (sd = 2.14) Individual Ethnicity		
	White	Black	Hispanic	White	Black	Hispanic	White	Black	Hispanic
White	.28	.37	−.12	.30	.56	.12	−.37	−.90	−.15
Black	−.86	.20	−.40	−.22	.06	−.65	−.50	−.27	.24
Hispanic	.19	−.14	−.17	.32	−.33	−.15	−.34	−.21	−.41
White/Hispanic	.06	−.21	−.15	−.17	.23	−.18	.08	.60	.92
Tests of Significance (F)									
Regression	9.58**			.14			7.16**		
Predominant Race	8.71**			17.67**			5.44**		
Individual Ethnicity	5.43**			12.31**			1.35		
Interaction	6.48**			9.94**			1.85		

* $p \leq .05$; ** $p \leq .01$.
Tests of significance are inflated due to weighting (increased sample size) and disparities in group sizes and variances.

306

TABLE A4.3. *Homogeneity of Individual Success Outcomes by Type of Neighborhood: An Intraclass Correlation Analysis*

Denver

Success Outcomes	All		Age										Gender				Race/Ethnicity					
			10[a]		12		14		16		18		Males		Females		White		Black		Hispanic	
	Dis[b]	Det[b]	Dis	Det	Dis	Det	Dis	Det	Dis	Det	Dis	Det	Dis	Det	Dis	Det	Dis	Det	Dis[c]	Det	Dis	Det
Personal Competence	.117	.039	.049	.005	.116	−.005	.041	−.007	.077	.083	.310	.208	.065	.005	.161	.077	.134	.113		.091	−.011	.000
Prosocial Behavior	.097	.049	.205	.105	.019	.014	.046	.053	.056	.063	.323	.035	.009	.009	.196	.101	.104	.022		.234	.012	−.003
On Track	.054	.017	.006	−.010	.021	−.010	−.019	.003	.075	.027	.185	.074	.006	−.003	.103	.042	.083	.204		.020	−.006	.005
Problem Behavior	.003	.002	.028	−.010	.004	−.009	.019	−.008	.133	−.002	.016	.053	−.001	.019	−.003	.001	.078	.035		−.036	.027	.056

Chicago

Success Outcomes	All		Age												Gender			
			11		12		13		14		15		16		Males		Females	
	Pov[b]	Det	Pov	Det	Pov	Det	Pov	Det	Pov	Det	Pov	Det	Pov	Det	Pov	Det	Pov	Det
Prosocial Competence	.136	.144	.067	.093	.279	.308	.032	.012	.127	.131	.044	.063	.239	.229	.194	.211	.092	.108
Problem Behavior	.027	.043	−.003	.020	.011	.054	.044	.022	−.011	−.013	−.030	−.004	.138	.219	.025	.038	.036	.076

[a] Scale reliabilities do not vary significantly by age.
[b] Dis = Neighborhood Disadvantage Typology; Det = Neighborhood Deterioration Typology; Pov = Neighborhood Poverty Typology.
[c] Cell sizes too small for calculation.

TABLE A4.4. *Mean Adolescent Developmental Outcomes by Levels of Neighborhood Disadvantage and Individual SES: Controlling for Individual Race/Ethnicity*

	Denver														
	Prosocial Competence			Problem Behavior			On Track			Personal Competence			Prosocial Behavior		
	Individual SES			Individual SES			Individual SES			Individual SES			Individual SES		
Neighborhood Disadvantage	Low	Mod.	High	Low	Mod.	High	Low	Mod.	High	Low	Mod.	High	Low	Mod.	High
Low	.329[a]	−.386	.679	−.272[a]	−.336	−.017	.557[a]	.567	.595	.621[a]	−.029	.597	.401[a]	.431	.536
Moderate	−.103	−.299	.211	−.274	.147	.037	.561	.512	.571	−.026	−.284	.102	−.043	−.297	.298
High	−.332	−.151	.372	−.200	−.036	.002	.557	.534	.570	−.463	.045	.515	−.087	−.372	.280
Tests of Significance (F)															
Regression		2.49			2.01		4.43**				3.24*			.80	
Neighborhood		4.99**			.49		1.11				5.78**			4.16**	
Individual SES Disadvantage		18.31**			7.31**		6.22**				9.65**			14.94**	
Interaction		2.26			.85		.26				5.80**			.75	

[a] Only 2 cases in cell.
* $p \leq .05$; ** $p \leq .01$.

TABLE A4.5. *Individual, Compositional, and Physical Neighborhood Effects on Youth Development: Unique, Shared, and Total Variance Explained*

Older Youth: (Denver, Ages 16–18; Chicago, Ages 15–16)

Individual Youth Developmental Outcomes

Disaggregated Neighborhood Effect	Personal Competence	Prosocial Behavior	Prosocial Competence		On Track	Problem Behavior	
	Den	Den	Den	Chi	Den	Den	Chi
Unique Physical Effect[a]	.06	.04	.03	.02	.10	.00	.02
Unique Compositional Effect[b]	.00	.00	.00	.00	.00	.00	.02
Unique Individual Effect[c]	.01	.13	.09	.07	.05	.18	.06
Unique Interactional Effect[d]	.02	.03	.01	.00	.01	.00	.02
Shared Effect	.15	.03	.15	.09	.03	.00	.05
TOTAL EXPLAINED VARIANCE	.24	.23	.28	.17[e]	.19	.18	.17

[a] The unique proportion of variance explained by neighborhood physical condition.
[b] The unique proportion of variance explained by Neighborhood Disadvantage/Poverty.
[c] The unique effect of a set of individual compositional/selection variables which includes: age, gender, race/ethnicity, socioeconomic status, family structure and length of residence in the neighborhood.
[d] The unique effect of the following individual by Neighborhood Disadvantage/Poverty interactions: age by Disadvantage/Poverty, gender by Disadvantage, race/ethnicity by Disadvantage, and socioeconomic status by Disadvantage.
[e] Figures for the unique and shared effects may not sum to equal the total explained variance due to rounding.

TABLE A6.1. *Neighborhood Organization Clusters: Group Centroids*

Variables	η^2 (p): Denver	Cluster 1: "Good" (n = 9 Chicago, 8 Denver): Chicago/Denver	Cluster 2: "Average" (n = 13 Denver): Chicago/Denver	Cluster 3 "Low-Mixed" (n = 6 Denver): Chicago/Denver	Cluster 4: "Bad" (n = 31 Chicago, 6 Denver): Chicago/Denver
Institutional Effectiveness	.61 (.000)/.69 (.000)	1.4349/1.0734	n/a/0.2417	n/a/−0.7486	−0.4166/−1.2063
Informal Networks	.01 (.592)/.37 (.004)	0.1599/0.7513	n/a/0.1794	n/a/−0.9841	−0.0464/−0.4064
Bonding and Control	.79 (.000)/.78 (.000)	1.6310/1.2844	n/a/−0.5100	n/a/0.1712	−0.4735/−0.7788
Normative/Value Consensus	.26 (.001)/.64 (.000)	0.9275/1.3221	n/a/0.0487	n/a/−0.7374	−0.2693/−1.1309
Illegal Modeling	.25 (.000)/.84 (.000)	−1.5888/−1.1253	n/a/−0.2696	n/a/0.5699	0.4612/1.5146
Illegal Performance	.17 (.008)/.62 (.000)	−0.7537/−0.8523	n/a/0.8177	n/a/−0.9356	0.2188/0.2643

TABLE A6.2. *Bivariate Correlations: Organization, Disadvantage, and Deterioration*

Cell Entries: Pearson's r (p)	Institutional Effectiveness		Informal Networks		Normative/ Value Consensus		Bonding/ Control		Illegal Modeling		Illegal Performance	
	Chi	Den	Chi	Den	Chi	Den	Chi	Den	Chi	Den	Chi	Den
Informal Networks	.235 (.145)	.616 (.000)										
Normative/Value Consensus	.468 (.002)	.488 (.004)	.134 (.409)	.371 (.033)								
Bonding/Control	.851 (.000)	.871 (.000)	.033 (.840)	.625 (.000)	.585 (.000)	.662 (.000)						
Illegal Modeling	-.750 (.000)	-.813 (.000)	.054 (.743)	-.347 (.048)	-.438 (.005)	-.470 (.006)	-.846 (.000)	-.821 (.000)				
Illegal Performance Opportunities	-.520 (.001)	.035 (.845)	-.088 (.589)	.023 (.898)	-.267 (.096)	-.531 (.001)	-.422 (.007)	-.167 (.352)	.558 (.000)	.079 (.663)		
Neighborhood Organization (Summary Measure)	.894 (.000)	.883 (.000)	.336 (.034)	.682 (.000)	.676 (.000)	.720 (.000)	.874 (.000)	.950 (.000)	-.828 (.000)	-.816 (.000)	-.668 (.000)	-.189 (.291)
Neighborhood Disadvantage	-.419 (.007)	-.766 (.000)	.353 (.025)	-.515 (.002)	-.400 (.010)	-.685 (.000)	-.591 (.000)	-.903 (.000)	.527 (.000)	.798 (.000)	.353 (.025)	.263 (.140)
Physical Deterioration	-.708 (.000)	-.859 (.000)	.032 (.847)	-.464 (.007)	-.400 (.010)	-.359 (.040)	-.741 (.000)	-.741 (.000)	.865 (.000)	.792 (.000)	.480 (.002)	-.061 (.738)

TABLE A6.3. *Regression Results: Neighborhood Organization–Neighborhood Level Analysis*

Dependent Variable	Percent Explained Variance (R^2)	Independent Variable	Standardized Coefficient (b^*)	Unstandardized Coefficient (b)	Statistical Significance (p)
DENVER					
Institutional	82	Disadvantage	−.365	−.365	.001
Effectiveness		Deterioration	−.626	−.626	.000
Informal	30	Disadvantage	−.370	−.370	.074
Networks		Deterioration	−.227	−.227	.264
Neighborhood	86	Disadvantage	−.725	−.725	.000
Bonding and Control		Deterioration	−.277	−.277	.004
Normative/Value	48	Disadvantage	−.771	−.771	.000
Consensus		Deterioration	.134	.134	.438
Illegal Modeling	77	Disadvantage	.493	.493	.000
		Deterioration	.476	.476	.000
Illegal	16	Disadvantage	.511	.511	.026
Performance Opportunities		Deterioration	−.388	−.388	.086
Neighborhood	83	Disadvantage	−.681	−.681	.000
Organization		Deterioration	−.312	−.312	.003
CHICAGO					
Institutional	52	Poverty	−.161	−.716	.200
Effectiveness		Deterioration	−.643	−.643	.000
Informal	14	Poverty	.406	1.800	.020
Networks		Deterioration	−.131	−.131	.435
Neighborhood	65	Poverty	−.350	−1.552	.002
Bonding and Control		Deterioration	−.601	−.601	.000
Normative/Value	23	Poverty	−.286	−1.267	.078
Consensus		Deterioration	−.286	−.286	.078
Illegal Modeling	79	Poverty	.215	.952	.014
		Deterioration	.779	.779	.000
Illegal	26	Poverty	.192	.850	.222
Performance Opportunities		Deterioration	.403	.403	.013
Neighborhood	58	Poverty	−.187	−.827	.119
Organization		Deterioration	−.665	−.665	.000

TABLE A6.4. *Bivariate Correlations between Neighborhood Organization and Youth Development Outcomes (Continuous Measures)*

Correlations: Pearson's r (p)	Personal Competence (Denver)	Prosocial Behavior (Denver)	Prosocial Competence (Chicago)	Problem Behavior (Denver)	Problem Behavior (Chicago)	On Track (Denver)
Institutional Effectiveness	.729 (.000)	.598 (.000)	.579 (.000)	-.157 (.383)	-.298 (.062)	.510 (.002)
Informal Networks	.628 (.000)	.638 (.000)	.151 (.353)	-.035 (.846)	.226 (.161)	.262 (.141)
Neighborhood Bonding/Control	.869 (.000)	.725 (.000)	.426 (.006)	-.225 (.209)	-.373 (.018)	.613 (.000)
Normative/Value Consensus	.702 (.000)	.581 (.000)	.224 (.164)	-.485 (.004)	-.113 (.487)	.655 (.000)
Illegal Modeling	-.612 (.000)	-.424 (.014)	-.449 (.004)	.069 (.704)	.401 (.010)	-.427 (.013)
Illegal Performance Opportunities	-.137 (.447)	-.280 (.115)	-.418 (.007)	.450 (.009)	.427 (.006)	-.209 (.244)
General Organization (Summary Measure)	.847 (.000)	.706 (.000)	.526 (.000)	-.303 (.086)	-.324 (.041)	.581 (.000)

TABLE A7.1. *Bivariate Correlations for Family Characteristics*

Cell Entries: Pearson's r (p)	Family Income	Parental Network Size	Family Dysfunction	Parenting Practices	Parental Moral Beliefs	Parental Conventional Values
DENVER						
Parental Network Size	.076 (.037)					
Family Dysfunction	−.065 (.076)	.004 (.908)				
Parenting Practices	.112 (.002)	.080 (.028)	.028 (.442)			
Parental Moral Beliefs	−.068 (.061)	−.012 (.734)	−.082 (.022)	.104 (.004)		
Parental Conventional Values	−.157 (.000)	−.051 (.158)	−.092 (.010)	−.036 (.320)	.177 (.000)	
Institutional Effectiveness	.481 (.000)	.110 (.002)	.055 (.129)	.167 (.000)	.007 (.850)	−.257 (.000)
Informal Networks	.366 (.000)	.123 (.001)	.043 (.233)	.067 (.057)	.012 (.747)	−.270 (.000)
Normative/Value Consensus	.290 (.000)	.011 (.762)	−.081 (.024)	.145 (.000)	.092 (.010)	.032 (.373)
Neighborhood Bonding/ Control	.553 (.000)	.139 (.000)	−.043 (.233)	.171 (.000)	.019 (.603)	−.264 (.000)
Illegal Modeling	−.524 (.000)	−.122 (.001)	.019 (.599)	−.136 (.000)	.023 (.522)	.225 (.000)
Illegal Performance	−.052 (.154)	.041 (.251)	.187 (.000)	−.096 (.006)	−.089 (.014)	−.061 (.089)
General Organization (Summary Measure)	.549 (.000)	.121 (.001)	−.085 (.019)	.163 (.000)	.052 (.148)	−.209 (.000)
Neighborhood Disadvantage	−.462 (.000)	−.108 (.003)	.089 (.013)	−.174 (.000)	−.047 (.196)	.185 (.000)
Physical Deterioration	−.442 (.000)	−.109 (.002)	−.098 (.006)	−.110 (.002)	.011 (.759)	.283 (.000)
CHICAGO						
Parental Network Size	−.047 (.191)					
Family Dysfunction	−.137 (.000)	.109 (.003)				
Parenting Practices	.162 (.000)	.114 (.002)	−.152 (.000)			
Parental Moral Beliefs	.098 (.006)	−.011 (.751)	−.277 (.000)	.232 (.000)		
Parental Conventional Values	.115 (.001)	.055 (.124)	−.277 (.000)	.312 (.000)	.432 (.000)	

(*continued*)

TABLE A7.1. *Bivariate Correlations for Family Characteristics (continued)*

Cell Entries: Pearson's r (p)	Family Income	Parental Network Size	Family Dysfunction	Parenting Practices	Parental Moral Beliefs	Parental Conventional Values
Institutional Effectiveness	.478 (.000)	−.121 (.001)	−.199 (.000)	.288 (.000)	.093 (.009)	.196 (.000)
Informal Networks	−.079 (.027)	.214 (.000)	.088 (.017)	.079 (.032)	−.091 (.011)	.093 (.000)
Normative/Value Consensus	.327 (.000)	−.039 (.275)	−.197 (.000)	.276 (.000)	.093 (.009)	.141 (.000)
Neighborhood Bonding/ Control	.509 (.000)	−.129 (.000)	−.187 (.000)	.275 (.000)	.090 (.011)	.128 (.000)
Illegal Modeling	−.525 (.000)	.095 (.007)	.202 (.000)	−.268 (.000)	−.089 (.012)	−.147 (.000)
Illegal Performance	−.348 (.000)	.152 (.000)	.248 (.000)	−.262 (.000)	−.127 (.000)	−.238 (.000)
General Organization (Summary Measure)	.486 (.000)	−.080 (.024)	−.214 (.000)	.322 (.000)	.092 (.010)	.221 (.000)
Neighborhood Disadvantage	−.444 (.000)	.241 (.000)	.183 (.000)	−.150 (.000)	−.070 (.049)	−.052 (.147)
Physical Deterioration	−.389 (.000)	−.008 (.825)	.187 (.000)	−.272 (.000)	−.144 (.000)	−.190 (.000)

TABLE A7.2. *Regression Results: Family Characteristics (Neighborhood Level Analysis)*

Dependent Variable	Percent Explained Variance (R²)	Independent Variable	Standardized Coefficient (b*)	Unstandardized Coefficient (b)	Statistical Significance (p)
DENVER					
Family Income	70	Informal Networks	.311	.311	.001
		Bonding and Control	.326	.326	.001
		Normative/Value Consensus	.257	.257	.006
Parental Network Size	72	Informal Networks	.532	.532	.000
		Bonding and Control	.272	.272	.002
		Illegal Performance	.307	.307	.022
Family Dysfunction	25	Illegal Performance Squared	-.244	-.259	.063
Parenting Practices	39	Institutional Effectiveness	.298	.298	.015
		Bonding and Control	.272	.272	.026
Parental Moral Beliefs	30	Informal Networks	.297	.297	.021
		Illegal Performance	-.343	-.343	.009
Parental Conventional Values	47	Institutional Effectiveness	-.278	-.278	.018
		Bonding and Control	-.419	-.419	.001
		Normative/Value Consensus	.223	.223	.062
CHICAGO					
Family Income	54	Poverty	-.206	-.912	.003
		Institutional Effectiveness	.102	.102	.073
		Bonding and Control	.154	.154	.002
Parental Network Size	35	Illegal Modeling	-.225	-.225	.000
		Poverty	.166	.736	.032
		Informal Networks	.245	.245	.003
		Illegal Performance	.184	.184	.032
Family Dysfunction	27	Institutional Effectiveness	-.206	-.206	.012
		Illegal Performance	.219	.219	.008
Parenting Practices	40	Institutional Effectiveness	.128	.128	.046
		Bonding and Control	.142	.142	.026
		Normative/Value Consensus	.195	.195	.011
		Illegal Performance	-.164	-.164	.032
Parental Moral Beliefs	3	n/a	–	–	–
Parental Conventional Values	19	Informal Networks	.211	.211	.018
		Illegal Performance	-.166	-.166	.058

TABLE A7.3. *HLM Results: Family Characteristics (Individual Level Analysis)*

Dependent Variable	Sample	Percent Explained Variance (R^2)	Independent Variable	Unstandardized HLM Coefficient (b)	Statistical Significance (p)
Family Income	Denver	52	Intercept	.230	.037
			Neighborhood Disadvantage	−.026	.919
			Deterioration	.147	.356
			Organization	.719	.010
			Age	.013	.218
			Gender (male)	−.043	.452
			Ethnicity: Black	−.220	.098
			Hispanic	−.190	.029
			Other	−.014	.918
			Socioeconomic Status	.102	.000
			Family Structure (intact)	.202	.003
			Length of Residence	.007	.062
	Chicago	27	Intercept	.124	.263
			Poverty	−.563	.044
			Deterioration	−.032	.695
			Organization	.098	.266
			Age	.010	.528
			Gender (male)	.035	.552
			Socioeconomic Status	.117	.000
			Family Structure (intact)	.367	.000
			Length of Residence	.005	.190
Parental Network Size	Denver	15	Intercept	.031	.584
			Neighborhood Disadvantage	.086	.472
			Deterioration	−.058	.465
			Organization	.034	.797
			Age	−.050	.001
			Gender (male)	−.024	.740
			Ethnicity: Black	−.402	.012
			Hispanic	−.348	.002
			Other	−.492	.008
			Socioeconomic Status	−.051	.025
			Family Structure (intact)	.193	.019
			Length of Residence	.038	.000

(*continued*)

TABLE A7.3. *HLM Results: Family Characteristics (Individual Level Analysis)* *(continued)*

Dependent Variable	Sample	Percent Explained Variance (R²)	Independent Variable	Unstandardized HLM Coefficient (b)	Statistical Significance (p)
	Chicago	9	Intercept	−.379	.014
			Poverty	1.071	.006
			Deterioration	−.045	.676
			Organization	.010	.930
			Age	−.000	.986
			Gender (male)	.016	.813
			Socioeconomic Status	.017	.353
			Family Structure (intact)	.010	.903
			Length of Residence	.027	.000
Family Dysfunction	Denver	5	Intercept	.002	.974
			Neighborhood Disadvantage	.041	.763
			Deterioration	−.200	.034
			Organization	−.253	.102
			Age	−.012	.360
			Gender (male)	.087	.236
			Ethnicity: Black	−.130	.398
			Hispanic	−.248	.022
			Other	−.200	.257
			Socioeconomic Status	.025	.251
			Family Structure (intact)	−.349	.000
			Length of Residence	−.002	.588
	Chicago	4	Intercept	−.081	.528
			Poverty	.126	.688
			Deterioration	−.000	.999
			Neighborhood Organization	−.094	.355
			Age	−.019	.341
			Gender (male)	−.023	.753
			Socioeconomic Status	−.059	.004
			Family Structure (intact)	−.145	.108
			Length of Residence	.002	.692
Parenting Practices	Denver	5	Intercept	.045	.427
			Neighborhood Disadvantage	−.173	.144

(continued)

TABLE A7.3. *HLM Results: Family Characteristics (Individual Level Analysis)* *(continued)*

Dependent Variable	Sample	Percent Explained Variance (R^2)	Independent Variable	Unstandardized HLM Coefficient (*b*)	Statistical Significance (*p*)
Parenting			Deterioration	−.042	.586
Practices			Organization	.055	.668
			Age	−.060	.000
			Gender (male)	.031	.676
			Ethnicity: Black	−.020	.897
			Hispanic	.140	.196
			Other	.233	.202
			Socioeconomic Status	−.014	.530
			Family Structure (intact)	.070	.389
			Length of Residence	−.003	.537
	Chicago	17	Intercept	−.192	.058
			Poverty	.506	.042
			Deterioration	.042	.557
			Organization	.280	.001
			Age	−.100	.000
			Gender (male)	−.267	.001
			Socioeconomic Status	.080	.000
			Family Structure (intact)	.201	.023
			Length of Residence	−.001	.807
Parental	Denver	12	Intercept	−.020	.677
Moral Beliefs			Neighborhood Disadvantage	−.052	.609
			Deterioration	.009	.892
			Organization	.134	.233
			Age	−.126	.000
			Gender (male)	−.095	.201
			Ethnicity: Black	.294	.052
			Hispanic	.336	.003
			Other	.124	.480
			Socioeconomic Status	−.004	.863
			Family Structure (intact)	.090	.256
			Length of Residence	.000	.917
	Chicago	3	Intercept	−.066	.636
			Poverty	.141	.680

(continued)

TABLE A7.3. *HLM Results: Family Characteristics (Individual Level Analysis)* (continued)

Dependent Variable	Sample	Percent Explained Variance (R^2)	Independent Variable	Unstandardized HLM Coefficient (b)	Statistical Significance (p)
Parental Moral Beliefs	Chicago		Deterioration	−.087	.395
			Organization	−.048	.661
			Age	−.016	.414
			Gender (male)	−.148	.039
			Socioeconomic Status	.043	.026
			Family Structure (intact)	.194	.030
			Length of Residence	.014	.002
Parental Conventional Values	Denver	13	Intercept	−.014	.843
			Neighborhood Disadvantage	.045	.757
			Deterioration	.088	.377
			Organization	.141	.395
			Age	.039	.005
			Gender (male)	−.222	.003
			Ethnicity: Black	.555	.001
			Hispanic	.534	.000
			Other	.472	.008
			Socioeconomic Status	−.081	.001
			Family Structure (intact)	.101	.183
			Length of Residence	−.005	.287
	Chicago	5	Intercept	−.183	.284
			Poverty	.579	.176
			Deterioration	.119	.349
			Organization	.295	.032
			Age	.033	.073
			Gender (male)	−.017	.786
			Socioeconomic Status	.039	.030
			Family Structure (intact)	.191	.023
			Length of Residence	−.002	.692

TABLE A7.4. *Bivariate Correlations: Family Characteristics and Youth Development Outcomes*

Cell Entries: Correlation (p)	Family Income	Parental Network Size	Family Dysfunction	Parenting Practices	Parental Moral Beliefs	Parental Conventional Values
Neighborhood level:						
Personal Competence	.786 (.000)	.616 (.000)	-.032 (.860)	.671 (.000)	.249 (.163)	-.387 (.028)
Prosocial Behavior	.742 (.000)	.581 (.000)	-.073 (.688)	.704 (.000)	.387 (.026)	-.240 (.178)
Prosocial Competence	.340 (.032)	.040 (.798)	-.662 (.000)	.711 (.000)	.298 (.062)	.575 (.000)
On Track	.491 (.004)	.320 (.069)	-.165 (.360)	.428 (.013)	.035 (.845)	-.292 (.099)
Problem Behavior (Denver)	-.280 (.115)	-.108 (.551)	.364 (.037)	-.319 (.070)	-.156 (.385)	-.146 (.419)
Problem Behavior (Chicago)	-.517 (.001)	.059 (.718)	.387 (.014)	-.325 (.041)	-.341 (.031)	-.062 (.701)
Individual level:						
Personal Competence	.252 (.000)	.162 (.000)	.039 (.288)	.496 (.000)	.104 (.004)	-.052 (.156)
Prosocial Behavior	.229 (.000)	.151 (.000)	.051 (.163)	.381 (.000)	.219 (.000)	-.189 (.000)
Prosocial Competence	.294 (.000)	.099 (.005)	-.234 (.000)	.498 (.000)	.281 (.000)	.416 (.000)
On Track	.158 (.000)	.124 (.001)	.001 (.976)	.382 (.000)	.049 (.181)	-.048 (.190)
Problem Behavior (Denver)	-.003 (.944)	-.082 (.026)	.070 (.057)	-.127 (.000)	-.153 (.000)	-.075 (.040)
Problem Behavior (Chicago)	-.094 (.008)	.023 (.523)	.164 (.000)	-.244 (.000)	-.122 (.001)	-.068 (.060)

TABLE A7.5. *Explained Variance in Youth Development Outcomes: Neighborhood Level*

Dependent Variable	Personal Competence	Prosocial Behavior	Prosocial Competence	Problem Behavior Denver	Problem Behavior (Chicago)	On Track
Percent Explained Variance (R^2):						
Disadvantage and Deterioration	58	45	19	6	19	32
Disadvantage, Deterioration, and Organization (Separate Measures)	78	65	33	33	29	51
Disadvantage, Deterioration, Organization (Separate Measures) and Family Characteristics	90	78	68	55	44	62
Increase Attributable to Family Characteristics	12	13	35	22	15	11

TABLE A8.1. *Bivariate Correlations for School and Peer Group Characteristics*

Cell Entries: Pearson's r (p)	Student Status (Non-Dropout) Denver only	Positive School Environment		School Violence and Safety		Positive Peer Group Environment	
		Chi	Den	Chi	Den	Chi	Den
Positive School Environment	NA						
School Violence and Safety	NA	−.248 (.000)	−.491 (.000)				
Positive Peer Group Environment	.264 (.000)	.277 (.000)	.367 (.000)	−.440 (.000)	−.271 (.000)		
Family Income	.085 (.021)	.088 (.014)	.039 (.305)	−.180 (.000)	−.309 (.000)	.228 (.000)	−.024 (.530)
Parental Network Size	.087 (.017)	.051 (.155)	.046 (.223)	.072 (.043)	−.076 (.044)	−.084 (.020)	.067 (.071)
Family Dysfunction	.004 (.906)	−.229 (.000)	.063 (.096)	.139 (.000)	.005 (.887)	−.158 (.000)	−.052 (.160)
Parenting Practices	.250 (.000)	.285 (.000)	.388 (.000)	−.181 (.000)	−.259 (.000)	.359 (.000)	.324 (.000)
Parental Moral Beliefs	.107 (.003)	.239 (.000)	.037 (.330)	−.151 (.000)	.028 (.451)	.218 (.000)	.241 (.000)
Parental Conventional Values	−.053 (.143)	.291 (.000)	.035 (.347)	−.008 (.814)	.081 (.030)	.055 (.130)	.081 (.028)
Institutional Effectiveness	.127 (.000)	.202 (.000)	.056 (.120)	−.251 (.000)	−.247 (.000)	.275 (.000)	−.030 (.408)

(continued)

TABLE A8.1. *Bivariate Correlations for School and Peer Group Characteristics (continued)*

Cell Entries: Pearson's r (p)	Student Status (Non-Dropout) Denver only	Positive School Environment		School Violence and Safety		Positive Peer Group Environment	
		Chi	Den	Chi	Den	Chi	Den
Informal Networks	.074 (.035)	.061 (.089)	-.026 (.467)	.115 (.001)	-.131 (.000)	-.077 (.031)	-.084 (.019)
Normative and Value Consensus	.074 (.033)	.181 (.000)	.067 (.067)	-.220 (.000)	-.217 (.000)	.244 (.000)	.177 (.000)
Neighborhood Bonding/Control	.140 (.000)	.174 (.000)	.084 (.021)	-.287 (.000)	-.311 (.000)	.291 (.000)	-.002 (.963)
Illegal Modeling	-.102 (.003)	-.198 (.000)	-.068 (.060)	.317 (.000)	.287 (.000)	-.312 (.000)	.037 (.302)
Illegal Performance	-.007 (.838)	-.197 (.000)	-.021 (.565)	.241 (.000)	.140 (.000)	-.252 (.000)	-.191 (.000)
Neighborhood Organization (Summary Measure)	.119 (.001)	.226 (.000)	.061 (.090)	-.276 (.000)	-.319 (.000)	.297 (.000)	.037 (.301)
Neighborhood Disadvantage	-.156 (.000)	-.055 (.127)	-.113 (.002)	.218 (.000)	.311 (.000)	-.256 (.000)	-.047 (.186)
Physical Deterioration	-.123 (.000)	-.196 (.000)	-.013 (.722)	.235 (.000)	.191 (.000)	-.263 (.000)	.110 (.002)

TABLE A8.2. *Ridge Regression Results: School and Peer Group Characteristics–Neighborhood Level Analysis*

Dependent Variable	Percent Explained Variance (R^2)	Independent Variable	Standardized Coefficient (b^*)	Unstandardized Coefficient (b)	Statistical Significance (p)
DENVER					
Student Status (School Enrollment/Graduation)	55	Deterioration	−.276	−.012	.021
		Neighborhood Disadvantage	−.261	−.011	.020
		Bonding/Control	.349	.015	.002
		Illegal Modeling	.234	.010	.046
		Parenting Practices	.316	.316	.011
Positive School Environment	42	Conventional Values	.205	.205	.085
		Family Income	.347	.347	.006
School Violence/Safety	87	Neighborhood Disadvantage	.128	.128	.050
		Bonding/Control	−.152	−.152	.008
		Illegal Modeling	.125	.125	.053
		Illegal Performance	.102	.102	.092
		Parenting Practices	−.257	−.257	.000
		Parental Network Size	−.162	−.162	.015
		Family Income	−.223	−.223	.002

(continued)

TABLE A8.2. *Ridge Regression Results: School and Peer Group Characteristics–Neighborhood Level Analysis (continued)*

Dependent Variable	Percent Explained Variance (R^2)	Independent Variable	Standardized Coefficient (b^*)	Unstandardized Coefficient (b)	Statistical Significance (p)
Positive Peer Group Environment	37	Parenting Practices	.330	.330	.010
		Family Dysfunction	-.349	-.349	.007
		Conventional Values	.205	.205	.098
CHICAGO					
Positive School Environment	43	Parenting Practices	.224	.224	.003
		Family Dysfunction	-.249	-.249	.001
		Conventional Values	.125	.125	.075
School Violence/Safety	49	Informal Networks	.135	.135	.056
		Illegal Modeling	.214	.214	.002
		Illegal Performance	.149	.149	.030
		Parenting Practices	-.260	-.260	.000
Positive Peer Group Environment	48	Normative/Value Consensus	.140	.140	.051
		Illegal Modeling	-.136	-.136	.038
		Illegal Performance	-.213	-.213	.004
		Family Income	.120	.120	.080
		Parenting Practices	.119	.119	.085
		Conventional Values	-.174	-.174	.018

TABLE A8.3. *HLM Results: School and Peer Group Characteristics–Individual Level Analysis*

Dependent Variable	Sample	Percent Explained Variance (R^2)	Independent Variable	Unstandardized HLM Coefficient (b)	Statistical Significance (p)
Student Status (enrolled or graduated)	Denver	NA	Intercept	7.345	.000
			Neighborhood Disadvantage	−.957	.154
			Deterioration	−1.387	.009
			Organization	−1.235	.126
			Family Income	1.527	.059
			Parental Network Size	.890	.137
			Family Dysfunction	−.386	.194
			Parenting Practices	.843	.006
			Parental Moral Beliefs	.094	.694
			Parental Conventional Values	.464	.135
			Age	−.848	.000
			Gender (male)	.255	.665
			Ethnicity: Black	3.553	.022
			Hispanic	.468	.624
			Other	2.727	.125
			Socioeconomic Status	−.052	.773
			Family Structure (intact)	.116	.859
			Length of Residence	.018	.596
Positive School Environment	Denver	23	Intercept	−.035	.478
			Neighborhood Disadvantage	−.235	.030
			Deterioration	.100	.149
			Organization	−.055	.651

(continued)

327

TABLE A8.3. *HLM Results: School and Peer Group Characteristics–Individual Level Analysis (continued)*

Dependent Variable	Sample	Percent Explained Variance (R^2)	Independent Variable	Unstandardized HLM Coefficient (b)	Statistical Significance (p)
Positive School Environment	Denver	23	Family Income	.065	.164
			Parental Network Size	.082	.073
			Family Dysfunction	.075	.055
			Parenting Practices	.370	.000
			Parental Moral Beliefs	−.095	.026
			Parental Conventional Values	.069	.091
			Age	−.094	.000
			Gender (male)	−.072	.328
			Ethnicity: Black	−.067	.656
			Hispanic	.216	.053
			Other	−.095	.585
			Socioeconomic Status	.005	.815
			Family Structure (intact)	−.046	.565
			Length of Residence	−.006	.221
	Chicago	15	Intercept	−.202	.083
			Poverty	.530	.067
			Deterioration	.024	.774
			Organization	.178	.062
			Family Income	−.070	.147
			Parental Network Size	−.008	.845
			Family Dysfunction	−.118	.005
			Parenting Practices	.138	.002

(continued)

TABLE A8.3. *HLM Results: School and Peer Group Characteristics–Individual Level Analysis (continued)*

Dependent Variable	Sample	Percent Explained Variance (R^2)	Independent Variable	Unstandardized HLM Coefficient (b)	Statistical Significance (p)
Positive School Environment	Chicago	15	Parental Moral Beliefs	.094	.042
			Parental Conventional Values	.127	.009
			Age	−.009	.682
			Gender (male)	−.046	.532
			Socioeconomic Status	.018	.386
			Family Structure (intact)	.083	.381
			Length of Residence	.008	.084
School Violence and Safety	Denver	18	Intercept	.007	.880
			Neighborhood Disadvantage	.130	.166
			Deterioration	−.083	.171
			Organization	−.106	.330
			Family Income	−.144	.006
			Parental Network Size	−.031	.498
			Family Dysfunction	−.022	.577
			Parenting Practices	−.194	.000
			Parental Moral Beliefs	.066	.126
			Parental Conventional Values	−.052	.217
			Age	.030	.066
			Gender (male)	.014	.857
			Ethnicity: Black	.370	.021
			Hispanic	.313	.009
			Other	.342	.062
			Socioeconomic Status	−.042	.075
			Family Structure (intact)	.029	.728
			Length of Residence	.007	.146

(continued)

329

TABLE A8.3. *HLM Results: School and Peer Group Characteristics–Individual Level Analysis (continued)*

Dependent Variable	Sample	Percent Explained Variance (R^2)	Independent Variable	Unstandardized HLM Coefficient (b)	Statistical Significance (p)
School Violence and Saftey	Chicago	14	Intercept	.084	.522
			Poverty	−.040	.902
			Deterioration	.083	.390
			Organization	−.190	.073
			Family Income	.002	.973
			Parental Network Size	.058	.147
			Family Dysfunction	.063	.103
			Parenting Practices	−.033	.430
			Parental Moral Beliefs	−.120	.009
			Parental Conventional Values	.101	.033
			Age	.109	.000
			Gender (male)	.036	.614
			Socioeconomic Status	.012	.566
			Family Structure (intact)	−.113	.223
			Length of Residence	−.007	.106
Positive Peer Group Environment	Denver	29	Intercept	.012	.787
			Neighborhood Disadvantage	−.118	.200
			Deterioration	.127	.034
			Organization	.012	.911
			Family Income	−.025	.561
			Parental Network Size	.026	.540

(continued)

TABLE A8.3. *HLM Results: School and Peer Group Characteristics–Individual Level Analysis (continued)*

Dependent Variable	Sample	Percent Explained Variance (R^2)	Independent Variable	Unstandardized HLM Coefficient (b)	Statistical Significance (p)
Positive Peer Group Environment	Denver	23	Family Dysfunction	.007	.832
			Parenting Practices	.227	.000
			Parental Moral Beliefs	.055	.137
			Parental Conventional Values	.074	.053
			Age	-.138	.000
			Gender (male)	-.177	.013
			Ethnicity: Black	.188	.178
			Hispanic	-.018	.853
			Other	.052	.745
			Socioeconomic Status	-.006	.777
			Family Structure (intact)	.296	.000
			Length of Residence	.006	.195
	Chicago	26	Intercept	.048	.591
			Poverty	-.284	.195
			Deterioration	-.061	.336
			Organization	.091	.217
			Family Income	.028	.523
			Parental Network Size	-.071	.059
			Family Dysfunction	-.059	.106
			Parenting Practices	.213	.000
			Parental Moral Beliefs	.173	.000
			Parental Conventional Values	-.109	.015
			Age	-.123	.000
			Gender (male)	-.194	.008
			Socioeconomic Status	.022	.243
			Family Structure (intact)	.073	.408
			Length of Residence	.001	.855

TABLE A8.4. *Bivariate Correlations: School and Peer Group Characteristics and Youth Development Outcomes*

Cell Entries: Correlations (*p*)	Student Status	Positive School Environment	School Violence/ Safety	Positive Peer Group Environment
Neighborhood level:				
Personal Competence	.560	.427	−.821	.347
(Denver)	(.001)	(.013)	(.000)	(.048)
Prosocial Behavior	.616	.594	−.792	.409
(Denver)	(.000)	(.000)	(.000)	(.018)
Prosocial Competence	NA	.637	−.317	.228
(Chicago)		(.000)	(.046)	(.157)
On Track (Denver)	.607	.264	−.512	.503
	(.000)	(.137)	(.002)	(.003)
Problem Behavior	−.292	−.169	.308	−.769
(Denver)	(.099)	(.346)	(.082)	(.000)
Problem Behavior	NA	−.294	.366	−.377
(Chicago)		(.066)	(.020)	(.016)
Individual level:				
Personal Competence	.198	.381	−.437	.252
(Denver)	(.000)	(.000)	(.000)	(.000)
Prosocial Behavior	.242	.269	−.287	.425
(Denver)	(.000)	(.000)	(.000)	(.000)
Prosocial Competence	NA	.369	−.149	.270
(Chicago)		(.000)	(.000)	(.000)
On Track (Denver)	.458	.184	−.349	.311
	(.000)	(.000)	(.000)	(.000)
Problem Behavior	−.097	−.210	.195	−.477
(Denver)	(.006)	(.000)	(.000)	(.000)
Problem Behavior	NA	−.227	.306	−.474
(Chicago)		(.000)	(.000)	(.000)

TABLE A9.1. *Neighborhood Level Reduced Models for Youth Development Outcomes*

Dependent Variable	R^2: Full Model	R^2: Reduced Model	Reduced Model Independent Variables	b*: Standardized Coefficient	b: Unstandardized Coefficient	p: Statistical Significance	d: Directly Explained Variance
Personal Competence (Denver)	89	88	Bonding and Control	.284	.284	.000	25
			Normative/Value Consensus	.191	.191	.005	13
			Illegal Performance[a]	.149	.149	.016	2
			Parenting Practices	.154	.154	.016	11
			Family Income	.217	.217	.002	18
			School Violence/Safety	-.157	.157	.010	13
			Positive Peer Group Environment	.155	.155	.012	6
			Constant	n/a	.000	1.000	n/a
Prosocial Behavior (Denver)	88	86	Deterioration	-.141	-.141	.052	8
			Informal Networks	.152	.152	.040	10
			Parenting Practices	.130	.130	.069	10
			Parental Moral Beliefs	.118	.118	.082	5
			Family Income	.148	.148	.034	12
			Student Status	.126	.126	.082	8
			Positive School Environment	.176	.176	.015	11
			School Violence/Safety	-.146	-.146	.043	12
			Positive Peer Group Environment	.212	.212	.003	9
			Constant	n/a	-2.747	.082	n/a
Prosocial Competence (Chicago)	71	68	Deterioration	-.092	-.152	.085	5
			Institutional Effectiveness	.121	.199	.023	8

(continued)

333

TABLE A9.1. *Neighborhood Level Reduced Models for Youth Development Outcomes (continued)*

Dependent Variable	R²: Full Model	R²: Reduced Model	Reduced Model Independent Variables	b*: Standardized Coefficient	b: Unstandardized Coefficient	p: Statistical Significance	d: Directly Explained Variance
			Family Dysfunction	-.172	-.284	.002	14
			Parenting Practices	.224	.369	.000	19
			Parental Conventional Values	.142	.233	.013	10
			Positive School Environment	.157	.258	.006	12
			Constant	n/a	-.319	.055	n/a
Problem Behavior (Denver)	73	62	Normative/Value Consensus	-.234	-.234	.016	13
			Positive Peer Group Environment	-.549	-.549	.000	49
			Constant	n/a	.000	1.000	n/a
Problem Behavior (Chicago)	45	36	Deterioration	.140	.090	.064	8
			Illegal Performance	.154	.099	.047	8
			Family Income	-.197	-.126	.011	13
			Parental Moral Beliefs	-.156	-.100	.050	7
			Constant	n/a	.088	.309	n/a
On Track (Denver)	73	67	Bonding and Control	.198	.011	.048	13
			Normative/Value Consensus	.307	.017	.004	22
			Parental Moral Beliefs[a]	-.162	-.009	.087	1
			Student Status	.237	.299	.020	16
			Positive Peer Group Environment	.269	.015	.006	15
			Constant	n/a	.267	.030	n/a

[a] Relationship in opposite direction than expected.

TABLE A9.2. *Individual Level Reduced Models for Youth Development Outcomes*

Dependent Variable	R²: Full Model	R²: Reduced Model	Reduced Model Independent Variables	b*: Standardized Coefficient	b: Unstandardized Coefficient	p: Statistical Significance	d: Directly Explained Variance
Personal Competence (Denver)	42	43	Organization	.140	.116	.057	4
			Age	.133	.058	.000	1
			Black	.025	.060	.628	0
			Hispanic	−.099	−.224	.020	2
			Other	−.005	−.036	.808	0
			SES	.096	.040	.034	2
			Family Structure (intact)	−.141	−.303	.000	0
			Residential Stability	.098	.008	.042	1
			Parental Network Size	.068	.107	.009	1
			Parenting Practices	.341	.346	.000	16
			Positive School Environment	.179	.185	.000	7
			School Violence/Safety	−.155	−.161	.000	6
			Positive Peer Group Environment	.088	.112	.009	2
			Constant	n/a	.060	.194	
Prosocial Behavior (Denver)	39	39	Disadvantage	−.050	−.043	.558	1
			Deterioration	−.215	−.206	.002	5
			Age	−.162	−.064	.000	4
			Male	−.035	−.066	.297	0
			Black	.157	.472	.001	0
			Hispanic	.031	.084	.375	1
			Other	−.087	−.355	.022	1
			SES[a]	−.116	−.050	.014	1
			Family Structure (intact)	.159	.292	.000	3

(continued)

TABLE A9.2. *Individual Level Reduced Models for Youth Development Outcomes (continued)*

Dependent Variable	R²: Full Model	R²: Reduced Model	Reduced Model Independent Variables	b*: Standardized Coefficient	b: Unstandardized Coefficient	p: Statistical Significance	d: Directly Explained Variance
			Residential Stability	.081	.008	.034	1
			Family Income	.068	.069	.085	1
			Family Dysfunction[a]	.063	.064	.056	1
			Parenting Practices	.160	.173	.000	5
			Conventional Values[a]	-.135	-.132	.001	2
			School Violence/Safety	-.080	-.072	.051	2
			Positive Peer Group Environment	.276	.284	.000	9
			Male × Disadvantage	.181	.317	.000	2
			Constant	n/a	.118	.019	
Prosocial Competence (Chicago)	43	43	Neighborhood Organization	.037	.036	.411	1
			Male	-.126	-.251	.000	2
			SES	.168	.068	.000	7
			Residential Stability[a]	-.067	-.007	.038	0
			Family Income	.153	.151	.000	5
			Parental Network Size	.077	.074	.021	1
			Parenting Practices	.249	.247	.000	11
			Parental Conventional Values	.205	.211	.000	8
			Positive School Environment	.191	.189	.000	7
			Male × Organization	.071	.141	.014	2
			Constant	n/a	.007	.847	
Problem Behavior (Denver)	31	32	Age	.063	.020	.095	2
			Male	.130	.195	.001	2
			Black	.092	.194	.048	0

(continued)

TABLE A9.2. *Individual Level Reduced Models for Youth Development Outcomes (continued)*

Dependent Variable	R²: Full Model	R²: Reduced Model	Reduced Model Independent Variables	b*: Standardized Coefficient	b: Unstandardized Coefficient	p: Statistical Significance	d: Directly Explained Variance
Problem Behavior (Denver)			Hispanic	.066	.081	.217	0
			Other	.080	.247	.042	0
			Family Dysfunction	.065	.052	.051	0
			Parental Moral Beliefs	−.101	−.081	.009	2
			Parental Conventional Values	−.061	−.049	.090	1
			Positive Peer Group Environment	−.470	−.380	.000	25
			Constant	n/a	−.046	.157	
Problem Behavior (Chicago)	29	30	Neighborhood Organization	.014	.014	.723	0
			Age	.156	.091	.000	3
			Family Structure (intact)	.086	.194	.027	0
			Family Dysfunction	.070	.076	.057	1
			Parenting Practices	−.075	−.077	.056	2
			Positive School Environment	−.091	−.094	.018	2
			School Violence/Safety	−.088	−.091	.029	2
			Positive Peer Group Environment	−.377	−.386	.000	17
			Age × Organization	−.122	−.071	.001	2
			Constant	n/a	.021	.571	
On Track (Denver)	18	18	Disadvantage	.014	.002	.850	0
			Age	−.023	−.001	.520	0
			Male	−.128	−.039	.002	2
			Black	−.007	−.005	.812	0
			Hispanic	−.115	−.034	.030	2
			Other	−.112	−.074	.008	1
			Parenting Practices	.220	.032	.000	5
			School Violence/Safety	−.272	−.036	.000	7
			Age × Disadvantage	−.107	−.006	.031	1
			Constant	n/a	.561	.000	

[a] Relationship in opposite direction than expected.

337

TABLE A9.3. *Predictors of Success in Disadvantaged Neighborhoods**
A: *Personal Competence*

Predictors	Standardized Coefficient (b^*)	Unstandardized Coefficient (b)	Statistical Significance (p)	Comments and Interpretation $R^2 = .48$ (6% increase over Table A9.2)
Intercept	NA	.122	.287	– On average, Disadvantaged Neighborhoods have lower levels of Personal Competence (PC).
Advantaged vs. Disadvantaged Neighborhood	–.108	–.261	.018	
Neighborhood Organization	.238	.240	.000	– PC is higher where Neighborhood Organization is higher.
Age (compared to age 10)	.128	.048	.001	– PC tends to increase with age (but see ethnicity).
Gender (male compared to female)	–.044	–.089	.142	– (Not statistically significant)
Ethnicity (compared to White):				– Initially, PC tends to be higher for African American and Other ethnic groups than for Whites, but while the general tendency is for PC to increase with age, it tends to *decrease relative to whites* for all three minority ethnic groups. By age 18, all three minority ethnic groups have lower scores on PC than whites.
African American	.145	.376	.050	
Hispanic	.019	.040	.751	
Other	.186	.697	.003	
Ethnicity × Age:				
African American × Age	–.139	–.074	.055	
Hispanic × Age	–.122	–.054	.038	
Other × Age	–.280	–.278	.001	
Intact Family Structure	–.142	–.287	.000	– PC is lower for adolescents in intact families.
Residential Stability	.273	.032	.000	– PC is higher for adolescents who are residentially stable, but the effect decreases with age.
Residential Stability × Age	–.196	–.005	.002	

(continued)

TABLE A9.3. *Predictors of Success in Disadvantaged Neighborhoods** (continued)

A: Personal Competence

Predictors	Standardized Coefficient (b*)	Unstandardized Coefficient (b)	Statistical Significance (p)	Comments and Interpretation $R^2 = .48$ (6% increase over Table A9.2)
Parental Network Size	-.019	-.022	.801	– Parental Network Size has a *negative* effect on PC for males in Disadvantaged neighborhoods, and a *positive* effect on PC for females in Advantaged Neighborhoods.
Parental Network Size × Disadvantage	.171	.211	.018	
Parental Network Size × Gender	-.107	-.159	.036	
Good Parenting Practices	.569	.611	.000	– Good Parenting Practices have a strong positive effect on PC that declines (but remains strong) with age and is higher in Disadvantaged Neighborhoods.
Good Parenting Practices × Disadvantage	-.190	-.243	.002	
Good Parenting Practices × Age	-.110	-.024	.072	
Positive Peer Group Environment	-.038	-.041	.548	– Positive Peer Group Environment has a positive effect on PC, but only in non-Disadvantaged neighborhoods.
Positive Peer Group Environment × Disadvantage	.162	.202	.014	
Positive School Environment	.382	.357	.000	– Positive School Environment has a positive effect on PC, more for females than for males; the effect declines with age.
Positive School Environment × Age	-.128	-.025	.057	
Positive School Environment × Gender	-.163	-.226	.003	
School Violence/Safety	.024	.024	.741	– School Violence/Safety has a negative effect on PC, stronger for males and non-Disadvantaged neighborhoods and weaker for females and Disadvantaged neighborhoods.
School Violence/Safety × Disadvantage	-.151	-.167	.028	
School Violence/Safety × Gender	-.131	-.181	.012	

* Disadvantaged Neighborhoods are coded as zero and non-Disadvantaged Neighborhoods as one.

TABLE A9.3B. *Prosocial Behavior*

Predictors	Standardized Coefficient (b*)	Unstandardized Coefficient (b)	Statistical Significance (p)	Comments and Interpretation R² = 42 (3% increase over Table A9.2)
Intercept		.345	.008	– No average difference between Advantaged and Disadvantaged Neighborhoods.
Advantaged vs. Disadvantaged Neighborhood	.016	.036	.761	– Less Prosocial Behavior in Deteriorated Neighborhoods.
Neighborhood Physical Deterioration	-.195	-.185	.001	– Prosocial Behavior tends to decline with age.
Age (compared to age 10)	-.166	-.059	.000	– No unconditional gender difference.
Gender (male compared to female)	-.042	-.081	.192	
Ethnicity (compared to white):				– Prosocial Behavior (ProsocialB) is lower for Hispanic and Other ethnic groups than for white or African American ethnic groups, more so for females than for males. African American and Hispanic males actually have higher levels of ProsocialB than white males.
African American	.074	.181	.282	
Hispanic	-.211	-.408	.003	
Other	-.225	-.790	.000	
Ethnicity × Gender:				
African American × Gender	.047	.172	.417	
Hispanic × Gender	.261	.690	.000	
Other × Gender	.137	.652	.024	
Socioeconomic Status	.012	.005	.847	– As adolescents get older, Socioeconomic Status becomes negatively associated with ProsocialB.
Socioeconomic Status × Age	-.152	-.017	.025	
Intact Family Structure	.184	.349	.000	– ProsocialB is higher in intact families.
Residential Stability	-.062	-.007	.338	– ProsocialB becomes higher for residentially stable adolescents as they get older.
Residential Stability × Age	.140	.003	.035	
Family Income	-.060	-.047	.513	– ProsocialB becomes positively associated with family Income as adolescents get older.
Family Income × Age	.183	.030	.063	

(continued)

TABLE A9.3B. *Prosocial Behavior (continued)*

Predictors	Standardized Coefficient (b*)	Unstandardized Coefficient (b)	Statistical Significance (p)	Comments and Interpretation $R^2 = .42$ (3% increase over Table A9.2)
Family Dysfunction	−.087	−.082	.177	– ProsocialB is *positively* associated with Family Dysfunction in *non-Disadvantaged* Neighborhoods.
Family Dysfunction × Disadvantage	.203	.222	.004	
Good Parenting Practices	.154	.156	.000	– ProsocialB is positively related to good parenting.
Parental Conventional Values	−.134	−.129	.001	– ProsocialB is negatively related to conv. values.
Positive Peer Group Environment	.249	.252	.000	– ProsocialB is positively related to good peer climate.
Positive School Environment	.290	.258	.004	
Positive School Environment × Disadvantage	−.128	−.132	.053	– ProsocialB is positively related to school environment, more for Disadvantaged Neighborhoods, and the relationship declines with age.
Positive School Environment × Age	−.200	−.037	.014	
School Violence/Safety	.252	.231	.003	– ProsocialB is a weakly *positively* related to school violence for females, at younger ages, but relationship is negative for both females and males at older ages.
School Violence/Safety × Age	−.321	−.066	.000	
School Violence/Safety × Gender	−.133	−.173	.012	

TABLE A9.3C. *Prosocial Competence*

Predictors	Standardized Coefficient (b^*)	Unstandardized Coefficient (b)	Statistical Significance (p)	Comments and Interpretation $R^2 = .45$ (2% increase over Table A9.2)
Intercept	NA	.037	.614	
Advantaged vs. Disadvantaged Neighborhood	.014	.028	.730	No difference between low and high Disadvantaged Neighborhoods.
Age (compared to age 11)	.062	.035	.045	Older kids have higher Prosocial Competence.
Gender (male compared to female)	-.101	-.202	.002	Males have lower Prosocial Competence.
Socioeconomic Status	.183	.074	.000	Kids from higher SES families have higher PC.
Residential Stability	-.077	-.017	.001	Longer term residents have lower PC in Disadvantaged Neighborhoods, but no effect in Advantaged Neighborhoods.
Residential Stability × Disadvantage	.076	.017	.015	
Family Income	.149	.147	.000	Kids from higher income households have higher PC.
Parental Network Size	.089	.085	.008	Kids whose parents have larger networks have high PC.
Good Parenting Practices	.248	.245	.000	PC is higher in families with Good Parenting Practices.
Parental Conventional Values	.316	.324	.000	PC is higher when mothers have conventional values
Parental Conventional Values × Age	-.126	-.049	.011	...but the effect declines with age.
Positive School Environment	-.028	-.028	.611	Good school environments increase PC
Positive School Environment × Age	.213	.070	.000	...but only for older kids
Positive School Environment × Gender	.078	.112	.060	...and more for males than for females.

TABLE A9.3D. *On Track*

Predictors	Standardized Coefficient (b^*)	Unstandardized Coefficient (b)	Statistical Significance (p)	Comments and Interpretation $R^2 = .27$ (8% increase over Table A9.2)
Intercept	NA	.592	.000	– No average difference in On Track between Disadvantaged and Advantaged neighborhoods.
Advantaged vs. Disadvantaged Neighborhood	.009	.003	.887	– Males are less likely than females to be On Track initially, but for On Track males trend upward while females trend downward.
Age (compared to age 10)	–.046	–.002	.448	
Age × Gender	.169	.009	.034	
Gender (male compared to female)	–.247	–.069	.001	– There is a complex interaction among ethnicity, age, and gender, as predictors of being On Track. For all three ethnic minority groups, females are less likely to be On Track than males. Hispanic and Other females are less likely to be On Track than white or African American females, and African American females become less likely to be On Track than white females as they get older. Males from all three minority ethnic groups start off as likely to be On Track as white males, but become relatively less likely to be On Track with age compared to white males.
Ethnicity (compared to White):				
African American	.074	.027	.514	
Hispanic	–.224	–.064	.032	
Other	–.205	–.106	.035	
Ethnicity × Age:				
African American × Age	–.234	–.017	.017	
Hispanic × Age	–.037	.023	.653	
Other × Age	–.016	–.022	.876	
Ethnicity × Gender:				
African American × Gender	.133	.072	.066	
Hispanic × Gender	.219	.085	.003	
Other × Gender	.140	.098	.057	
Socioeconomic Status	.111	.007	.284	– Individuals with higher SES are more likely to be On Track, but this is more true of younger age groups and individuals in Advantaged Neighborhoods.
Socioeconomic Status × Disadvantage	.187	.014	.045	
Socioeconomic Status × Age	–.268	–.004	.002	

(continued)

TABLE A9.3D. *On Track* (continued)

Predictors	Standardized Coefficient (b^*)	Unstandardized Coefficient (b)	Statistical Significance (p)	Comments and Interpretation $R^2 = .27$ (8% increase over Table A9.2)
Intact Family Structure	.161	.045	.067	– Individuals with intact family structure are more likely to be On Track, especially in Disadvantaged Neighborhoods.
Intact Family Structure × Disadvantage	−.191	−.054	.053	
Residential Stability	.099	.002	.407	– The positive association between residential stability and being On Track increases with age, and is higher in Disadvantaged Neighborhoods.
Residential Stability × Disadvantage	−.176	−.003	.077	
Residential Stability × Age	.145	.0005	.070	
Family Income	−.349	.040	.004	– At early ages, Income is negatively associated with being On Track, but at later ages, there is a strong positive relationship between Income and being On Track.
Family Income × Age	.305	.007	.014	
Parental Network Size	−.232	−.036	.012	– Parental Network Size is *negatively* related to being On Track, but only in Disadvantaged Neighborhoods.
Parental Network Size × Disadvantage	.204	.035	.029	
Family Dysfunction	−.078	−.011	.201	– Family Dysfunction becomes *positively* related with being On Track as adolescents get older.
Family Dysfunction × Age	.136	.004	.034	
Good Parenting Practices	−.096	−.014	.176	– Good Parenting Practices are unrelated to being On Track at early ages, but strongly positively related to being On Track at older ages.
Good Parenting Practices × Age	.358	.011	.000	
Parental Beliefs	.091	.012	.247	– Parental Beliefs are positively related to being On Track, but only in Disadvantaged Neighborhoods.
Parental Beliefs × Disadvantage	−.141	−.022	.078	
Parental Conventional Values	.131	.019	.038	– Conventional Values are positively related to being On Track for females but not for males.
Parental Conventional Values × Gender	−.114	−.022	.055	
Positive Peer Group Environment	.092	.014	.054	– Positive Peer Group Environment is positively related to On Track.
School Violence/Safety	−.197	−.027	.002	– School Violence/Safety is negatively related to being On Track, for both males and females, but more for males than for females.
School Violence/Safety × Gender	−.125	−.024	.039	

TABLE A9.3E. *Problem Behavior (Denver)*

Predictors	Standardized Coefficient (b*)	Unstandardized Coefficient (b)	Statistical Significance (p)	Comments and Interpretation $R^2 = .35$ (4% increase over Table A9.2)
Intercept	NA	-.384	.001	– On average there is no difference between Advantaged and Disadvantaged Neighborhoods.
Advantaged vs. Disadvantaged Neighborhood	.041	.087	.367	– Problem Behavior (ProblemB) increases with age.
Age (compared to age 10)	.078	.026	.031	– ProblemB is higher for males.
Gender (male compared to female)	.107	.192	.001	
Ethnicity (compared to White):				– At early ages there is no difference among ethnic groups in ProblemB but some minority ethnic groups, particularly Hispanic and Other in this analysis, show higher rates of increase in ProblemB than whites as they get older.
African American	.073	.169	.298	
Hispanic	-.037	-.068	.528	
Other	-.071	-.238	.176	
Ethnicity × Age:				
African American × Age	.046	.022	.499	
Hispanic × Age	.116	.046	.050	
Other × Age	.242	.213	.002	– There is a weak *positive* relationship between SES and ProblemB at older ages.
Socioeconomic Status (SES)	-.017	-.007	.178	
Socioeconomic Status × Age	.093	.010	.097	– At older ages, there is a weak negative relationship between Intact Family Structure and ProblemB.
Intact Family Structure	.075	.134	.178	
Intact Family Structure × Age	-.106	-.042	.049	
Family Income	-.228	-.170	.124	

(*continued*)

TABLE A9.3E. *Problem Behavior (Denver) (continued)*

Predictors	Standardized Coefficient (b^*)	Unstandardized Coefficient (b)	Statistical Significance (p)	Comments and Interpretation $R^2 = .35$ (4% increase over Table A9.2)
Family Income × Disadvantage	.274	.216	.052	– ProblemB is (nonsignificantly) related to Income, *positively* in Advantaged Neighborhoods and *negatively* in Disadvantaged Neighborhoods; the difference, but neither of the coefficients, is significant.
Family Dysfunction	.064	.057	.037	– Family Dysfunction is weakly positively related to ProblemB.
Good Parenting Practices	–.104	–.100	.054	– Good Parenting Practices are negatively related to ProblemB, but the relationship reverses for older ages.
Good Parenting Practices × Age	.139	.027	.011	
Parental Beliefs	–.085	–.072	.017	– Parental Beliefs are negatively related to ProblemB.
Positive Peer Group Environment	–.021	–.020	.787	
Positive Peer Group Environment × Age	–.250	–.045	.001	– Positive Peer Group is negatively related to ProblemB.
Positive Peer Group Environment × Gender	–.165	–.206	.001	– Positive Peer Group, more so for males than females and for older than for younger ages.
School Violence/Safety	.099	.086	.006	– School Violence/Safety is positively related to ProblemB.

TABLE A9.3F. *Problem Behavior (Chicago)*

Predictors	Standardized Coefficient (b^*)	Unstandardized Coefficient (b)	Statistical Significance (p)	Comments and Interpretation $R^2 = .43$ (14% increase over Table A9.2)
Intercept	NA	-.256	.006	
Advantaged vs. Disadvantaged Neighborhood	-.010	-.021	.840	On average, no difference between Advantaged and Disadvantaged Neighborhoods.
Physical Deterioration	.136	.141	.033	Higher PB in Deteriorated Neighborhoods.
Neighborhood Organization	.121	.125	.090	Higher PB in *more* Organized Neighborhoods.
Age (compared to age 11)	.114	.067	.001	PB increases with age.
Gender (male compared to female)	.038	.079	.231	No average difference between males and females.
Intact Family Structure	-.081	-.182	.137	
Intact Family Structure × Age	.161	.124	.004	Only younger kids benefit from being in intact families; kids 13 and older have *higher* PB in intact families.
Length of Residence	.075	.009	.150	
Length of Residence × Age	-.097	-.004	.058	PB higher for longer term residents, but only for younger kids; 14 and older, PB lower with longer Residence.
Family Dysfunction	.070	.077	.045	PB higher for kids of dysfunctional mothers.
Good Parenting Practices	-.060	-.176	.003	
Good Parenting Practices × Disadvantage	.111	.227	.003	Good Parenting reduces PB in Disadvantaged Neighborhoods, but *increases* PB in Advantaged Neighborhoods.
Parental Beliefs	.036	.103	.044	
Parental Beliefs × Disadvantage	-.064	-.131	.064	

(continued)

347

TABLE A9.3F. *Problem Behavior (Chicago)* (continued)

Predictors	Standardized Coefficient (b*)	Unstandardized Coefficient (b)	Statistical Significance (p)	Comments and Interpretation R² = .43 (14% increase over Table A9.2)
Positive School Environment	.099	.011	.866	Moms with strong beliefs have higher PB kids in Disadvantaged Neighborhood, but lower PB in Advantaged Neighborhoods.
Positive School Environment × Disadvantage	.090	.182	.014	
Positive School Environment × Age	−.217	−.074	.000	Positive School Environment associated with lower PB for older kids in Disadvantaged Neighborhoods, but may have the reverse effect for younger kids in Advantaged Neighborhoods.
School Violence Safety	−.024	−.136	.072	
School Violence/Safety × Disadvantage	.109	.223	.003	
School Violence/Safety × Age	−.116	−.040	.067	School Violence/Safety decreases PB for older kids in Disadvantaged Neighborhoods, but the advantage is wiped out for kids in Advantaged Neighborhoods.
Positive Peer Group Environment	.104	.107	.178	
Positive Peer Group Environment × Age	−.428	−.132	.000	
Positive Peer Group Environment × Gender	−.161	−.231	.001	Positive Peer Group Environment reduces PB more for males than for females and more for older than for younger kids.

Appendix B

Directly Explained Variance as an Estimate of the Influence of a Predictor on an Outcome

Unstandardized regression coefficients estimate the influence of a predictor on an outcome using whatever units the variables were originally measured in (feet, pounds, inches, number of people, or an arbitrary scale score, for instance). If we denote the unstandardized regression coefficient as b, then a one unit increase in the predictor is associated with a b unit change in the outcome. For example, from Table A8.2, a one unit change in the index of Neighborhood Deterioration is associated with a $-.012$ unit change in student status, and a one unit change in Neighborhood Bonding/Control is associated with a 0.015 unit change in student status. Because both Neighborhood Deterioration and Neighborhood Bonding/Control are measured as standard deviations (in other words, the standard deviation is the unit of measurement), and because student status is measured as a proportion of respondents in the neighborhood enrolled in school, then a one standard deviation increase in Neighborhood Deterioration is associated with a *decrease* (because of the negative sign) of .012, or 1.2 percent, in the proportion or percentage, respectively, of respondents who are either enrolled in school or have graduated high school; and a one standard deviation increase in Neighborhood Bonding/Control is associated with an *increase* (positive coefficient) of .015, or 1.5 percent, in the proportion or percentage of respondents either enrolled in school or graduated from high school.

When both the predictor and the outcome are measured as standard deviations, the resulting coefficient is a standardized coefficient. There are other ways to calculate a standardized coefficient (see, e.g., Agresti and Finlay 1986), but for present purposes, it is enough to know that if b^* is a standardized coefficient, then a *one standard deviation increase* in the predictor is associated with a b^* *standard deviation change* in the outcome. All that has happened is that we have changed the unit of measurement to standard deviations, from some other unit of measurement. Using standard deviations and returning to Table A8.2, a one standard deviation increase in Neighborhood Deterioration is associated with a *decrease* (negative sign) of .276 *standard deviations* in student status, and a one standard deviation increase in Neighborhood Bonding and Control is associated with a .349 standard deviation *increase* in student status. Notice that student status, with respect to the standardized coefficient, is now being measured as a standard deviation instead of a proportion or percentage.

If we multiply the standard deviation times itself, $s \times s$, we get s^2, the variance. If both the predictor and the outcome are measured as variances rather than as standard deviations, and if d is the directly explained variance, then a one variance change in the predictor is associated with a d variance change in the outcome, or a $100 \times d$ *percent* change in the outcome. Another way of saying this is to say that the predictor *directly* explains $100 \times d$ percent of the variance in the outcome. It may explain more, if it influences other variables that in turn influence the outcome, but like the unstandardized and standardized regression coefficients, d is an estimate of how strongly the predictor influences the outcome, *statistically controlling* for any other variables that may be in the model.

In ordinary least squares multiple regression (OLS), with its closed form solution, the directly explained variance can be calculated as the product of the standardized regression coefficient, b^*, and the correlation coefficient, r: $d = b^* \times r$. If the standardized regression coefficient and the correlation have the same sign, then d will be positive; if they have the opposite sign, then d will be negative. (Negative d coefficients are usually close to zero in empirical research.) Either way, in OLS, the sum of the d coefficients for all of the variables in the model will be precisely equal to the explained variance, R^2. For iterative techniques, including ridge regression and hierarchical linear modeling (HLM), the sum of the d coefficients will not necessarily add up to the explained variance, but should be very close.

Because a negative contribution to explained variance makes no sense substantively (mathematically, it makes sense only because it ensures that the sum of the d coefficients will add up to R^2), it seems reasonable to adjust the d coefficients when one or more of them is negative. This can be done by adding the absolute value of the d coefficients (in other words, disregarding the negative signs), which will result in a number larger than R^2, then multiplying each d coefficient by the quantity $R^2 / \Sigma \ |d|$, where $\Sigma |d|$ is the sum of the absolute values of the d coefficients. This same adjustment may be used for d coefficients calculated from ridge regression, HLM, or other techniques that do not have the same closed form solution as OLS. In Tables 9.1, A9.1, and A9.2, we include the directly explained variance, d, and we focus on directly explained variance as the most reasonable estimate of the direct impact of each predictor on each of the youth development outcome variables. This allows us to partition the explained variance in a way that eliminates shared explained variance and is totally consistent with the unstandardized and standardized coefficients from OLS, ridge regression, or HLM. The rank ordering of the size of the coefficients b, b^*, and d will be different, partly because b is sensitive to the unit of measurement (measuring in feet instead of inches reduces b, but has no effect on b^* or d), but the ordering of b^* and d will usually be similar, especially when d is greater than 5 percent or b^* is greater than about .200.

References

Aber, J. L., Mitchell, C., Garfinkel, L., Allen, L., and Seidman, E. (1992). *Indices of Neighborhood Impoverishment: Their Associations with Adolescent Mental Health and School Achievement.* Paper presented at the Conference on the Urban Underclass: Perspectives from the Social Sciences, Ann Arbor, MT.

Adlaf, E. M., and Iris, F. J. (1996). Structure and relations: The influence of familial factors on adolescent substance use and delinquency. *Journal of Child and Adolescent Substance Abuse,* 5(3):1–19.

Adler, P. A., and Adler, P. (1995). Dynamics of inclusion and exclusion in preadolescent cliques. *Social Psychology Quarterly,* 58(3):145–162.

Agresti, A., and Finlay, B. (1986). *Statistical Methods for the Social Sciences.* Second Edition. San Francisco: Dellen/Macmillan.

Ahlbrandt, R. S., Jr., and Cunningham, J. V. (1980). *Pittsburgh Residents Assess Their Neighborhoods.* Pittsburgh: School of Social Work and University Center for Social and Urban Research, University of Pittsburgh (December).

Aldenderfer, M. S., and Blashfield, R. K. (1984). *Cluster Analysis.* Beverly Hills, CA: Sage.

Alex-Assenson, Y. (1995). Myths about race and the underclass. *Urban Affairs Review,* 31:3–19.

Alexander, J. F., Pugh, C., Parsons, B. V., Sexton, T., Barton, C., Bonomo, J., Gordon, D., Grotpeter, J. K., Hansson, K., Harrison, R., Mears, S., Mihalic, S. F., Ostrum, N., Schulman, S., and Waldron, H. (2000). *Functional Family Therapy.* In D. S. Elliott (series ed.), *Blueprints for Violence Prevention* (Book 3). Boulder, CO: Center for the Study and Prevention of Violence, Institute of Behavioral Science, University of Colorado.

Allen, J. B., and Turner, E. (1995). Ethnic Differentiation by Blocks within Census Tracts. *Urban Geography,* 16:344–364.

Anderson, D. C. (1998). Curriculum, Culture, and Community: The Challenge of School Violence. In M. Tonry and M. H. Moore (eds.), *Youth Violence.* Chicago: University of Chicago Press, pp. 317–363.

Anderson, E. (1976). *A Place on the Corner.* Chicago: University of Chicago Press.

Anderson, E. (1991). *Streetwise: Race, Class, and Change in an Urban Community.* Chicago: University of Chicago Press.

353

Anderson, E. (1994). The code of the streets. *The Atlantic Monthly* (May):81–94.

Anderson, E. S., and Keith, T. Z. (1997). A longitudinal test of a model of academic success for at-risk high school students. *Journal of Educational Research*, 90:259–268.

Anderson, M. (2001). School-associated violent deaths in the United States, 1994–1999. *Journal of the American Medical Association*, 286:2695–2702.

Arnette, J. L., and Walsleben, M. C. (1998). Combating fear and restoring safety in schools. *Juvenile Justice Bulletin*. Washington, DC: Office of Juvenile Justice and Delinquency Prevention.

Aseltine, R. H., Jr. (1995). A reconsideration of parental and peer influences on adolescent deviance. *Journal of Health and Social Behavior*, 36:103–121.

Astone, N. M., and McLanahan, S. S. (1991). Family structure, parental practices and high school completion. *American Sociological Review*, 56 (June):309–320.

Baldwin, A. L., Baldwin, C., and Cole, R. E. (1990). Stress-Resistant Families and Stress-Resistant Children. In J. Rolf, A. S. Masten, D. Cicchetti, K. H. Neuchterlein, and S. Weintraub (eds.), *Risk and Protective Factors in the Development of Psychpathology*. New York: Cambridge University Press, pp. 257–280.

Bandura, A., (ed.). (1995). *Self-Efficacy in Changing Societies*. New York: Cambridge University Press.

Bank, L., Forgatch, M. S., Patterson, G. R., and Fetrow, R. A. (1993). Parenting practices of single mothers: Mediators of negative contextual factors. *Journal of Marriage and the Family*, 55:371–384.

Bankston, C. L., III, and Caldas, S. J. (1998). Family structure, schoolmates, and racial inequalities in school achievement. *Journal of Marriage and the Family*, 60(August):715–723.

Battin, S. R., Hill, K. G., Abbott, R. D., Catalano, R. F., and Hawkins, J. D. (1998). The contribution of gang membership to delinquency beyond delinquent friends. *Criminology*, 36:93–115.

Battistich, V., and Hom, H. (1997). The relationship between students' sense of their school as a community and their involvement in problem behaviors. *American Journal of Public Health*, 87:1998–2001.

Battle, J. J. (1997). Academic achievement among Hispanic students from one-versus dual-parent households. *Hispanic Journal of Behavioral Sciences*, 19(2):156–170.

Baumrind, D. (1966). Effects of authoritative parental control on child behavior. *Child Development*, 37:887–907.

Baumrind, D. (1989). Rearing Competent Children. In W. Damon (ed.), *Child Development Today and Tomorrow*. San Francisco: Jossey-Bass, pp. 349–378.

Baumrind, D. (1991). The influence of parenting style on adolescent competence and substance abuse. *Journal of Early Adolescence*, 11:56–94.

Baumrind, D. (1994). The social context of child maltreatment. *Family Relations*, 43:360–368.

Bellair, P. E. (1997). Social interaction and community crime: Examining the importance of neighbor networks. *Criminology*, 35(4):677–704.

Belsky, J. (1984). The determinants of parenting: A process model. *Child Development*, 55:83–96.

Berry, W. D., and Feldman, S. (1985). *Multiple Regression in Practice*. Beverly Hills, CA: Sage.

Beyers, J. M., Bates, J. E., Pettit, G. S., and Dodge, K. A. (2003). Neighborhood structure, parenting processes, and the development of youths' externalizing behaviors: A multilevel analysis. *American Journal of Community Psychology*, 13: 35–53.

Beyers, J. M., Loeber, R., Wikstrom, P.-O. H., and Stouthamer-Loeber, M. (2001). What predicts adolescent violence in better-off neighborhoods? *Journal of Abnormal Child Psychology*, 29(5):369–381.

Birch, D. L., Brown, E. S., Coleman, R. P., DaLomba, D. W., Parsons, W. L., Sharpe, L. C., and Weber, S. A. (1979). *The Behavioral Foundations of Neighborhood Change*. Cambridge, MA: Joint Center for Urban Studies.

Blankston, C. L., III, and Caldas, S. J. (1998). Family structure, schoolmates, and racial inequalities in school achievement. *Journal of Marriage and the Family*, 60(August):715–723.

Blau, P. M., and Duncan, O. D. (1967). *The American Occupational Structure*. New York: Wiley.

Blum, R. W., and Rhinehart, P. M. (1997). *Reducing the Risks: Connections That Make a Difference in the Lives of Youth*. Minneapolis, MN: Division of General Pediatrics and Adolescent Health, University of Minnesota.

Blumstein, A. (1995). Violence by young people: Why the deadly nexus? *National Institute of Justice Journal*, 229:2–9.

Blumstein, A., Cohen, J., Roth, J. A., and Visher, C. A. (1986). *Criminal Careers and "Career Criminals," Volume I*. Washington, DC: National Academy Press, National Academy of Sciences.

Booth, A., and Crouter, A. C. (2001). *Does It Take a Village?* Mahwah, NJ: Lawrence Erlbaum Associates.

Braddock, J. H., and McPartland, J. (1992). *Education of At-Risk Youth: Recent Trends, Current Status, and Future Needs*. Washington, DC: Panel on High-Risk Youth. Commission on Behavioral and Social Sciences and Education, National Research Council.

Bratton, W. (1998). *Turnaround*. New York: Random House.

Brewster, K. L., Billy, J. O. G., and Grady, W. R. (1993). Social context and adolescent behavior: The impact of community on the transition to sexual activity. *Social Forces*, 71(3):713–740.

Bronfenbrenner, U. (1979). *The Ecology of Human Development*. Cambridge, MA: Harvard University Press.

Bronfenbrenner, U. (1986). Ecology of family as a context for human development. *Developmental Psychology*, 22(6):732–742.

Brooks-Gunn, J., Duncan, G. J., and Aber, J. L. (eds.). (1997a). *Neighborhood Poverty: Volume 1, Context and Consequences for Children*. New York: Russell Sage.

Brooks-Gunn, J., Duncan, G. J., and Aber, J. L. (eds.). (1997b). *Neighborhood Poverty: Volume II, Policy Implications in Studying Neighborhoods*. New York: Russell Sage Foundation.

Brooks-Gunn, J., Duncan, G. J., Klebanov, P. K., and Sealand, N. (1993). Do neighborhoods influence child and adolescent development?" *American Journal of Sociology*, 99:353–395.

Brooks-Gunn, J., Duncan, G. J., Levanthal, T., and Aber, J. L. (1997). In J. Brooks-Gunn, G. J. Duncan, and J. L. Aber (eds.), *Neighborhood Poverty*. New York: Russell Sage Foundation, pp. 279–298.

Brown, B. B. (1990). Peer Groups and Peer Cultures. In S. S. Feldman and G. R. Elliott (eds.), *At the Threshold: The Developing Adolescent*. Cambridge, MA: Harvard University Press, pp. 171–196.

Bryk, A. S., and Driscoll, M. E. (1988). *The High School as Community: Contextual Influences and Consequences for Students and Teachers*. Madison, WI: National Center on Effective Schools.

Bryk, A. S., and Raudenbusch, S. W. (1992). *Hierarchical Linear Models: Applications and Data Analysis Methods*. Newbury Park, CA: Sage Publications.

Burgess, E. W. (1925). The Growth of the City. In Robert E. Park, Ernest W. Burgess, and Rodrick D. McKenzie (eds.), *The City*. Chicago, IL: University of Chicago Press, pp. 47–62.

Buri, J. R. (1989). Self-esteem and appraisals of parental behavior. *Journal of Adolescent Research*, 4:33–49.

Bursik, R. J., Jr. (1984). Urban dynamics and ecological studies in delinquency. *Social Forces*, 63:393–413.

Bursik, R. J., Jr. (1989). Political Decision-Making and Ecological Models of Delinquency: Conflict and Consensus. In S. F. Messner, M. D. Krohn, and A. E. Liska (eds.), *Theoretical Integration in the Study of Deviance and Crime*. Albany, NY: State University of New York Press, pp. 105–117.

Bursik, R. J., Jr., and H. G. Grasmick (1993). *Neighborhoods and Crime: The Dimensions of Effective Community Control*. New York: Lexington Books.

Bursik, R. J., Jr., and Webb, J. (1982). Community change and patterns of delinquency. *American Journal of Sociology*, 88(1):24–42.

Burton, L. M. (1997). Ethnography and the meaning of adolescence in high-risk neighborhoods. *Ethos*, 25(2):208–217.

Burton, L. M. (2001). One Step Forward and Two Steps Back: Neighborhoods, Adolescent Development, and Unmeasured Variables. In A. Booth and A. C. Crouter (eds.), *Does It Take a Village?* Mahwah, NJ: Lawrence Erlbaum Associates, pp. 149–160.

Burton, L. M., Allison, K., and Obeidallah, D. (1995). Social Context and Adolescence: Perspectives on Development among Inner-City African-American Teens. In L. Crockett and A. C. Crouter (eds.). *Pathways Through Adolescence: Individual Development in Relation to Social Context*. Hillsdale, NH: Erlbaum, pp. 119–138.

Burton, L. M., Hernandez, D., and Hofferth, S. (1998). *Families, Youth, and Children's Well-being*. Washington, DC: American Sociological Association.

Burton, L. M., Price-Spratten, T., and Spencer, M. B. (1997). On Ways of Thinking about Measuring Neighborhoods: Implications for Studying Context and Developmental Outcomes for Children. In J. Brooks-Gunn, G. J. Duncan, and J. L. Aber (eds.). *Neighborhood Poverty: Policy Implications in Studying Neighborhoods Volume II*. New York: Russell Sage Foundation, pp. 132–144.

Cairns, R. B., Cairns, B. D., Neckerman, H. J., Gest, S. C., and Gariepy, J. L. (1988). Social networks and aggressive behavior: Peer support or peer rejection. *Developmental Psychology*, 24:815–823.

Cairns, R. B., Leung, M., Buchanan, L., and Cairns, B. D. (1995). Friendships and social networks in childhood and adolescence: Fluidity, reliability, and interrelations. *Child Development*, 66:1330–1345.

Campbell, E., Henley, J., Elliott, D. S., and Irwin, K. (2003). *The Meaning and Measurement of Neighborhood Boundaries: Lessons from a Qualitative Study of Five Neighborhoods.* Paper presented at the American Sociological Association Meeting: San Francisco, CA.

Carmines, E. G., and Zeller, R. A. (1979). *Reliability and Validity Assessment.* Beverly Hills, CA: Sage.

Carnegie Corporation (1992). *A Matter of Time.* New York: Carnegie Corporation.

Carnegie Corporation (1995). *Great Transformations: Preparing Youth for a New Century.* New York: Carnegie Corporation.

Caspi, A., Moffitt, T. E., Entner-Wright, B. R., and Silva, P. A. (1998). Early failure in the labor market: Childhood and adolescent predictors of unemployment in the transition to adulthood. *American Sociological Review,* 63:424–451.

Cattarello, A. M. (2000). Community-level influences on individuals' social bonds, peer associations, and delinquency: A multilevel analysis. *Justice Quarterly,* 17(1):33–60.

Chaiken, M. R. (1998). Tailoring Established After-School Programs to Meet Urban Realities. In D. S. Elliott, B. Hamburg, and K. R. Williams (eds.). *Violence in American Schools.* New York: Cambridge University Press, pp. 348–375.

Chase-Lansdale, P. L., Cherlin, A. J., and Kiernan, K. E. (1995). The long-term effects of parental divorce on the mental health of young adults: A developmental perspective. *Child Development,* 66:1614–1634.

Chase-Lansdale, P. L., Gordon, R., Brooks-Gunn, J., and Klebanov, P. (1997). Neighborhood and Family Influences On the Intellectual and Behavioral Competence of Preschool and Early School Age Children. In J. Brooks-Gunn, G. J. Duncan, and J. L. Aber (eds.). *Neighborhood Poverty.* New York: Russell Sage Foundation, pp. 79–118.

Chilcoat, H. D., and Anthony, J. C. (1996). Impact of parent monitoring on initiation of drug use through late childhood. *Journal of the American Academy of Child Adolescence and Psychiatry,* 35:(1):91–100.

Clark, R. L. (1992). *Neighborhood Effects of Dropping Out of School among Teenage Boys.* Washington, DC: Urban Institute (Mimeograph.)

Clay, P. L. (1998). *Urban Neighborhoods and the Generation of Opportunity: An Assessment of Impact.* Cambridge, MA: Massachusetts Institute of Technology. (Unpublished.)

Cloward, R. A., and Ohlin, L. E. (1960). *Delinquency and Opportunity: A Theory of Delinquent Gangs.* Glencoe, NY: Free Press.

Cochran, W. G. (1977). *Sampling Techniques,* 3rd ed. New York: John Wiley.

Cohen, B. (1980). *Deviant Street Networks: Prostitution in New York City.* Lexington, MA: Lexington Books.

Cohen, J. M. (1977). Sources of peer group homogeneity. *Sociology of Education,* 50:227–241.

Coie, J., Terry, R., Zakriski, A., and Lochman, J. (1995). Early Adolescent Social Influences on Delinquent Behavior. In J. McCord (ed.), *Coercion and Punishment in Long Term Perspectives.* New York: Cambridge University Press, pp. 229–244.

Coleman, J. S. (1988). Social capital in the creation of human capital. *American Journal of Sociology,* 94:S95–S120.

Coleman, J. S. (1990). *Foundations of Social Theory*. Cambridge, MA: Harvard University Press.

Coley, R. L. (1998). Children's socialization experiences and functioning in single-mother households: The importance of fathers and other men. *Child Development*, 69(1):219–230.

Comer, J. P., and Haynes, N. M. (1991). Parent involvement in schools: An ecological approach. *Elementary School Journal*, 91:271–277.

Conger, R., and Elder, G. B. (1994). *Families in Troubled Times: Adapting to Change in Rural America*. New York: Aldine de Gruyter.

Connell, J. P., and Halpern-Felsher, B. L. (1997). How Neighborhoods Affect Educational Outcomes in Middle Childhood and Adolescence: Conceptual Issues and an Empirical Example. In J. Brooks-Gunn, G. J. Duncan, and J. L. Aber (eds.), *Neighborhood Poverty, Volume 1*, pp. 174–199.

Cook, T. D., Herman, M. R., Phillips, M., and Settersten, R. A., Jr. (2002). Some ways in which neighborhoods, nuclear families, friendship groups, and schools jointly affect changes in early adolescent development. *Child Development*, 73 (4):1283–1309.

Cook, T. D., Shagle, S. C., and Degirmencioglu, S. M. (1997). Capturing Social Process for Testing Mediational Models of Neighborhood Effects. In J. Brooks-Gunn, G. J. Duncan, and J. L. Aber (eds.), *Neighborhood Poverty, Volume II*. New York: Russell Sage Foundation, pp. 94–119.

Corcoran, M. (1995). Rags to rags: Poverty and mobility in the United States. *Annual Review of Sociology*, 21:237–267.

Corcoran, M., Gordon, R., Laren, D., and Solon, G. (1987). *Intergenerational Transmission of Education, Income, and Earnings*. (Unpublished paper).

Costa, F. M., Jessor, R., Turbin, M., Dong, Q., Zhang, H., and Wang, C. (2003). *Protection and risk in the social contexts of adolescent life: A cross-national study of problem behavior in China and the U.S.* Boulder: Institute of Behavioral Science, University of Colorado.

Coulton, C., Korbin, J., Chan, T., and Su, M. (1997). Mapping Resident Perceptions of Neighborhood Boundaries: A Methodological Note. Center on Urban Poverty and Social Change, Cleveland, OH: Case Western Reserve University. (Unpublished paper).

Coulton, C. J., and Pandey, S. (1992). Geographic concentration of poverty and risk to children in urban neighborhoods. *American Behavioral Scientist*, 35:238–257.

Covey, H. C., Menard, S., and Franzese, R. J. (1997). *Juvenile Gangs*, 2nd ed. Springfield, IL: Charles C. Thomas.

Cowen, E. L., and Work, W. C. (1988). Resilient children, psychological wellness, and primary prevention. *American Journal of Community Psychology*, 16:591–607.

Crane, J. (1991). The epidemic theory of ghettos and neighborhood effects on dropping out and teenage childbearing. *American Journal of Sociology*, 96:1226–1259.

Cunningham, J. V., and Kotler, M. (1983). *Rebuilding Neighborhood Organizations*. Notre Dame, IN: University of Notre Dame Press.

Curran, P. J., and Chassin, L. (1996). A longitudinal study of parenting as a protective factor for children of alcoholics. *Journal of Studies on Alcohol*, 57:305–313.

Curran, P. J., Stice, E., and Chassin, L. (1997). The relation between adolescent alcohol use and peer alcohol use: A longitudinal random coefficients model. *Journal of Consulting and Clinical Psychology*, 65:130–140.

Curtner-Smith, M. E., and MacKinnon-Lewis, C. E. (1994). Family process effects on adolescent males' susceptibility to antisocial peer pressure. *Family Relations*, 43:462–468.

Datcher, L. (1982). Effects of community and family background on achievement. *Review of Economics and Statistics*, 64:32–41.

David, C., Steele, R., Forehand, R., and Armistead, L. (1996). The role of family conflict and marital conflict in adolescent functioning. *Journal of Family Violence*, 11(1):81–91.

Delaney, M. E. (1996). Across the transition to adolescence: Qualities of parent/ adolescent relationships and adjustment. *Journal of Early Adolescence*, 16(3):274–300.

Denton, B. A., and Massey, D. S. (1991). Patterns of Neighborhood Transitions In a Multiethnic World: U.S. Metropolitan Areas, 1970–1980. *Demography*, 28:41–63.

Dishion, T. J., Patterson, G. R., Stoolmiller, M., and Skinner, M. L. (1991). Family, school, and behavioral antecedents to early adolescent involvement with antisocial peers. *Developmental Psychology*, 27:172–180.

Dornbusch, S. M., Ritter, P. L., Leiderman, P. H., Roberts, D. F., and Fraleigh, M. J. (1987). The relation of parenting style to adolescent school performance. *Child Development*, 58(5):1244–1257.

Dornbusch, S. M., Ritter, L. P., and Steinberg, L. (1991). Community influences on the relation of family status to adolescent school performance: Differences between African Americans and Non-Hispanic Whites. *American Journal of Education*, 38:543–567.

Downs, R. M., and Stea, D. (1973). Cognitive Maps and Spatial Behavior: Process and Products. In R. M. Downs and D. Stea (eds.), *Image and Environment*. Chicago: Aldine, pp. 8–26.

Dumka, L. E., Roosa, M. W., Michaels, M. L., and Suh, K. W. (1995). Using research and theory to develop prevention programs for high-risk families. *Family Relations*, 44:78–86.

Duncan, G. J. (1994). Families and neighbors as sources of disadvantage in the schooling decisions of Black and White adolescents. *American Journal of Education*, 103:20–53.

Duncan, G. J. (1995). How nonmarital childbearing is affected by neighborhoods, marital opportunities and labor-market conditions. *Report to Congress on Out-of-Wedlock Childbearing*. [DHHS Pub. No. (PHS) 95-1257] Hyattsville, MD: U.S. Department of Health and Human Services.

Duncan, G. J., and Brooks-Gunn, J., (eds.) (1994). *Consequences of Growing Up Poor*. New York: Russell Sage Foundation.

Duncan, G. J., Brooks-Gunn, J., Yeung, W. J., and Smith, J. R. (1998). How much does childhood poverty affect the life chances of children? *American Sociological Review*, 63:406–423.

Duncan, G. J., and Raudenbush, S. W. (2001). Neighborhoods and Adolescent Development: How Can We Determine the Links? In A. Booth and A. C.

Crouter (eds.), *Does It Take a Voillage?* Mahwah, NJ: Lawrence Erlbaum Associates, pp. 105–135.

Duncan, T. E., Duncan, S. C., and Hops, H. (1994). The effects of family cohesiveness and peer encouragement on the development of adolescent alcohol use: A cohort sequential approach to the analysis of longitudinal data. *Journal of Studies in Alcohol,* 55:588–599.

Duncan, T. E., Duncan, S. C., Okut, H., Strycker, L. A., and Hix-Small, H. (2003). A multilevel contextual model of neighborhood collective efficacy. *American Journal of Community Psychology,* 32:245–252.

Duncan, T. E., Tildesley, E., Duncan, S. C., and Hops, H. (1995). The consistency of family and peer influences on the development of substance use in adolescence. *Addiction,* 90:1647–1660.

Dunteman, G. H. (1989). *Principal Components Analysis.* Newbury Park, CA: Sage.

Dunworth, T., and Saiger, A. (1994). *Drugs and Crime in Public Housing: A Three-City Analysis.* Washington, DC: U.S. Department of Justice, Office of Justice Programs.

Eccles, J. S., and Gootman, J. (2002). *Community Programs to Promote Youth Development.* Washington, DC: National Academy Press.

Eccles, J. S., Lord, S. E., Roeser, R. W., Barber, B. L., and Jozefowicz, D. M. H. (1997). The Association of School Transitions in Early Adolescence with Developmental Trajectories through High School. In J. Schulenberg, J. Maggs, and K. Hurrelman (eds.), *Health Risks and Developmental Transitions during Adolescence.* New York: Cambridge University Press, pp. 283–320.

Eccles, J. S., Midgley, C., Buchanan, C., Wigfield, A., Reuman, D., and MacIver, D. (1993). Development during adolescence: The impact of stage/environment fit on young adolescents' experiences in schools and in families. *American Psychologist,* 48:90–101.

Elder, G. H., Jr. (1974). *Children of the Great Depression: Social Change in Life Experience.* Chicago: University of Chicago Press.

Elder, G. H., Jr., and Conger, R. D. (2000). *Leaving the Land: Rural Youth at Century's End.* Chicago: University of Chicago Press.

Elder, G. H., Jr., Eccles, J. S., Ardelt, M., and Lord, S. (1995). Inner-city parents under economic pressure: Perspectives on the strategies of parenting. *Journal of Marriage and the Family,* 57:771–784.

Elliott, D. S. (1982). A review essay of Measuring Delinquency by M. Hindelang, T. Hirschi, and J. Weis. *Criminology,* 20(3):527–537.

Elliott, D. S. (1993). Longitudinal Research in Criminology: Promise and Practice. In E. Weitekamp and H. Kerner (eds.), *Cross-National Longitudinal Research on Human Development and Criminal Behavior.* Dordrecht, The Netherlands: Kluwer Academic Publishers, pp. 189–201.

Elliott, D. S. (1994). Serious violent offenders: Onset, developmental course and termination. The American Society of Criminology 1993 Presidential Address. *Criminology,* 32(1):1–21.

Elliott, D. S. (1995). *Lies, Damn Lies, and Arrest Statistics.* The Edwin H. Sutherland Award Presentation, American Society of Criminology Annual Meeting, Boston.

Elliott, D. S. (1998). Prevention Programs That Work for Youth: Violence Prevention. Aspen Institutes' Congressional Program, Education and The Development of American Youth. Washington, DC: Aspen Institute.

Elliott, D. S. (2000). Violent Offending over the Life Course. In N. A. Krasnegor, N. B. Anderson, and B. A. Bynum (eds.), *Health and Behavior, Volume 1*. Rockville, MD: National Institutes of Health, pp. 191–204.

Elliott, D. S., and Ageton, S. S. (1980). Reconciling race and class differences in self-reported and official estimates of delinquency. *American Sociological Review*, 45:95–110.

Elliott, D. S., and Huizinga, D. (1983). Social class and delinquent behavior in a National Youth Panel. *Criminology*, 21:149–177.

Elliott, D. S., and Huizinga, D. (1989). Improving Self-Reported Measures of Delinquency. In M. W. Klein (ed.), *Cross-National Research in Self-Reported Crime and Delinquency*. Boston: Kluwer Academic Publishers, pp. 155–186.

Elliott, D. S., and Huizinga, D. (1990). The Mediating Effects of Social Structure in High-Risk Neighborhoods. Paper presented at the 84th Annual Meeting of the American Sociological Association, Washington, DC, August.

Elliott, D. S., and Menard, S. (1996). Delinquent Friends and Delinquent Behavior: Temporal and Developmental Patterns. In J. D. Hawkins (ed.), *Delinquency and Crime: Current Theories*. Cambridge, UK: Cambridge University Press, pp. 28–67.

Elliott, D. S., and Tolan, P. H. (1999). Youth Violence Prevention, Intervention, and Social Policy: An Overview. In D. J. Flannery and C. R. Huff (eds.), *Youth Violence: Prevention, Intervention, and Social Policy*. Washington, DC: American Psychiatric Press, pp. 3–46.

Elliott, D. S., and Voss, H. L. (1974). *Delinquency and Dropout*. Lexington, MA: D.C. Heath.

Elliott, D. S., Hamburg, B. A., and Williams, K. R. (1998a). *Violence in American Schools*. Cambridge, UK: Cambridge University Press.

Elliott, D. S., Hamburg, B. A., and Williams, K. R. (1998b). Violence in American Schools: An Overview. In D. Elliott, B. Hamburg, and K. Williams (eds.) *Violence in American Schools: New Perspectives and Solutions*. New York: Cambridge University Press, pp. 1–28.

Elliott, D. S., Huizinga, D., and Ageton, S. S. (1985). *Explaining Delinquency and Drug Use*. Beverly Hills, CA: Sage Publications.

Elliott, D. S., Huizinga, D., and Menard, S. (1989). *Multiple Problem Youth: Delinquency, Substance Use, and Mental Health Problems*. New York: Springer-Verlag.

Elliott, D. S., Williams, K. R., and Hamburg, B. A. (1998). An Integrated Approach to Violence Prevention. In D. Elliott, B. Hamburg, and K. Williams (eds.), *Violence in American Schools*. New York: Cambridge University Press, pp. 379–386.

Ellis, A. L. (1992). Urban youth economic enterprise zones: An intervention strategy for reversing the gang crisis in American cities. *The Urban League Review*, 15:29–40.

Ennis, P. H. (1967). *Criminal Victimization in the United States: A Report of a National Survey*. Washington, DC: U.S. Department of Justice.

Ensminger, M. E., Lawkin, R. P., and Jacobson, N. (1996). School leaving: A longitudinal perspective including neighborhood effects. *Child Development*, 67:2400–2416.

Entwisle, D. R. (1990). Schools and the Adolescent. In S. Feldman and G. Elliott (eds.), *At the Threshold: The Developing Adolescent*. Cambridge, MA: Harvard University Press, pp. 197–224.

Epstein, J. L., and McPartland, J. M. (1977). Family and School Interactions and Main Effects on Affective Outcomes. Center for Social Organization of School Reports, Johns Hopkins University, No. 235.

Esbensen, F., and Huizinga, D. (1993). Gangs, drugs, and delinquency in a survey of urban youth. *Criminology*, 31:565–589.

Everitt, B. (1980). *Cluster Analysis*. Second Edition. New York: Halsted Press.

Farrington, D. (1993). Have Any Individual Family or Neighborhood Influences on Offending Been Demonstrated Conclusively? In D. Farrington, R. Sampson, and P. O. Wikstrom (eds.), *Integrating Individual and Ecological Aspects of Crime*. Stockholm: National Council on Crime Prevention, pp. 7–37.

Farrington, D. P. (2000). *Explaining and preventing crime: The globalization of knowledge*. The American Society of Criminology 1999 Presidential Address. *Criminology*, 38:1–24.

Felson, M., and Cohen, L. E. (1980). Human Ecology and Crime: A Routine Activity Approach. *Human Ecology*, 8:389–406.

Felson, R., Liska, A., South, S., and McNulty, T. (1994). The subculture of violence and delinquency: Individual vs. school context effects. *Social Forces*, 73, 155–173.

Figueira-McDonough, J. (1992). Community structure and female delinquency rates: A hueristic discussion. *Youth and Society*, 24:3–30.

Finnegan, W. (1998). *Cold New World: Growing Up in Harder County*. New York: Random House.

Fisher, R., and Romanofsky, P. (eds.). (1981). *Community Organization for Urban Social Change–A Historical Perspective*. San Diego, CA: Greenwood Press.

Fletcher, A. C., Darling, N., and Steinberg, L. (1995). Parental Monitoring and Peer Influences on Adolescent Substance Use. In J. McCord (ed.), *Coercion and Punishment in Long-Term Perspectives*. New York: Cambridge University Press, pp. 259–271.

Foley, D. L. (1973). Institutional and Contextual Factors Affecting the Housing Choice of Minority Residents. In A. Hawley and V. P. Rock (eds.), *Segregation in Residential Areas*. Washington, DC: National Academy of Sciences, pp. 85–147.

Fordham, S., and Ogbu, J. U. (1986). Black students school success: Coping with the burden of "acting-white." *Urban Review*, 18(3):176–206.

Furstenberg, F., Jr. (1990). How Families Manage Risk and Opportunity in Dangerous Neighborhoods. Paper presented at the 84th Annual Meeting of the American Sociological Association, Washington, DC: August.

Furstenberg, F., Jr. (1996). On the Role of Fathers. In *Fostering Successful Families*. Washington, DC: Consortium of Social Science Associations, pp. 11–14.

Furstenberg, F., Jr., Brooks-Gunn, J., and Morgan, S. (1987). *Adolescent Mothers in Later Life*. New York: Cambridge University Press.

Furstenberg, F., Jr., and Crawford, D. B. (1978). Family support: Helping teenagers to cope. *Family Planning Perspectives*, 11:322–333.

Furstenberg, F., Jr., Cook, T. D., Eccles, J., Elder, Jr., G. H., and Sameroff, A. (1999). *Managing to Make It*. Chicago: University of Chicago Press.

Furstenberg, F., Jr., and Harris, K. M. (1993). When and Why Fathers Matter: Impact of Father Involvement on the Children of Adolescent Mothers. In Lerman, R. J. and Ooms (eds.), *Young Unwed Fathers: Changing Roles and Emerging Policies*. Philadelphia: Temple University Press, pp. 117–138.

Furstenberg, F., Jr., and Hughes, M. E. (1997). The Influence of Neighborhoods on Childrens' Development: A Theoretical Perspective and Research Agenda. In J. Brooks-Gunn, G. J. Duncan, and L. Aber (eds.), *Neighborhood Poverty, Policy Implications in Studying Neighborhoods*. New York: Russell Sage Foundation, pp. 23–47.

Furstenberg, F., Jr., and Tietler , (1994). Reconsidering the effects of marital disruption. *Journal of Family Issues*, 15:173–190.

Gans, A. (1962). *The Urban Villagers: Group and Class in the Life of Italian-Americans.* New York: The Free Press.

Garafalo, J., and McLeod, M. (1989). The structure and operations of neighborhood watch programs in the United States. *Crime and Delinquency*, 35:326–344.

Garbarino, J. (1976). A preliminary study of some ecological correlates of child abuse: The impact of socioeconomic stress on mothers. *Child Development*, 47:178–185.

Garbarino, J., and Ganzel, B. (2000). (1989). The Human Ecology of Early Risk. In J. Shonkoff and R. Meisels (eds.), *The Handbook of Early Intervention*. New York: Cambridge University Press, pp. 76–93.

Garmezy, N. (1985). Stress-Resistant Children: The Search for Protective Factors. In J. E. Stevenson (ed.), *Recent Research in Developmental Psychopathology*. New York: Pergamon, pp. 213–233.

Garner, C. L., and Raudenbush, J. W. (1991). Neighborhood effects on educational attainment: A multilevel analysis. *Sociology of Education*, 64:251–262.

Gaziel, H. (1997). Impact of school culture on effectiveness of secondary schools with disadvantaged students. *Journal of Educational Research*, 90:310–318.

Geerken, M. (1994). Rap sheets in criminological research. *Journal of Quantitative Criminology*, 10:3–21.

Gelles, R. J. (1973). Child abuse as psychopathology: A sociological critique and reformulation. *American Journal of Orthopsychiatry*, 43:611–662.

Gelles, R. J. (1992). Poverty and violence toward children. *American Behavioral Scientist*, 35:258–274.

Gephart, M. A. (1997). Neighborhoods and Communities as Contexts for Development. In J. Brooks-Gunn, G. J. Duncan, and J. L. Aber (eds.), *Neighborhood Poverty, Volume 1*. New York: The Russell Sage Foundation, pp. 1–43.

Gerard, J. M., and Buehler, C. (1999). Multiple risk factors in the family environment and youth problem behaviors. *Journal of Marriage and the Family*, 61(May):343–361.

Gibbs, J. (1986). Assessment of depression in urban adolescent females: Implications for early intervention strategies. *American Journal of Social Psychiatry*, 6: 50–56.

Gilmore, S. (1992). Culture. In E. Borgatta and M. L. Borgatta (eds.), *Encyclopedia of Sociology*. New York: MacMillan & Co., pp. 404–411.

Goodenow, C., and Grady, K. E. (1993). The relationship of school belonging and friends' values to academic motivation among urban adolescent students. *Journal of Experimental Education*, 62:60–71.

Gorman-Smith, D., Tolan, P. H., Zelli, A., and Huesmann, L. R. (1996). The relation of family functioning to violence among inner-city minority youths. *Journal of Family Psychology*, 10(2):115–129.

Gottfredson, D. C. (2001). *Schools and Delinquency*. Cambridge, UK: Cambridge University Press.

Gottfredson, D. C., McNeil, R. J., and Gottfredson, G. D. (1991). Social area influences on delinquency: A multi-level analysis. *Journal of Research in Crime and Delinquency*, 28:197–226.

Greenberg, S. W., Williams, J. R., and Rohe, W. M. (1982). Safety in Urban Neighborhoods: A Comparison of Physical Characteristics and Informal Territorial Control in High- and Low-Crime Neighborhoods. *Population and Environment*, 5:151–165.

Grolick, W., and Ryan, R. (1989). Parent styles associated with children's self-regulation and competence in school. *Journal of Educational Psychology*, 81:143–154.

Grotevant, H. D. (1998). Adolescent Development in Family Context. In F. N. Eisenberg (ed.), *Handbook of Child Psychology: Social, Emotional, and Personality Development*. New York: John Wiley and Sons, Inc., pp. 1097–1149.

Guerra, N., Huesmann, L. R., Tolan, P. H., VanAcker, R., and Eron, L. D. (1995). Stressful events and individual beliefs as correlates of economic disadvantage and aggression among urban children. *Journal of Consulting and Clinical Psychology*, 63:518–528.

Haapsalo, J., Tremblay, R. E., Boulerice, B., and Vitaro, F. (2000). Relative advantages of person- and variable-based approaches for predicting problem behaviors from kindergarten assessments. *Journal of Quantitative Criminology*, 16:145–168.

Hagan, J. (1993). The social embeddedness of crime and unemployment. *Criminology*, 31:465–491.

Hagan, J. (1998). Life Course Capitalization and Adolescent Behavioral Development. In R. Jessor (ed.), *New Perspectives on Adolescent Risk Behavior*. New York: Cambridge University Press, pp. 499–517.

Hallman, H. W. (1984). *Neighborhoods: Their Place in Urban Life*. Beverly Hills, CA: Sage.

Halpern-Flesher, B. L., Connell, J. P., Spencer, M. B., Aber, J. L., Duncan, G. J., Clifford, E., Crichlow, W. E., Usinger, P. A., Cole, S. P., Allen, L., and Seidman, E. (1997). Neighborhood and Family Factors Predicting Educational Risk and Attainment in African-American and White Children and Adolescents. In J. Brooks-Gunn, G. L. Duncan, and J. L. Aber (eds.), *Neighborhood Poverty*, volume I. New York: Russell Sage, pp. 146–173.

Harris, L. (1998). *Violence in America's Public Schools: A Survey of the American Teacher*. New York: Metropolitan Life Insurance Company.

Hauser, S. T., Powers, S. J., and Noam, G. G. (1991). *Adolescents and Their Families: Paths of Ego Development*. New York: The Free Press.

Haveman, R., and Wolf, B. (1995). The determinants of children's attainments: A review of methods and findings. *Journal of Economic Literature*, 33:1829–1878.

Havighurst, R. J. (1953). *Human Development and Education*. New York: McKay.

Hawkins, J. D., Farrington, D. P., and Catalano, R. F. (1998). Reducing Violence through the Schools. In D. S. Elliott, B. A. Hamburg, and K. R. Williams. *Violence in American Schools*. Cambridge, UK: Cambridge University Press, pp. 188–216.

Hawkins, J. D., Guo, J., Hill, K. G., Battin-Pearson, S., and Abbott, R. (2001). Long Term Effects of the Seattle Social Development Intervention on School Bonding Trajectories. *Applied Developmental Science: Special Issue: Prevention as Altering the Course of Development*, 5:225–236.

Hawkins, J. D., Catelano, R. F., Kosterman, R., Abbot, R. D., and Hill, K. G. (1999). Preventing adolescent health-risk behavior by strengthening protection during childhood. *Archives of Pediatrics and Adolescent Medicine*, 153:226–234.

Haynie, D. L. (2002). Friendship networks and delinquency: The relative nature of peer delinquency. *Journal of Quantitative Criminology*, 18(2):99–134.

Heffgot, J. H. (1981). *Professional Reforming: Mobilization for Youth and the Failure of Social Science*. Lexington, MA: D.C. Heath.

Heimer, K. (1997). Socioeconomic status, subcultural definitions, and violent delinquency. *Social Forces*, 75:799–833.

Henggeler, S. W., Mihalic, S. F., Rone, L., Thomas, C., and Timmons-Mitchell, J. (2001). Multisystemic Therapy. In D. S. Elliott (series ed.), *Blueprints for Violence Prevention* (Book 6), Center for the Study and Prevention of Violence, Institute of Behavioral Science, University of Colorado, Boulder, CO.

Herman, M. R., Dornbusch, S. M., Herron, M. C., and Herting, J. R. (1997). The influence of family regulation, connection, and psychological autonomy on six measures of adolescent functioning. *Journal of Adolescent Research*, 12(1):34–67.

Herrenkohl, T. I., Huang, B., Kosterman, R., Hawkins, J. D., Catalano, R. F., and Smith, B. H. (2001). A comparison of the social development processes leading to violent behavior in late adolescence for childhood initiator and adolescent initiators of violence. *Journal of Research in Crime and Delinquency*, 38(1):45–63.

Herrenkohl, T. I., Maguin, E., Hill, K. G., Hawkins, J. D., Abbott, R. D., and Catalano, R. F. (2000). Developmental risk factors for youth violence. *Journal of Adolescent Health*, 26:176–186.

Hester, R. T. (1975). *Neighborhood Space*. Stroudsburg, PA: Dowden, Hutchinson and Ross.

Hetherington, E. M. (1989). Coping with family transitions: Winners, losers, and survivors. *Child Development*, 60:1–14.

Hetherington, E. M., Cox, M., and Cox, R. (1978). The Aftermath of Divorce. In J. Stevens, Jr., and M. Matthew (eds.), *Mother–Child, Father–Child Relations*. Washington, DC: National Association for the Education of Young Children.

Hill, J. P. (1980). *The Family*. Yearbook of the National Society for the Study of Education, 79:274–314.

Hill, K. G., Howell, J. C., Hawkins, J. D., and Battin, S. R. (1999). Risk factors for adolescent gang membership: Results from the Seattle Social Development Project. *Journal of Research in Crime and Delinquency*, 36:300–322.

Hindelang, M. J. (1976). *Criminal Victimization in Eight American Cities*. Cambridge, MA: Ballinger.

Hindelang, M. J., Hirschi, T., and Weis, J. G. (1981). *Measuring Delinquency*. Beverly Hills, CA: Sage.

Hirsch, A. R. (1983). *Making the Second Ghetto: Race and Housing in Chicago*. New York: Cambridge University Press.

Hirschi, T. (1969). *Causes of Delinquency*. Berkeley: University of California Press.

Hoerl, A. E., and Kennard, R. W. (1970). Ridge regression: Biased estimation for nonorthogonal problems. *Technometrics*, 12:55–68.

Hofferth, S. L., Shauman, K. A., Henke, R. P., and West, J. (1998). Characteristics of Children's Early Child Care and Educational Programs: Data from the 1995 National Household Education Survey, NCES 98-128. Washington, DC: U.S. Department of Education, National Center for Education Statistics.

Hogan, D. P., and Kitagawa, E. M. (1985). The impact of social status, family structure and neighborhood on the fertility of black adolescents. *American Journal of Sociology*, 90:825–855.

Huff, C. R. (1998). Comparing the Criminal Behavior of Youth Gangs and At-Risk Youths. *National Institute of Justice Research Brief*. Washington, DC: U.S. Department of Justice.

Huizinga, D., and Elliott, D. S. (1986). Re-assessing the reliability and validity of self-reported delinquency measures. *Journal of Quantitative Criminology*, 2:293–327.

Huizinga, D., and Elliott, D. S. (1987). Juvenile offenders: Prevalence, offender incidence, and arrest rates by race. *Crime and Delinquency*, 33:206–223.

Huizinga, D., Loeber, R., and Thornberry, T. P. (1995). *Recent Findings from the Program of Research on Causes and Correlates of Delinquency*. Washington, DC: Office of Juvenile Justice and Delinquency Prevention.

Hunter, A. (1985). Private, Parochial and Public Social Orders: The Problem of Crime and Incivility in Urban Communities. In G. Suttles and M. Zald (eds.), *The Challenge of Social Control*. Norwood, NJ: Ablex, pp. 230–242.

Hunter, A. G. (1997). Counting on Grandmothers: Black Mothers' and Fathers' Reliance on Grandmothers for Parenting Support. *Journal of Family Issues*, 18(3):251–269.

Ireland, T. O., Thornberry, T. P., and Loeber, R. (2003). Violence among adolescents living in public housing: A two site analysis. *Criminology and Public Policy*, 3:3–38.

Irwin, K. (2004). The violence of adolescent life: Experiencing and managing everyday threats. *Youth and Society*, 35:452–479.

Jackson, A. W., and Davis, G. A. (2000). *Turning Points 2000: Educating Adolescents in the 21st Century*. New York: Teachers College Press.

Jacobs, J. (1961). *The Death and Life of the American City*. New York: Vintage Press.

Jargowsky, P. A. (1996). Take the money and run: Economic segregation in U.S. Metropolitan areas. *American Sociological Review*, 61:984–998.

Jargowsky, P. A. (1997). Beyond the street corner: The hidden diversity of high-poverty neighborhoods. *Urban Geography*, 17:579–603.

Jarrett, R. L. (1995). Growing up poor: The family experiences of socially mobile youth in low income African-American neighborhoods. *Journal of Adolescent Research*, 10:111–135.

Jarrett, R. L. (1997). Bringing Families Back In: Neighborhood Effects on Child Development. In J. Brooks-Gunn, G. J. Duncan, and J. L. Aber (eds.), *Neighborhood Poverty, Volume II Policy Implications in Studying Neighborhoods*. New York: The Russell Sage Foundation, pp. 48–64.

Jencks, C., and Mayer, S. (1990). The Social Consequences of Growing Up in a Poor Neighborhood. In L. E. Lynn, Jr., and M. G. H. McGeary (eds.), *Inner-City Poverty in the United States*. Washington, DC: National Academy Press, pp. 111–186.

Jencks, C., and Peterson, P. E. (eds.) (1991). *The Urban Underclass*. Washington, DC: The Brookings Institution.

Jencks, C., Smith, M., Acland, H., Bane, M. J., Cohen, D., Gintis, H., Heyns, B., and Michelson, S. (1972). *Inequality: A Reassessment of the Effect of Family and Schooling in America*. New York: Harper and Row.

Jessor, R., and Jessor, S. L. (1975). Adolescent development and the onset of drinking: A longitudinal study. *Journal of Studies of Alcohol*, 36:27–51.

Jessor, R., Donovan, J. E., and Costa, F. M. (1991). *Beyond Adolescence: Problem Behavior and Young Adult Development*. Cambridge, UK: Cambridge University Press.

Johnston, L. D., O'Malley, P. M., and Bachman, J. G. (1998). *National Survey Results on Drug Use from the Monitoring the Future Study, 1975–1997. Volume II*. Rockville, MD: National Institutes on Drug Use.

Johnston, L. D., O'Malley, P. M., and Bachman, J. G. (2000a). *Monitoring the Future: National Survey Results on Drug Use, 1975–1999. Volume I: Secondary School Students*. Bethesda, MD: NIDA.

Johnston, L. D., O'Malley, P. M., and Bachman, J. G. (2000b). *Monitoring the Future: National Survey Results on Drug Use, 1975–1999. Volume II: College Students and Adults Ages 19–40*. Bethesda, MD: NIDA.

Jussim, L., and Osgood, D. W. (1989). Influence and similarity among friends: An integrative model applied to incarcerated adolescents. *Social Psychology Quarterly*, 52:98–112.

Kandel, D. B. (1996). The parental and peer contexts of adolescent deviance: An algebra of interpersonal influences. *Journal of Drug Issues*, 26:289–315.

Kao, G., and Tienda, M. (1998). Educational aspirations of minority youth. *American Journal of Education*, 106:349–384.

Kasarda, J. D., and Janowitz, M. (1974). Community attachment in mass society. *American Sociological Review*, 39:328–339.

Kasen, S., Cohen, P., and Brook, J. S. (1998). Adolescent school experiences and dropout, adolescent pregnancy, and young adult deviant behavior. *Journal of Adolescent Research*, 13:49–72.

Kaufman, P., Chen, X., Choy, S. P., Chandler, K. A., Chapman, C. D., Rand, M. R., and Ringel, C. (1998). *Indicators of School Crime and Safety 1998: Executive Summary*. Washington, DC: U.S. Departments of Education and Justice.

Kaufman, P., Chen, X., Choy, S. P., Ruddy, S. A., Miller, A. K., Fleury, J. K., Chandler, K. A., Rand, M. R., Klaus, P., and Planty, M. G. (2000). *Indicators of School Crime and Safety, 2000*. U.S. Departments of Education and Justice. NCES 2001-017/NCJ-184176. Washington, DC.

Keenan, K., Loeber, R., Zhang, Q., Stouthamer-Loeber, M., and VanKammen, W. (1995). The influence of deviant peers on the development of boys' disruptive and delinquent behavior: A temporal analysis. *Development and Psychopathology*, 7:715–726.

Kellam, S. G., Ensminger, M. A., and Turner, J. T. (1977). Family structure and the mental health of children. *Archives of General Psychiatry*, 34:1012–1022.

Keller, S. (1968). *The Urban Neighborhood*. New York: Random House.

Kingston, B. (2005). *The Effects of Neighborhood Context on Adolescent Delinquency and Drug Use*. Dissertation. Boulder, CO: University of Colorado.

Kipke, M. (ed.) (1999). *Risks and Opportunities: Synthesis of Studies in Adolescence*. Washington, DC: National Academy Press. Board on Children, Youth and Families, National Research Council and Institute of Medicine.

Klebanov, P. K., Brooks-Gunn, J., and Duncan, G. J. (1994). Does neighborhood and family poverty affect mother's parenting, mental health, and social support? *Journal of Marriage and the Family*, 56(May), 441–455.

Klebanov, P. K., Brooks-Gunn, J., Chase-Lansdale, P. L., and Gordon, R. A. (1997). Are Neighborhood Effects on Young Children Mediated by Features of the Home Environment? In J. Brooks-Gunn, G. J. Duncan, and J. L. Aber (eds.), *Neighborhood Poverty: Volume 1*. New York: Russell Sage, pp. 119–145.

Klein, M. W. (1995). *The American Street Gang*. New York: Oxford University Press.

Klein, M. W., and Maxon, C. L. (In press). *Street Gang Patterns and Policies*. New York: Oxford University Press.

Knight, D. K., Broome, K. M., Cross, D. R., and Simpson, D. D. (1998). Antisocial tendency among drug-addicted adults: Potential long-term effects of parental absence, support, and conflict during childhood. *American Journal of Drug, Alcohol, and Abuse*, 24:361–375.

Kobrin, S. (1951). The conflict of values in delinquency areas. *American Sociological Review*, 16:653–661.

Korbin, J. E. (2001). Context and Meaning in Neighborhood Studies of Children and Families. In A. Booth and A. C. Crouter (eds.), *Does It Take a Village?* Mahwah, NJ: Lawrence Earlbaum Associates, pp. 79–86.

Korbin, J. E., and Coulton, C. (1996). The role of neighbors and the government in neighborhood-based child protection. *Journal of Social Issues*, 52:163–176.

Kotlowitz, A. (1991). *There Are No Children Here*. New York: Doubleday.

Kozol, J. (1995). *Amazing Grace*. New York: Crown.

Kroeber, A. and Parsons, T. (1958). The concepts of culture and social systems. *American Sociological Review*, 23:582–583.

Kruttschnitt, C., McLeod, J. D., and Dornfeld, M. (1994). The economic environment of child abuse. *Social Problems*, 41(2):299–315.

Kubrin, C. E., and Weitzer, R. (2003). New directions in social disorganization theory. *Journal of Research in Crime and Delinquency*, 40(4):374–402.

Lamborn, S. D., and Steinberg, L. (1993). Emotional autonomy redux: Revisiting Ryan and Lynch. *Child Development*, 64:483–499.

Land, K., McCall, P., and Cohen, L. (1990). Structural covariates of homicide rates: Are there any invariances across time and space? *American Journal of Sociology*, 95:922–963.

Larson, R. W., Moneta, G., Richards, M. H., Holmbeck, G., and Duckett, E. (1996). Changes in adolescents' daily interactions with their families from ages 10 to 18: Disengagement and transformation. *Developmental Psychology*, 32:744–754.

Laub, J., and Lauritsen, J. L. (1998). The Interdependence of School Violence with Neighborhood and Family Conditions. In Elliott, D. S., Hamburg, B. A., and Williams, K. R. *Violence in American Schools*. Cambridge, UK: Cambridge University Press, pp. 127–155.

Laub, J., and Sampson, R. (1988). Unraveling families and delinquency: A re-analysis of the Gluecks' data. *Criminology*, 26:355–380.

Leahy, R. L. (1981). Parental practices and the development of moral judgment and self-image disparity during adolescence. *Developmental Psychology*, 17(5):580–594.

LeClere, F. B., Rogers, R. G., and Peters, K. D. (1997). Ethnicity and mortality in the United States: Individual and community correlates. *Social Forces*, 76:169–198.

LeClere, F. B., Rogers, R. G., and Peters, K. D. (1998). Neighborhood social context and racial differences in women's heart disease mortality. *Journal of Health and Social Behavior*, 39:91–107.

Lee, B. A. (2001). Taking Neighborhoods Seriously. In A. Booth and A. C. Crouter, (eds.), *Does It Take a Village?* Mahwah, NJ: Lawrence Erlbaum Associates, pp. 31–40.

Lee, B. A., and Campbell, K. E. (1998). Neighborhood Networks of Black and White Americans. In Wellman, B. (ed.), *Networks in the Global Village*. Boulder, CO: Westview, pp. 119–146.

Lee, B. A., Campbell, K. E., and Miller, O. (1991). Racial differences in urban neighborhoods. *Sociological Forum*, 6:525–550.

Lempers, J., Clark-Lempers, D., and Simons, R. (1989). Economic hardship, parenting, and distress in adolescence. *Child Development*, 60: 25–49.

Leventhal, T. J., and Brooks-Gunn, J. (2000). The neighborhoods they live in: The effects of neighborhood residence upon child and adolescent outcomes. *Psychological Bulletin*, 126:309–337.

Leventhal, T., and Brooks-Gunn, J. (2003). Children and youth in neighborhood contexts. *Current Directions in Psychological Science*, 12:27–31.

Leventhal, T. J., Brooks-Gunn, J., and Kammerman, S. (1997). Communities As Place, Face and Space: Provision of Services to the Poor Urban Children and Their Families. In J. Brooks-Gunn, G. J. Duncan, and J. L. Aber (eds.), *Neighborhood Poverty, Volume II*. New York: Russell Sage Foundation, pp. 182–206.

Lewis, D. A., and Salem, G. (1986). *Fear of Crime, Incivility and the Production of a Social Problem*. New Brunswick, NJ: Transaction Books.

Liebow, E. (1967). *Tally's Corner: A Study of Negro Street Corner Men*. Boston: Little Brown.

Lipsey, M. W., and Derzon, J. H. (1998). Predictors of Violent or Serious Delinquency in Adolescence and Early Adulthood: A Synthesis of Longitudinal Research. In R. Loeber and D. P. Farrington (eds.), *Serious and Violent Juvenile Offenders*. Thousand Oaks, CA: Sage, pp. 86–105.

Loeber, R., and Stouthamer-Loeber, M. (1986). Family Factors as Correlates and Predictors of Juvenile Conduct Problems and Delinquency. In Tonry, M. and Morris, N. (eds.), *Crime and Justice: An Annual Review of Research, Volume 7*, Chicago: University of Chicago Press.

Loeber, R., and Stouthamer-Loeber, M. (1998). Juvenile Aggression at Home and at School. In D. S. Elliott, B. A. Hamburg, and K. R. Williams. *Violence in American Schools*. Cambridge, UK: Cambridge University Press, pp. 94–126.

Loeber, R., and Wickstrom, P. H. (1993). Individual Pathways to Crime in Different Types of Neighborhoods. In D. P. Farrington, R. J. Sampson, and P. H. Wickstrom (eds.), *Integrating Individual and Ecological Aspects of Crime*. Stockholm: National Council for Crime Prevention, pp. 169–204.

Loeber, R., Green, S. M., Keenan, M. S., and Lahey, B. B. (1995). Which boys will fare worse? Early predictors of the onset of conduct disorder in a six-year longitudinal study. *Journal of the American Academy of Child and Adolescent Psychiatry*, 34:499–509.

Logan, J. R., and Moloch, H. L. (1987). *Urban Frontiers: The Political Economy of Place*. Berkeley: University of California Press.

Lorion, R. P. (1998). Exposure to Urban Violence: Contamination of the School Environment. In D. S. Elliott, B. Hamburg, and K. R. Williams, *Violence in American Schools*. Cambridge, UK: Cambridge University Press, pp. 293–311.

Lukas, J. (1985). *Common Ground: A Turbulent Decade in the Lives of Three American Families*. New York: Knopf.

Lundman, R. J. (1993). *Prevention and Control of Juvenile Delinquency*, 2nd ed. New York: Oxford University Press.

Luster, T., and McAdoo, H. (1996). Family and child influences on educational attainment: A secondary analysis of the High/Scope Perry Preschool data. *Developmental Psychology*, 32(1):26–39.

Luthar, S. S. (1995). Social competence in the school setting: Prospective cross-domain associations among inner-city teens. *Child Development*, 66:416–429.

MacLeod, J. (1987). *Ain't No Makin' It*. Boulder, CO: Westview Press.

MacLeod, J. (1995). *Ain't No Making It. Leveled Aspirations in a Low Income Community*, 2nd ed. Boulder, CO: Westview Press.

McAdoo, H. P. (1982). Stress absorbing systems in black families. *Family Relations*, 31:479–488.

McCahey, R. M. (1986). Economic Conditions, Neighborhood Organization, and Urban Crime. Pp. 221–270. In A. J. Reiss, Jr. and M. Tonry (eds.), *Communities and Crime*. Chicago: University of Chicago Press.

McCarthy, B., and Hagan, J. (1995). Getting into street crime: The structure and process of criminal embeddedness. *Social Science Research*, 24:63–95.

McCord, J. (1991). Family relationships, juvenile delinquency, and adult criminality. *Criminology*, 3:397–417.

McLanahan, S. (1985). Family structure and the reproduction of poverty. *American Journal of Sociology*, 90:873–901.

McLoyd, V. C. (1990). The impact of economic hardship on black families and children: Psychological distress, parenting and socioemotional development. *Child Development*, 61:311–346.

McLoyd, V. C., and Wilson, L. (1991). The Strain of Living Poor: Parenting, Social Support, and Child Mental Health. In A. C. Huston (ed.), *Children in Poverty*. New York: Cambridge University Press, pp. 105–135.

McNeely, C. A. (1999). *Parenting Strategies and Health-Risk Behaviors across Urban Contexts: Does it Matter Where Black Families Live?* Minneapolis: University of Minnesota Medical School.

Maccoby, E. E., and Martin, J. A. (1983). Socialization in the Context of the Family: Parent–Child Interaction. In E. M. Hetherington (ed.), *Handbook of Child Psychology, Volume 4, Socialization, Personality, and Social Development*, 4th ed. New York: Wiley, pp. 1–101.

Maccoby, E. E., Johnson, J. P., and Church, R. M. (1958). Community integration and the social control of juvenile delinquency. *Journal of Social Issues*, 14:38–51.

Maden, M. F., and Wrench, D. F. (1977). Significant findings in child abuse research. *Victimology*, 2:196–224.

Magnusson, D. (1988). *Individual Development from an Interactional Perspective: A Longitudinal Study*. Hillsdale, NJ: Erlbaum.

Manski, C. F. (1995). *Identification Problems in the Social Sciences*. Cambridge, MA: Harvard University Press.

Massey, D. S. (1993). *American Apartheid. Segregation and the Making of the Underclass.* Cambridge, MA: Harvard University Press.

Massey, D. S. (2001). The Prodigal Paradigm Returns: Ecology Comes Back to Sociology. In A. Booth and A. C. Crouter (eds.), *Does It Take a Village?* Mahwah, NJ: Lawrence Erlbaum Associates, pp. 41–47.

Massey, D. S., and Denton, N. A. (1989). Hypersegregation in U.S. Metropolitan Areas: Black and Hispanic Segregation along Five Dimensions. *Demography*, 26:373–391.

Massey, D. S., and Denton, N. A. (1993). *American Apartheid.* Cambridge, MA: Harvard University Press.

Massey, D. S., Gross, A. B., and Eggers, M. L. (1991). Segregation, the concentration of poverty, and the life chances of individuals. *Social Science Research*, 20:397–420.

Masten, A., Best, K., and Garmezy, N. (1990). Resilience and development: Contributions from the study of children who overcame adversity. *Development and Psychopathology*, 2:425–444.

Masten, A., and Coatsworth, J. D. (1998). The development of competence in favorable and unfavorable environments: Lessons from research on successful children. *American Psychologist*, 53:205–220.

Matsueda, R. L., and Anderson, K. (1998). The dynamics of delinquent peers and delinquent behavior. *Criminology*, 36:269–308.

Mayer, S., (1997). *What Money Can't Buy: The Effect of Parental Income on Children's Outcomes.* Cambridge, MA: Harvard University Press.

Mayer, S., and Jencks, C. (1989). Growing up in poor neighborhoods: How much does it matter? *Science*, 243:1441–1446.

Melby, J. N., and Conger, R. D. (1996). Parental behaviors and adolescent academic performance: A longitudinal analysis. *Journal of Research on Adolescence*, 6(1): 113–137.

Menard, S. (1985). Inequality and fertility. *Studies in Comparative International Development*, 20:83–97.

Menard, S. (1986). Fertility, family planning, and development: Indirect influences. *Studies in Comparative International Development*, 21:32–50.

Menard, S. (1987a). Fertility, development, and family planning, 1970–1980: An analysis of cases weighted by population. *Studies in Comparative International Development*, 22:103–127.

Menard, S. (1987b). Short-term trends in crime and delinquency: A comparison of UCR, NCS, and self-report data. *Justice Quarterly*, 4:455–474.

Menard, S. (1995a). *Applied Logistic Regression Analysis.* Thousand Oaks, CA: Sage.

Menard, S. (1995b). A developmental test of Mertonian anomie theory. *Journal of Research in Crime and Delinquency*, 32:136–174.

Menard, S. (1997). A developmental test of Cloward's differential-opportunity theory. In N. Passas and R. Agnew (eds.), *The Future of Anomie Theory.* Boston: Northeastern University Press, pp. 142–186.

Menard, S. (2002). *Longitudinal Research.* Thousand Oaks, CA: Sage.

Menard, S., and Covey, H. C. (1987). Patterns of victimization, fear of crime, and crime precautions in non-metropolitan New Mexico. *Journal of Crime and Justice*, 10:71–100.

Menard, S., and Elliott, D. S. (1990). Longitudinal and cross-sectional data collection and analysis in the study of crime and delinquency. *Justice Quarterly*, 7:11–55.

Menard, S., and Elliott, D. S. (1994). Delinquent bonding, moral beliefs, and illegal behavior in a three-wave panel model. *Justice Quarterly*, 11:173–188.

Menard, S., and Morse, B. J. (1984). A structuralist critique of the IQ-delinquency hypothesis: Theory and evidence. *American Journal of Sociology*, 89:1347–1378.

Merry, S. E. (1981a). *Urban Danger: Life in a Neighborhood of Strangers*. Philadelphia: Temple University Press.

Merry, S. E. (1981b). Defensible space undefended: Social factors in crime prevention through environmental design. *Urban Affairs Quarterly*, 16:397–422.

Metropolitan Life Insurance Company (1993). *The Metropolitan Life Survey of the American Teacher, 1993: Violence in America's Public Schools*. New York: Louis Harris and Associates.

Miethe, T. D., and McDowall, D. (1993). Contextual effects in models of criminal victimization. *Social Forces*, 71(3):741–759.

Mihalic, S. W., and Elliott, D. S. (1997a). A social learning theory model of marital violence. *Journal of Family Violence*, 12:21–48.

Mihalic, S. W., and Elliott, D. S. (1997b). If violence is domestic, does it really count? *Journal of Family Violence*, 9(3):293–312.

Mihalic, S. W., Irwin, K., Elliott, D. S., Fagan, A., and Hansen, D. (2001). *Blueprints for Violence Prevention*. Juvenile Justice Bulletin, July. Washington, DC: Office of Juvenile Justice and Delinquency Prevention, U.S. Department of Justice.

Miller, W. B. (1962). The impact of a "total community" delinquency control project. *Social Problems*, 10:168–191.

Moffitt, T. E., Caspi, A., Rutler, M., and Silva, P. A. (2001). *Sex Differences in Antisocial Behavior: Conduct Disorder, Delinquency, and Violence in the Dunedin Longitudinal Study*. Cambridge, UK: Cambridge University Press.

Morenoff, J. D., Sampson, R. J., and Raudenbush, S. W. (2001). Neighborhood inequality, collective efficacy, and the spatial dynamics of homicide. *Criminology*, 39:517–560.

Morris, D., and Hess, K. (1975). *Neighborhood Power: The New Localism*. Boston: Beacon Press.

Murray, D. M. (1996). An ecological analysis of coital timing among middle-class African American adolescent families. *Journal of Adolescent Research*, 11:261–279.

Murray, D. M., and Short, B. (1995). Intra-class correlates, among measures related to alcohol use by young adults: Estimates, correlates, and applications in intervention studies. *Journal of Studies in Alcohol*, 56:681–694.

Myers, H. F., and King, L. (1983). Mental Health Issues in the Development of the Black American Child. In G. Powell, J. Yamamoto, A. Romero, and A. Morales (eds.), *The Psychosocial Development of Minority Children*. New York: Brunner/Mazel, pp. 275–306.

National Research Council (1993). *Losing Generations: Adolescents in High-Risk Settings*. Washington, DC: National Academy Press.

Neighbors, B. D., Forehand, R., and Bau, J.-J. (1997). Interparental conflict and relations with parents as predictors of young adult functioning. *Development and Psychopathology*, 9:169–187.

Newcomb, M. D., and Bentler, P. M. (1988). *Consequences of Adolescent Drug Abuse.* Beverly Hills, CA: Sage.

Newman, K. (1999). *No Shame In My Game: The Working Poor in the Inner City.* New York: Russell Sage Foundation.

Newman, O. (1972). *Defensible Space.* New York: MacMillan.

Newman, O. (1979). *Community of Interest.* New York: Doubleday.

NICHD (2005). *Child Care and Child Development.* New York: The Guilford Press.

O'Brien, R. M. (1996). Police productivity and crime rates: 1973–1992. *Criminology,* 34:183–207.

O'Brien, S. F., and Bierman, K. L. (1988). Conceptions and perceived influence of peer groups: Interviews with preadolescents and adolescents. *Child Development,* 59:1360–1365.

O'Donnell, J. O., Hawkins, J. D., and Abbott, R. D. (1995). Predicting serious delinquency and substance use among aggressive boys. *Journal of Consulting and Clinical Psychology,* 63:529–537.

Ogbu, J. U. (1985). A Cultural Ecology of Competence Among Inner-City Blacks. In M. Spencer, G. Brookins, and W. Allen (eds.), *Beginnings: The Social and Affective Development of Black Children.* Hillsdale, NJ: Lawrence Erlbaum, pp. 45–66.

Ogbu, J. U. (1994). From Cultural Differences to Differences in Cultural Frame of Reference. In P. M. Greenfield and R. R. Cooking (eds.), *Cross-Cultural Roots of Minority Child Development.* Hillsdale, NJ: Lawrence Erlbaum, pp. 365–391.

OJJDP (2001). School violence: An overview. *Juvenile Justice,* 8(1):1–35.

Olds, D. L., Eckenrode, J., Henderson, C. R., Jr., Kitzman, H., Powers, J., Cole, R., Sidora, K., Morris, P., Pettitt, L., and Luckey, D. (1997). Long-term effects of home visitation on maternal life course and child abuse and neglect: 15 year follow-up on a randomized trial. *Journal of the American Medical Association,* 278(8):637–643.

Park, R. E. (1926). The Urban Community as a Special Pattern and Moral Order. In E. W. Burgess (ed.), *The Urban Community,* Chicago, IL: University of Chicago Press, pp. 3–18.

Park, R. E., and Burgess, E. W. (1924). *Introduction to the Science of Sociology,* 2nd ed. Chicago, IL: University of Chicago Press.

Park, R. E., Burgess, E. W., and McKenzie, R. D. (1925). *The City.* Chicago: University of Chicago Press.

Patterson, G. R. (1982). *Coercive Family Process: Volume 3, A Social Learning Approach,* Eugene, OR: Castalia.

Patterson, G. R. (1992). Developmental Changes in Antisocial Behavior. In R. D. Peters, R. J. Mahon, and V. L. Quinsey (eds.), *Aggression and Violence through the Life Span.* Newbury Park, CA: Sage, pp. 52–82.

Patterson, G. R., and Bank, L. (1987). When is a Nomological Network a Construct? In D. R. Peterson and D. B. Fishman (eds.), *Assessment for Decision,* New Brunswick, NJ: Rutgers University Press, pp. 249–279.

Patterson, G. R., and Dishion, T. J. (1985). Contributions of families and peers to delinquency. *Criminology,* 23:63–79.

Patterson, G. R., Reid, J. B., and Dishion, T. J. (1992). *Antisocial Boys.* Eugene, OR: Castalia.

Peeples, F., and Loeber, R. (1994). Do individual factors and neighborhood context explain ethnic differences in juvenile delinquency? *Journal of Quantitative Criminology*, 10:141–158.

Prior-Brown, L., and Cowen, E. L. (1989). Stressful life events, support, and children's school adjustment. *Journal of Clinical Child Psychology*, 18:214–220.

Putnam, R. D. (1995). Bowling alone: America's declining social capital. *Journal of Democracy*, 6:65–78.

Rainwater, L. (1970). *Beyond Ghetto Walls: Black Families in a Federal Slum*. Chicago: Aldine Publishing Co.

Rapoport, A. (1997). *Human Aspects of Urban Form*. Oxford, UK: Pergamon.

Reckless, W., Dinitz, S., and Murray, E. (1957). The good boy in a high delinquency area. *Journal of Criminal Law, Criminology, and Police Science*, 48:18–26.

Reinarman, C., and Fagan, J. (1988). Social organization and differential association: A research note from a longitudinal study of violent juvenile offenders. *Crime and Delinquency*, 34:307–327.

Reiss, Jr., A. J., and Tonry, M. (eds.). (1986). *Communities and Crime*. Chicago, IL: University of Chicago Press.

Reynolds, A. J., and Gill, S. (1994). The role of parental perspectives in the school adjustment of inner-city Black children. *Journal of Youth and Adolescence*, 23(6):671–691.

Rice, K. G., Cunningham, T. J., and Young, M. B. (1997). Attachment to parents, social competence, and emotional well-being: A comparison of Black and White late adolescents. *Journal of Counseling Psychology*, 44(1):89–101. American Psychological Association, Inc.

Rivlin, L. G. (1987). The Neighborhood, Personal Identity, and Group Affiliation. In I. Altman and A. Wandersman (eds.), *Neighborhood and Community Environments*, New York: Springer, pp. 1–34.

Robert, S. (1998). Community-level socioeconomic effects on adult health. *Journal of Health and Social Behavior*, 39:18–37.

Roth, I., and Brooks-Gunn, J. (2000). *What Do Adolescents Need For Healthy Development?: Implications for Youth Policy (Social Policy Report 16)*. Ann Arbor, MI: Society for Research in Child Development.

Rutter, M. (1979). Protective Factors in Children's Responses to Stress and Disadvantage. In M. W. Kent and J. E. Rolf (eds.), *Primary Prevention of Psychopathology, Volume 3*. Hanover, NH: University Press of New England, pp. 49–74.

Ryan, R. M., and Lynch, J. H. (1989). Emotional autonomy versus detachment: Revisiting the vicissitudes of adolescence and young adulthood. *Child Development*, 6:340–356.

Ryan, T. P. (1997). *Modern Regression Methods*. New York: Wiley.

Ryan-Arredondo, K., Renouf, K., Egyed, C., Doxey, M., Dobbins, M., Sanchez, S., and Rakowitz, B. (2001). Threats of violence in schools: The Dallas Independent School District's Response. *Psychology in the Schools*, 38(2):185–196.

Sackney, L. (1988). *Enhancing School Learning Climate: Theory Research and Practice*. Report #180. Saskatchewan, Canada: Saskatchewan School Trustees Association Research Center.

Sameroff, A. J., Seifer, R., Zax, M., and Barocas, R. B. (1987). Early indices of developmental risk. The Rochester Longitudinal Study. *Schizophrenia Bulletin*, 13:383–394.

Sameroff, A. J., Seifer, R., Baldwin, A. L., and Baldwin, C. A. (1993). Stability of intelligence from preschool to adolescence: The influence of social and family risk factors. *Child Development*, 64:80–97.

Sampson, R. J. (1985). Neighborhood and crime: The structural determinants of personal victimization. *Journal of Research in Crime and Delinquency*, 22:7–40.

Sampson, R. J. (1986). Crime in the Cities: The Effects of Formal and Informal Control. In A. J. Reiss, Jr. and M. Tonry (eds.), *Communities and Crime*. Chicago: University of Chicago Press, pp. 271–310.

Sampson, R. J. (1987a). Communities and Crime. In M. Gottfredson and T. Hirschi (eds.), *Positive Criminology*, Beverly Hills, CA: Sage, pp. 91–114.

Sampson, R. J. (1987b). Urban Black violence: The effect of male joblessness and family disruption. *American Journal of Sociology*, 93:348–382.

Sampson, R. J. (1992). Family Management and Child Development: Insights From Social Disorganization Theory. In Joan McCord (ed.), *Advances in Criminological Theory, Volume 3: Facts, Frameworks, and Forecasts*. New Brunswick, NJ: Transaction.

Sampson, R. J. (1993). Family and Neighborhood Level Influences on Crime: A Contextual Theory and Strategies for Research Testing. In D. P. Farrington, R. J. Sampson, and P. Wikstrom (eds.), *Integrating Individual and Ecological Aspects of Crime*. Stockholm: National Council for Crime Prevention, pp. 153–168.

Sampson, R. J. (1995). The Community. In J. Q. Wilson and J. Petersilia (eds.), *Crime*. San Francisco: ICS Press, pp. 193–216.

Sampson, R. J. (2001). How do Communities Undergird or Undermine Human Development? Relevant Contexts and Social Mechanisms. In A. Booth and A. C. Crouter (eds.), *Does It Take a Village?* London: Lawrence Erlbaum Associates, pp. 3–30.

Sampson, R. J., and Groves, W. B. (1989). Community structure and crime: Testing social disorganization theory. *American Journal of Sociology*, 94:774–802.

Sampson, R. J., and Laub J. H. (1991). Crime and deviance over the life course: The salience of adult bonds. *American Sociological Review*, 55:608–627.

Sampson, R. J., and Laub, J. H. (1993). *Crime in the Making: Pathways and Turning Points through Life*. Cambridge, MA: Harvard University Press.

Sampson, R. J., and Laub, J. H. (1997). A Life Course Theory of Cumulative Disadvantage and the Stability of Delinquency. In T. P. Thornberry (ed.), *Developmental Theories of Crime and Delinquency, Volume 7: Advances in Criminological Theory*. New Brunswick, NJ: Transaction, pp. 133–161 .

Sampson, R. J., and Lauritsen, J. L. (1994). Violent Victimization and Offending: Individual, Situational, and Community-Level Risk Factors. In A. J. Reiss and J. A. Roth (eds.), *Understanding and Preventing Violence: Social Influences on Violence, Volume 3*, Washington, DC: National Academy Press, pp. 1–114.

Sampson, R. J., and Morenoff, J. (1997). Ecological Perspectives on the Neighborhood Context of Urban Poverty, Past and Present. In J. Brooks-Gunn, G. Duncan, and L. Aber (eds.), *Neighborhood Poverty: Policy Implications in Studying Neighborhoods*. New York: Russell Sage Foundation, pp. 1–22.

Sampson, R. J., Morenoff, J., and Gannon-Rowley, T. (2002). Assessing "Neighborhood Effects:" Social Processes and New Directions in Research. *Annual Review of Sociology*, 28:443–478.

Sampson, R. J., Raudenbush, S. M., and Earls, F. (1997). Neighborhood, and violent crime: A multilevel study of collective efficacy. *Science*, 277, 918–924.

Sampson, R. J., Raudenbush, S. M., and Earls, F. (1998). Neighborhood Efficacy– Does it Really Help Reduce Violence? *NIJ Research Preview*, April 1998. Washington, DC: The National Institute of Justice.

Sampson, R. J., and Wilson, W. J. (1995). Toward a Theory of Race, Crime, and Urban Inequality. In J. Hagan and R. Peterson (eds.), *Crime and Inequality*. Stanford: Stanford University Press.

Scales, P. C., and Leffert, N. (1999). *Developmental Assets: A Synthesis of Scientific Research on Adolescent Development*. Minneapolis, MN: Search Institute.

Schmid, C. (1960). Urban crime areas: Part I. *American Sociological Review*, 25:527–542.

Schmitz, S., Fulker, D. W., and Mrazek, D. A. (1995). Problem behavior in early and middle childhood: An initial behavior genetic analysis. *Journal of Child Psychology and Psychiatry*, 36:1443–1457.

Schuerman, L. A., and Kobrin, S. (1983). *Crime and Urban Ecological Processes: Implications for Public Policy*. Paper presented at the Annual Meeting of the American Society of Criminology. Denver, CO, November.

Schuerman, L. A., and Kobrin, S. (1986). Community Careers in Crime. In A. J. Reiss, Jr., and M. Tonry (eds.), *Communities and Crime*. Chicago: University of Chicago Press, pp. 67–100.

Sebald, H. (1989). Adolescents' peer orientation: Changes in the support system during the past three decades. *Adolescence*, 24(96):937–946.

Seidman, E., Yoshikawa, H., Roberts, A., Chesir-Teran, D., Allen, L., Friedman, J. L., and Aber, J. L. (1998). Structural and experimental neighborhood contexts, developmental stage, and antisocial behavior among urban adolescents in poverty. *Development and Psychopathology*, 10:259–281.

Shaw, C. R., and McKay, H. D. (1942). *Juvenile Delinquency and Urban Areas*. Chicago, IL: University of Chicago Press.

Shaw, C. R., and McKay, H. D. (1969). *Juvenile Delinquency and Urban Areas*. Revised Edition. Chicago: University of Chicago Press.

Sherman, L. W. (1997). Communities and Crime Prevention. In L. W. Sherman, D. Gottfredson, D. MacKenzie, J. Eck, P. Reuter, and S. Bushway (eds.), *Preventing Crime: What Works? What Doesn't? What's Promising?* Washington, DC: U.S. Department of Justice, pp. 2.1–2.32.

Sherman, L. W., Gottfredson, D., MacKenzie, D., Eck, J., Reuter, P., and Bushway, S. (eds.), (1997). *Preventing Crime: What Works? What Doesn't? What's Promising?* Washington, DC: U.S. Department of Justice.

Shihadeh, E. S., and Steffensmeier, D. J. (1994). Economic inequality, family disruption and urban Black violence: Cities as units of stratification and social control. *Social Forces*, 73(2):729–751.

Short, J. F. (1996). *Gangs and Adolescent Violence*. Boulder, CO: Center for the Study and Prevention of Violence, University of Colorado.

Sickmund, M., Snyder, H. N., and Poe-Yamagata, E. (1997). *Juvenile Offenders and Victims: 1997 Update on Violence*. Washington, DC: Office of Juvenile Justice and Delinquency Prevention.

Sim, H.-O., and Vuchinich, S. (1996). The declining effects of family stressors on antisocial behavior from childhood to adolescence and early adulthood. *Journal of Family Issues*, 17(3):408–427.

Simcha-Fagan, O., and Schwartz, J. E. (1986). Neighborhood and delinquency: An assessment of contextual effects. *Criminology*, 24:667–703.

Simons, R. L., Johnson, C., Beaman, J., Conger, R., and Whitbeck, L. B. (1996). Parents and peer group as mediators of the effect of community structure on adolescent problem behavior. *American Journal of Community Psychology*, 24:145–171.

Skogan, W. G. (1986). Fear of Crime and Neighborhood Change. In A. J. Reiss, Jr. and M. Tonry (eds.), *Communities and Crime*. Chicago, IL: University of Chicago Press, pp. 203–229.

Skogan, W. G. (1990). *Disorder and Decline: Crime and the Spiral of Decay in American Neighborhoods*. New York: Free Press.

Small, S., and Supple, A. (2001). Communities as Systems: Is a Community More Than the Sum of its Parts? In A. Booth, and A. C. Crouter (eds.), *Does It Take a Village?* London: Lawrence Erlbaum Associates, pp. 161–174.

Smith, D. A., and Jarjoura, G. R. (1988). Social structure and criminal victimization. *Journal of Research in Crime and Delinquency*, 25:27–52.

Snow, D., and Anderson, L. (1993). *Down on Their Luck: A Study of Homeless Street People*. Berkley: University of California Press.

Snyder, H. N. (2005). *Juvenile Arrests 2003*. Juvenile Justice Bulletin. Washington, DC: U.S. Department of Justice.

Snyder, H. N., and Sickmund, M. (1999) *Juvenile Offenders and Victims: 1999 National Report*. (NCJ 178257) Washington, DC: Office of Juvenile Justice and Delinquency Prevention. U.S. Government Printing Office.

Sokol-Katz, J., Dunham, R., and Zimmerman, R. (1997). Family structure versus parental attachment in controlling adolescent deviant behavior: A social control model. *Adolescence*, 32(125):199–215.

Sorrentino, A. (1977). *Organizing against Crime: Redeveloping the Neighborhood*. New York: Human Sciences Press.

Spencer, M. B. (2001). Resiliency and Fragility Factors Associated with the Contextual Experiences of Low-Resource Urban African-American Male Youth and Families. In A. Booth and A. C. Crouter (eds.), *Does It Take a Village?* London: Lawrence Erlbaum Associates, pp. 51–78.

Spencer, M. B., Dupree, D., and Hartman, T. (1997). A Phenomenological Variant in Ecological Systems Theory (PVEST): A self-organization perspective in context. *Development and Psychopathology*, 9:817–833.

Stack, C. B. (1974). *All Our Kin: Strategies for Survival in a Black Community*. New York: Harper and Row.

Stark, R. (1987). Deviant place: A theory of the ecology of crime. *Criminology*, 25:893–909.

Steinberg, L. (2001). We know some things: Parent–adolescent relations in retrospect and prospect. *Journal of Research in Adolescence*, 11:1–19.

Steinberg, L., Catelano, R., and Dooley, D. (1981). Economic antecedents of child abuse and neglect. *Child Development*, 52:975–985.

Steinberg, L., Elmen, J. D., and Mounts, N. S. (1989). Authorative parenting, psychosocial maturity, and academic success among adolescents. *Child Development*, 60:1424–1436.

Steinberg, L., Lamborn, S., Dornbusch, S., and Darling, N. (1992). Impact of parenting practices on adolescent achievement: Authoritative parenting, school involvement, and encouragement to succeed. *Child Development*, 63:1266–1281.

Steinberg, L., Mounts, N. S., Lamborn, S. D., and Dornbusch, S. M. (1991). Authoritative parenting and adolescent adjustment across varied ecological niches. *Journal of Research on Adolescence*, 1(1):19–36.

Steinberg, L., and Silverberg, S. B. (1986). The vicissitudes of autonomy in early adolescence. *Child Development*, 57:841–851.

Stephens, R. (1998). Safe School Planning. In D. S. Elliott, B. A. Hamburg, and K. R. Williams (eds.), *Violence in American Schools*, New York: Cambridge University Press, pp. 253–292.

Stern, S. B., and Smith, C. A. (1995). Family processes and delinquency in an ecological context. *Social Sciences Review*, 69:703–731.

Stewart, E. A., Simons, R. L., and Conger, R. D. (2002). Assessing neighborhood and social psychological influences on childhood violence in an African-American sample. *Criminology*, 40:801–830.

Stouthamer-Loeber, M., Loeber, R., Farrington, D. P., Zhang, Q., Van Kammen, W. B., and Maguin, E. (1993). The double edge of protective and risk factors for delinquency: Interrelations and developmental patterns. *Development and Psychopathology*, 5:683–701.

Stouthamer-Loeber, M., Loeber, R., Homish, D. L., and Wei, E. H. (2002). Maltreatment of boys and the development of disruptive and delinquent behavior. *Development and Psychopathology*, 13:941–955.

Suarez, R. (1999). *The Old Neighborhood*. New York: Free Press.

Sullivan, M. (1989). *"Getting Paid": Youth Crime and Work in the Inner City*. Ithaca, New York: Cornell University Press.

Sutherland, E. H. (1939). *Principles of Criminology*. New York: Lippincott.

Suttles, G. D. (1968). *The Social Process of the Slum*. Chicago, IL: University of Chicago Press.

Suttles, G. D. (1972). *The Social Construction of Communities*. Chicago: University of Chicago Press.

Swindler, A. (1986). Culture in action: Symbols and strategies. *American Sociological Review*, 51:273–286.

Taylor, R. B. (1981). *Informal Control in the Urban Residential Environment*. Report from the Center for Metropolitan Planning and Research, Johns Hopkins University to the U.S. Department of Justice, National Institute of Justice, Washington, DC Baltimore: Johns Hopkins University.

Taylor, R. B. (1996). Adolescents' perceptions of kinship support and family management practices: Association with adolescent adjustment in African American families. *Developmental Psychology*, 32(4):687–695.

Taylor, R. B. (1997). Social order and disorder of street blocks and neighborhoods: Ecology, microecology, and the systemic model of social disorganization. *Journal of Research in Crime and Delinquency*, 34(1):113–155.

Taylor, R. B. (2001). *Breaking Away from Broken Windows*. Boulder, CO: Westview Press.

Taylor, R. B., and Browser, S. (1981). Territorial cognition and social climate in urban neighborhoods. *Basic and Applied Social Psychology*, 2(4):289–303.

Taylor, R. B., Casten, R., and Flickinger, S. (1993). The influence of kinship social support on the parenting experiences and psychosocial adjustment of African-American adolescents. *Developmental Psychology*, 29:382–388.

Taylor, R. B., and Covington, J. (1988). Neighborhood changes in ecology and violence. *Criminology*, 26:553–589.

Taylor, R. B., and Covington, J. (1993). Community structural change and fear of crime. *Social Problems*, 40:374–387.

Taylor, R. B., and Harrell, A. V. (1996). *Physical Environment and Crime*. Washington, DC: NIJ, U.S. Department of Justice.

Taylor, R. B., and Roberts, D. (1995). Kinship support and maternal and adolescent well-being in economically disadvantaged African-American families. (1995). *Child Development*, 66:1585–1597.

Tedeschi, J. T., and Felson, R. B. (1994). *Violence, Aggression, and Coercive Actions*. Hyattsville, MD: American Psychological Association.

Thornberry, T. P. (1998). Membership in Youth Gangs and Involvement in Serious and Violent Offending. In R. Loeber and D. P. Farrington (eds.), *Serious and Violent Juvenile Offenders*. Thousand Oaks, CA: Sage Publications, pp. 147–166.

Thornberry, T. P., Krohn, M. D., Lizotte, A. J., and Chard-Wierschem, D. (1993). The role of juvenile gangs in facilitating delinquent behavior. *Journal of Research in Crime and Delinquency*, 30:55–87.

Thornberry, T. P., Krohn, M. D., Lizotte, A. J., Smith, C. A., and Tobin, K. (2003). *Gangs and Delinquency in Developmental Perspective*. New York: Cambridge University Press.

Thornberry, T. P., Lizotte, A. J., Krohn, M. D., Farnworth, M., and Jang, S. J. (1994). Delinquent peers, beliefs, and delinquent behavior: A longitudinal test of interactional theory. *Criminology*, 32:47–83.

Thrasher, F. M. (1927). *The Gang*. Chicago: University of Chicago Press.

Tienda, M. (1991). Poor People and Poor Places: Deciphering Neighborhood Effects on Poverty Outcomes. In J. Huber (ed.), *Macro-Micro Linkages in Sociology*, Newbury Park, CA: Sage, pp. 244–262.

Tittle, C. R. (1989). Influences on urbanism: A test of three perspectives. *Social Problems*, 36:270–288.

Trump, K. S. (2004). *School-Related Deaths, School Shootings, and School Violence Incidents*. Cleveland, OH: National School Safety and Security Services.

Turner, R. H., and Killian, L. M. (1987). *Collective Behavior*, 3rd ed. Englewood Cliffs, NJ: Prentice Hall.

U.S. Department of Health and Human Services (2001). *Youth Violence: A Report of the Surgeon General*. Rockville, MD: U.S. Government Printing Office.

Wacquant, L. (2002). Scrutinizing the street: Poverty, morality, and the pitfalls of urban ethnography. *American Journal of Sociology*, 107(6):1468–1532.

Weatherburn, D., Lind, B., and Forsythe, L. (1999). *Drug Law Enforcement: Its Effect on Treatment Experience and Injection Practices*. Sydney: Bureau of Crime Statistics and Research.

Wellman, B., and Leighton, B. (1979). Networks, neighborhoods, and communities: Approaches to the study of the community question. *Urban Affairs Quarterly*, 14:363–390.

Werner, E. E., and Smith, R. S. (1992). *Overcoming the Odds: High Risk Children from Birth to Adulthood*. Ithaca, NY: Cornell University Press.

Whyte, W. F. (1955). *Street Corner Society*, 3rd ed. Chicago: University of Chicago Press.

Widom, C. S. (1994). Childhood Victimization and Risk for Adolescent Problem Behavior. In R. Ketterlings and M. J. Lamb (eds.) *Adolescent Problem Behaviors*. New York: Erlbaum, pp. 127–164.

Williams, T., and Kornblum, W. (1985). *Growing Up Poor*. Lexington, MA: Lexington Books.

Williams, T., and Kornblum, W. (1994). *Uptown Kids*. New York: G. P. Putnam's Sons.

Wilson, J. Q., and Kelling, G. (1982). Broken windows. *Atlantic Monthly*, (March):29–38.

Wilson, W. J. (1987). *The Truly Disadvantaged: The Inner-City, the Underclass, and Public Policy*. Chicago, IL: The University of Chicago Press.

Wilson, W. J. (1991). Studying the inner-city social dislocations: The challenge of public agenda research. *American Sociological Review*, 56(1):1–14.

Wilson, W. J. (1997). *When Work Disappears: The World of the New Urban Poor*. Seventh Publishing. New York: Alfred A. Knopf.

Windle, M. (1994). A study of friendship characteristics and problem behaviors among middle adolescents. *Child Development*, 65:1764–1777.

Winiarski-Jones, T. (1988) Adolescent peer groups: Their formation and effects on attitudes towards education and academic performance. *Research in Education*, 40:51–58.

Wirth, L. (1928). *The Ghetto*. Chicago: University of Chicago Press.

Wirth, L. (1938). Urbanism as a way of life. *American Journal of Sociology*, 44:1–24.

Wright-Atkinson, D. (1995). *An Ethnographic Exploration of Parenting Dimensions across High Economically Disadvantaged Neighborhoods*. Boulder, CO: Institute of Behavioral Science, University of Colorado. (Unpublished.)

Wolkow, K., and Ferguson, H. B. (2001). Community factors in the development of resiliency: Considerations and future directions. *Community Mental Health Journal*, 37:489–498.

Woodson, R. L., Sr. (1998). *The Triumphs of Joseph*. New York: Free Press.

Yancey, W., and Ericksen, E. P. (1979). The antecedents of community: The economic and institutional structure of urban neighborhoods. *American Sociological Review*, 44:253–263.

Zorbaugh, H. (1976). *The Gold Coast and The Slum*. Chicago: University of Chicago Press.

Author Index

Subject Index

DATE DUE

GAYLORD | No. 2333 | | PRINTED IN U.S.A.